THE VIOLENCE OF LIBERATION

Charlene E. Makley · THE VIOLENCE
OF LIBERATION

*Gender and Tibetan Buddhist Revival
in Post-Mao China*

University of California Press

Berkeley   Los Angeles   London

University of California Press, one of the most distinguished university presses in the United States, enriches
lives around the world by advancing scholarship in the
humanities, social sciences, and natural sciences. Its
activities are supported by the UC Press Foundation
and by philanthropic contributions from individuals
and institutions. For more information, visit
www.ucpress.edu.

University of California Press
Berkeley and Los Angeles, California

University of California Press, Ltd.
London, England

Library of Congress Cataloging-in-Publication Data

Makley, Charlene E., 1964–.
    The violence of liberation : gender and Tibetan
Buddhist revival in post-Mao China / Charlene E.
Mackley.
        p.   cm.
    Includes bibliographical references and index.
    ISBN: 978-0-520-25059-8 (cloth : alk. paper)
    ISBN: 978-0-520-25060-4 (pbk : alk. paper)
    1. Tibet (China)—History—1951–.   I. Title.
DS786.M295   2007
951'.45—dc22   2007020212

Manufactured in the United States of America

16   15   14   13   12   11   10   09   08   07
10   9   8   7   6   5   4   3   2   1

This book is printed on New Leaf EcoBook 50, a 100%
recycled fiber of which 50% is de-inked post-consumer
waste, processed chlorine-free. EcoBook 50 is acid-free
and meets the minimum requirements of ANSI/ASTM
D5634-01 (Permanence of Paper).

For Cain, my partner in all things, and
For my Amdo Tibetan friends and colleagues

CONTENTS

List of Illustrations   ix

Acknowledgments   xi

Notes on Transliteration   xv

Abbreviations   xvii

Introduction: Bodies of Power   1

1. Fatherlands: Mapping Masculinities   29

2. Father State: Socialist Transformation and
    Gendered Historiography   76

3. Mother Home: Circumambulation,
    Femininities, and the Ambiguous Mobility
    of Women   135

4. Consuming Women: Consumption,
    Sexual Politics, and the Dangers
    of Mixing   180

5.   Monks Are Men Too: Domesticating
Monastic Subjects   225

Epilogue: Quandaries of Agency   285

Notes   293

References Cited   315

Index   349

ILLUSTRATIONS

MAPS

1. The People's Republic of China and Inner Asia   xviii

2. Gannan Zangzu Autonomous Prefecture, Gansu province   44

3. Tibetan regions in the PRC   47

FIGURES

1. Labrang monastery complex   3

2. Tourism brochure for Xiahe   9

3. Maṇḍala of Yama Dharmarāja   35

4. Painted mural, Śākyamuni temple   41

5. Fifth Jamyang Shepa, Apa Alo, and Apa Alo's son Amgon   51

6. Last Cham Chen before CCP intervention   63

7. Christian missionary Wayne Persons   71

8. New shops on Labrang's main street   83

9. Detail, "Wrath of the Serfs"   94

10. Young women showing off new headdresses   119

11. Images of local trulkus and deities for sale   133

12. Tibetan women turn newly rebuilt prayer wheels   139

13. "Mother Love," by Ji Mei   149

14. Labrang monastery from the southeast   151

15. Cautionary tale cartoon in *Tibet Daily* newspaper   211

16. Massive thangka of Donpa   229

17. Crowd-controlling "wild yak" attacks crowd at Shampa (Maitreya)
    procession   233

18. The Great Liberation Stupa   263

ACKNOWLEDGMENTS

A project as long and involved as this one is truly a collective endeavor. Over the fifteen years of research and language work this book entailed, many, many people have been crucial allies, colleagues, and supporters, even when the sensitive nature of the project posed potential political difficulties. I consider this work to be a lifelong endeavor, one that created boundary-crossing relationships and obligations that extend far beyond the fieldwork and the publication of the book. In the making, family became collaborators and colleagues, while friends and colleagues became family. My husband and children have Tibetan names and are learning Chinese, while many of my Tibetan friends and colleagues now speak English.

Family here in the United States were, of course, my foundation. My first, most heartfelt thanks go to my husband, Cain. As my dedication indicates, his committed partnership in Labrang and at home made all this possible. His gender-bending capacity to take up the work of the household has helped to create a home in the midst of academic chaos, as well as three of the most beautiful, curious children imaginable—Noah, Anna, and Rosa. I also thank my sister, Mary, and her husband, Kevin, for all their computer and photography support along the way. My parents, John and Kathryn Makley, as always, were a great source for me of personal strength and self-esteem. I could not have come this far without their constant emotional and occasional, yet crucial, financial support throughout the hills and valleys of this journey.

I have been extremely fortunate to have benefited from the guidance and support of a group of extraordinary scholars at the University of Michigan. My deepest respect and thanks go to my advisors and mentors in anthropology, Norma Diamond, Jennifer Robertson, Bruce Mannheim, Webb Keane, Erik Mueggler, and the late Roy ("Skip") Rappaport. Each has, in insistence on theoretical and historical rigor, his or her commitment to nuanced area and language studies, and compassionate mentorship profoundly influenced the work I produced here, as well as the kind of scholar and teacher I have tried to be.

I also benefited immensely from my time in the Buddhist Studies Department at the University of Michigan. Luis Gomez's unparalleled knowledge of Buddhist traditions and ritual practices challenged me to contextualize what I was seeing in Labrang in a much broader linguistic and historical milieu. Donald Lopez's knowledge of the Tibetan language and the complex traditions of Tibetan Buddhism is perhaps unique in its breadth and critical incisiveness. His wry wit and high scholarly standards pushed me to both a more sophisticated understanding of Tibetans in all their historical color and a deeper sense of the ironies inherent in the cultural politics swirling around them.

Many colleagues, teachers, and friends at Michigan and elsewhere took their valuable time to help me at various stages of this project over the years. I would like to thank members of the Linguistic Anthropology Lab at Michigan: Laura Ahearn, Laada Bilaniuk, Coralynn Davis, Jennifer Dickinson, Anjun Ghosh, Bridget Hayden, James Herron, Leila Hudson, Oren Kosansky, Mandana Limbert, Colleen O'Neal, and Krista Van Vleet—for reading my papers, debating my conclusions, contributing their varied perspectives, and thereby challenging me to rethink the relationship between language and culture in creative ways.

I have also taken much inspiration and encouragement from the constructive criticisms and insightful work of my colleagues in the Department of Anthropology at Reed College: Robert Brightman, Anne Lorimer, Paul Silverstein, Rupert Stasch, and Marko Zivkovic—as well as of my colleagues elsewhere, David Akin, Ann Anagnost, Emily Chao, Keith Dede, Larry Epstein, Janet Gyatso, Toni Huber, Carole Macgranahan, Chas Mackhann, Paul Nietupski, Peng Wenbin, Beth Notar, Louisa Schein, Mona Schrempf, Kevin Stuart, Janet Upton, and Emily Yeh. Further, I thank my students at Reed College in my courses on China and Tibet for their brilliance and unique capacity to challenge my comfortable professorial assumptions. Our courses have been just as much a learning experience for me. Beth Notar and Chas Mackhann valiantly read the entire manuscript and gave me detailed comments that contributed to a much tighter book. My brilliant and dedicated Reedie research assistants, Adam Sargent and Caitlin Shrigley, were indispensable in helping to get the manuscript in final shape. Of course, all remaining errors, incomprehensible jargon, and run-on sentences are entirely my own.

I must especially thank my good friend and teacher Amdo Lekshay Gyamtsho. Born on the grasslands northwest of Labrang, and a former monk at Labrang monastery, Lekshay ended up in Portland, a truly karmic friend. I have learned so much from our long conversations about Amdo and our collaborations over Tibetan Buddhist and secular texts. My spoken and written Tibetan-language skills have improved greatly only because of him.

I would like to thank Mona Schrempf for allowing me to use her phrase describing tantric ritual, "the violence of liberation," as the title of my book. I also thank Paul Nietupski and Gandan Thurman at the Tibet House in New York City for making it possible for me to use the photo, taken by the American missionary Marion Griebenow, of Apa Alo and Jamyang Shepa. I am also grateful to Wayne and Minnie Persons, who shared with me their experiences as a young missionary couple in the Griebenow mission compound in Labrang between 1947 and 1949, on the very eve of the CCP takeover. They generously bequeathed to me their collection of photos from their time in Labrang, and five of them appear here. Their daughter, Marjie Persons, was instrumental in making that happen. Thanks also go to Andreas Gruschke for allowing me to reproduce his gorgeous photograph of the rare wall painting of the first Jamyang Shepa. Finally, the Rubin Museum of Art generously allowed me to reproduce their image of the Yama Dharmaraja mandala, which appears on the wonderful website Himalayan Art Resources.

Rackham Graduate School at the University of Michigan funded a huge part of my research in the form of a Regents' Fellowship for graduate study, summer preliminary research money, and a Predoctoral Fellowship. In addition, the Center for Chinese Studies at the University of Michigan provided me with invaluable support, granting me a FLAS for graduate study and an Endowment Award for dissertation write-up. Finally, the University of Michigan Institute for Research on Women and Gender's "Community of Scholars" Fellowship allowed me to complete the writing of this dissertation. I am also grateful to the Committee on Scholarly Communication with China and the Wenner-Gren Anthropology Foundation, without whose financial help and logistical support I could not have undertaken the complicated fieldwork upon which this book is based. The massive effort of expanding and rewriting the research for the book was funded in part by a Reed College Paid Leave Award, the Levine and Stillman-Drake funds for faculty research and materials, and Freeman Foundation funds for research in Chinese studies.

I reserve my most humble gratitude for the Tibetans with whom I worked and lived in China. I always assumed that I would be able to acknowledge my Tibetan friends and colleagues by name, but the current political situation requires that I do not. I do thank the Gansu Province Tibetan Studies Institute (Ch. Gansu Sheng Zangxue Yanjiusuo) in Labrang for hosting my time there in 1995–96. As for local Tibetans, I can say only that in their genuine kindness toward a lonely American in their midst, and in their lively interest in me and the world I represented, Tibetans I came to know took me into their lives, sometimes at great personal risk. With dignity and vigorous humor, they showed me how they live and cope in the PRC, and for that I am eternally grateful. I can only hope that through the ongoing relationships I maintain with many of them, I can continue to find ways to give back.

NOTES ON TRANSLITERATION

This book is based on research conducted in both Chinese and Amdo Tibetan, a dialect that is pronounced quite differently from the better-known dialect spoken in and around Lhasa. Therefore, I want to be very clear about how I rendered those languages in print. In the main text and endnotes, all foreign-language terms, except proper names, are italicized. In parenthetical glosses of words I rendered in English, I identify the language with an abbreviation before the word: "Tib." for Tibetan words, "Ch." for Chinese words, and "Skt." for the occasional Sanskrit word. For Chinese words, I used the standard pinyin transliteration system, minus tone markers for ease of printing.

At present, there is no commonly accepted system for writing Tibetan phonetically. Recent efforts to develop such a system have for the most part been based on the pronunciation of Lhasa dialects. I felt strongly though that I should represent, as clearly as possible, the Amdo dialect spoken in Labrang. Yet I also wanted to preserve the etymological relationships of words spoken in Amdo Tibetan for readers unfamiliar with those dialects. Thus, for the Tibetan terms and important proper names that I emphasize for discussion here, I render them in forms approximating their pronunciation in the Labrang Amdo dialect. But I also use the Wylie transliteration system in parenthetical notes to include the exact spellings of most Tibetan words I mention.

Since geographic nomenclature in this frontier region is notoriously complex, I include both Tibetan and Chinese names only for the most important sites and geographic features mentioned. For the sake of simplicity however, I for the most part use the name (rendered phonetically) that is most commonly used by Tibetan locals. In my view, it would obscure locals' experience of space there to insist on using all Tibetan names. In many cases the Chinese term, especially for administrative units newly demarcated with the establishment of the PRC, is the one both Tibetans and Chinese use most frequently. This is reflected on my maps and photos.

In the text, when I quote directly from my fieldnotes as I originally wrote them, I specify this and the quote appears as an indented paragraph. When I draw on my fieldnotes to construct a narrative of an interaction, the narrative appears as an indented paragraph with the heading "FROM FIELD NOTES."

All names of Tibetan interlocutors I mention here are pseudonyms. The particularly tense atmosphere in Labrang since the tightening of state security around the monastery during the "patriotic education" campaign, begun in 1998, makes this more imperative than ever (see the epilogue). In order to render them more generic, the pseudonyms I chose are all disyllabic, extremely common names among Tibetans in the region. In writing this account, I encountered the tension between my desire to portray my Tibetan interlocutors as the nuanced individuals who personally influenced me in so many ways and the need to mask their identities. Thus I do not give any key identifying information about them, such as specific home regions, occupations or work units.

ABBREVIATIONS

CBA	China Buddhist Association
CCP	Chinese Communist Party
Ch.	Chinese
CPPCC	Chinese People's Political Consultative Committees
KMT	Guomindang
NSB	National Security Bureau
PLA	People's Liberation Army
PRC	People's Republic of China
PSB	Public Security Bureau
Skt.	Sanskrit
Tib.	Tibetan
TAR	Tibetan Autonomous Region (Xizang Zangzu Autonomous Region)

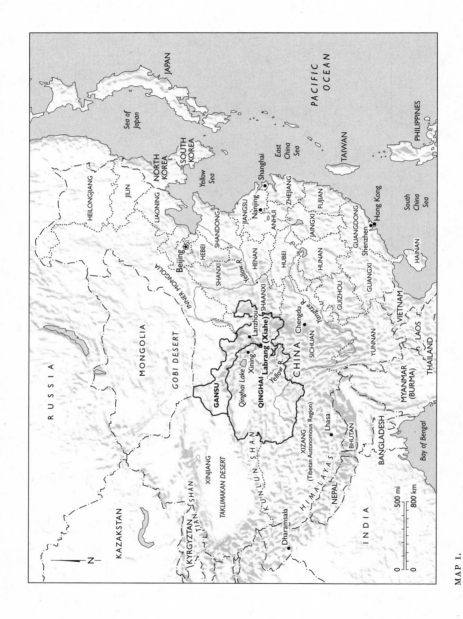

MAP 1.

The People's Republic of China (PRC) and Inner Asia.

Introduction

Bodies of Power

"We young people sometimes can't believe the stories; it's like some sort of nightmare torture." That is how my good friend the young monk Akhu Konchok wincingly referred to the story an elderly monk had told me about state violence in Tibetan regions after the Chinese Communist revolution in 1949. In this book I examine the gendered cultural politics that separated the two monks by the mid-1990s. I ask: How did gendered inequalities structure the revitalization of the famous Tibetan Buddhist monastery of Labrang Tashi Khyil during post-Mao reforms? What were the exigencies of great gendered changes for Tibetans who lived under the nightmare shadow of state terror even as they encountered utopian dreams of pleasurable consumption in a new market economy? And what were the implications of my analytic interest in gender difference as a contingent and translocal social process in a community that was vigorously invested in rebuilding stable and coherent local worlds after the collective trauma of socialist transformation? These are the main questions and unresolved tensions of this book.

FOREIGN PHANTOMS: UNINTELLIGIBLE BODIES

Foreign tourists in the southwestern Gansu province town of Labrang, the seat of Xiahe county in Gannan Tibetan Autonomous Prefecture, moved through its streets like phantoms. They were hypervisible to locals and yet barely noticed by them; they observed local people and yet never coexisted substantially with them. In the 1990s, thousands of foreign visitors, mostly from Europe, Canada, the United States, and Australia, joined the westward flow of Han Chinese tourists to travel through Labrang every year (cf. Yang Ming 1992: 14). They were attracted by the Tibetan culture of the town, famous for its huge Buddhist monastery and the beauty of its mountain locale. Indeed, this narrow river valley at the edge of the region known to Tibetans as Amdo was touted in the *Lonely Planet Travel Survival Kit* for China as "one of the most enchanting places to visit in China, especially if you can't get to Tibet" (1996: 900). By the mid-1990s, Labrang was a long strip of development hemmed in by fairly steep, treeless mountains, a valley divided administratively into Labuleng town (Ch. *zhen*) and Jiujia township (Ch. *xiang*). According to many of the foreign tourists I surveyed between 1992 and 1996, they sought an experience there of "authentic Tibetanness" that was more accessible than that in central Tibet and Lhasa far away over the Amnye Machen mountain range to the southwest.[1] During the summer months, when tourist traffic reached its peak, foreign visitors could be seen strolling up and down the main road that bifurcated the monastery and linked it to the town and farming villages to its east and to the grassland plateaus to its west (see map 1).

Such foreign tourists traveled great distances to absorb the ambiance of Buddhist piety in and around the newly reconstructed monastery, and to interact with local Tibetans and pilgrims. Gilles, a young French tourist, rapturously described to me how he loved to sit and watch Tibetans circumambulate the monastery. "It's like a movie, but it isn't," he said; and it made him feel (sucking in his breath with a wind-rushing noise), "that's why I keep coming back to Tibet." Foreign visitors like Gilles strove to experience the promise of global connectedness offered by international tourism trajectories, and thereby to expand personal horizons or to benefit from others' ritual technologies. Indeed, since the death of Mao Zedong and Deng Xiaoping's subsequent "reform and opening up" (Ch. *gaige kaifang*) policies of the 1980s, the tourism industry in Labrang was integrating the town and monastery with the global economy to an unprecedented extent.

Yet during my four research trips to the region, I was frequently struck by the vast cultural and economic distance that separated foreign tourists from locals, even as they walked the same roads and pilgrimage paths. Among foreigners and locals alike, sheer ignorance coexisted tensely with assumptions each held deeply about the other. In addition, the dissident discourse of the Dalai Lama's exile government in India still loomed large in this region, where Tibetans had strong ties to friends and relatives abroad. In this context, Chinese state anxiety about the

FIGURE I.
Labrang monastery complex surrounded by prayer-wheel
buildings in the summer of 2002. On the right, to the east and
downriver, are recently constructed homes and buildings in town.

potential for Tibetan separatism fomented by foreign support translated to restrictive residence policies and surveillance aimed at maintaining a "safe" distance between locals and foreigners. Thus despite their desire to see past the "Chinese" trappings of Tibetan lifestyles in China and penetrate to true Tibetanness, foreign visitors—myself included—in reality haunted the peripheries of Tibetan lives in Labrang, embodying the imagined possibilities of a larger world and the realities of rapid change locally.

Indeed, this was no mere station in a global ecumene, where geographic distance crossed meant cultural difference overcome. I arrived in the mid-1990s hoping to conduct anthropological fieldwork on gender and the post-Mao revitalization of the lay-monastic relationship in town. By then, I found that a decade of state-supervised tourism in the region had actually solidified a certain distance between locals and foreign visitors, in that assumptions each held about the other's nature and interests had become anchored in stereotypes, often-cited rumors, and certain patterned interactions. For many Tibetans I knew, the recent appearance in their homes and streets of images of wealthy, hyperempowered white people in pirated videos or in imported television programs (*Baywatch* had recently aired) mirrored the ideal translocal mobility of foreign tourists arriving in town. Consequently, as against the far more numerous Han Chinese visitors there, "foreigners" (Tib. *phyi rgyal pa*, lit. "outside-country ones")[2] were the preferred consumers of local ethnic commodities. For Tibetans they were the models of powerful and pleasurable consumption to both cultivate and emulate. "Foreigners," one old former monk declared in my presence, pointing to an image of the Buddha, "are like deities" (Tib. *lha 'dra mo red*).

I of course found myself implicated in and constrained by these difficult dynamics in Labrang. After all, my interest in Tibetans had originally been piqued after a trip to central Tibet as a "Lonely Planeteer" in 1987. I had then felt the powerful longing to communicate across the distance separating foreigners and Tibetans in China. This longing I now know was often mutual, since I had arrived at precisely the time when the Dalai Lama was taking the international stage by addressing the United States Congress on human rights and the Chinese occupation of Tibet, thus heightening hope among Tibetans in China for help from Americans in particular (cf. Goldstein 1997).

In this charged context, I discovered that transcending the status of foreign phantom for locals to find any mutual grounds for communication was a deeply *gendered* process, one that I myself, despite my years of training in feminist anthropology, had not anticipated. When in March 1995 my official status was finally secured as a social science researcher doing "on-the-spot fieldwork" (Ch. *shidi diaocha*), and my husband, Cain, and I at long last moved into our apartment at the Tibetan Studies Institute in town for a year and a half's stay, I thought I would finally be able to get past the world of tourists and enter the lives of local Tibetans. After all, we were to my knowledge the first foreigners in Labrang since reforms who were granted official permission to take up residence outside the few state-designated foreign tourist hotels. As a "married" couple,[3] we were able to set up a household in the institute's two-story family-residence building along with the mostly Tibetan and a few Muslim Chinese (Ch. Hui) families renting the cold, cement-block apartments there. In addition, my language skills had progressed, and I was at last able to speak and understand the local dialect of Tibetan in addition to Mandarin Chinese well enough to eliminate the need for the translators who had always kept me steps removed from interacting with people on my own.

But I was stunned to find that my language skills at the outset allowed me instead to experience what felt like a radical, visceral difference from the locals. As my husband and I ventured out to see friends, make acquaintances, go to the market, and circumambulate the monastery, for the first time I was able to understand the many conversations about us passing Tibetans engaged in within inches of our bodies. What interested passersby in us in those early days was not that we were foreigners per se, but that we were unfamiliar gendered beings. Time and again, Tibetan men and women across the community, as well as some Hui, wondered to each other as we passed or, in several embarrassing episodes, to our faces, whether we were men or women, or which one of us was a man and which was a woman. I will not forget my shock the first time I heard a passing Tibetan man ask his companion if we were men or women (Tib. *de cho byis mo red byis lu red?*); or when Ama Lhamo, an eccentric woman I came to know who was herself a particularly androgynous, hardy old retired cadre in a Mao suit, was taken aback when I introduced Cain to her as my husband. "He's a man?!" (Ch. *ta shi nande?!*), she exclaimed.

Even the Hui proprietor of the public showers we used to frequent expressed this gender confusion about us. (There were no sex-segregated showers, only private stalls.) Here is an excerpt from my field notes about the incident:

At the shower owned by a Hui family, I had finished showering, and as I was leaving the man asked me if I was alone here. I said, "No, my husband was here too; you've seen him, he came before, has brown hair." (In spoken Chinese, pronouns are not inflected for gender.) He seemed perplexed, and I thought he didn't understand *xiansheng* ("husband"), so I said *zhangfu* (the word used locally for "husband") instead. He said, *Zhangfu?* and then finally asked straight out: "You're a woman, and he's a man?!" (Ch. *ni shi nude? ta shi nande?*). I was blown away and said, "Of course! Can't you tell?" He shook his head and said "I can't tell." Someone snorted from inside the showers. How embarrassing.

My shock and embarrassment, and the confusion and derision of my interlocutors about the unintelligibility of my gender, indexed the space of cultural exclusion in which I initially found myself in Labrang. Being deemed unintelligible as a woman brought home to me just how basic to my personhood my gender identity was. I had never personally encountered such gender confusion or been mistaken for a man at home, and in Labrang, I had not set out to deliberately "scramble" markers of gender in the manner of drag queens and stage performers. To the contrary, I had intentionally (if somewhat unconsciously) set out to gender myself "woman" in ways I thought would be most comprehensible to Tibetans—by growing my hair long ahead of time, wearing large gold hoop earrings, and calling my fiancé my "husband." I even wondered to Cain whether or not our bulky winter coats had hidden our bodies enough to obscure our gender identities.

The gender confusion I initially experienced in Labrang faced me with the depth of my unconscious assumptions about gender. My shock pointed up that I had still been assuming both the universal translatability (across cultural, linguistic, and economic differences) of at least my gender identity as a biologically female body, *and* the universal efficacy of my own intentions to present my personhood to others. But such moments of awkward misrecognition provided critical object lessons that ultimately structured my approach in my fieldwork and in this book. I was to learn that becoming more substantial in Tibetans' lives than an apparition haunting public spaces would entail not an eradication of my difference from them but an ongoing negotiation and mutual reinterpretation of what I, as a privileged American and an educated woman, embodied to them. And this process, I discovered, had everything to do with the constitution of and potential threats to gendered "bodies of power" in Labrang amidst the rising stakes of interethnic politics (Zito 1994: 107).

PARTICIPATION AND EMBODIMENT: THE CULTURAL POLITICS OF GENDERED RECOGNITION

With the development of the tourism industry since the mid-1980s, Tibetan-foreigner relationships in Labrang could not escape the new terms of an intensifying commodity aesthetics that relied on older, state-mediated forms of ethnic difference to produce "culture" as an object for sale. Far from an ideal leveling of regional and sociocultural or economic difference, globalizing Labrang, as in other rural regions in China, meant everyday practical training for citizens in new modes of recognizing discrete, hierarchically arranged cultures as clusters (or, better, packages) of visible features of language, lifestyle, and beliefs fixed in particular locales. As many have recently pointed out, "backward" (Ch. *luohou*), rural, yet colorful ethnicity has been an entailed Other in the reform-era market economy and in the model of modern progress that urban Han state planners hoped to build on the foundation of the socialist state infrastructure (Gladney 1994, 2004; Oakes 1997, 1998; Blum 2000; Litzinger 2000; Schein 2000; Mueggler 2001; Bulag 2002).

Thus, like other groups defined and regulated as "minority nationalities" (Ch. *shaoshu minzu*) in China, Tibetans were ambivalently situated vis-à-vis the therapeutic consumption that state officials offered China's citizens in order to effect the transition from the violence, deprivation, and radical politics of the Maoist years

(1949–79). In post-Mao Labrang, to *be* ethnic was to be left behind, the object of a backward-looking gaze; to *consume* ethnicity was to get behind the lens—to participate simultaneously in capitalist development and in the remedial revival of a Tibetanness that (ostensibly) erased the state-sponsored violence of decades of forced assimilation to a Han Chinese and Communist model of modernity. In the 1980s and 1990s, capitalist forms of vision were eminently compatible with (or in fact constitutive of) an emergent politics of identity among Tibetans and other minorities in China.

This is not a case, then, of an isolated people being flattened by the juggernaut of external capitalist interests, as some earlier Western theorists of globalization, development, and tourism assumed (cf. Oakes 1997, 1998). Instead, in Labrang, state officials, local Tibetans, and foreigners all participated in this new commodity voyeurism in the valley. Further, the bilingual English-Chinese tourism brochure I picked up in the summer of 1993 at the then recently completed Labrang Hotel wonderfully illustrates how this process played out in competing efforts at *gendered recognition*.

The Labrang Hotel, not coincidentally, was also featured that same year, a time when national and provincial efforts to promote tourism in Labrang intensified, in a Han scholar's survey of Tibetan Buddhist sites in the valley. The author frames such sites as "resources" (Ch. *ziyuan*) for the development of the tourism industry in Xiahe and notes that the Labrang Hotel's value depended on its status as the original site of the villa (built in 1943) of the ruling lama at Labrang monastery (Geng 1993: 220). The hotel's 1993 brochure was designed by Tshering, a young local Tibetan man who at the time was the hotel manager. It touts the state-run hotel as an official branch of the state's international travel service (CITS) and presents the region as the destination of a "romantic" tour setting out from provincial capitals to see the folk customs (Ch. *minsu*) of "Little Tibet."

Despite the valley's large population of Han and Hui residents, who indeed outnumbered Tibetan residents in town, not a single one is pictured, and the only tourists represented are foreigners. According to the 1990 census, around eighty-seven thousand (or 62%) of the population in Xiahe county were Tibetan, the largest Tibetan population in any county in Tibetan autonomous districts outside the TAR (cf. Marshall and Cooke 1997: 1443). By my estimates, in 1990 there were about seventeen thousand people registered as living in the nineteen or so agricultural and urban villages comprising the administrative units of Labrang town and Jiujia township, all of them concentrated in the narrow valleys of the Sang river and its tributaries. In town, though actual percentages are unclear, lay Tibetans were a minority (at least in the early reform years), with Han and Hui making up equal proportions of the rest, while in villages outside and to the west of the valley, Tibetans were still the vast majority (Ma Denghun and Wanma 1994: 177; and see below, chapter 3).[4]

But in the brochure's vision of the valley, the enticing realism of its colorful photos recognizes only two categories of gendered subjects for tourists' gaze: immobile and smiling rural "Tibetan women" in traditional lay garb, and red-robed and costume-clad monk ritualists performing in front of monastic buildings. Meanwhile, the hotel's modern facilities are pictured served up by pretty young Tibetan village women (several of whom I knew) as maids and waitresses projecting more urbane and sexualized ethnicity in colorful, form-fitting Lhasa-style dresses. And Tshering presents himself as the manager, a modern, urban agent of the tourism industry, *not* its object, nattily dressed in a monochrome Western suit and tie.

The brochure's representations of ethnic difference thus already exceed the ideal enclosure of an unchanging and monolithic Tibetan ethnicity in a rural locale that the tourism commodity would offer. As such, it indexes everyday struggles with representations of selves and Others in town, even as it attempts to definitively locate ethnic color in and around a "sacred" place called "Labrang monastery." Disappointed foreign tourists I spoke to, whose search for authentic Tibetanness was frustrated in Labrang at the sight of "modernized" Tibetans (not to mention Han and Hui), did not recognize locals', especially young people's, intense ambivalence toward representations of ethnicity. Tibetanness in this region was after all first widely objectified not by commodity fetishism but by the increasingly violent disciplinary strategies of the Chinese Communist state that constructed it as a reactionary hindrance to socialist advance. By the 1990s, relations between Tibetans and foreigners in town thus relied on an often self-conscious process of each recognizing essential ethnic differences in the other. But more importantly, such relationships most often relied on powerful fantasies of alliance and mutual aid through assumptions of differences between conspiratorial selves and a notion of a monolithic and dominating Han Chinese society and state.

The Tibetan-Chinese divide was thus decidedly overdetermined in Tibetan-foreigner relations in Labrang, as elsewhere in the Tibetan diaspora since the Dalai Lama's flight to India in 1959. This meant that attention to essential ethnicities often worked to obscure interlocutors' awareness of other forms of social difference at work. Yet, as the tourism brochure and my early "gender troubles" in town make clear, in both conscious and unconscious ways, gender differences cru-

FIGURE 2.
Tourism brochure for Xiahe, summer 1993.

cially shaped asymmetric local-translocal encounters in Labrang. Like many other
county seats in China's minority regions, the Labrang valley was not the unchanging, ideally rural node that tourism networks constructed it to be (cf. Stevenson
1999, Upton 1999). It was a rapidly urbanizing locale where the premises for
power, value, and morality were shifting, and many residents thus deeply felt that
boundaries among persons, spaces, and agencies were dangerously blurring.

As Louisa Schein has argued, throughout China by the 1990s the "imagined
cosmopolitanism" associated with the urban and touted by state development
officials held out great promise to men *and*, increasingly, to women of an unprecedented escape from subsistence production to leisurely, self-confirming consumption (2001: 225). As a result, I found that gender difference was increasingly highlighted for locals as an *ontological ground* for recognizing types of moral persons
and valued actions. That is, practices of gender recognition worked to ground and
to hierarchically order valued "ways of being" (Desjarlais 1992) amidst the flux
and perceived chaos of rapid change on the rural-urban and interethnic frontier.

For a variety of reasons, Tibetans in Labrang across generations tended to vigorously insist on an essentially gendered social order and cosmology. And this
despite their participation in new institutions and practices that, like the tourism

brochure, drew on a posited male-female sex binary in new ways to challenge and change notions of gender (and thereby ethnic, regional, and class) difference. In the brochure, Tshering positions himself as a modern urban subject by adopting the markers of a translocal masculinity and thereby distinguishing himself from visibly Tibetanized monks and rural laywomen. At the same time, then, he reiterates a now global pattern, one that had particular salience in reform-era China, by presenting the rural ethnic tourist commodity (including monks) as a feminized Other (cf. Enloe 1989, Gladney 1994, Lin 1999, Schein 2000, Hyde 2001; and see below, chapter 5).

In this way, the dilemmas and difficulties of ethnic authenticity and modernity in Labrang were fundamentally *embodied* through competing recognitions of sex and gender differences, and foreign men and women were only two of many categories of gendered Others pressing in on the narrow valley. It is not surprising then that foreign tourists were kept at a distance not only by state policies but also by local (mis)apprehensions. Foreign bodies for harried Tibetans most often represented not substantial, known individuals but glimpsed surfaces indexing powerful gendered stereotypes and envious or resentful fantasies. One of the most frequent opening conversations in which Tibetans engaged me consisted of questions about the cost and time required to get me there, miraculously (for a woman) free of household responsibilities. For many villagers shrewdly calculating the numbers I gave them, such leisure time, disposable income, and the capacity to move beyond household and Chinese state discipline seemed far out of their reach. I could then read the ambivalence of hinted resentment or sarcasm in the old ex-monk's remark to me about foreigners' godlike nature—deities for Tibetans, as we will see, were not at all unproblematic agents in their lives.

Thus, against the unique allure in Tibetan studies of a conscious focus on ethnicity, I argue in this book that to make any sense of the extremely fraught encounters and their differential stakes in urbanizing spaces in China, we simply cannot ignore the ways shifting relationships were gendered for Tibetans and their interlocutors. In fact, it is very often the case that people vehemently deny the importance of gender in shaping key social relations in direct proportion to its actual consequence. "Gender," as Judith Butler put it, "is a construction that regularly conceals its genesis" (1988: 522). I follow Butler and others in asserting that we cannot conflate forms of social difference (like ethnicity, race, class, and gender) as merely analogous or structurally equivalent relations merging in a chaos of difference (Butler 1993: 18; cf. de Lauretis 1987, Stoler 1991, Bordo 1993, Tsing 1993). Doing so would be to miss the historically particular ways that local categories of social difference articulate to shape people's participation in asymmetric social fields.

Importantly, such theorists argue that gender is a key analytic for understanding the risks and stakes for people of the increasing variety and *scales* of social contexts amidst globalizing capitalist relations—as the minutely local and personal come to take on unprecedented *trans*local implications. That is, globalization processes (like "reform and opening up" in the PRC) underscore the precariously foundational nature of gender categories. As I discovered in those first weeks in Labrang, gender categories (in this case, "woman/female") are eminently constitutive at the same time as they are eminently constructed. Their variously understood links to primary or natural essences associated with presumed biological facts (i.e., sex) make them a means par excellence for recognizing selves and others as socially intelligible subjects who are legitimately (or not) located in shifting contexts of power and prestige. As Julia Epstein and Kristina Straub put it, "gender definition is one of the primary principles by which binary structures are socially maintained as hierarchical relations" (1991: 4; cf. Scott 1988: 42; Lancaster 2003). Yet that process critically relies on subtle mutual recognitions (on a variety of scales) that individuals can never completely regulate. We could then consider gender to be a dynamic politics of personhood that is uniquely implicated in the ongoing production of the widest range of salient social contexts for people: "attention to gender, as both an imaginative construct and a point of divergent positionings, brings wider cultural negotiations to the center of local affairs" (Tsing 1993: 9; cf. Judd 1994).

In emphasizing the indeterminacy and intersubjectivity of recognition (*not* "identification") as the core of gender dynamics, I take my primary inspiration in this book from sociolinguists and linguistic anthropologists. To my mind, it is that group of theorists who provide the most effective analytic tools for conceptualizing all signs or representations as dialogic (i.e., mutually construed) and thus socially situated practices (cf. Silverstein 1976, 1997; Bakhtin 1981; Goffman 1981; Hanks 1990; Keane 1997). This perspective on the production of meaning rules out easy assumptions that decontextualized individuals construct gender "identities" only through their intentioned "performances" (cf. Butler 1990, 1993; Bordo 1993; Weston 1993; R. Morris 1995). Considering gendered subjectivity as an ongoing and unstable process of recognition or mutual interpretation allows us to foreground the insight, developed (I think) most powerfully by recent linguistic anthropologists, that in practice there is no direct and universal relationship between any instance of a representation and its particular effects or meanings.

Gender recognition directs our attention instead to the cultural politics of *contextualization*—that is, the subtle and emergent (i.e., patterned yet unpredictable) processes of embodiment and boundary definition that are the effects of people's mutual interpretations framed by particular activities and encounters (Keane 1997: i).

This approach then entails an alternative social ontology that can be profoundly counterintuitive, one that I attempt in this book to bring to readers not necessarily versed in the sometimes arcane methodologies of linguistic anthropologists. I do this by rethinking people in Labrang as first and foremost *participants*. That designation refers to the constant and hazardous location of people and social meanings in hierarchically arranged and co-produced discourse genres and speech events, or what Erving Goffman famously referred to as "participation frameworks" (1981: 137; cf. Hanks 1990, 1996; Irvine 1996; Duranti 1997: 281). As Goffman pointed out, every current version of a self is a representation that must be recognized in actual social situations (by selves as well as others) as an instance of a repeatable type (1981: 147). Goffman's spatial metaphor of participation frameworks, originally conceptualized in terms of face-to-face interactions, directs our attention to the particular, embodied processes (like the automatic removal of a hat for a passing lama) by which interlocutors invoke local schemas of valued action to position themselves as types of persons/participants. We could then see frameworks of participation as embodying competing *metapragmatics* (theories and rules of socially appropriate and valued action) that, by linking certain behaviors and speech to imagined constellations of persons in space and time, attempt to foreground and privilege certain values over others (cf. Graeber 2001, Silverstein 2001).

In the chapters to come, I use the phrase "participation framework" in a perhaps broader way than did Goffman himself in order to apply his insights on the micropolitics of face-to-face talk to more macro scales of interaction that globalization processes entail. I take larger schemas of action, like discourse genres (e.g., forms of narrative) and formalized speech events (e.g., tantric Buddhist rituals), as themselves participation frameworks that *in practice* work to encode and substantialize links among varied scales of time and space—Goffman's phrase helps us to conceptualize these social processes *not* as two-dimensional sets of ideas or principles abstracted for analysis, but as three-dimensional (even multidimensional) social worlds brought into being on a variety of scales. Indeed, as many have pointed out, frameworks for translocal action within larger imagined scales and communities are very often put into practice locally as modeled on idealized frameworks for interpersonal interaction and exchange (e.g., hosting guests or kinship obligations; cf.

Graeber 2001, Bulag 2002, Mills 2003). This perspective then sheds light on the crucial role of gender categories amidst the ramifying complexity of local-translocal relations. I am arguing that gender signs (in behavior and in discursive or visual representations) very often operate as key *framing cues* (cf. Gumperz 1992) to participants, markers that index relevant subjectivities and, most importantly, their appropriate contexts and scales of action in particular social situations.

This linguistic anthropological approach to gender dynamics then leads us to some perhaps disorientingly counterintuitive understandings of sex versus gender. In this view, we must see gender and gendered sexualities as preceding sex. That is, sex, even under the most "scientific" of conditions, does not designate fixed or "natural" attributes of bodies. Instead, people *attribute* sex to bodies by drawing on particular models of male and female corporality that are always dialectically constituted by preexisting (and not necessarily binary) notions of gendered and sexualized subjectivity (cf. Kessler and McKenna 1978, Fausto-Sterling 1997, Yuval-Davis 1997, Lancaster 2003). From the other side of the dialectic, then, gender is the process of contextualizing sexed bodies as subjects (categories of appropriate personhood and agency) participating in social frameworks. This dialectic, as it intersects with sociocultural structures at particular historical junctures, is what Gayle Rubin (1975) famously referred to as a "sex/gender system." From this perspective we can also appreciate that there is no entailed one-to-one relationship between notions of sexed bodies and types of gendered subjects—masculinities and femininities in practice are a function not so much of embodied individuals but of the particular, mutually construed *contexts* in which recognition takes place: "social relations are gendered, not persons or things" (Weston 1993: 17). Thus, for example, as I discovered in Labrang, self-recognized females can draw on, invest in, and participate in masculine subjectivities in a variety of ways.

Amidst the great social inequities of urbanizing Labrang, the recognition of bodies as types of gendered subjects depended on the capacities of unequally positioned participants to invoke contexts of power and authority that far surpassed the spatial and temporal bounds of contemporary encounters (Mannheim and Tedlock 1995: 9; Keane 1997: i). In post-Mao Labrang, then, the inherent instability of perceived links between categories of sex and gender could clash with people's strong compulsion to posit naturalized boundaries between bodies, embodied acts, and proclivities that justified unequal access to resources and authority. In such a context, we need to ask, along with William Hanks, what kind of co-participation is possible amidst fundamental social and interpretive asymmetries (1996: 160).

FIELDWORK IN THE INTERSTICES:
ON BEING REGENDERED

In the Sino-Tibetan frontier zone, conducting fieldwork through unproblematic "participant observation" was of course out of the question. To the contrary, my own substantialization as a recognizable gendered subject in Labrang brought to the fore the particular hazards of my personhood and research focus, for myself as well as for my interlocutors. Indeed, the crucial role of gender categories in ontologizing sociocultural worlds by positing natural links and distinctions among persons and contexts depends in part on their remaining uniquely *unremarked* for people—that is, unavailable to metalinguistic reflection. Yet I arrived decades after the state's modernist agendas had violently objectified Tibetanness, in fact, as we will see, targeting for conscious attack the gendered foundations of local power. Further, my arrival coincided with the intensified objectification of Tibetanness in tourism amidst increasing rural-to-urban migration. Thus while locals came to know me as a foreign female anthropologist explicitly researching the role of sex and gender in the revitalization of the lay-monastic relationship in town, I both embodied and explicitly demanded awareness of seismic shifts in relationships among key social contexts in town, even as I tried to observe them.

In such a situation, my research could develop as fieldwork only in the interstices between sanctioned public discourses and conflicting realms of power, a project that could be seen as both trivial and intensely threatening to citizens and state officials alike. Since the early 1980s, when the PRC State Council named Labrang monastery a national center for the preservation of "cultural relics," Deng Xiaoping's regime took a risk in supporting the revitalization of the monastery as a tourist site and as a monument to the benevolence of the Party's post-Mao guarantee of "freedom of religious belief." That risk arose because the state's focus on Labrang allowed for the (partial) restoration of its historical status as a Tibetan regional center controlled by powerful male monastic elites, especially those recognized as *lama*s (lit. "high ones," teachers). Labrang in the 1990s was not only "in the palm of the state," as Akhu Konchok once remarked to me, but it was also the center of what was arguably the most authoritative Buddhist monasticism Tibetans in the region had mustered within the Chinese state. As a state-sanctioned social science researcher operating outside both the managed contexts of foreign tourists and the authoritative contexts of monastic learning, my presence and research agendas then threatened to lay bare the *emasculating seculariza-*

tion of knowledge and power that maintained the uneasy existence of the Labrang monastic community under Chinese state domination since reforms.

When the beloved lama Gongtang Tshang completed the rebuilding of his great stupa in his estate grounds at Labrang in 1993 (it had been demolished during the Cultural Revolution), the artful calligraphy of the banner reading "Love Your Country; Love Your Religion" (Ch. *aiguo aijiao*) adorned the wall above the circumambulation gallery—to both claim and call for the harmonious coexistence of the nation-state and "religion" in Labrang (see chapter 5). Yet the primacy given the nation-state in the slogan indexed the Chinese Communists' victory over Tibetan monastic elites as an unprecedented process that reduced monasticism to a circumscribed and regulated local realm of Tibetan "religion" (Ch. *zongjiao*), encompassed by the secular and translocal nation-space of a Chinese "nation" (Ch. *guojia*) and "society" (Ch. *shehui*). "Religion" by then was definitively a category of the state. By the mid-1990s, the continued vitality of the spatiotemporal opposition between "feudal religion" and "modern society" rested on the ongoing political economic dominance of the Chinese state. This, I found, created everyday conundrums in which local Tibetans (especially young intellectuals) and state officials had to negotiate the disturbing inadequacy of those categories to actually delineate safely separate social contexts.

I was then precariously situated under the auspices of the newly established Tibetan Studies Institute in town. The Beijing-educated half-Tibetan founder, himself a former Xiahe Party and county deputy head, had enthusiastically set it up as the center of "Labrang studies," making the monastery and its environs the objects of a rationalist social history research (Ch. *shehui lishi yanjiu*). In some ways, he and his largely Tibetan lay male underlings compensated for their relative alienation from Tibetan Buddhism by focusing their research on the monastery's prestigious great men. My own social science orientation and the translocal prestige of hosting a foreigner jibed well enough with the director's goals that I was, after much negotiation, able to live in the Institute's apartment building.

With my file open at the Public Security Bureau (PSB), a work unit to take responsibility for me, and various government offices benefiting from my income, I was considered to be appropriately ensconced in the supervisory networks of the state. Our cement-block apartment with its tiny coal stove gave us a degree of privacy unheard of in those parts. That space became an ideal home base from which to go out into the monastery, town, and village, and in which to conduct interviews and language exchanges, or just to converse with friends with a minimum of state or neighborhood scrutiny. In this I think I greatly benefited from my male colleagues' trivialization of me as a woman doing gender (read "women's") studies. As such, I was largely ignored by them, left to conduct my research as I pleased, with no direct intervention or mandatory "research assistants" accompanying me. Some days I got quite complacent.

Yet in Labrang, being ignored was also the effect of locals' well-honed communicative strategies to cope with the routinization of fear and resentment under current and remembered state repression (cf. Taussig 1987). Secrecy was vital, not only to the workings of ritual, power, and knowledge in the monastic community (cf. Campbell 1996: 98), but also for preserving the everyday frameworks of "harmonious" coexistence, an unconscious habitus, in which *everyone* was arguably invested, that constructed the semblance of apolitical public spaces in the valley. Social science fieldwork, with its emphasis on interview techniques that record informants' own accounts on paper or on tape, was associated for many locals with the methods used by outsiders to reveal and manipulate hidden realities that could gravely threaten that uncertain everyday accommodation (see chapter 2). In fact, contrary to the pretensions of post-Mao tourism and "patriotic religion" policies, Tibetan monasteries in the PRC were acutely repoliticized spaces after demonstrations against Chinese rule led by monks and nuns in Lhasa in the late 1980s (cf. Schwartz 1994). Labrang was thus one of the few subprefecture-level regions in Gansu province to have a branch of the National Security Bureau (NSB), the national-level office in charge of investigating and rooting out any signs of antistate dissent.

As I discovered, I had my own NSB official secretly assigned to keep tabs on me—the hard-drinking Tibetan cadre who lived downstairs with his long-suffering wife, herself a local PSB cadre. In this climate, no state bureau, not even the Women's Federation, would go out on a limb and officially support my research by giving me direct access to data. I was never able to conduct a systematic household survey, for example, and any research materials (Chinese- and Tibetan-language books, survey data, censuses, maps) I collected were obtained through private negotiations or in bookstores.[5]

In this context, it did not take me long to accept that there was no way to ultimately eradicate my difference from local Tibetans, or to neutralize fully the political difficulties of my subject position. Thus, anything I eventually learned there was shaped by Tibetans' vigorous efforts to either keep me at bay as an unfamiliar subject or to *regender* me across ethnic categories. That is, they worked to substantialize me in their lives by recontextualizing me as a participant in local Tibetan genres of discourse and action befitting my eventual assignment to femaleness, in ways I did not always want or control. As a foreign researcher, my femaleness was particularly problematic vis-à-vis the accommodation of the monastic intelligentsia with the state over the status of "religion."

Since the monastery was reopened in 1980, lamas and their monk and lay male students had been deeply invested in reframing Buddhism first and foremost as prestigious, rationalized knowledge production. And that status depended on reproducing the Buddha Dharma through the participation framework of the hierarchical lama-student relationship based in male celibate monasticism. I was not much surprised, then, when I heard from young Tibetan men that some lamas and monks at the monastery and the monastery-affiliated Buddhist Studies Institute in town were resentful and derisive of the secular Tibetan Studies Institute, founded as it was on very different premises for knowledge and prestige under state auspices, and competing for limited state funds earmarked in the reform era for "preserving" Tibetan cultural heritage.

But as a female member of that work unit, I particularly embodied the emasculating usurpation of lamas that the establishment of the Tibetan Studies Institute seemed to carry forward. As I set out to talk with Tibetans of every stripe about local history, and their opinions about gender and ritual practices, I learned that there were no general Tibetan terms in everyday use for "religion" and "ritual" that would cover all the practices constituting the lay-monastic relationship (cf. Huber 1994b: 34). Tibetans across the community instead referred to a vast repertoire of efficacious practices with particular terms depending on the task to be accomplished, the target of the practice, and whether or not it conferred benefits to future lifetimes. But in the face of state regulation that divided institutionalized and Party-supervised "religion" from dangerously irrational "superstition" (Ch. *mixin;* cf. Welch 1972, Anagnost 1987, Duara 1995), what most structured this complex ritual life in Labrang was locals' heightened insistence on a *gendered social ontology* that attributed highest efficacy to the rational knowledge of Tibetan Buddhist scholar-adepts (Tib. *mkhas pa*) initiated in the monastic system (see chapter 5).

Despite my interlocutors' strong pride in all manner of local custom as markers of Tibetanness contained in "the way we do things" (Tib. *nga cho'i bca' srol las srol*), I was never more Other than when I was initially asking the uninitiated to teach me on tape about topics of Buddhism and gender. Most of my interlocutors awkwardly found ways to refuse the tape recorder, not only out of fear of the state, but also because taped speech was associated with the authoritative words of lamas. In those encounters, I both made explicit and upended the gendered participant statuses that constructed the hierarchical relationship between lay and monastic worlds in town. Thus, Dargye (about 27 years old), a highly educated lay male friend and a teacher at a prefecture Tibetan school, could barely contain his condescension and gentle mockery during our long debates about my research methods. For him what was at stake here was nothing less than my scholarly reputation, and he thus took it upon himself to regender me appropriately.

To him, my efforts to learn about ritual practices from the perspective of Tibetans at various levels of the community, and especially my interest in talking to laywomen and nuns, threatened to muddle seriously the crucial distinction between folk knowledge and authentic Buddhist knowledge. Despite his own position as a lay teacher under secular state auspices, Dargye was appalled that I was working outside the monastic contexts of initiation (Tib. *dbang*) and oral instructions on a canon of Buddhist texts (Tib. *lung*) under a lama qualified to confer them (Tib. *bka' drin gsum ldan bla ma*), especially since Labrang was one of the few places left where one could find such a lama. In his view, any knowledge I produced through social science methods was trivial at best and mistaken at worst, and rendered suspect the quality of my scholarship.

Dargye's absolutist position in that early conversation glossed over the difficulties for any female to gain access to the most qualified and sought-after Tibetan lamas, who rarely left monastic space. Instead, he offered as a model for my appropriate gendered participation a foreign woman he had known. He enthused about how she had come to Labrang as a tourist and, despite her inability to understand or read Tibetan, had learned a lot just by going every day to the main assembly hall of the monastery and listening at the threshold. To my eternal frustration, the knowledge she gained from her appropriately peripheral position in the gendered participation frameworks of Tibetan monasticism seemed to count much more for Dargye than my years of study outside them. Yet encounters like that one were only one aspect of the productive tensions of mutual recognition that structured my experience in Labrang. What mattered most for my Tibetan interlocutors, including Dargye, was the gradual yet contested process of what Jennifer Robertson has referred to as (gendered) "cross-ethniking" (1998: 77), by which I came to be (partially) regendered as a Tibetan-inflected laywoman. For most, this was greatly enabled by the commitment I had demonstrated by learning to speak (however imperfectly) the local dialect of Amdo Tibetan. "If you did not speak our language," said one old woman, her friends nodding in agreement, "we would not be friends with you."

Eight months after my arrival, I was circumambulating the monastery during a lay festival. On that occasion, the only visible bodily marker that distinguished my appearance from those first months were my heavy gold-and-turquoise earrings, like those worn by local Tibetan laywomen. I had had them made and had painstakingly worked them through my tiny pierced ear holes. Passersby, many of them now my friends and acquaintances, were delighted to see me out, and many commented on my earrings, joking that I had now changed into a (lay) Tibetan woman (Tib. *da khyod bod mo la brjes dang*).

But it was not merely the earrings that so clearly marked my gender as intelligible to Tibetans and transformed me (in those interactions) from a foreign body to a recognizable gendered subject—Why *had* I felt compelled to shove those huge things through my earlobes? And why did Tibetans focus on them as emblematic? It was the history those earrings (as a recently key public marker of local femininity) indexed of my (partial) incorporation into gendered interactions on Tibetan terms. It was in the subtle sociolinguistic cues and gestures associated with Labrang Tibetan femininity I gradually took on in encounters, such as the way I came to talk and think about my "husband"—feeling extremely uncomfortable with public displays of heterogender affection, yet learning to participate in and expect the micropractices of bodily touch signifying homogender affection. It was also in the way I found myself drawn into feeling a deep sense of existential vulnerability as lay and monastic interlocutors spoke to me of the capriciousness of life, luck, and deities, the dizzying momentum of economic changes, and the overwhelming power of the state.

People often didactically addressed me as a fellow seeker of guidance and happiness, and like Dargye instructed me in the proper way to orient myself vis-à-vis Buddhist deities' abodes or "power centers" (Tib. *gnas*), and I gradually assimilated a sense of the everyday efficacy of ritual technologies that focused on an orienting and grounding corporeal proximity to such Buddhist centers (see chapter 3). My regendering was then also manifest in my (still awkward) participation in worship practices around the monastery and at home appropriate to a married laywoman; it was in the feeling of awe I came to experience in Buddhist contexts, and my automatically deferential behavior upon meeting male religious elites. And it was in the way I came to respect gender exclusions in and around the monastery and to feel profoundly uncomfortable if they were transgressed.[6]

It was only when I became subject to a gendered Tibetanness publicly reproducing vital distinctions between lay and monastic contexts that my Tibetan interlocutors, at all levels of the community, began to share with me more openly their own critical or ironic detachment from both ritual and state contexts. As my lan-

guage skills improved, and I took on the obligations of various reciprocity relations throughout the community, Tibetan men and women shared with me in
broad-ranging gossip sessions, and, as Cain and I began to teach English in our
apartment, in various teacher-student exchanges, their life stories, their opinions
about gender relations and Buddhism, and their anxieties and angers about the
changes they felt to be happening all around them. From this ground, I was eventually able to conduct some thirty formal, taped interviews with nuns, monks, and
laypeople. Over time, as I moved between household, monastery, and state contexts, trying not to attract undue attention to myself or to my interlocutors, I came
to understand some of the multiple and often competing interests swirling around
the revitalizing monastery under state scrutiny, as well as some of the ways in
which local Tibetans continued to construct themselves as a community in contradistinction to (threatening) outsiders.

BODIES OF POWER: CULTURAL POLITICS
AND EMBODIMENT IN THE FRONTIER ZONE

Agents of tourism's new "exhibitionary order" (Mitchell 1992) in Tibetan regions
like Labrang attempted, with the alluringly simple realism of photographs, to fix
Tibetanness in space and time as an ancient yet timeless (in the sense of unchanging) tradition. Such representations implicitly claimed that the commodity they
offered was both ideal and real, and their persuasiveness was in large part due to
their wide appeal to Tibetans and non-Tibetans alike (cf. Makley 1994, 1998;
Upton 1996). Yet the Labrang region, with its centuries-old Geluk-sect Buddhist
monastery, seat of the region's former rulers, would seem to present both ordinary
citizens and state officials with particular challenges in defining and managing the
persistent gap between the ideal and the real. In the 1990s the national status of
Labrang as an exemplary site for ethnic tourism and harmonious state-minority
relations actually depended on its historical position as both a multiethnic periphery *and* as a uniquely autonomous Buddhist and political economic center.

In recent years, social theorists have been fascinated with "borderlands" or "marginal" regions. For many these are privileged sites for rethinking earlier notions of
"cultures" as static social and ideological orders confined to a place, and for focusing
instead on elucidating the "cultural politics" among people attempting to define
boundaries between persons, ethnicities, and spaces in an increasingly interconnected world (e.g., Anzaldua 1987, Limón 1991, Gupta and Ferguson 1992, Behar
1993, Tsing 1993, Ortner 1996). Since the monastery of Labrang Tashi Khyil was

founded in 1709, this region has indeed been an important borderland, located in what Michael Aris has called the north-south "frontier zone" on the western edges of Chinese worlds (1992: 13; cf. Gaubatz 1996: 28). The monastery and its networks of lay supporters and branch monasteries flourished in the foothills of the towering mountain ranges that rise to the Tibetan plateau, at the edges of both the Manchu Qing empire in China and the central Tibetan regime under the ascendant Dalai Lamas (see map 1).

Situated near the major trade and pilgrimage routes west to Xinjiang along the Silk Road, north to Mongolia and southwest to Lhasa, Labrang's lama hierarchs marshaled a Buddhist monastic order that grew to be the largest in the region (with up to 4,000 monks in its heyday). That order encompassed Tibetans, Mongols, and various Muslim groups even after People's Liberation Army (PLA) troops marched into the valley in September 1949 to establish it as part of a new nation, the People's Republic of China (PRC) under the Chinese Communist Party (CCP). In the ensuing decades, Communist ideologies justified the wholesale destruction of the monastic community and the social nexus that supported it. Yet in the context of the 1990s revitalization of the monastery and lay-monastic relationships, the reduction of Labrang to a marginal county seat of the Chinese nation-state was arguably incomplete. It was instead an ongoing, politically fraught process implicated in locals' everyday lives.

Thus, when social theorists pose such borders and margins in a new global world as exemplary counterpoints to "culture-as-order," they risk eliding as much as they reveal. Focusing on a place as a "border" risks reifying spatial and political economic marginality that is most often produced through local manifestations of the power and violence of states and transnational corporations (cf. Tsing 1993: x). Indeed, the "frontier zone" retained its peripheral status into the 1990s largely because of political economic policies since the establishment of the PRC that had set up alternative forms of governance in the west, extracting resources there in order to target eastern regions for rapid economic "development" (Ch. *fazhan;* cf. Gaubatz 1996: 28). Most importantly, though, in emphasizing "borders" as extreme or atypical cases in social theory, it is all too tempting to continue to assume radical disjunctures in time and space, so that the contemporary flux, "hybridity," and cultural politics on the margins are not to be found in some posited center, or in the imagined past. These sorts of assumptions of course are comfortably compatible with Chinese state historiography since the founding of the PRC. In those narratives, reproduced paradigmatically in State Council White Papers, 1949 marks a Communist "revolution" that establishes a coherently centralized, rational, and democratic state radically different from all previous regimes; "modern" history starts then. Further, bolstered by the findings of an emergent Han Chinese social science, state narratives depict Han urbanites as the unmarked norm, heirs to centuries of "Chinese" rule over "minority nationalities," who are largely confined to the less cultured hinterlands (see chapter 2).

In my fieldwork and in the writing of this book, I attempted to work against such deeply assumed homologies between places, cultures, and times. As many have pointed out, forms of geographic fixing have been primary techniques in imperial and national ruling strategies past and present (cf. Axel 2002) By the nineteenth and twentieth centuries, Westerners' longing for Tibet as an inaccessible colonial domain or economic market helped to generate potent images of Tibet as an enclosed and static cultural Other par excellence (Lopez 1998). In the face of various modernist trajectories, "Tibet" was then available for condemnation or idealization (i.e., "Shangri-la") as a reified periphery, a counterpoint to historical progress, especially after the Chinese Communist takeover in the early 1950s (cf. Bishop 1989, 1993, 1994; Harris 1999; Dodin and Rather 2001). By contrast, I consider Labrang to be a complex cultural and political nexus centered on the monastery, but one that was fundamentally translocal and vigorously historical. Local lay and monastic interests always relied on and competed with a range of (human and divine) agents and polities based elsewhere, and history making was arguably the ground of Tibetans' ongoing existence there.

As we will see, Tibetans at various positions in their communities worked to manage the often tense relationship between perceived stasis and change, drawing on ritual and discourse genres that linked them to peoples (not all of whom identified themselves with names translatable as "Tibetan," Tib. *bod*) spread out over a vast area of Inner Asia and the Himalayas. After all, contrary to tourism claims as to the "ancientness" of Tibetan tradition there, the founding lama of Labrang monastery actually intervened, at the behest of a Mongol lord, relatively recently in the region, taking over land that for centuries had been the contested pasturelands of Mongolian, Tangut, and Tibetan nomads in various relations with dynastic regimes. Major Tibetan settlement there did not occur until the monastery was founded in the early eighteenth century. That was a particular moment in history with strong implications for the shaping of the space and its peoples—at the height of the Qing, when, as the power of local Mongol suzerains waned, the Manchu empire had expanded to rival other expansionist states globally (cf. Millward 1999, Perdue 2005), and Tibetan and Mongol factions vied for control of the Tibetan Buddhist polity under the Dalai Lamas' Geluk sect in Lhasa (cf. Petech

1950). Yet nineteenth century local Tibetan Buddhist histories posited an ultimately timeless relationship between Tibetans, Labrang monastery, and the local landscape through the power of prophecy (Tib. *lung bstan*) wielded by the omniscient Buddha and his Dharma heirs, tantric Buddhist yogins and lamas. Labrang monastery in these narratives is the foreseen end result of a specifically Tibetan spread of Buddhism north from its cradle in India (dkon mchog rgyal mtshan 1985, dkon mchog bstan pa rab rgyas 1987).

In the light of such complex intersections of discourse and practice, we could consider "culture" not as unitary ideological or social orders, but as the *tensions* between all participation frameworks that come into play in particular historical encounters. The frontier zone only makes more explicit the dialogic or intersubjective interpretive politics at the heart of all sociocultural worlds (cf. Silverstein 1976, 1997; Bakhtin 1981; Mannheim and Tedlock 1995). In this view, "cultural politics" is constituted by people's quotidian struggles with interpretive dilemmas and practical predicaments vis-à-vis themselves and others, a process that unfolds as familiar categories prove inadequate in the face of competing pressures to recognize them as real and unassailable (cf. Hannerz 1996). In the Labrang region, especially after the fall of the Qing in 1911 and the establishment of new Han Chinese regimes as "modern" nation-states, those interpretive frames available to locals increasingly came to be shaped by the dialogue between competing frameworks for the ideal management of values and selves in time and space—Tibetan Buddhist monasticism, tantric Buddhist liberation paths, Maoist communism, and nationalist economic development (cf. Tuttle 2005). Thus, for Labrang residents, their eventual incorporation into the Chinese nation meant an extremely stressful *re*incorporation as new types of moral selves located on a linear road of socialist advance.

In the chapters to follow, I treat the state as an ongoing cultural project that was crucially manifest in practices of embodiment (cf. Foucault 1977). My account of local processes here is in some ways a story of state officials' and ordinary citizens' efforts to reify or substantialize in bodies the Chinese state as a monolithic agent, despite the massive, often disorganized, and dispersed nature of Party and government personnel and institutions over time and space (cf. Corrigan and Sayer 1985, Cohn and Dirks 1988, A. Alonso 1994, Mueggler 2001; and see below, chapter 2). From this perspective we can appreciate the inherent dangers for state authorities in the project of constructing state agency among its multiethnic citizens, even given the unprecedented "success" of the Chinese Communist state in dominating a massive area of Inner Asia once claimed by the Qing. In the 1990s,

Tibetans and other groups now regulated as national minorities occupied 60 percent of the PRC's landmass, an area containing precious raw materials for state and economy building in that country of 1.3 billion citizens. For Tibetans in Labrang, the stakes of this process of imputing state agency to bodies were also extremely high, as they coped with memories of the brutal violence of Maoist bodily discipline, a particular culture of state violence that was arguably refigured in post-Mao policing techniques (cf. Dutton 1992, 1995), or as they themselves embodied the state as officials, representing a selfhood and a moral order profoundly at odds with those asserted in (newly objectified) Tibetan Buddhist cosmologies (see chapter 2).

From the linguistic anthropological perspective on participation I have been developing here, we have to consider power and authority in China's frontier zone to be the emergent effects of the contested recognition of bodies. Insistent claims as to the novel scientific rationality of the Maoist state notwithstanding, new PRC state leaders, much as did previous dynastic regimes, had to find ways to substantialize their dominance locally by getting citizens to recognize corporeal individuals (selves as well as Others) as embodiments of an awesome power and legitimate authority whose unseen sources were based far away in Beijing. But in Labrang, PRC national body–building came up against Tibetans' own elaborately ramified frameworks for the embodiment of power and authority, and those processes, of course, were fundamentally gendered.

In this book, I argue that national incorporation in the Labrang region was in large part a dialogue and a clash between very different androcentric social orders—forms of masculine dominance were the sites of major conflict *and* the frames for important state-local collusions. After the seats of the Communist Party and PRC government were established in the market town downriver from the monastery, the most authoritative bodies of power in state-local encounters were male—Han and Tibetan state cadres on the one hand and on the other, Tibetan incarnate lamas or *trulku*s (Tib. *sprul sku*, lit. "miraculously transformed bodies"). Unlike those who earn the title of *lama* through ritual or scholarly prowess, trulkus are recognized (usually as children) to be current incarnations in lineages of previously enlightened Buddhist lamas, themselves often said to be physical emanations of Buddhas or bodhisattvas. Thus trulkus in Labrang epitomized a uniquely Tibetan form of substantialization through embodiment that has been problematic for Tibetan and non-Tibetan regimes alike—but especially for Chinese Communist authorities.

Trulkus will be very important protagonists in this story, because since the fourteenth century, when all Tibetan Buddhist sects adopted the practice of recognizing a child as the reincarnation of their revered lamas, trulkus played pivotal roles in the most grounding participation frameworks throughout regions converted to Tibetan forms of Buddhism.[7] As Toni Huber and others have noted, the ascendance of the tantric lama as culture hero in Tibet and intensified competition among trulku lineages were historically associated with the increased importance of monastic sectarian interests, especially after the monastic-based Geluk sect rose to power in the sixteenth and seventeenth centuries under the great fifth Dalai Lama (1999: 29; cf. Samuel 1993). The power of incarnate lamas, whose main "seats" or "thrones" (Tib. *gdan pa*) were located in monasteries, was thus intimately connected with that of male monasticism throughout Tibetan regions (cf. Mills 2003: 81).

In Labrang, trulkus were paradigmatically male and uniquely purified bodies. As such, I argue, they could both embody and tame the semiotic and existential indeterminacy that ordinary Tibetans so acutely felt. Their status as categories of the human divine (divinity in human form) positioned in uniquely intimate relationships to their lay and monastic constituencies in the Labrang region meant that their bodies and actions operated as crucial *indexes*—that is, signs interpreted as naturally presupposing (i.e., being part of or caused by) both a Buddhist history locally and a divine cosmos beyond—and thus also as entailing hoped-for outcomes (cf. Silverstein 1997: 268).

As many have pointed out, we cannot take huge Geluk monastic communities like Labrang to be typical of Tibetan cultures (Samuel 1993, Germano 1998, Kapstein 1998). Indeed, as we will see, in many ways Labrang was extremely atypical in eastern Tibetan regions especially. Yet I would also argue that in the everyday worship of trulkus there, we can see a particularly Tibetan emphasis on physicality, substance, and contiguity as frameworks for ideal participation invoked by people across lay, monastic, or sectarian communities throughout Tibetan regions, in ways that did not necessarily jibe with the analytic distinctions of Buddhist exegesis (cf. Huber 1994a, 1994b, 1999; Mills 2003).

Thus, as against the monastic scholarly ideal in places like Labrang, revered trulkus were not necessarily the most learned or ritually accomplished lamas, yet they were the preferred objects of devotional practices, everyday merit-making, and "purity" harvests (collecting objects people felt to be empowered to heal or protect through contact with the trulku's pure body), all to a variety of this-worldly and otherworldly ends (cf. Huber 1999). Much to the consternation of CCP public security officials, the sixth Gongtang Tshang (1926–2000), one of the four highest-ranked "Golden Throne" trulkus at Labrang, was arguably the most widely known and beloved lama in the region. His public ceremonies in Labrang in the 1990s were huge interregional events, and when he emerged from a building I had to be careful not to be trampled as people struggled for proximity to him (see chapter 5). If we take into account the very different things trulkus like Gongtang mean to people at such events, trulkus were positioned as key shifters—the meanings their bodies and actions indexed for people crucially depended on the particulars of social situation (cf. Silverstein 1976). In other words, they were interpretive pivots whose recognition in a variety of contexts could thereby causally and semiotically link a range of spatial and temporal frameworks in contrasting ways.

Trulkuhood, then, directs our attention back to the importance of recognition processes for understanding (gendered) cultural politics. By "recognition" here I mean not merely the rituals for finding and confirming a reborn incarnate lama (Tib. *yang srid ngos 'dzin gnang ba*), but also the everyday processes by which differently motivated worshippers and (lamas themselves) interpreted (or rejected) individuals as trulkus. In this light, the divine charisma of a Tibetan trulku perhaps epitomizes what Keane has called the "quandary of agency": the most authoritative agents are often precisely those whose grounds for power and authority most elude individuals' control (1997: 16). Despite people's strong assertions about the intrinsic nature of such persons' agency, in actuality it depends on the vicissitudes of co-created meanings in particular contexts (cf. Mannheim and Tedlock 1995, Ahearn 2001).

Yet, in the coming chapters, I argue that it was the *unmarked* nature of maleness (versus femaleness as relatively marked and impure) as the ontological ground for transcendent bodies and minds that crucially enabled Tibetan trulkus' local *and* translocal authority. The less corporeal quality of their purified (male) bodies allowed for the recognition (and manipulation) of their powers not as gender attributes but as the manifestation of an absolute and abstract (i.e., *dis*embodied) Dharma. It was arguably only with an unprecedented political challenge that trulkus were violently and *categorically* resexed in the Labrang region. We will see that the (painful) transition to nationhood in this region did not occur when the Qing dynasty fell, but almost fifty years later, in 1958, when Han CCP authorities finally dispensed with earlier efforts to appropriate the charisma of locally centered trulkus and attempted to radically displace them instead (see chapter 2). At the beginning of the Cultural Revolution, in the summer of 1966, multiple images of Mao Zedong marched into Labrang monastery carried by drum-beating Red

Guards bent on desecrating the space (Tenzin Palbar 1994: 203). That was the outcome of an almost decade-long process of PRC officials' attempts to supplant local trulkus and expropriate their wealth and constituencies by replacing them with the national body of Mao—when I was there some Tibetan cadres still hung portraits of Mao in the high places in their homes once reserved for images of lamas and deities (cf. Harris 1999: 82).

To really grasp the post-Mao stakes of gendered social change among Tibetans in Labrang, we have to understand that this usurpation was accomplished through state-local collaboration in *(re)sexing* trulkus by violently desecrating them in public. That is, trulkus were sexed as ordinary males (along with other "class enemies") in the new participation frameworks of compulsory public meetings. There, Chinese and Tibetan conveners attempted to deny trulkus' innate superhuman bodily purity and agency in accusations and demonstrations of their human moral and sexual corruption. The hyperrealism of Mao images in demolished or emptied monastic spaces then modeled the new national (male) body: one that refused the irrationality of trulkus' indexical links to a local lamaist historicity and to a Buddhist cosmos beyond, and asserted the superior legitimacy of a radically "rational" and socially located power instead. For most Tibetan men *and* women in Labrang, socialist transformation was thus not only a forced secularization of their lives; it was also a fundamentally *emasculating* process.

WRITING FROM THE INTERSTICES

The shape of this book reflects the exigencies of fieldwork in an urbanizing locale under a still-repressive state. The six chapters do not constitute a simple chronological narrative, nor do they form an old-style anthropological "ethnography" that separates out different "systems" constituting a "social structure" and presumes to represent a community in its (static) entirety. Instead, my account of the ongoing incorporation of Labrang into the PRC nation-state is partial and episodic. That is, the chapters are linked analyses of particular episodes in gendered contestations and collusions in the valley, and are organized in order to demonstrate the actual diversity and global connectedness of Tibetan experiences of Geluk monastic revitalization under Chinese rule. Moving from larger spatiotemporal and political economic contexts to the particulars of gendered ritual and everyday encounters in and around the monastery, the chapters build an increasingly nuanced account of the exigencies of life in post-Mao Labrang for Tibetan men and women. In the telling, I try to find a middle ground between abstract theory and narratives, interweaving relevant fieldwork stories with historical accounts as a way to demonstrate how history, for my Tibetan interlocutors, was always in the making.

At the same time, I attempt to bring key insights from linguistic anthropology to nonspecialist readers by taking up Goffman's master trope of participation frameworks especially. That spatial metaphor is an ideal way to get at the fundamentally co-produced yet situated nature of all social powers, values, and meanings, even in the absence of the complex transcripts and diacritics of linguistic anthropological analyses. In this way, over the six chapters, I progressively develop a theory of the locally salient categories of sex, gender, and sexuality as key framing cues deployed by Tibetans and their interlocutors amidst radically shifting values set in motion with the advent of globalizing capitalism under reforms. In this, my goal was not so much to produce an exhaustive study of the microprocesses of local interactions among Tibetans and others, but to demonstrate the ways in which such encounters are inextricably linked with the macropolitics of the translocal.

My focus on gender as an analytic tool in the chapters to follow will hopefully counter essentialized accounts of "Tibetans," in contradistinction to "Chinese," that tend to portray Tibetans either as passive victims of Chinese state violence and colonialist expansions, or as determined (peaceful) resisters. But I have no illusions that so doing will be enough to foreclose the politics in which any representation of Tibetans is inevitably ensconced. Thus my arguments here will not seek to resolve or to mitigate the inherently controversial nature of my approach to the process of Buddhist revival among Tibetans in the PRC. Instead, I can only present the politics generated by my (ultimately immutable) difference from locals as integral to the entire research process and the analyses in the following chapters. Only such an approach would be true to the ongoing and very personal way I have struggled with such issues throughout my fieldwork and beyond.

ONE

Fatherlands

Mapping Masculinities

GOMPO'S MOVE

Perhaps one of the reasons for the initial gender confusion about me in Labrang was that when I arrived my large gold hoop earrings and long unbraided hair evoked the self-conscious bodily markers of an important category of local Other in town: young nomad men. Gompo, a quiet and respectful student of Cain's in his early twenties, had always defiantly presented himself that way, insisting, in contrast to young village men, on marking his origins in a nomad region historically subject to Labrang monastery by sporting a style that had been popularized since the late 1980s by idolized Tibetan male singers marketing their talents in popular cassettes and local performances—long hair, a large hoop earring, robes, and high boots.

Amidst the bustling press of multiethnic bodies clothed in pants and jackets on the main street, Tibetan nomad men and women, with their long hair, jewelry, and distinctive wool and felt robes (knee-length for men, ankle-length for women), stood out as they browsed the shops looking for necessities to take back up to the grasslands, attended public events at the monastery, or haggled prices with Hui merchants over sheep or wool they were selling. At night, the local bars and dance halls filled with young nomad men seeking a good time. But Gompo's fashionable nomad style indexed his more cosmopolitan ambitions. As I came to know him that year, it seemed to me that Gompo's personal trajectories over space and time illustrated important processes in struggles over Tibetan lay and monastic masculinities in the frontier zone. And those contests had figured importantly in intensifying struggles over defining and controlling spaces in the region as Labrang by the early twentieth century came to be tied ever closer to Chinese interests.

Like many young Tibetan men living in Labrang town, Gompo was there seeking opportunity, and his moves relied on networks of men who forged alliances across regions and across lay and monastic contexts. While in Labrang, Gompo depended for housing and emotional guidance on his affectionate relationship with Akhu Sherap, an old monk and lama (teacher) living in the monastery. As Akhu Sherap later explained it to me, he supported Gompo and took on his younger brother as a monk student out of loyalty and affection for their nomad father. Akhu Sherap said that during "the frightening time" (post 1958), when monks in Labrang monastery were forcibly returned to lay life, Gompo's father had taken him in to live with them in their region, so that, against policy, the monk could retain his vows and remain unmarried. To Akhu Sherap's consternation however, Gompo's ambitions in the 1990s took him far beyond Labrang and out of the purview of those networks. He had just returned from two and a half years in Shenzhen, that coastal Chinese city and "special economic zone" from which Deng Xiaoping had famously reaffirmed China's commitment to market reforms in 1992. In Ann Anagnost's words, Shenzhen by then was "the showplace of China's economic reforms" that had been set in motion by the Dengist regime in the early 1980s (1997: 161).

As Gompo sardonically described it to me, his opportunity to move east and participate in that "economic miracle" came when Chinese recruiters traveled to Labrang seeking young Tibetan men and women as dancers for the newly established "Folk Cultural Village" in Shenzhen. He described how the recruiters watched a line of young Tibetans dance in front of them, choosing the ones who looked best. Gompo insisted that they must have chosen him because of his looks (Tib. *tshug ka*) alone, since he didn't even know how to dance! But the job did not turn out the way he and his fellow dancers had thought, he said. Even though the pay was not bad compared to Labrang, they had no say in anything. When they raised complaints, they were told, in terms echoing Maoist socialist education, that they had bad attitudes (Tib. *rnam gyur mi sra gi*) and could leave. He said that the park's vision of Tibetan history and that of Tibetans didn't agree (Tib. *tho mi thug gi*), so it was too difficult for him to stay. Yet by his account, Gompo continued to dance in the park for several years before Akhu Sherap sent word to him that Cain and I were teaching English in Labrang and he should return to take advantage of that rare opportunity.

MASCULINITY AND TRANSLOCALITY:
GENDER, SPACE, AND CONTEXTUALIZATION

What can such a mobile personal history as Gompo's tell us about the locale that was Labrang in the mid-1990s? I begin with an account of some of the main local premises for Gompo's move east to dance in an ethnic park in a Chinese coastal city, in order to highlight the crucial role of Tibetan men's *translocal* networking in the dynamic construction of Labrang as a locality, past as well as present.

In that community, there were very good reasons for reifying the past. As we will see, for many Tibetans I spoke to, the unprecedented state violence and velocity of socialist transformation during the Maoist years seemed, in line with Communist rhetoric, to have abruptly sealed in the past a timeless and monolithic "Old Society" (Tib. *'jig rten rnying pa*, Ch. *jiu shehui*). In this chapter, however, my focus on the cultural politics of masculinity and space will illustrate the seething dynamism of Labrang as a particularly important frontier polity that was subject to an extraordinary range of jurisdictional claims from the time Labrang monastery was founded. "Labrang," as a place and a jurisdiction, has always been a moving target.

Here, I argue that attention to gender dynamics can elucidate important spatial processes that shaped the Labrang locality even after the Communist "revolution" and the incorporation of the region into the PRC nation-state. Gender, as a contested process of recognizing bodies to be intrinsically linked to hierarchized personas, discourse genres, and social contexts, is an important lens through which to understand space as a cultural politics of contextualization. In this, I consider gender in conjunction with a refigured notion of "context." Rather than a fixed "background" for social action, I take context to be an ongoing *interpretive process* in order to work against prevalent views of space as an immobile backdrop for time, and to explore instead what Soja, following Foucault, called the "triple dialectic of time, space and social being" (1989: 12; cf. Bauman and Briggs 1990, C. Goodwin and Duranti 1992).

In other words, the seeming permanence of key aspects of sociocultural life, such as categories of space and personhood, actually depends on people's differential capacities to contextualize those categories in and across historically situated events. "Contexts" in this view are in actuality frameworks for social participation negotiated in everyday interactions (cf. Goffman 1981; Hanks 1996: 161; Silverstein 1997: 264). I would say, then, that space and time emerged as mutually constitutive contexts or "places" in the frontier zone only as asymmetrically positioned people worked to situate themselves as types of gendered subjects (cf. de Certeau 1984: 117).[1]

My focus on gendered contextualization processes here will illuminate the triple dialectic of geography, history, and power in the Labrang region as various authorities, for increasingly high stakes, sought to map Labrang residents as loyal constituents within competing jurisdictional fields. In this chapter, I focus on relevant masculinities in this process as categories of subjectivity defining premises for authoritative agency and capacities for violence exercised *translocally*—that is, across sociospatial contexts—and always in relation to subordinated masculine and feminine Others. Thus, to recall the mutual misrecognitions of Gompo's Tibetan masculinity during his audition for the Chinese ethnic-park recruiters, the contested interpretation of masculinities had all along been at the center of efforts to define and control the Labrang region and its residents in relation to larger social and spatial units, yet the frameworks for such contests had radically shifted by the 1990s (see chapters 2 and 5).

For Tibetans, the strategic (mis)interpretation of masculinities had offered precarious avenues for actively forging translocal alliances and for recruiting residents to subjecthood. As we will see, Tibetan trulkus and Qing emperors expediently misinterpreted each other in order to claim very different kinds of jurisdiction locally. Yet by the time Gompo strategically sold the image of his ethnicized nomad masculinity to the Chinese ethnic theme park, he was recruited to participate most directly in a new nation-space that had profoundly remapped the Labrang region as a marginalized administrative unit and a passive repository of "resources" (including people) to be exploited in the interest of national "progress." Thus in this and the coming chapters, I consider the incorporation of Labrang into the People's Republic of China as a fundamentally emasculating process by exploring the ways Tibetans in the region (men *and* women) struggled to define the locality as first and foremost a homeland constituted by crucial masculine relationships ultimately centered on the monastery.

PHAYUL: TRULKUS AND GENDERED EMBODIMENT IN AMDO TIBETAN FATHERLANDS

In the 1990s, notions of *phayul,* or "fatherland," among Tibetans in the frontier zone posed a countergeography to that asserted in Chinese state discourse about the multiethnic "family of the nation" (Ch. *duo minzu guojia*) headed by paternal Han authorities (cf. Munson 1999: 2). In the face of what many experienced as the overwhelming power of the Chinese state and the unprecedented regulation of their everyday lives, recourse to phayul for Tibetans was a primary framework for an intensely nostalgic repositioning of selves to home regions, even for those who grew up under Chinese rule. As such, their invocations of phayul indexed a self-consciously Tibetan and patrifocal historicity that reterritorialized people by asserting natural links between selves, male authorities, imagined pasts, and topographic places through an idiom of patrilineal kinship (cf. Malkki 1997: 57). Indeed, the profoundly deterritorialized perspective of Tibetans in the diaspora had arguably lent acute new meaning, for Tibetans both in and outside the PRC, to *land* as the roots of Tibetan home and nation: "Few people in the world," asserted the noted exiled writer and fervent nationalist Jamyang Norbu in his recent manifesto for Tibetan sovereignty, "are so distinctly defined by the kind of land they live in as the Tibetans" (1999: 4; cf. Yuval-Davis 1997: 18).[2]

In this chapter, I situate Labrang in the broader cultural politics of mapping the difficult terrain of the Tibetan frontier zone as a historical legacy of efforts to control the region against Tibetan men's resistance especially. Here, I consider maps broadly as particular types of representations of (social) space, but most importantly as situated assertions of ideal participation frameworks for masculine power and authority. From this perspective, we can understand the violent shift to PRC nationhood in Labrang as, in part, the outcome of a clash between very different framing "maps" for male authorities' legitimately superior relationships to the subjects they claimed, a clash that could be seen as a confrontation between divergent "civilizing projects" in the frontier zone (Harrell 1995; cf. M. Yang 1999: 45).

In Labrang, the recognition of trulkus (and by extension, lamas in general) as the highest masculine authorities in an extensive interregional monastic polity depended on an ongoing Geluk sectarian "mandalization" process that constituted the primary tantric ritual frameworks linking contemporary situations to a Buddhist heritage of civilizing endeavors throughout Tibetan regions. Mandalization efforts were aimed at mapping Labrang as a *centered* place, on the model of a tantric deity's circular palace or maṇḍala, by establishing the region as essentially the field of action of Jamyang Shepa, the founding trulku and transcendent Buddhist agent enthroned at its center and empowered to teach and protect his subjects by taming deities to his will. In practice however, centricity at Labrang was always constructed relative to particular embodied trulkus (e.g., the five historical emanations of Jamyang Shepa) in emergent relationships with other powerful men in a complex frontier-zone political economy.

I argue in this chapter that the specifically tantric Buddhist processes of trulku embodiment crucially established the region as a Tibetan fatherland: that is, as a patrifocal mandalic sphere, one that continually worked to recruit subjects amidst intensifying competition for their loyalties. As I mentioned in the introduction, trulkus or incarnate lamas are supposed to be recognized at birth as human instantiations of an already perfect Buddha mind with a particular relationship to the physical body and to the mundane world. In monastic settings, their rebirth, formal recognition, and enthronement extends an originating lama's agency, and hence his monastic authority and control of the personnel and economic assets of his personal estate (Tib. *bla brang*), across generations. In Labrang, incarnate lama-monks thus embodied a particular *place*-based historicity that attempted to resolve the fundamental Buddhist opposition between the pure timeless Buddha mind and the impure human body subject to karmic history. As many have pointed out, all Buddhist communities have struggled, in relation to indigenous notions of corporality, with the tradition's strong ambivalence toward the body (cf. Faure 1998, 2002; Gyatso 2005).

In much Buddhist exegesis, the human body, as a temporary housing for the mind, is at once an indispensable tool for the ultimate liberation of the mind and a defiling obstacle to it (cf. Lopez 1995). To the amazement or disgust of many an orientalist observer, tropes of the body were arguably one of the principal ways that Mahāyāna forms of Buddhism in India ontologically grounded and rendered materially manifest highly abstract notions of the Buddha's realizations in universes replete with Buddha body-forms. But of all the Buddhist traditions that emerged in Asia, Tibetans alone developed the incarnate lama as the quintessential human Buddhist agent, whose intentionality is said to derive from a transcendent mind that acts through and across extraordinarily pure bodies.

In a wide variety of contexts, Tibetans built on earlier Mahāyāna theories of the "three bodies" of a Buddha, a schema that categorized (and hierarchized) Buddha forms according to degree of corporality and worldly presence, to situate trulkus as the "emanation bodies" of a Buddha (Skt. *nirmaṇakāya*) acting in the mundane world. Unlike the "enjoyment bodies" of Buddhas (Skt. *saṃbhogakāya*) teaching and residing in pure lands inaccessible to ordinary humans in this degenerate age, trulkus are figured as compassionate enlightened beings (Skt. *bodhisattva*) who choose to incarnate in successive mortal bodies to help others escape the sufferings of karmic existence. Tibetan trulkuhood, then, in important ways embodied the dialectic between absolute truth and relative situation that crucially enabled Buddhist intervention in the mundane world of humans. That is, as an emanation body, a trulku's body and actions were supposed to index the ultimately *dis*embodied,

FIGURE 3.

Maṇḍala of Yama Dharmarāja (Tib. Chegyal *or* chos rgyal). Eighteenth century, Geluk lineage: 30.48 × 30.48 cm (12" × 12"), ground mineral pigment on cotton. The deity and his consort are represented in the center only by the implements they usually hold. (Photo courtesy of the Rubin Museum of Art)

pure, and timeless truth of the Buddha's "Dharma body" or Dharmakāya, a notion that tropes corporality to categorize the truth of the historical Buddha's teachings as existing far beyond his physical body and historical time (cf. Keane 1997; Lopez 1997: 22).

I found that in Labrang the historiography of the monastery as a supreme Buddhist abode (Tib. *gnas mchog*), and as one of the six great Geluk Tibetan monasteries,[3] was based on its status as the seat (Tib. *gdan sa*) of the ruling Jamyang Shepa lineage of incarnate lamas. In the 1990s, the narratives I heard from lay and monastic residents alike explained the interregional fame and prestige of the monastery as the fruits of the miraculous deeds of the five previous Jamyang Shepa lamas (see chapter 2). Their status as emanations of Jampiyang (Skt. Mañjuśrī), the bodhisattva of wisdom associated with Buddhist monastic scholarship, linked them to Tshongkhapa, founder of the Geluk sect and also recognized as an emanation of Jampiyang. The name "Labrang" (Tib. *bla brang*, lit. "Great House"), used by local Tibetans instead of the Chinese county name (Xiahe), is after the palace of the founder, and historically it referred to the whole region subject to the monastery (cf. Gu and Lu 1938; Sun 1993: 2). As the monastery expanded its scope, the community included increasing numbers of trulku lineages, the most important of which began with Jamyang Shepa's main disciples who followed him back to the region from Lhasa.

I found that Tibetans across the community recognized high-status trulkus as unique categories of the human divine. Unlike mediums (Tib. *lha pa*), whose bodies are temporarily possessed by deities (cf. Aziz 1976), trulkus for lay and monastic worshippers alike embodied the human possibility for purified mind and body to suffuse each other indefinitely. In this way, they manifested the human capacity to transcend physical limitations and exercise material power across mundane and divine spaces and times—a goal toward which much of the Vajrayāna, the tantric form of Buddhism Tibetans adopted from India, is arguably directed. As humans innately empowered to wield tantric ritual technologies, trulkus embodied an intentional agency that contrasted sharply with most ordinary Tibetans' sense of being subject to both the coercive forces of karma and the capricious intervention of outside (demonic or human) agents (cf. Lichter and Epstein 1983: 253).

Thus historically, Tibetan trulkuhood as a contested locus of authoritative agency provided a participation framework for embodiment that was particularly unmanageable from the perspective of Tibetan and non-Tibetan authorities alike. Monastic scholars and trulkus themselves could not completely control how trulkus were recognized. At Labrang, disputes over whether and how the first Jamyang Shepa would be reincarnated left the throne empty for over twenty years (Dan Qu 1993: 23). The indexical nature of trulkuhood as an agency linking divine and worldly realms thus made the institution a double-edged sword for Tibetan authorities. Geluk trulkus literally embodied the Buddhist rule (Tib. *chos srid gnyis 'dzin*, lit. "Buddhism and government together") that constituted local regimes, yet trulku recognition in practice was fundamentally *trans*local, requiring complex networking among supporters across regions to confirm a candidate against competitors. These politics throughout Tibetan regions by the sixteenth century were the central locus of both internecine conflict and the intervention of outside authorities in efforts to influence locals—a dynamic that I argue had reemerged in post-Mao China (see chapter 5). "Incarnate gods [i.e., trulkus]," said Marion Griebenow, the frustrated American Christian missionary who took advantage of trulku succession struggles in the 1920s to build a compound in Labrang, "are Satan's greatest counterfeit" (1938: 1).

What then of the role of gender? Trulkus in Labrang were one permutation of a complex mind-body nexus among Tibetans that in rituals devoted to multitudes of male and female deities, and in a vast Buddhist commentarial literature, presupposed a wide range of possible relationships between attributes of sex and the proclivities of gendered and sexualized subjects (cf. Huber 1999; Gyatso 2000, 2003, 2005). Indeed, the seemingly excessive flexibility of Tibetan sex-gender systems, including the sexual imagery basic to tantric Buddhist ritual, bewildered or disgusted Western and Chinese observers in the nineteenth and twentieth centuries. There were in fact several lineages of female trulkus throughout Tibetan regions. Yet of the infinite possibilities for Buddha minds to choose incarnation in types of corporeal bodies, the vast majority of Tibetan trulkus have been male.[4]

I argue that if we consider trulkuhood from the perspective of recognition as an inherently unstable and intersubjective process, we can appreciate the crucial role of sex and gender difference locally and translocally. Tibetan historiography and Buddhist exegesis ignore or play down the sex of trulku bodies as inconsequential. In Labrang, I found that their maleness was largely an unconscious given. Yet since trulkus were most often chosen as male children, their recognition as superior beings and pure bodies (Tib. *skyes bu dam pa*) hinged on the recognition of what were assumed to be the inherent qualities of male sex. In this, trulku recognition illustrates a process that I would say operates generally in Tibetan Buddhist practice—Tibetans have always drawn on the unmarked nature of maleness (as against femaleness marked as relatively impure) to mediate the pure mind–impure body antithesis and produce powerful human Buddhist subjects (cf. Campbell 1996; Gyatso 2000, 2003; and see below, chapter 4). Trulku worship thus had a particular role to play in the gendered life of the valley past and present.

Trulku recognition practices in Labrang grounded the local sex-gender system by continually reestablishing a hierarchical male-female sex polarity over time and space, a polarity locals referred to in conversation as *phomo nyi* (lit. "the two," males and females). Those categories of (biological and karmic) sex difference, I found, were widely considered to be at the base of various categories of gendered subjects, like "layman" (Tib. *byis lu* or *gsar bu, rgan po*), "laywoman" (Tib. *byis mo, ayas*), "monk" (Tib. *a khu, grwa pa*), and "nun" (Tib. *a ne, jo mo*).[5] Trulkuhood then powerfully linked maleness with purified bodies and with the most authoritative Buddhist and translocal forms of agency and power. In fact, as I discovered from the wider judgmental leeway Tibetans tended to allow trulkus for their actions, trulkus in Labrang embodied the powerfully flexible masculine agency of "skillful means" (Skt. *upāya*) that in Buddhist exegesis identifies the bodhisattva and tantric ritualist as superior human agents who can tailor their benevolent actions to fit the requirements of persons and situations. Thus in a way, a kind of "calculated ambiguity" (Berger 2003: 184) was essential to trulku masculinity in the frontier zone. In the coming chapters, I argue that this process took on heightened importance and danger in the context of the much-compromised status of male monasticism after reforms.

My monk friend Akhu Konchok's sarcastic reaction to my mention of the only female trulku in the region, Alak Gungru Tshang, perhaps makes sense in this light. After months of conversations with me about changing gender behavior in town, perceptions of flagging monastic discipline, and the (to him) embarrassingly ambivalent role of sex and gender in Buddhism, Akhu Konchok was quick to dismiss Gungru Tshang as an inconsequential regional trulku, and, as a female, "in no way" (Ch. *bu keneng*) the appropriate object of worship in Labrang. His initial smirking sarcasm did give way to respect when we read about her female predecessor's yogic accomplishments, but I was nonetheless struck by the contrast between his initial response to her sex and his usual expressed reverence for incarnate lamas in general.

Trulkuhood in practice could then be seen to be the apotheosis of both lamahood and maleness, a reciprocal process that enabled Tibetans' attempts to impose a specifically local order on the multi-Buddha and multiethnic flux of the frontier zone. *Iconicity*, or the assumed resemblance between a sign and its referent, was in fact a crucial aspect of trulku recognition among Tibetans (cf. Duranti 1997: 205). That is, the iconicity of *maleness* was one of the most powerful existential links for Tibetans between bodies of living lamas and the visualized (in meditation techniques) or materialized representations of the bodies of lama predecessors and Buddhas (cf. Harris 1999). At the same time, while that iconicity linked Tibetan trulkus with the highest authorities in a male-dominated world of interregional politics, its unmarked nature allowed them to represent themselves in their encounters with Mongol, Manchu, or Chinese authorities as transmitters of universal Buddhist knowledge and thus as superior purveyors of the highest values, in "patron-preceptor" relationships that in turn stood for relationships between entire regions (Tib. *yon mchod*).

For example, a wall painting in what was the newly built private temple of the Jamyang Shepa lamas at Labrang—probably dating from the early twentieth century, a time when pressures on Labrang from outside interests were increasing—depicts the mustached founder of the monastery receiving the worship of his original patron, the Qosot Mongol lord. In the prevalent visual idiom for superior moral and political status, the painting places Jamyang Shepa above his patrons, so that the Mongol lord, clearly clad in sumptuous garments marked as gifts from the Qing court, humbly kneels with his lay male retinue at the lama's feet (see fig. 4).[6]

Such representations could then claim primacy locally even as outside authorities turned the powerful indexicality of trulkus to their own ends.[7] In fact, the rise of Labrang monastery as a local power center in the eighteenth and nineteenth centuries hinged on the collaboration of its main trulkus with Mongol and Manchu leaders in efforts to garner the loyalties of Tibetan and Mongol tribal alliances. In the frontier zone especially, Geluk Tibetan trulkus and their monastic bases benefited greatly from the ascendant Qing emperors' patronage, a crucial form of imperial "indebtedness engineering" (Firth, cited in Appadurai 1986: 19) that positioned trulkus as subordinates and pivots against Mongol influence in the Inner Asian regions they claimed (cf. Rahul 1969: 220; Berger 2003: 36). In this context, the most successful Tibetan trulkus were those who learned to mediate competing interests while carving out privileges and relative autonomy for their monasteries and estates. Indeed, especially since the Geluk Jangjya trulku, whose lineage was based at a famous monastery just north of Labrang, took up duties as imperial preceptor and lama minister at the Qing court, Geluk trulkus from Amdo regions in particular parlayed patron-preceptor relations with the court to shore up local autonomy, from Qing as well as from Lhasa government intervention (cf. Chen Qingying 1991, Dan Qu 1993, X. Wang 2000, Berger 2003, Tuttle 2005).

At Labrang, the unique status of the monastery as the center of a powerful local polity throughout the eighteenth and nineteenth centuries owed much to the way in which monastic officials successfully negotiated the Qing courts' interests in pacification (versus costly wars) and positioned themselves as neutral parties amidst various regional uprisings against Qing overlordship.[8] Their tribal constituencies thus relatively insulated from outside expropriation, the Jamyang Shepas were among the most mobile of translocal agents in the region, yet their place-based charisma allowed them to build their political economic power center based in the valley. Most high trulkus at Labrang continued the regional practice, begun long before the founding of the monastery, of studying and making offerings at the great Geluk monasteries in Lhasa and traveling frequently to visit patron tribes.

Yet, just as during the Mongol Yuan and the Chinese Ming dynasties, by the mid-eighteenth century seals and titles from the Qing court, received and displayed with great ceremony, were among the most coveted markers of trulkus' translocal prowess and crucial signs indexing the grand scale of their authorized local supremacy. Both the second and the fourth Jamyang Shepas, the most ambitious trulkus of that lineage, spent time at the Manchu court in Beijing. As James Hevia (1995) and others have noted however, those elaborate journeys and encounters always had emergent consequences within shifting configurations of power at court and in the frontier zone. Just as in the wall painting of the first Jamyang Shepa at Labrang, within the intricate orchestrations of guest ritual at Qing courts, lamas and emperors "vied to hierarchize each other" (Hevia 1995: 48) by asserting the transcendence of the participation frameworks they embodied to a variety of ends, even as they recognized each other as powerful men—that is, as vitally *commensurate* agents operating at the upper reaches of authority.

From this perspective we can better grasp that in the Labrang region, a sense of being a Buddhist "insider" (Tib. *nang pa*) was established through relative proximity to an embodied center, not by a fixed position inside a boundary line (cf. Hanks 1996: 180). Thus Tibetan Buddhist mandalization centered on trulkus produced the shifting and relative sociospaces of the polity that, since the early twentieth century, defied the absolute, distinctly bounded spaces Chinese nationalist officials attempted to impose so as to control and "develop" the region. I argue however that, in order to grasp the complex relationship between change and continuity in this process, attention to gendered contextualization, especially here the cultural politics of Tibetan fatherlands, will help us to avoid analytic dichotomies between "ritual" contexts and those of "rational" power and politics. In actuality, such easy dichotomies ultimately construct and reify temporal *and* spatial divides between the "premodern" and the "modern," in both influential social theorists' writings *and* in consequential state policies.

DOMESTICATING MASCULINITIES:
MAPPING NATIONAL SPACE

The crisp fold-out map in the huge two-volume gazetteer of Gannan (Tibetan Autonomous) prefecture (GZZ 1999), recently produced under Tibetan coeditors

FIGURE 4.
The first Jamyang Shepa accepts the worship of his main patron, the
Qosot Mongol lord. Śākyamuni temple, Labrang monastery, early
twentieth-century wall painting. (Photo by Andreas Gruschke)

in the prefecture capital, does not even use the name Labrang (Ch. Labuleng). The
only suggestion of the rocky peaks and narrow gorges of the mountain ranges that
extend across the high Tibetan plateau and shape the Labrang landscape are the
map's winding boundary lines. At three thousand meters above sea level, the
Labrang valley is at the lower edge of the dramatic terrain carved out by the
Machu (Ch. Huanghe: Yellow river) and its tributaries, the Luchu (Ch. Tao) and
the Sang (Ch. Daxia) rivers. Yet this map of administrative districts (Ch. *xing-*
zheng qu) depicts the town as simply the seat of Xiahe county, one of seven color-
coded counties of the prefecture in the southwesternmost corner of Gansu province bordering on Qinghai. These contemporary boundaries, thin and distinct, are,
however, just the most recent move in a long history of contending "maps of
power" over the region (see map 2; cf. Sun 1993: 2).

As a growing number of theorists have pointed out, we have to consider cartography, even the most "scientific" of mapping projects, *not* as simple reflections

of geographic reality but as historically particular contextualization strategies deeply implicated in political economy (cf. Millward 1999: 62). In fact, the positivist authority of maps as visual representations of the precise extent and structure of political sovereignty arguably emerged relatively recently with the rise of Western scientific knowledge production and the global shift to adjacent national states (cf. A. Alonso 1994: 383). Statist mapping, as officially sponsored efforts to reconstitute lived space under state auspices, can thus be seen as an important form of what Foucault called "bio-power"—resituating and disciplining bodies as localized subjects of translocal rule (1977, 1984).

Tibetans had for centuries produced written and visual representations mapping sociocosmological spaces—in various historiographic works, as well as in wall paintings and scrolls of individual maṇḍalas, or of the Buddhist universe, with Mount Meru as a maṇḍala palace at its center surrounded by the four continents (the southern one, Dzambuling, being the abode of humans), the gods' heavens above and the hell realms below. And at least since the nineteenth century, Tibetans drew "strip maps" depicting pilgrimage routes that positioned sacred sites relative to a viewer's position on a central axis (cf. Aziz 1975, 1978b; Huber 1992).

But it was arguably with the rise of Geluk hegemony in conjunction with Qing imperial expansion that Tibetans increasingly came to participate in new universalizing and segmenting views of territory and identity. As many historians of the Qing have recently pointed out, Qing emperors, just as did their rivals in European and Russian states, made use of new cartographic technologies for accurately mapping broad expanses of terrain as part of their multifaceted efforts to know and control the empire on an unprecedented scale (cf. Hevia 1995, R. Smith 1998, Millward 1999, Elliot 2000, Hostetler 2001, Berger 2003, Perdue 2005). Indeed, the first such positivist maps of central Tibet as a Qing protectorate were produced in the early eighteenth century by Jesuit missionaries at the behest of the ambitious Kangxi emperor (Petech 1950: 13). As Mark Elliot and others argue, depictions such as that of Tibet as a known space unequivocally a part of the Qing were enormously influential in Europe, and eventually in China, so that current representations of the Chinese national "geobody" extending far into Inner Asia (i.e., encompassing the provinces of Tibet, Inner Mongolia, Qinghai, and Xinjiang) are based on those Qing claims (Elliot 2000: 637; cf. Thongchai 1994, Bulag 2002; and see above, map 1).

The main Tibetan texts mapping broad expanses of Tibetan territory in relation to other countries (Tib. *yul;* see n. 9 below), often cited as examples of an essentially "Tibetan" worldview (e.g., ICT 1996), were actually written by Geluk trulkus from eastern Tibetan regions and date only from the nineteenth century. Lama Tsanpo (1789–1839), the trulku who wrote the first Tibetan comprehensive geography of Tibet and the world around 1820, was from a region just north of Labrang. His global worldview and encyclopedic impulse to describe all Tibetan regions must be seen in the context of his position at the time as a lama in the service of the Qing emperor in Beijing (cf. Petech 1950: 242). As Turrell Wylie notes, the lama states in his colophon that the text was commissioned by the "high one" (Tib. *gongma*, the emperor; blama bstan po 1962: xiv).

Indeed, by the time those Tibetan geographic histories were written, the regions northeast of Lhasa, settled by Tibetans since the expansion of the Tibetan Yarlung dynasty (7th–9th centuries), had been divided into Qing administrative districts separate from central Tibet under an *amban* (Qing official) in Xining (cf. Ren and Zewang 1989). The Labrang region, partitioned into twenty-one *zhai* (camps) of the "Nanbo" (southern Tibetans), had been placed under Xunhua Ting (Tib. Yardzi). In actuality, as I mentioned in the previous section, the rel-ative adminis-trative autonomy and most importantly the *tax-exempt* status of great Geluk monasteries like Labrang, factors that contributed to locals' strong sense that the region was "outside the fortresses" (Ch. *saiwai*) of the Qing (cf. Sun 1993), were originally due to the close accommodations Geluk trulkus from Amdo regions had made with Qing emperors against Mongol expansionist interests (cf. Fletcher 1978: 105; Zha Zha 1994; Tuttle 2005).

The Sino-Tibetan frontier zone was thus always a space of hybrid masculine authorities. Translocal alliances among Tibetan, Manchu, and Mongol men cru-cially enabled both local political economic autonomy in the Labrang region *and* the power of Tibetans there to proudly recontextualize globalizing mapping strategies in a triumphalist vision of Geluk-sect Buddhist hegemony. Both Lama Tsanpo and Konchok Tanpa Rabgye (b. 1801), the trulku author of the best-known Tibetan history of the region and Labrang monastery, barely mention Qing administration and instead draw on earlier genres of Tibetan sectarian historiog-raphy to situate their homelands in a broad yet partitioned view of Tibetan regions vis-à-vis other countries, including China (Tib. *rgya nag*).[9]

They do this by orienting the Tibetan Buddhist civilizing project of *taming* (Tib. *'dul pa*) and conversion to the mountainous terrain of the plateau through the movements and activities of lamas, monks, and laymen between mountains and monasteries. (Women appear mostly as wives and mothers of great men.) In their accounts, the spread of Geluk Buddhist monasticism is inexorable, ultimately unhindered by the difficult terrain of the plateau. Tshongkhapa (1357–1419), the

MAP 2.

Gannan Zangzu Autonomous Prefecture, Gansu province (GZZ 1999). The two closest nomad regions formerly subject to Labrang were Sangkok, to the southwest, and Gangya, to the northeast.

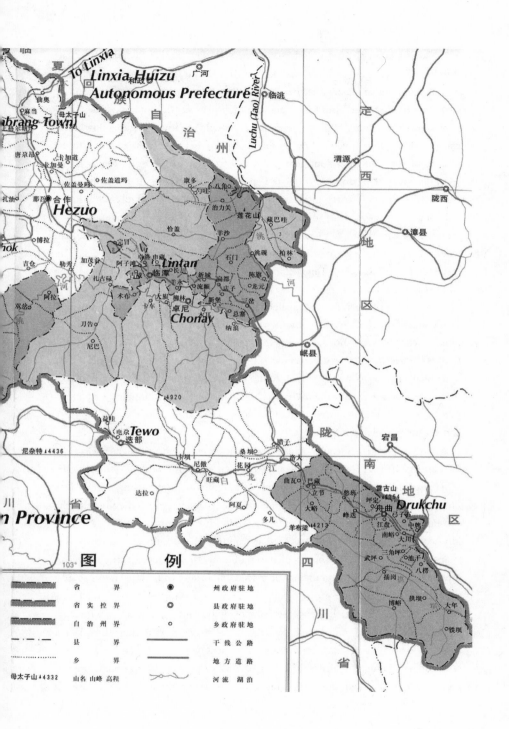

夏河 To Linxia
Linxia Huizu
Autonomous Prefecture

曲奥
麻当
(brang Town)
唐尕昂   加道
加曼
扎油   那哈   佐盖曼日玛   佐盖道玛
博拉   **Hezuo**
hok   勒秀
吉仓   加茂萨
阿拉   扎古碌
双岔
阿拉
刀告
尼巴

康多   八角
可哇
治力关   莲花山
怡盖   羊沙   藏巴哇
定旦   溢申藏   石门   洮砚
阿子滩   **Lintan**   柏林
临潭   羊永   新城   新堡
木仔   大族 楼村   庄子   尼元
卡车   **Chonay**   总寨   谷
纳浪

▲4920

菊哇   腊子
Tewo 电尕 桑坝   范大
尼杂特▲4436   迭部
尼傲   花园
旺藏   龙   曲瓦   巴藏   雷古山▲4154
达拉   白   整坪   坪定   **Drukchu**
阿夏   大峪   峰迭   舟曲 子山
多儿   羊布梁▲4213   江盘 中牌
南峪   大川
武坪   三角坪   池干
插岗   八楞
拱坝   大年
博峪   铁坝

川   四
n Province   川
省

103°   **图   例**

省   界   ◉ 州政府驻地
省实控界   ◎ 县政府驻地
自治州界   ○ 乡政府驻地
县   界   ━ 干线公路
乡   界   ━ 地方道路
母太子山▲4332 山名 山峰 高程   河流 湖泊

定
西
地
区

渭源
陇西
漳县
岷县

陇
南
地
区
宕昌

great lama claimed as the founder of the Geluk sect, is the second (historical) Buddha (Tib. *rje rgyal pa gnyis pa*), whose birthplace far east of Lhasa glorifies the region. Labrang monastery is then a magnificent extension and culmination of Geluk monastic order from Lhasa and the high plateau (the source of the continent's major rivers and thus the center of the world) to lower regions downriver called Amdo. There, the winding Machu (Yellow river) sculpts the region into the auspicious shape of a precious gem (dkon mchog bstan pa rab rgyas 1987: 366).

In the 1990s, Tibetan male scholars I spoke with at lowland "nationalities" colleges or at Tibetan research institutes under state auspices were avidly poring over those Tibetan texts as a way to recuperate relationships to their mountainous Amdo fatherlands, which they felt had been abruptly altered since the Maoist years. And when I brought out a copy of the hand-drawn map a Tibetan scholar in exile had created based on Konchok Tanpa Rabgye's text, they would invariably spend time enthusiastically locating their home regions in relation to the monasteries and mountain ranges depicted there, labeled in Tibetan, as situated to the north or south of the Machu river. One trulku, by then a lay scholar, asked me to make a copy for him. "Such a map does not exist here," he said bitterly. As lay scholars at state institutions located in Chinese urban centers, these men were painfully aware that they embodied a profound remapping of Amdo regions under the CCP, a recontextualization or *domestication* of themselves as "Zangzu" (Tibetan nationality), a process that they knew the post-Mao revitalization of monasteries could not completely contravene (see chapter 2).

As Gompo's trip to Shenzhen illustrates, monastic communities since "reform and opening up" had to contend with the new spatial premises for locals to exercise desirable masculine subjectivity through forms of mobility. Aspiring young Tibetan laymen like Gompo and the urban Tibetan scholars I knew grappled daily with the dilemmas of their subjecthood as (ethnicized minority) citizens of the PRC in a rapidly expanding market economy. Tibetan cultural revitalization in the post-Mao years was thus far from a simple return to tradition. For these men it was instead an often painful process of negotiating the essential hybridity of their positions as subordinated ethnic Others on the national margins (cf. Gupta 1992, Yuval-Davis 1997). And this, I argue, they experienced most importantly as a struggle with masculinity—their compromised roles as Tibetan men in relation to their fatherlands. In many long and passionate conversations, aspiring young men expressed to me a sense of being stuck or incapacitated (Tib. *bkod pa med gi*) by everyday realities requiring their deep collusion with Chinese ways and state interests, even as they felt

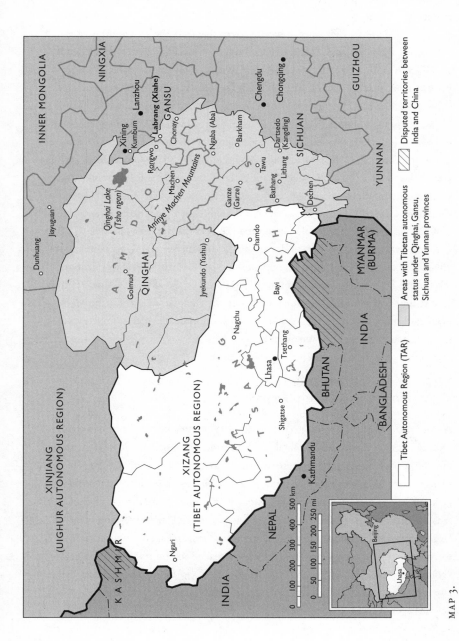

MAP 3.
Tibetan regions in the PRC.

Legend:
- Tibet Autonomous Region (TAR)
- Areas with Tibetan autonomous status under Qinghai, Gansu, Sichuan and Yunnan provinces
- Disputed territories between India and China

Labels on map:

INNER MONGOLIA
NINGXIA
XINJIANG (UIGHUR AUTONOMOUS REGION)
GANSU
QINGHAI
SICHUAN
GUIZHOU
YUNNAN
XIZANG (TIBET AUTONOMOUS REGION)
KASHMIR
NEPAL
INDIA
BHUTAN
BANGLADESH
MYANMAR (BURMA)
A M D O
K H A M
G T S A N G
U

Place names:
Lanzhou
Xining
Kumbum
Labrang (Xiahe)
Rongwo
Chonay
Chengdu
Chongqing
Ngaba (Aba)
Barkham
Machen
Amnye Machen Mountains
Qinghai Lake (Tsho ngon)
Dunhuang
Jiayuguan
Golmud
Jyekundo (Yushu)
Ganze (Garze)
Dartsedo (Kangding)
Tawu
Lithang
Bathang
Dechen
Chamdo
Bayi
Nagchu
Tsethang
Lhasa
Shigatse
Kathmandu
Ngari

Scale: 0 50 100 150 200 250 mi
0 100 200 300 400 500 km

Inset map: Beijing, Lhasa

the weight of great personal responsibility for the future integrity of a Tibetan community as a whole.

In fact, the military violence and state terror that over the previous decades had established the new nation-space of CCP rule in Amdo had inescapably alienated all Tibetans from their phayul even as they inhabited the same spaces. It is not surprising then that when reforms allowed for an unprecedented outpouring of Tibetan secular media production spearheaded by young Tibetan men in the mid-1980s, "Nostalgia Songs" (Tib. *dran glu*) eulogizing key gendered categories marking oppositional Tibetanness became widely popular in Amdo regions (see chapter 3).[10] In this context, "Nostalgia Songs for Fatherlands" (Tib. *pha yul dran glu*), in which the author (wistfully) extols the marvelous virtues of his homeland, its topography, and the achievements of its great men, most often reflected the ambivalent alienation of young Tibetan men, whose pursuit of opportunity and education had led them to reside in lowland urban centers (cf. Upton 1996).

Thus, in the backward and rural-looking gaze of such nostalgic representations, Tibetans could not help but participate in the intensifying objectification of Tibetanness that in part constituted a refigured map of the modern Chinese nation. And that process, I argue, was fundamental in the Dengist state's efforts to domesticate and recruit recalcitrant Tibetans to its development projects while avoiding the mass violence of the Maoist years.

THE VIOLENCE OF LIBERATION: SOCIALIST TRANSFORMATION

As Chinese state officials sought to stabilize the country in the early 1980s, and to mollify angry minority leaders finally able to officially protest their treatment during the Maoist years (cf. Herberer 1989: 41), the new pedagogical role of the Dengist state to improve the "civility" (Ch. *wenming*) of the masses in a developed (Ch. *fazhan, fada*) nation was particularly important in Tibetan regions (cf. Anagnost 1997: 79). In the Labrang region, where the Tibetan economy was still largely primary (i.e., pastoralist and agricultural), this meant a refigured approach to "civilizing" Tibetans that focused local cadres' efforts on training Tibetans in a "commodity production vision" (Ch. *shangpin shengchan yanguang*) necessary to participate in a newly liberated or "opened" (capitalist) market economy (GGK 1987: 119; cf. Teng 1990).

Yet if we consider these new policy directives of the 1980s in terms of gendered spatial politics, we can discern continuities in state-local relations in the frontier zone that belie the radical break with the Maoist past that reform-era historiography sought to create. Just as during the Maoist years, in the 1980s and 1990s an important part of Chinese state civilizing efforts was the need to domesticate local Tibetan men. This was so because the unmanageable power and violence of Tibetan men embedded in monastic-tribal alliances continued to hinder the smooth "development" (Ch. *fazhan*) and exploitation of the region's many natural resources under the direction of Han state industry leaders in the Han-dominated Gannan prefecture capital, Hezuo (formerly Heicuo; cf. Teng 1990, Ma Jiang 1993, Marshall and Cooke 1997). In fact, it was arguably due to the violent resistance of Tibetan men loyal to local Tibetan leaders that the Gannan prefecture capital had been moved from Labrang to Hezuo in 1956.[11]

Many of the elderly Tibetan men and women who had lived through Maoist socialist transformation in Labrang spoke to me of that time. Their faces often registered expressions of intense disbelief and incomprehension when they described the state violence that had been largely directed at Tibetan men during the first decade of Communist rule (see chapter 2). Those conversations confirmed my sense that profound misrecognitions of Tibetan masculinities had been at the heart of the brutal violence that erupted between Tibetan men and Chinese forces in the mid-1950s. Those struggles culminated with a military crackdown in 1958, in which state officials arrested and imprisoned much of the monk and lay male population in the valley. I would say, though, that simply calling this process "colonialism" and likening it to European forms of domination in overseas colonies would foreclose more nuanced understandings of the particular cultural politics of CCP intervention in Labrang (cf. Osterhammel 1997, Tuttle 2005). It seems clear from the sources that many of the battle-weary CCP cadres who first came to the Labrang region did not think of themselves as colonizers; many were very sincere social reformers who looked forward to a modicum of social order under centralized Chinese rule after decades of civil war and battles with Japanese invaders.

Yet the Communist agendas and nationalist spatial frameworks of the Han workteam members sent to Labrang in the 1950s led them to grossly misapprehend the nature of Tibetan male power and legitimate violence in Labrang. As they discovered, bringing the Communist revolution to the frontier zone and "liberating" (Ch. *jiefang*) Labrang was not at all a peaceful process. Ya Hanzhang was a Han special officer in the Linxia PLA and one of the original members of Xiahe's Party Committee. His 1950 report to the Party leadership in Linxia (formerly Hezhou) criticized earnest Han cadres in Labrang for misinterpreting the local status and intentions of ambitious young Tibetan men seeking to ally with them (1991: 40).

Those young collaborators did not in fact represent a broad reorientation of local Tibetan selves to Communist frameworks. Cadres learned instead that the loyalties of locals and control of their regions could not be easily won just by applying a Maoist class analysis that reduced lamas and tribal leaders to feudal landlords and thus justified immediately expropriating and redistributing their properties. In September 1949, the first Party Secretary in Labrang was Huo Deyi, a former poor Han farmer from Shanxi and then a People's Liberation Army veteran. As he bitterly complained in his memoir decades later, "we would redistribute land to the peasants in the daytime, and by the nighttime they would return it as gifts [to the original owners]" (1991: 55).

At that time, Labrang monastery and its subject territories had been ruled for almost thirty years by powerful lay-monastic alliances embodied in the brothers of the aristocratic Tibetan family known by the Chinese surname Huang. That cosmopolitan family had moved to Labrang from Litang in Kham, a Tibetan region to the south, after one of the brothers had been recognized as the fifth Jamyang Shepa, Lozang Jamyang Yeshe Tanpa (1916–47). The oldest brother, Apa Alo (Ch. Huang Zhengqing, 1903–2000), was the lay military commander, and two other younger brothers were also important monk trulkus at Labrang. Jamyang Shepa had died suddenly of smallpox in 1947 at the young age of thirty-two, and when Huo Deyi headed his new CCP Party Committee in Labrang two years later, Apa Alo and his only remaining trulku brother, Amang Tshang, then the monastery's main minister (Tib. *phyag mdzod*), held power in that uncertain interim period (cf. Huang 1989: 57).

In his account, Huo Deyi insists that he thought of Apa Alo as a "feudal despot" (Ch. *ba*), and he contends that against the CCP's "United Front" policies to ally with local minority elites, at the time, he himself opposed the entire "exploitative system" of the monastery and could not bear the sight of Buddha worship (1991: 56). Huo had good reason to be defensive in his memoir so many years later. He and his committee in Labrang, aided by several young Tibetan male reformers, had had little patience for the niceties of United Front policies and, with Apa Alo and Amang Tshang safely in Lanzhou receiving "socialist education," they had immediately attempted to usurp their authority while confiscating private property (often for themselves) and implementing land reforms.

They had even less patience for Tibetan men's violent resistance to those efforts, and within months CCP cadres had to huddle in their guarded headquarters at night as armed Tibetan laymen and monks raided the CCP's commandeered buildings. The main Tibetan collaborator, a local village man named Jamyang Nagri

FIGURE 5.
The fifth Jamyang Shepa (left), his older brother, Apa Alo
(middle), and Apa Alo's son Amgon, mid-1940s. (Photo by
Marion Griebenow, courtesy of the Tibet House, New York.)

(Ch. Wu Zhengang), was assassinated by monks, and the Party Committee's presence was secured only with the aid of PLA troops garrisoned in Apa Alo and his
son's mansions and on the mountaintops overlooking the valley. As the situation
deteriorated through 1950, Huo's Party superiors in Linxia conducted an investiga-
tion and found that Xiahe Party Committee members and the Han and Tibetan
leaders of almost all the new government bureaus in Labrang had bullied locals
while embezzling large sums of tax and bribe monies (Ya Hanzhang 1991, Zhang
Qingyou 1991). Huo Deyi was reprimanded for ignoring both "local nationality
customs" and Party policies for gradual intervention in "minzu regions" and was

transferred away in disgrace. Ultimately, as Apa Alo tells it in his 1989 memoir, by February 1950, months after Mao Zedong had declared the establishment of the PRC in Beijing, Han Party leaders in Labrang could stabilize the situation and appease angry monks and laymen only by (temporarily) bringing him and his trulku brother back to Labrang from Lanzhou (cf. Ya Hanzhang 1991).

Consider in this light then the bland statement of Zhang Qingyou, the Han historian who headed the Xiahe office of county history in the 1990s. He states that when Xiahe was "peacefully liberated" and the first Party Committee was established in Labrang, Xiahe county was divided into seven districts (Ch. *qu*) and thirty-six townships (Ch. *xiang*) as its main administrative units (1991: 48). Such casual retrospective mapping claims deny the immediate difficulties Han cadres encountered in attempting to extend the participation frameworks of a Communist sociospatial order west from the "old [liberated] regions" (Ch. *laoqu*) into Tibetan areas. Indeed, as Keane writes, "much of the work of power is aimed at, and is registered in" attempts to transform or constrict the relevant loci of agency, be they individual, collective, human, or divine (1997: 8). I find this to be a fruitful way to understand early CCP efforts on the Sino-Tibetan frontier. In the Communist takeover of Labrang, Han cadres utilized radically positivist mapping strategies to reject indexical links between male-bodied Tibetans and the agencies of deities, and to thereby constrict legitimate, authoritative masculine agency to cadres embodying a secular, paternal state refigured as *pervading* social space and time in the form of a nation-family (Ch. *guojia;* see chapter 2).

In the frontier zone, Mao's historical materialism in practice meant constructing a civilizing discourse of excess and lack that both legitimated and constituted the unprecedented pervasion of state regulation into Tibetans' lives, nonetheless cast as aid offered by Han urbanites (cf. Dreyer 1976, Karan 1976). Communist "thought work" (Ch. *sixiang gongzuo*) introduced Tibetans to the reductionist category of "feudal superstition" (Ch. *fengjian mixin*), a notion that constructed faith in divine agencies as an irrational emotional investment in excess of the material truth of socioeconomic structure, thus establishing "religion" as a category opposed to the liberation achievable through rationalized modern progress (cf. GZZ 1999: 115; and see below, chapter 2).

That objectification of Tibetan Buddhism as "religion," drawing as it did on earlier genres of Western scientific discourse, was in fact powerfully influential among some Tibetans even before 1949, providing some ambitious young men like Jamyang Nagri (and eventually, women) a framing discourse for embracing modernity—though *not* necessarily in concert with Chinese Communist interests (cf.

Stoddard 1985, Duara 1995). I would argue, however, that throughout the Maoist years and beyond, reformers' attempts to map Labrang Tibetans' loyalties to the abstract translocal space of the nation, by dividing them within the distinct political boundaries of CCP administrative units, always came up against locally anchored, centered spaces constructed relative to embodied persons, and reproduced through Tibetans' great respect for Tibetan men's privileged relationships to divine agencies.

THE VIOLENCE OF LIBERATION: MANDALIZING LABRANG

What Han cadres like Huo Deyi did not recognize was that the basis for Tibetan masculine authority in Labrang was the "violence of liberation" (Schrempf 1994: 106) at the heart of Tibetan tantric Buddhist ritual agency. As Mona Schrempf and others argue, throughout Buddhist Tibet, lamas, as enlightened beings, asserted control over spaces by violently subjugating the earth and its associated enemy agencies (Tib. *sa btul*). They did this through tantric ritual practices that asserted lama bodies as structuring microcosms. That is, lamas were ritually recognized as divinized embodied agents operating from the center of a mandala, and thereby pervading and encompassing space and time in order to dominate deities toward particular contemporary ends, a process I refer to here as "mandalization."

Mandalization was thus the key participation framework for constructing the reciprocal link between the purified (and unmarked) maleness of lamas and authoritative masculine subjectivity. Indeed, Tibetan Buddhists were unique in adapting Indian forms of tantric Buddhism to indigenous understandings of masculine efficacy as the conquest or taming (Tib. *'dul ba*) of wildness (Tib. *rgod po*) embodied by malevolent or capricious non-Buddhist deities (Samuel 1993: 217; Gibbons 1995: 284). *Duwa*, with its nexus of connotations—to subdue, tame, and conquer, as well as to cultivate (fields and minds), convert, discipline, and even kill—thus encapsulates a particularly Tibetan Buddhist relationship to social and topographic space that underwrote Geluk monastic hegemony by the seventeenth century (cf. Huber 1999, Mills 2003).[12]

The importance of mandalization at Labrang, and especially the magnificent grandeur of the monastery's public ceremonies during its heyday, suggest that there were important similarities between that polity and other "premodern" states of the exemplary center, such as the Indonesian Negara described by Clifford Geertz (1980), or the Thai Buddhist "galactic polity" analyzed by Stanley Tambiah (1976). As both Geertz and Tambiah argue for their cases, in the emphasis on centered control over people, not land, the Labrang monastic polity was indeed based on a very different notion of sovereignty than nation-states. However, a focus on gendered contextualization processes at Labrang will allow us to avoid the objectifying dichotomy Geertz and Tambiah ultimately set up between "ritual" and "real politics," an opposition that to them seemed to encapsulate the spectacular Otherness of those "premodern" states versus "modern" ones.

In fact, Geertz and Tambiah were participating in a broad-reaching "revolution in political epistemology" (Corrigan and Sayer 1985: 205) among Western social theorists, in which theorists called for a nuanced understanding of power as much more than just the imposition of coercion or bodily violence (cf. Williams 1977; Foucault 1984; C. Bell 1992: 194). This line of inquiry among anthropologists took the very productive step of insisting that rituals "actively create reality" (Taussig 1980: 102) in projects of domination and resistance. But, as many have pointed out, the perennial problem is that "ritual," even in those writings, is still associated with radically *Other*, "symbolic" or irrational action and meaning, operating separately from rational or pragmatic "politics" to produce unifying, collective representations for all participants (cf. Giddens 1971, Asad 1993, Kaplan and Kelly 1990, C. Bell 1992, Bulag 2002, Kapferer 2003).

By contrast, from the perspective of everyday recognition and contextualization processes, "ritual" becomes a *situated event*, an instance of a particularly formal or high-stakes local performance genre, in which, just as in less formal contexts, differently positioned participants simultaneously draw on a wide range of signifying resources (not just "symbols") to contextualize themselves and others in emergent ways (cf. Bauman and Sherzer 1975, Irvine 1979, Hanks 1989, Bauman and Briggs 1990). Thus as we will see, the main locus of difference before and after CCP intervention at Labrang was not "ritual" versus "politics" but the (violent) shift in predominant participation frameworks for masculine authority and asymmetric exchange. To paraphrase Keane, mandalizing rituals did not exert power over Labrang's subjects merely through mimesis (that is, by symbolizing or modeling an ideal sociocosmological order for people). Instead, just like the new nationalist public events and media forms under Guomindang (KMT) or Chinese Communist Party (CCP) regimes, taming rituals at Labrang were also particularly important forms of space making—attempts to arbitrate hierarchical arrangements of humans and deities that "imposed material and organizational requirements on people" (Keane 1997: 18; cf. Hanks 1996) against contravening forces and in the interest of the continuity of rule.

Further, if we consider these processes in conjunction with gender as key framing cues for embodied subjectivity, affiliation, and exchange, we can breach the seemingly hermetically sealed world of ritual and conceptualize the inherent links between the high formality of ritual genres and everyday contexts, between dramatized and physical violence, or between ritual and economic exchange. From this angle, mandalizing rituals at Labrang were efforts, amidst the hazards inherent to performance in an extremely complex locale, to regiment sex and gender recognition so as to produce forms of hierarchized masculine affiliation in contradistinction to the categorical abjectness of the female Other (cf. Hanks 1996, Keane 1997).[13]

The theme of heroic enlightened lamas conquering and taming the enemies of Buddhism, and thereby purifying spaces for the reproduction of the Buddha Dharma (Tib. *chos*), is pervasive in Tibetan literature and ritual, forming the narrative backbone of Buddhist Tibet's origin stories. The Tibetan translation for the Sanskrit term *bodhisattva*, an enlightened being who remains in the mundane world to benefit sentient beings, is after all "a hero in striving for enlightenment" (Tib. *byang chub sems dpa'*). The paradigmatic lama is thus Guru Rinpoche (Skt. Padmasambhava), the eighth-century Indian tantric master who is said to have come to Tibet on the invitation of the Tibetan king and tamed the indigenous gods to the service of Buddhism so that the first Buddhist monastery, Samye, could be built (cf. Stein 1972; Gyatso 1987; Tucci 1988: 169; Kohn 1997).

In Labrang, as elsewhere, Tibetans were acutely aware that this masculine taming process had to be continually renewed, as purified spaces were constantly vulnerable to infiltration by a vast array of human and demonic agencies (cf. Huber 1999: 32). The masculine might of lamas was thus regularly exercised and displayed in the cult of wrathful protector deities, a crucial aspect of the ritual calendar, keyed to the lunar year and the rhythms of the monastic curriculum, that formed the spatiotemporal framework for everyday participation in the valley, both before *and* after the Maoist years. By the heyday of the monastery in the late nineteenth century, all major units of the huge monastic community, trulkus' mansions and "colleges" had temples (Tib. *mgon khang* or *btsan khang*) in which resided their special oath-bound protector deities—chanting their texts and exhorting them to protect particular lineages of teachings and smooth the way to masculine achievement was an integral part of both routine assemblies and special ceremonies. Importantly, those temples, adorned with weapons and housing the shrouded images of the fierce deities, were among the most guarded of spaces in the monastic complex; only males and only the initiated entered to make daily offerings (see chapters 2 and 3).

Restricted spaces of protector-deity temples thus point up the importance of sex as a key contextualization cue (cf. Gumperz 1992) for linking maleness to the expert frameworks necessary for wielding the extraordinary yet dangerous power of tantric ritual.[14] At great Geluk monastic institutions like Labrang, the secrecy associated with such spaces for wrathful deities restricted to male initiates was an important component of ongoing efforts to extend powerful masculine authority across time and social contexts.[15] Spatial restrictions were one element of the elaborate regulations on the transmission of knowledge and legitimate ritual agency reproduced in the practice of initiation, in which the lama admitted a worthy student to a tantric teaching lineage (Tib. *rgyud*) by allowing him to "enter the maṇḍala" of a particular deity. Such regulated revelation helped to construct the awesomeness of tantric masculine prowess at Labrang over time. But it also indexed the profound ambivalence of Geluk celibate monasticism toward the antinomian directness, ritualized sexuality, and dramatized violence of tantric ritual. An important part of claims that Buddhism had tamed Tibetans was after all the claim that Buddhism had eliminated the violence of live animal sacrifice to non-Buddhist deities (cf. Huber 1999: 174). And, as famously advocated by Tshongkhapa, Geluk celibate monasticism was supposed to be the most disciplined, ethical, and appropriately gradual approach to tantric soteriological and worldly achievement.

In actuality, particular contextualization practices allowed locals to take for granted that such monastic sentiments could coexist with fierce deities capable of violently intervening in worldly affairs in order to protect monastic interests against human enemies, including lay male tantrists who scoffed at monastic pretensions (e.g., dge 'dun chos 'phel 1990). From this angle, we can appreciate that an opposition between lay and monastic tantric ritual orientations has been overdrawn in both Tibetan and Western discourses. At Labrang, just as in nonmonastic settings, maṇḍalas were the contextualization tool par excellence. Maṇḍalas (Tib. *dkyil 'khor*, lit. "center and surroundings"), in visualized or material forms, were extremely intricate, often highly abstract representations of a central deity and his or her palace and retinue, guarded at the peripheries by protector gods. In the principal tantric rituals (Skt. *sādhana*, Tib. *sgrub thabs*, lit. "means of achievement"), they were essentially repertoires of ordering tools for placing and exhorting vast pantheons of deities as co-participants nonetheless subordinated to the current event and goal of a practitioner (cf. Hanks 1996: 180; Berger 2003: 89; and see fig. 3 above).

Thus, in contrast to some Buddhist exegesis that reduces maṇḍalas and their deities to mere symbols of abstract concepts (e.g., R. Paul 1982, Samuel 1993, Marko 1994, Bryant 1993, Kohn 2001), I argue that in practice maṇḍalas were most importantly frameworks for vital *exchanges* between substantially coexistent human and divine agents (cf. Mills 2003). All ritual goals were pursued by first evoking deities in their maṇḍalas (ideally by visualizing them as one recited the relevant text), then making appropriate offerings and praises to them, and finally requesting (or demanding) their services. If we view tantric ritual as primarily a hoped-for exchange embedded in the historical exigencies of a particular embodied practitioner, who works to bind powerful divine Others to the obligations associated with receipt of the gift, we can appreciate how inherently *precarious* such rites have always been (cf. Ortner 1978: 86; Appadurai 1986: 12; Mauss 1990; Makransky 1996; Keane 1997).

Indeed, the work of recent theorists suggests that there has long been a profound ambivalence in Buddhist discourses about the nature of ritual gifts or "offerings" (Tib. *mchod pa;* Makransky 1996, Ohnuma 2005). That is, even though Buddhist specialists and monastic communities have always relied on economic exchanges with laity, the very basis of their numinous power and moral superiority was their capacity to give, to provide blessings and merit, *without* reciprocation. Theirs was supposed to be the purely generous gift, the highest possible values to transfer because they originated in such supremely purified intentions. Offerings then, were supposed to be merely tokens of praise and worship, to be recompensed only by the mechanical operations of karma that Buddhist specialists made possible as "fields of merit" (cf. Mills 2003).

Yet such ideals coexisted with the widespread *substantialization* of Buddhist deities as "guests" hosted and petitioned by ritual practitioners. Indeed, the presence and co-participation of supramundane beings as autonomous agents gravely challenge the effective supremacy of intentioned human actors at particular historical junctures. Deities, however they are incarnated, could then be said to embody the (threatening) *limits* of human participation and disciplinary efforts, secular or not (cf. Hanks 1996: 177). Thus human ritual practitioners could fail and cause offense, and some deities, especially protector deities (even the ones considered to be Buddhas themselves) were notoriously capricious—their reciprocation was not guaranteed (cf. Kohn 2001). And in all tantric ritual, just as in other genres of guest ritual, practitioners "hosting" deities were ambiguously positioned as both creditors and supplicants—humans needed deities much more than the other way around (cf. Makransky 1996). The ambiguity of such exchange politics at the heart of tantric practice is one way to understand the complex coexistence of various subject positions or "footings" (Goffman 1981) vis-à-vis deities that one finds in tantric texts (e.g., affectionate awe, flattery, cajoling, beseeching, or ordering). Of course the (dangerous) power and promise of tantric Buddhism was the possibility for an initiated practitioner to take the subject position of the central Buddha or *yidam* himself, thereby attempting to appropriate altogether the deity's transcendent agency (cf. Samuel 1993: 259).

At Labrang, it was arguably trulku embodiment, as the ongoing consequence of both everyday worship and mandalization ritual, that ultimately worked to trump those ritual ambiguities and shore up the monastery as a power center over time. As embodied heirs to both emanation and teaching lineages, as well as to the vows of deities sworn to protect them, the dominating masculine authority of trulkus was overdetermined, thus positioning them to be recognized as *inherently* successful tantrists, their intrinsic power (Tib. *byin rlabs*), like that of tantric deities, imagined to radiate from them like light or electricity. The fifth Jamyang Shepa, for example, received tantric initiations at the age of four and gave his first teachings at eight (zhabs drung 1952, Huang 1989). The majority of monastic inmates at Labrang however were not primarily tantric practitioners. In fact, according to Li Anzhai (1982: 33), over 85 percent of monks in the early 1940s belonged to the Thisamling college (Tib. *grwa tshang*), the original monastic college and by then one of six. Unlike the much smaller tantric colleges, the core of Thisamling academic activity was memorization and formal debate based on the synthesis of Indian Buddhist philosophy and Tibetan commentary presented in the first Jamyang Shepa's debate manuals (cf. Yonten Gyatso 1988, Newland 1996).

In this context, the power of lamas for monks (and as we will see, for laity) hinged on the embodiment of particular lamas as indispensable media of *transvaluation*. In the terms of Buddhist exegesis, lamas could be seen as central conduits to the field of merit for the accumulation of good karma toward better rebirths. But they were more than that in practice. As recent theorists of economics and value have argued, all exchange systems are actually dynamic "regimes of value" (Appadurai 1986: 4), in which the sources of the values that are seemingly attached to objects, persons, or acts (like pure compassion versus obligated blessings) are constantly negotiated through practices that assert their appropriate places in competing hierarchies of value (cf. Graeber 2001). At Labrang as elsewhere, the worship of lamas, but especially trulkus, through quotidian practices such as the tantric ritual of reciting Lama Chopa, or "Offerings to the Lama," was the central way to transform objects and acts of offering to desired future values, be they this-worldly well-being and protection, or progress on the path to enlightenment—the vital indexicality of trulkus operated, in practice, through the flux of situated exchange. In effect, trulkus were positioned both as benevolent central deities and as the most powerful participants in tantric exchanges with them (cf. Samuel 1993, Draper 1994, Huber 1999). Indeed, in the Lama Chopa offering ritual the visualized lama's footstool is said to be the worldly gods tamed to Buddhist service, and becoming Buddhist in practice meant "going for refuge" (Tib. *skyabs 'gro*) with a particular lama (ZDPG 1990s: 56; Lopez 1997: 379).

Here we cannot reduce the function of the lama to merely that of a "symbolic device" (Samuel 1993: 256) for the reciters' desired soteriological transformation. Such regular mandalizing rituals also set up key participation frameworks for understanding lamas as powerful, though not necessarily present, authoring agents in *everyday* contexts. They were subjects whose access to tantric power exercised as the compassionate "skillful means" of a teacher *and* a wise protector marked them as superior to those with recourse merely to physical violence, creating an essential "diarchy" of masculinities in the region (cf. Keane 1997: 44). Thus the offering text's recitation also regularly indexed particular lamas' transcendent *physicality* as supreme tantrists across contexts—just as the lama's feet press down and subjugate the non-Buddhist worldly gods, so too in enthusiastically cited lay and monastic narratives Tibetan localities were marked by revered lamas' footprints pressed in local rocks (cf. blama bstan po 1962, zhabs drung 1952). In the 1990s, finding and touching footprints and handprints left by the Jamyang Shepas or other trulkus as a way to absorb some of their residual blessing-power were important components of pilgrimage practices for monks and laity alike.

In this context, then, we can understand the great pageantry of annual monastic festivals during Labrang's heyday as only the grandest and most spectacular of mandalizing efforts there. Those festivals were initiated by various trulkus emulating the practices at the great Geluk monasteries of central Tibet, and they were presented as corporate productions of the monastic community. They were crucial because they were the performance genres that claimed the widest scope of participants (branch monasteries, monks, lay tribes, *and* deities) as beneficiaries of lamas', but especially Jamyang Shepa's, tantric masculine prowess, and thus as legitimate subjects of the monastery. As public events performed only once a year, they were rare occasions on which carefully guarded divine agents and empowered objects were disclosed to mass audiences (cf. Li Anzhai 1982; Luo 1987; Samuel 1993: 259). Linguistic anthropologists, following on the seminal work of Mikhail Bakhtin, have argued that discourse genres, or participation frameworks for discourse production and performance like monastic festivals, are always understood and deployed in relation to other genres within a particular system of language stratification (Bakhtin 1981: 289; Bauman and Briggs 1990: 63; Hanks 1996: 161). Thus the performative impact of public festivals at Labrang always depended on the ways they alluded to the higher-status but *hidden* genres of monastic ritual on the one hand and to the lower-status more public genres of lay ritual and everyday exchange on the other.

The Cham Chen, or Great Monastic Dance, was perhaps the most important of public mandalizing efforts at Labrang. That all-day event was held annually in the midst of the Great Prayer Festival at the beginning of the lunar year, a two-week period of intensive monastic assemblies and public events during which, by the 1930s, tens of thousands of laypeople and monks from subject tribes and monasteries would descend on the valley (Li Anzhai 1982). Held jointly by all monastic colleges, the Cham Chen were in effect attempts, through the corporate agency of the officiating lama, to both dramatize the tantric violence of liberation for Labrang's heterogeneous subjects *and* to recruit them to participation in it under the ultimate auspices of Jamyang Shepa. To use Ana Marko's words (1994: 137), in the circular dance space laid out in the main monastic courtyard, the dances "ritually disclosed" the wrathful protectors in the monastery's guarded *gonkhang* (protector-deity shrines), in order to publicly enlist their aid in eliminating evil spirits on behalf of the polity. After days of careful preparation inside, in which the monk assembly recited the texts setting up the main protector deity's maṇḍala and propitiated him and his retinue with offerings, on the day of the Cham Chen, the head lama led masked dancers and their accompanying musicians and monk assembly in invoking the buffalo-headed protector deity Damjen Chegyal (Tib. dam can chos rgyal, Skt. Yama Dharmarāja), the terrible Lord of Death, along with his consort and warrior retinue (see figs. 3 and 6).

As a wrathful emanation of the bodhisattva Jampiyang (Skt. Mañjuśrī), and thus an "otherworldly protector" (Tib. *'jig rten las 'das pa'i srung ma*) who is himself enlightened, Damjen Chegyal was one of the most important deities charged with protecting the Geluk lineage at Labrang.[16] On the day of the dance, a huge painted scroll was unfurled next to the dance space, depicting the ferocious deity on his lotus seat, holding a skull-topped staff and a lasso, dancing atop a bull who treads on a human corpse. Over the course of the day, as Jamyang Shepa and other trulkus watched from the veranda, the dancers animating the deities gave way to the "black hat" dancers, who, led by the principal lama, deployed the wrathful agency of Chegyal as the central deity to subjugate the ground under their feet and force evil spirits into a human-shaped effigy. Then, wielding their ritual daggers and making stabbing motions toward the effigy, they killed it and offered its remains to the maṇḍala deities, thereby, according to Buddhist exegesis, "liberating" the spirits to be reborn in a heaven (cf. Kohn 2001: 79). The day culminated with the procession of the effigy and the principal offerings—led by the monastery's main abbot and Chegyal, and accompanied by the audience—out of the courtyard for the final burnt offering, thus helping to ensure good fortune for the year (see fig. 6; cf. Li Anzhai 1982, Luo 1987).[17]

In the spring of 1949, while Communist forces advanced south and west after their victory against KMT forces in Beijing, and the Gansu Party Committee sent operatives to Labrang to pressure Apa Alo to support the CCP, the abbot and Chegyal presided over the last Cham Chen at Labrang before CCP occupation (cf. GGK 1987, Chang Qiuying 1991, Ya Hanzhang 1991).

MANDALIZING MOBILITY:
PATRIFILIALITY, VALUE, AND EXCHANGE

From this perspective on the Sino-Tibetan frontier zone, we must see the unprecedented transformation of Labrang that ultimately occurred with Chinese Communist intervention in the light of the gendered cultural politics of place making. A focus on gender and spatial contextualization in this way allows us to appreciate that while the spatial premises for Buddhist and Communist participation frameworks there were vastly different, both hinged on linking male bodies to highest authority and legitimate violence, while establishing hierarchies of masculinities aimed at controlling the mobility and loyalty of local Tibetan men. Tantric mandalizing rituals like the Cham Chen did not create hermetically sealed worlds of collective representations for all. Nor were they mere "spectacle" for ignorant audiences (*pace*, e.g., Snellgrove and Richardson 1986: 247). Instead, as pressures on Labrang from competing regimes and globalizing markets intensified through the early twentieth century, the Cham Chen, in conjunction with other ritual genres, were determined efforts to recruit heterogeneous participants to a Geluk monastic regime of value as patron beneficiaries (Tib. *sbyin bdag*) of lamas' taming power. The centering force of such rituals depended on the ways they indexed for participants the comforting and overarching intentional agency of Jamyang Shepa as an all-knowing and compassionate protector operating exclusively through the mysterious exchanges of tantric ritual violence[18]—in the Cham Chen after all even the Buddha Lord of Death, another emanation of Jampiyang, is subject to and encompassed by the (corporate) lama on behalf of the entire polity. Invoked in the tantric framework of deity yoga, the ferocious protector is in effect an extension of Jamyang Shepa's agency.

Thus, even as the frontier zone destabilized around the valley with the decline of the Qing and the splintering of rule in China, mandalization at Labrang provided flexible participation frameworks for locals to understand the expansion and protection of monastic interests to be the consequences of the intentions of trulkus, all the while insulating trulkus from direct implication in physical violence or asymmetric economic relations (cf. Huang 1989: 61–65).

Indeed, the exigencies of Labrang's rule in the frontier zone had intensified in the late nineteenth and early twentieth centuries, with decades of brutal clashes between shifting alliances of state and local Han, Hui, and Tibetans fighting for regional control, revenge, and, increasingly, ethnic hatred (cf. Lipman 1990, 1997). But those conditions only highlight the quandary of agency that was always basic to trulkus' recognition as intrinsically empowered individuals in Labrang. Indeed, the ambitious fourth Jamyang Shepa (1856–1916), whose reign coincided with these seismic upheavals, was moved when he reached adulthood to recentralize the expanding reach of the central trulku's taming power over subject tribes and monasteries. He reorganized the monastic government to place the monk assembly and other trulkus under his own estate organization and central committee, and established an eighty-man personal guard, a prison, and closer oversight of lay communities and the market by monk officials appointed by himself (cf. Luo 1987: 17; Huang 1989; Suo Dai 1992; Dan Qu 1993; Wang Zhouta 1996b). Importantly, Jamyang Shepa decreed that his personal guard would be constituted by the faithful lay sons of wealthy families, who after several years of service could serve on the all-monk central committee or be appointed representatives to subject tribes and monasteries (cf. Huang 1989: 109). That move points up the increasing importance of lay-monastic masculine alliances in the dispensation and control of legitimate violence as the frontier zone came to be tied ever closer to the Chinese interior.

Indeed, given the indeterminacy and inherent vulnerabilities of trulku recognition across incarnations, at Labrang perhaps the most important element of the co-creation of trulku agency over time were efforts to create participant obligations for laymen as forms of desirable exchange embedded in patrifilial relationships across generations. Yet the stakes of all spatial politics in the frontier zone revolved around the capacity to appropriate local wealth and labor in a region of mobile social groups. With the Mongol prince's initial transfer of land and five hundred nomad households as subjects (ibid. 111; cf. Ma Denghun and Wanma 1994), the monastery was founded in a valley straddling the geographic transition zone between lower arable plains and higher plateau suitable only for nomadic pastoralism (see fig. 1). Thus the expansion of Geluk mandalization from Labrang, a process that continued

FIGURE 6.
The last Cham Chen before CCP intervention is performed at
Labrang in the spring of 1949. Chegyal's thangka is displayed to
the right of the main assembly hall. A stick-wielding lay official
stands in the foreground. (Photo by Wayne Persons)

up until CCP intervention, could be seen as an ongoing process of Tibetan *sedentarism*—not only in settling nomads (Tib. *'brog pa*) as farmers (Tib. *rong pa*) in the
valley, but most importantly in orienting the flux of nomad alliances and mobility to
an expanding sedentary center.

As a civilizing project, Geluk mandalization in the frontier zone contrasted
sharply with the ways Han and Hui sedentary communities and would-be rulers
mapped relationships with Tibetan nomads. By the late 1920s and 1930s, Han, Hui,
and even foreign missionaries and observers throughout the region referred to all
Tibetans with the Chinese ethnonym *fanzi* (lit. "aborigine" or "barbarian"). That
term, in use for centuries, indexed the (frightening) Otherness of Tibetan nomadic
pastoralist lifeways as epitomizing the unsophisticated barbarity of Tibetans in
general, and it mapped degrees of civilization as a spatiotemporal progression
down and away from the "raw" Tibetans (Ch. *shengfan*) of the plateau to the
"cooked" Tibetans (Ch. *shoufan*) of the loess valleys and plains (cf. Petech 1988,
Sperling 1993).

Zhang Qiyun, a Han professor from Nanjing who wrote a gazetteer of the newly established Xiahe county in the 1930s, spatializes this schema by categorizing Labrang "Tibetans" (Ch. Zang) in terms of their cultural and geographic proximity to Han: the "Near Tibetans" (Ch. Jinzang), Tibetans settled near towns, who knew Chinese but still wore traditional Tibetan clothing; the "Half-Tibetans" (Ch. Banzang), descendants of marriages between Tibetan women and Han men, who spoke Chinese, lived in town, and wore Chinese clothes; and the "Far Tibetans" (Ch. Yuanzang), Tibetans who were "purely nomadic," did not speak Chinese and lived far from towns. In these schemas, temporal progress is read from spatial progress toward a Sinified sedentarism. Hence Robert Ekvall's vision of traveling upriver to the Sangkok grasslands west of Labrang monastery as like "a journey into the past" (1939: 30). By contrast, Tibetan sedentarism through Geluk mandalization at Labrang was a reorganization of Tibetan nomad fatherlands. Its success hinged on inserting lamas and monks into the intimacies of masculine personhood and kinship that constituted nomad *patrifiliality*—the structuring emphasis, among nomad communities in the region, on links between generations of men naturalized in an idiom of father-son relation.

The debates in Western and Chinese literature about whether or not Tibetans are "patrilineal" seem to stem from several sources (cf. Nakane 1966, Stein 1972, Aziz 1978a, Levine 1988, Samuel 1993, Draper 1994, Watkins 1996). Either "Tibet" is reified, so that theorists miss the great diversity of kinship ideologies and organization across Tibetan regions, or patrilineality is reified, so that theorists dismiss its importance among Tibetans as against assumed paradigmatic cases of patrilineal clanship (like Chinese surname villages; cf. Yu Xiangwen 1943). Perhaps most importantly though, the recent rethinking of kinship among feminist anthropologists especially has opened avenues for moving beyond the limitations of earlier structural-functionalist assumptions that have arguably limited understandings of the complexity of kinship among Tibetans (cf. Collier and Yanagisako 1987, Weston 1991, Peletz 1995, Maynes et al. 1996). From this perspective, kinship is not taken to be an isolable realm of primary biological relationships undergirding all social structure. Instead, it is understood as a realm of gendered cultural politics par excellence. Kinship, in this view, emerges in contested ideas about types and degrees of relatedness, affiliation, and obligation associated with particular notions of biology, sex, and reproduction—a process at the heart of the politics of gender recognition amidst the everyday flux of social groups.

In the Labrang region, as elsewhere, idioms of male lineage (Tib. *rgyud, rus brgyud*, lit. "bone line") were the main way that the ideal continuity of knowledge and authority was constructed and naturalized across generations—in both lay *and* monastic contexts (cf. Samuel 1993: 150; Stuchbury 1994; Gibbons 1995: 287; Mills 2003: 53). But in this largely pastoralist region, notions of patrilineage took on heightened importance, because tribes (Tib. *tsho ba* or *shog pa*), the main political units among nomads, relied on the historicity of patrilineage for claims of corporate identity, rights to pasturelands, and, in larger tribes with hereditary chiefs, to ensure the continuity of tribal control of pastures in alliance or conflict with other tribes (cf. Ekvall 1939, 1968; Carrasco 1959). Importantly, terms of familiar address in that region likened the members of one's community to the generations of one's stem family, so that men *and* women would address all unrelated male familiars a generation older as "father" (Tib. *a pa*). Phayul, or fatherland, thus indexed the importance of the "father" as a general trope for elder and ideally wiser and respected masculine authority intimately linked to and responsible for younger inferiors. In this light then, phayul could be seen as a relative term with which men and women placed themselves in localities defined by the contested grassland ranges of tribes under the auspices of "fathers and grandfathers" (Tib. *pha dang mes po, yab dang yang mes*).

By the nineteenth century, local Tibetan historiography utilized patrilineal descent to directly link the main tribal alliances subject to Labrang through three original immigrant brothers to the great aristocratic patrilines (Tib. *rus chen*) of the eighth-century central Tibetan dynasty (cf. dkon mchog bstan pa rab rgyas 1987: 547). In the 1980s and 1990s, Tibetan historians, along with Han counterparts, took up this interest in the patrilineal historicity of Tibetan tribes (cf. Chen Qingying 1990, 1995; Ma Denghun and Wanma 1994; Wang Zhouta 1996a; XXZ 1997). And locals in Labrang still referred to their phayul as constituted by the original settlements of patrilineally linked male nomad ancestors, even if they did not recognize themselves as direct descendants. But as Nancy Levine (1988: 30) points out, such origin stories impose order on extremely heterogeneous histories of migration and alliance. As groups of households moved in search of pasture or protection, tribes could encompass a variety of groups that did not claim patrilineal relation. In fact, Tibetan patriliny defined ideal male solidarity and continuity *against* both inherent tensions in tribal structure and the crucial flexibility of masculine alliance in the frontier zone. Patriliny for Tibetans in the Labrang region was essentially an ordering framework for the flux of patrifiliality in practice.

Most importantly, the respected authority of fathers was constructed relative to their roles as patriarchs of ideally independent households, or rather tentholds (Tib. *khyim tshang*), the main unit of livestock ownership and production and the locus of decision making about the specifics of movement and residence and the distribution of property (cf. Ekvall 1939, 1968; Hermanns 1953; Stubel 1958; Carrasco 1959; Mills 2003). The apparently wide variety of marriage arrangements and postmarital residence, the seemingly large number of households headed by matriarchs, and the relative independence of women—features of nomad life around Labrang that horrified some Chinese and Western missionary observers (e.g., Gu and Lu 1938, Gao Changzhu 1942, Yu Xiangwen 1943, Rijnhart 1901)—were in part due to the overriding importance of maintaining the household patrimony across generations in the face of shortages of sons as heirs (see chapter 4).

In this region, where long-distance trade was the purview of men, and sons could be sent to monasteries as children, daughters were important not only as household labor, but also as crucial conduits of what Levine, following Fortes, calls "complementary filiation" (1988: 46; and see below, chapters 3–5). Local Tibetan kin terms, almost identical for relatives on both sides, recognize both parents' relatives for several generations as equally important; these were all one's "flesh and blood" (Tib. *sha khrag*). But kinship was not reckoned bilineally. Instead, mothers provided links to other patrilines, and—where succession mattered, such as in wealthy households or those of hereditary chiefs—by bringing in a surrogate son (in-law: Tib. *mag pa*), a daughter could indirectly transmit the bone of her father's line to her children through her blood (Tib. *khrag*) or flesh (Tib. *sha;* cf. Hermanns 1953; Ekvall 1968: 27; Stein 1972: 108; Levine 1988: 49; Stuchbury 1994: 165).

As nomad population expanded in the nineteenth century, a patrilineal participation framework thus mediated the tensions between independent households and the need for tribal alliances among them to protect pasture rights. For men in that context, locating selves in the historicity of a father-son line (with either a household name or a lineage or bone name), and *not* the close control of women, was most important for authorizing their status as crucial *exchange specialists* representing and protecting the interests of corporate units vis-à-vis others. From this angle then, we can understand the particular form of masculine alliance across lay and monastic contexts that undergirded Geluk mandalization at Labrang amidst the increasingly high-stakes politics of the frontier zone. Trulkus' embodiment as supreme tantrists positioned them as paramount exchange specialists, indeed in a sense as ultra-fathers, at the top of a hierarchical regime of value that oriented all registers of exchange toward the monastic center.[19] Patrifilial patronage of trulkus, the monk assembly, and monk relatives thus provided frameworks for affiliation and obligatory production and exchange that came to be part and parcel of masculine personhood locally.

Indeed, in contrast to other regimes in the frontier zone by the early twentieth century, direct taxation of subjects was much less significant than in-kind donations to the monastery construed as freely given, a matter of pure faith in the karmically meritorious nature of the offering.[20] In the words of Tenzin Palbar, a monk trulku at Labrang writing from exile, Labrang monastery became the Buddhist ruler of the region due to the "pure offerings" (Tib. *gtsang 'bul*) of its patron tribes (1994: 45). But the power of the pious gift in a patrifilial status economy meant that status, sons, daughters, male alliance, and wealth among competing lay male and monastic elites could circulate *along with* the signs of trulkus' blessing power, which were arguably the highest "tokens of value" locally (cf. Appadurai 1986, Huber 1999, Graeber 2001, Ohnuma 2005).

Perhaps the most important participation framework for sedentarizing nomads as patrifilial subjects in this way was the *dewa* (Tib. *sde ba*), a named group of households and key administrative unit in both nomad and farming communities. The Tibetan term *dewa* is not directly translatable as "village" or "nomad encampment." Instead, *de* (Tib. *sde*) means "portion of a whole," and thus references to dewa always indexed the metonymic nature of local groupings of households (anywhere from 20 to over 500) as parts of larger tribes across the nomad-farming divide (cf. Ekvall 1939: 67).[21] But under Labrang, as more Tibetans settled in the valley to cultivate land owned by the monastery, dewa were institutionalized as the most important and most familiar corporate unit under the leadership of oftentimes patrilineally related male elders. They were the crucial intermediate groupings between the independence of property-owning households and the shifting politics of tribal alliances.

By the early twentieth century, nineteen Tibetan farming dewa, grouped under the fourth Jamyang Shepa's administration in the "Four Lhade Tribes" (Tib. lha sde shog bzhi), had developed in the valley around the monastery (see chapter 2). And as Labrang expanded its influence over branch monasteries and their lay patrons farther afield, those local "tribes" were in turn counted as belonging to the "Eight Great Lhade Tribes" (Tib. lha sde shog pa brgyad) of Labrang, an imagined community that encompassed almost all the major groupings of nomadic pastoralists working the surrounding grasslands and affiliated more locally with branch monasteries of Labrang.[22] Of all the types of relationship monastic officials individually negotiated with various multiethnic groupings, the *Lhade* (lit. "God Dewas") were supposed to be its closest patrons, residing in closest proximity to the monastery in the market town downriver (called Tawa, "Edge") or in neighboring villages, and supplying the monastery with most of its income and its monks. In exchange for protection, indefinite leases on farmland, or privileged status vis-à-vis the monastery, the headmen and patriarchs of those Tibetan dewa accepted direct oversight in all important affairs by a representative appointed from among Jamyang Shepa's trusted lay guard, and farming dewa handed over a portion of their harvests annually. Further, they had labor obligations that included annual ritual duties and military services provided by laymen (cf. Gao Changzhu 1942; Luo 1987: 111; Ji Wenpo 1993; Ma Denghun and Wanma 1994: 165).

If we go back and situate the great mandalizing pageants at Labrang like the Cham Chen in these gendered spatial politics, we can now grasp more clearly that, as Keane (1997) and others have recently emphasized, the very formality of such ritual events also produces the inherent *vulnerability* of their main meanings and goals. Formal frames like the Cham Chen, as public performance genres, invite participants to reflect on and evaluate the discourses and performances presented therein as reiterations of important values and meanings. But they also both construct and entail participants' reflection on what the extreme formality of the event would hope to thereby exclude: "by insisting too much, as it were, the [ritual] frame invites the watcher to imagine its vulnerability to breaking and to appreciate the difficulty of sustaining it" (Keane 1997: 17). In part, the grandeur, scale, and solemnity of the event worked to construct the unmarked and absolute nature of Jamyang Shepa's supreme tantric masculine prowess. But like all such hierarchizing efforts, the event created the corporate lama's Other (or Others) even as it tried to control and suppress them.

As the Geluk monastic regime of value at Labrang attracted settlers and traders to the valley and concentrated farmland and capital in trulkus' estates, the Cham Chen was an annual event always at odds with itself. It was an attempt to establish a centered sociospatial order based on the absolute symmetry of a maṇḍala (see fig. 3), and yet it also indexed a center relative to embodied trulkus ensconced in the precarious politics of asymmetric exchange with crucial lay male authorities (cf. Hanks 1996). In such a context, the tantric participation frameworks of such events were always amenable to misrecognition or appropriation by participants and competing agents for their own ends. In actuality, the very success of Geluk mandalization at Labrang heightened competition among trulkus for control of masculine alliances and tied the region ever closer to both the Chinese "interior" (Ch. *neidi*) and foreign economic interests (cf. Fletcher 1978: 48). Under Qing patronage, throughout the nineteenth and early twentieth centuries the most immediate threats to the center at Labrang were in fact the competing mandalizing efforts of *other* trulkus. Indeed, trulkus based there and elsewhere had, through patrifilial alliances with local leaders or Qing authorities, procured their own patron tribes among Tibetan nomads, thus building independent power bases in their own estates (Tib. *nang chen*, lit. "Great Houses").[23]

In this light, the Cham Chen by the early twentieth century must be seen as a culminating component of the greater mandalizing event that was the annual Great Prayer Festival at the lunar new year. That two-week period created participant obligations for both lay patrons and lesser trulkus that juxtaposed and hierarchized various registers and scales of exchange under corporate monastic auspices, so that the event itself constituted the peak of ritual and economic exchange framing the whole year (cf. Ekvall 1939; Zhang Guangda 1993a: 87). In effect, the Great Prayer Festival was a culminating "tournament of value" (Appadurai 1986: 21; cf. Mauss 1990: 27) in which the circulation of the highest Buddhist values (trulku blessings, merit) provided frameworks and networks for the circulation of other values and goods—everyone was invested, but not necessarily along preferred lines. Thus, since the Lhade tribes rotated responsibility for supporting the monk assembly during the assembly's annual intensive meetings, when it was their turn tribal leaders vied with one another to demonstrate their political prowess by donating the most and best items of food, butter, meat, and money successfully collected from their constituents (cf. Rock 1956: 38; Li Anzhai 1982: 7; Goldstein 1998a; Huber 1999: 160).[24]

In the context of such high political economic stakes, one of the most significant ways the Jamyang Shepas attempted to recruit and regulate the participation of lay male patrons in the event was to give gifts and allocate prestigious supporting ritual roles to publicly reward male heirs for the original faithful patronage of their male forebears (cf. Ma Denghun and Wanma 1994: 233). The highest-profile of these roles during the festival literally mandalized key laymen by recruiting heirs of the "six earliest households" (those said to have first settled in the valley as tenant farmers in support of the monastery) to patrol the town and monastery as six of the Eight Cavalrymen of Namtisay (Skt. Vaiśravaṇa; cf. Li Anzhai 1982: 84; Ma Denghun and Wanma 1994: 179; Tenzin Palbar 1994: 46). Namtisay, god of wealth and an oath-sworn worldly protector of the Geluk, leads the four guardians of the directions as protector of the North in Buddhist cosmology. Depicted as a fierce general, his image, along with the protector gods of the other three directions, protects the entrance to the inner temple of the main assembly hall at Labrang, and he is invoked as a key protector in most maṇḍala rites.

The six laymen representatives from the earliest households, along with two others representing dewa that also early on became patrons, were the only men allowed to ride horses in monastic space and bear arms during the festival, and they were empowered to shoot, beat, or fine transgressors. Elderly laypeople described to me their solemn power in the 1940s. Both men and women told me that everyone feared them because one could get hit even for exhibiting disrespect by failing to remove one's hat when they passed. The move to reward the earliest farming settlers in this way, a decision attributed to the second Jamyang Shepa (1728–91) when he initiated the Great Prayer Festival at Labrang, indexes the importance of sedentarization to the monastery. Further, since those households were said to be the prestigious ancestors of the *Tibetan* households of the (by that time) multiethnic Tawa dewa, the role of the Eight Cavalrymen in the Great Prayer Festival annually recruited Tibetan lay sons to model the appropriate peripheries of the maṇḍala amidst increasing ethnic diversification.[25] Their roles as Namtisay's warrior retinue linked the Tibetan Lhades' labor obligations as hereditary patrons to the faithful protection of the central deity-trulku and promised rich rewards for such service.

Such annual appeals to the intimate obligations and potential benefits of patrifilial exchange took on heightened importance and risk as Jamyang Shepa's offices struggled to maintain his position at the top of the polity's regime of value in an increasingly heterogeneous urbanizing valley. Indeed, like other Geluk monastic centers that expanded under Qing patronage in the frontier zone, the Lhade dewas in the valley developed into the Tawa market town that became a commercial hub between Chinese and Tibetan regions. European demand for Tibetan wool and leather in the nineteenth century had intensified the regional interests of Han and Hui migrant brokers (Ch. *xiejia*) who initially made enormous profits off of nomad Tibetans' relative naivete (cf. Lipman 1997). In the ferment of the late nineteenth century, Hui traders and refugees moved upriver and occupied an important niche as economic mediators between nomad Tibetan producers and Han and foreign buyers. Thus the thriving market also provided ample opportunities for some Tibetans, lay and monastic, to parlay capital into profit-making ventures (cf. Ekvall 1939).

As early as 1863, the concerned ministers of the seven-year-old fourth Jamyang Shepa felt compelled to issue an edict, framed by the lama's status as hereditary holder of a Qing title and head of the polity, warning all the monk

FIGURE 7.
The American Christian missionary Wayne Persons looks down
over Labrang monastery on the eve of CCP intervention, summer 1949. The largest monastic buildings in the foreground are
trulkus' mansions. (Photo courtesy of Wayne Persons)

officials and trulkus competing with one another in lucrative loan and long-
distance-trade businesses not to be greedy, exploit others, or embezzle communal
funds for personal profit.[26] The edict reminds Labrang's multiethnic subjects that
such behavior would "damage the good purposes of our Buddhism and directly
counter monks' cultivation of compassion and morality," and it threatens viola-
tors with public humiliation in a great assembly of monk and lay leaders, as well
as with terrible karmic retribution inflicted by the Dharma protectors (cited in
Zhang Guangda 1993a: 90). The ministers' invocation of both the Qing court and
the ferocious protector deities reasserts the child Jamyang Shepa's (hereditary)
access to their transcendent agency in the face of a devolution of power from the
monastic center in a rapidly expanding local economy. As part of his later recen-
tralizing efforts, the fourth Jamyang Shepa appointed monk officials to more
directly administer the town and market, hoping to ensure that lucrative taxes on
commerce would continue under monastic auspices, and he saw that the Great
Prayer Festival, the height of annual commercial activity, was a time for reiterat-
ing lay patrons' and merchants' duties to the monastery with a lecture in the mar-

ket by the monastic disciplinarian (Li Anzhai 1982: 59; Tenzin Palbar 1994: 46). But those efforts, as it turned out, were not enough to neutralize intensifying pressures on the region.

CONCLUSION: JAMYANG SHEPA'S DREAM

In the summer of 1934, the nineteen-year-old fifth Jamyang Shepa had a disturbing dream (zhabs drung 1952: 136.4):

> One morning, Jamyang Shepa said to his older brother the military commander [Apa Alo], [last] night, the 25th [of the 8th lunar month], "[I] dreamed that an airplane was circling the Front Mountain [opposite his palace in the monastery]. Beside the peak of Queen Mountain there stood a white and a blue foal. A rifle shot [from the plane] felled them. A man dressed in white robes rolled up high helped the blue one up." That very day a [KMT] plane sent from Lanzhou flew over the top of Front Mountain, up to Sangkok plain and back over the monastery, banking up and down to show off its might.

In those days, the young monk-trulku was keenly interested in global affairs, keeping abreast of them via his radio and his relationships with his cosmopolitan older brother and with Marion Griebenow, the American missionary by then living in Labrang (see fig. 5; cf. Nietupski 1999). I would say then that Jamyang Shepa's dream focusing on the inexplicable violence emanating from an airplane indicates his growing awareness of the imminent threat to the monastic center of a new spatial order with the unprecedented means to both envision and violently enforce it over the Tibetan tribal militiamen whom Apa Alo had worked so hard to muster in the previous decade (cf. Huang 1989).

Indeed, what the fifth Jamyang Shepa had to face as he reached adulthood was that with the fall of the Qing and the death of his predecessor at a young age, the very terms of Geluk mandalization at Labrang had opened the way to the incorporation of the region into an array of competing spatial frameworks. By the time of his reign, Tibetans there recognized Labrang's bustling cosmopolitanism as an essentially Tibetan urbanity centered on the monastery, an extension of that of Lhasa so that, contrary to Lhasans' stereotypes of Amdowans as rustic beggars (cf. Stoddard 1985: 284), they called the region the "Second Central Tibet" (cf. Pu 1990: 507). However, the Han merchants and officials arriving in increasing numbers considered the town to be an indispensable economic and administrative entree to the broader Tibetan plateau and referred to the region as an expansion of Chinese urbanity, calling it a "Little Beijing" or a "Little Shanghai in Tibetan Regions" (Zhang Guangda 1993a: 86; cf. Gesang Daji 1993: 52).

But the *permanent* presence of such outsiders with competing visions for Labrang's future had actually been secured in the negotiations of Apa Alo himself as he struggled in the face of devastating military defeats to regain control of Labrang. In 1917, Ma Qi, the Muslim warlord in Xining, in order to tax Labrang's lucrative market and finance his expansionist goals, took advantage of internecine conflict among Tibetan trulkus in the wake of the fourth Jamyang Shepa's death to marshal the first-ever (though brief) occupation of Labrang by non-Tibetans.[27] In Apa Alo's later account of those years—their detail and unabashedly pro-Tibetan tone contrasting sharply with his careful account of the CCP takeover—he depicts himself expanding the grounds of Tibetan masculinity by expediently embracing the modernist discourses of "promoting Tibetan culture" and working for "minorities'" equality, discourses that were advocated by the competing Han agents he cultivated as allies against Ma Qi and his Hui armies. But it is also clear from his account that, as representatives of the preteen Jamyang Shepa, Apa Alo and his formidable father parlayed the Buddhist indexicality of the central trulku to approach Han provincial officials on much the same grounds as previous Labrang officials had approached the Qing court. Amidst the escalating militarization of the region, they sought military support against local threats by appealing to an overarching central government that would act as a court of final appeal and support Labrang's regional autonomy on the grounds of its apolitical Buddhist mission and ethnic sovereign right (Huang 1989: 26).

But in the absence of such a central authority in China by that time, the strategic misrecognition of masculinities that had allowed for translocal alliance in the past this time resulted in a uniquely problematic compromise for Labrang authorities. Securing the military support of Han Gansu officials against Ma Qi meant that Apa Alo allowed them to establish a regional government headquarters (Ch. *shezhiju*, Tib. *srid skyong las shag*) in Labrang, complete with a security force of provincial troops. Since around the same time the Gansu provincial ruler Feng Yuxiang threw his lot in with the ascendant KMT head Jiang Jieshi (Chiang Kaishek), in 1928 Labrang was claimed as the seat of Xiahe county, an administrative unit of Gansu province under the KMT central government in Nanjing (ibid. 29). County officials lost no time in delegating people to survey the terrain and set boundaries, ultimately claiming twice as much territory under county jurisdiction as had originally been agreed upon (ibid. 31; cf. Ma Haotian 1942–47, Zhang

Qiyun 1969), and this period marked the intensification of private and statist mapping and census efforts throughout the Labrang region.[28] We can get a sense of both the traditional categories and Han county officials' unprecedented aspirations for the region in the couplet that adorned the government headquarters' main door in 1936: "Using the Xia [Chinese] to civilize the Yi [barbarians], mountains and forests are developed into a land of peace. / Taking the river as a boundary, wide territories are opened up that are better than Taoyuan [legendary place of peace]" (Ma Haotian 1942–47: 46).

Thereafter, the county headquarters gave provincial officials a base from which to heighten pressure on Apa Alo and monastic officials to participate in KMT development projects and in the escalating war with CCP forces. Yet ultimately, KMT plans in Labrang were a low priority for embattled KMT nationalist leaders, and eager Han social reformers who flocked to the region to "develop the Northwest" (Ch. *kaifa* Xibei) could do nothing in the face of the ongoing power of Geluk mandalization (cf. Upton 1999). After all, Apa Alo and his father had gained the attention of Han provincial officials in their battle with Ma Qi only when they had demonstrated the power of patrifilial alliance centered on Labrang by mustering over twenty thousand nomad troops from regions extending into Sichuan, camping them en masse on the Sangkok grasslands (Huang 1989: 23). Thus like many other Han visitors, in 1936 the KMT official Ma Haotian, urging Apa Alo to support KMT efforts to promote "cultural equality" through Chinese curriculum education, could only complain to Apa Alo that the new secular schools he had helped to establish a decade earlier had attracted only a very few Tibetan students, and the cash-poor county government could do nothing in the face of locals' loyalties to monastic officials. Apa Alo blandly replied that he wanted to help the county government, but since the boundaries were still unclear, there was nothing he could do (Ma Haotian 1942–47: 76; cf. Gu and Lu 1938; Gao Changzhu 1942; Zhang Qiyun 1969: 12).

In effect then, these confrontations between the monastic polity at Labrang and new nationalist spatial frameworks in the first half of the twentieth century cannot be understood as an encounter between a hermetically sealed ritual world and rationalist "politics." Instead, Ma Qi was defeated in part due to Apa Alo's capacity to embrace modernist discourses to his own ends, and KMT officials had no leverage with which to dislodge the preeminence of mandalic participation frameworks for masculine authority and alliance in Labrang. Indeed, under the fifth Jamyang Shepa's central office (Tib. *yig tshang*), the monastery collected its own census statistics among its patron dewa, counting households as the primary units ensconced in larger tribal units (Ma Denghun and Wanma 1994: 165). And Apa Alo's successes in mobilizing Tibetan nomads against Ma Qi had in fact heightened his (and by extension Jamyang Shepa's) prestige among Tibetans, pushing him into the realm of divine agency. Apa Alo was eventually said to be an incarnation of Namtisay himself, thus enhancing his appropriately subordinate status as a protector in and of Jamyang Shepa's mandalic order. Further, the institutionalization of Apa Alo's position as military commander in the new county only further insulated Jamyang Shepa's agency from contexts for physical violence and the projects of the county government.[29] Indeed, the summer when Jamyang Shepa had his ominous dream was precisely the time when KMT militarization intensified as the whole region anticipated the arrival of CCP Long-Marchers. But that was also the summer when he accepted, in gorgeous ceremony reminiscent of Qing practice, a seal from Jiang Jieshi proclaiming him a Sacred Teacher and Protector of the Nation—a gesture toward strategic misrecognition that had arguably short-lived efficacy, since a little over a decade later Jamyang Shepa died and Jiang Jieshi was defeated (cf. Tuttle 2005).

When the last Cham Chen before CCP intervention was held in the spring of 1949, the abbot and Chegyal tamed evil spirits on behalf of the polity in the absence of Jamyang Shepa. In the light of this analysis, we cannot reduce that event to evidence of Tibetans' conservative ignorance in the face of impending doom. Instead it indexed the crucial importance of masculine tantric prowess in the Buddhist mandalic regime of value at Labrang. The mysterious politics of tantric ritual exchange provided locals ways to construe the unprecedented compromises and arbitrary turns of frontier politics that had maintained a provisional autonomy at Labrang as the consequences of trulkus' absolute agency. But most importantly, mandalization provided for a great flexibility of frameworks for key laymen to recognize, affiliate with, and benefit from embodied trulkus. Jamyang Shepa's power over time was not the result of collective representations shared by all. It was instead the ongoing effect of strategic misrecognition within an uneasy and shifting hierarchy of masculinities. In this milieu, no one anticipated the Maoist state violence that within a decade would eradicate Jamyang Shepa's mandalic sphere and the Cham Chen entirely.

T W O   ·   Father State

Socialist Transformation
and Gendered Historiography

MINZU: NATIONAL INCORPORATION AND
THE POLITICS OF DECONTEXTUALIZATION

After the death of Mao Zedong in 1976 and the fall of the radical faction known as "the Gang of Four," Labrang monastery was officially reopened in 1979, just as soon as Deng Xiaoping's reform policies permitted. The only Tibetan Buddhist monastery in Gannan prefecture to have had any buildings left standing after the Cultural Revolution (1966–68), it was also the first place in the prefecture where, as locals told me, the "door to the Dharma was (re)opened" (Tib. *chos sgo phye dang*). That very year, monastic officials found the resources to hold the Great Prayer Festival again, and by 1996, when I was there, the magnificence of the Cham Chen, with its massive lay audience and procession of splendidly dressed village laymen representing wealthy patron households, seemed to indicate the great success of fifteen years of monastic "recovery" (Ch. *huifu*) at Labrang. But the event was also constituted by the transformed premises for its performance. As I discovered, my own ethnographic lens on the performance had to jostle for position with the camera lenses of Han and foreign photographers and television crews.

Monastic dances at Labrang had always been staged for the optimal viewing *not* of the lay audience but of the high lamas and officials on the main assembly hall veranda (see fig. 6). In 1996, then, the event unfolded within a new-pitched politics of access to the dance space. That year, state cadres and influential tourist visitors seeking optimal images of the photogenic performances parlayed local ties to negotiate with severe monastic officials and buy permits for new coveted positions with a view on the neighboring rooftops of trulkus' estates. After my own dogged attempts failed, I talked with a local Tibetan woman cadre from the Gansu Province Commission on Minzu ("Nationality") Affairs (Ch. Minzu Shiwu Weiyuanhui *or* Minwei). She said she was there supervising Han television crews from Lanzhou— colorful images of Tibetan performances were useful in the propaganda efforts of a wide range of provincial bureaus under the Minwei's authority. Indeed, images of the Cham Chen had been front and center in a variety of Minwei-sponsored tourism media about Labrang since the early 1990s (cf. Duozang Caidan 1992). In an exhausted and resentful tone, and using a term that alluded to Maoist revolutionary politics, the cadre described her long "struggle" (Ch. *douzheng*) with the monk officials in the monastery's management committee for access to the dance space without the requisite permits. Her resentment seemed to me to index the gendered fault lines of state-local conflict in post-Mao Labrang. Against her expectations, the purview of her provincial bureau's secular authority had faltered at the mandala's peripheries—unlike the wealthy lay "guests" of the monastery happily settled on the rooftops, she said that up until that very morning her crew was not going to be allowed to film up there.

The restaging of the Cham Chen under the gaze of both foreign tourists and the provincial Minwei at the reopened Labrang monastery raises important questions for understanding gender and Tibetan cultural revitalization there. How do competing authorities appropriate local discourses and participation frameworks in order to regulate populations from afar? In other words, what are the premises for the successful *de*contextualization of discourses, spaces, and subjects in the interests of power? (Cf. Bauman and Briggs 1990: 72.) Under what conditions are decontextualized discourses made newly meaningful to people, thereby effectively *re*contextualizing people as types of embodied subjects or "citizens" in the refigured participation frameworks of new "national" macrospaces *and* times? And what consequences would that process have for locals' abilities to situate themselves and to interpret their experiences to their own ends? These questions direct our attention back to the gendered cultural politics of national incorporation as they played out in the collective trauma of Maoist socialist transformation in Labrang.

We can understand this process past and present, I would argue, only if we consider state discipline directed at national citizens as a multilayered and often unconscious process. The multivalence of the term "incorporation" then serves us well. As exemplified in the emasculating force of the laywoman state agent's claim to an unprecedented point of view over male monastic authorities and ritualized spaces, "incorporation" encapsulates the essentially intertwined nature of legal, geo-graphic, social, and bodily transformations entailed in nationalization. Here I find analytic tools developed by linguistic anthropologists to be particularly illuminat-ing ways to operationalize theories about the process of achieving unconscious dominance or cultural "hegemony" (cf. Williams 1977). As Bauman and Briggs and other theorists of language, meaning, and power have pointed out, the capacity to *arbitrate* frameworks for social participation, and thus to continually reincorporate people in often subtle and unremarked ways, is an essential part of the reproduction of agencies authorized to discipline populations, violently or not (Bauman and Briggs 1990: 72; cf. Goffman 1981, McDermott and Tylbor 1995, Keane 1997).

Consider, then, the particular difficulties facing early Chinese Communist nation-state builders after decades of regional strife throughout the territories once claimed by the Qing. In order to claim those territories as fixed components of a newly emancipatory or "democratic" (Ch. *minzhu*) yet legitimately "Chinese" nation-state, CCP leaders had to work hard to recruit extraordinarily diverse peo-ples to recognize themselves in what Arjun Appadurai (1996: 162) refers to as the "fragile abstractions" of subjecthood in a new translocal community—*and* they had to do so in a way that would legitimize, as we will see, unprecedented state reg-ulation and expropriation of bodies and resources in the locale. As I argued in the previous chapter, in the Sino-Tibetan frontier zone this was not merely a process of transition from a "traditional" Buddhist ritual order to a "modern" rationalist polit-ical one. Instead, we need to conceptualize national incorporation in Labrang to be primarily the state's conflictual dialogue with Tibetan forms of masculine divinity, playing out in visions of a paternalist Chinese national "Fatherland" (Ch. *zuguo*, Tib. *mes rgyal*) versus mandalized Amdo Tibetan fatherlands (Tib. *pha yul*). Just as in Geluk mandalization efforts, CCP leaders also worked to posit natural corre-spondences for people between micro- and macrocosmic spaces by creating com-peting participation frameworks aimed at marginalizing (emasculating) local Tibetan trulkus and establishing rival masculine authorities. Crucially, those new national masculine authorities had to manifest as *unmarked*—that is, as disembod-ied or all-pervasive disciplinary and arbitrating agencies.

Unlike the Qing emperors in their relations with Tibetans, the secular and ratio-nalist discourse of Chinese Communists allowed them no explicit recourse to medi-ating divine embodiment as a way to link micro- and macrospaces in their radical vision of a new overarching social order.[1] But for CCP leaders both during and after the Maoist years, the secular category *minzu* (sometimes translated "national-ity" or "national ethnic group") was pivotal in this process.[2] Minzu envisioned a newly democratic and self-aware citizenry as primary moral and political agents (thus *backgrounding* state agency) in the new nation, at the same time as it provided tools for classifying the citizenry in fixed, hierarchically arranged ethnic or racial groups with specific, legally delimited "rights" (cf. Herberer 1989, Harrell 1995, Schein 2000, Bulag 2002). From the perspective I have been developing here, we have to conceptualize minzu politics in the PRC not just as state rhetoric but as three-dimensional participation frameworks, contested efforts to decontextualize and resituate persons in space and, especially for our purposes in this chapter, in time. That is, CCP leaders' harmonious (and almost stateless) vision of democratic "national unity" (Ch. *minzu tuanjie*) played out in Labrang as a fundamental *temporal contradiction* that made minzu a dangerous and shifting category vis-à-vis Tibetan masculine authority (cf. Duara 1995).

On one hand, the arduous process of CCP "minzu recognition" work (Ch. *minzu shibie*, lit. "recognize and distinguish") in the early 1950s sought to fix ethnic or racial groups (eventually 56 total, including Han Chinese) in a *timeless* national democracy, one that promised unprecedented categorical (legal) equality and political "autonomy" for non-Chinese Others, regardless of their minzu groups' numbers (cf. Dreyer 1976, Fei 1981).[3] Thus PRC minzu status promised to liberate non-Han men from local hierarchies of masculinities in new frameworks for men's translocal and social mobility. On the other hand, minzu recognition work was premised on the stage theories of nineteenth-century Western social Darwinisms that sought to *rehistoricize* sociocultural differences as stages of development toward a class society, while positing their eventual disappearance in a socialist nation appropriately led by the most advanced group, the Han majority. In effect, then, minzu labels were initially an effort at containing sociocultural solidarities inimical to the all-important one of class, the primacy of which justified taking the Communist revolution to the frontier zone (cf. Dreyer 1976). Thus, in times of key social reforms, less civilized, tradition-bound "minority minzu" (Ch. *shaoshu minzu*) could then be appropriately relegated to marginalized regions and defined as limited political actors within local minzu "autonomous" districts, such as Gannan Tibetan Autonomous Prefecture (established 1953), where a majority of the government (but not necessarily Party) cadres were supposed to be Tibetan (see map 2). Alternatively, in times of minority resistance (as in the 1950s) minzu differences (from a Han standard) could be targeted for brutal eradication.

Minzu citizenship was then a crucial decontextualizing tool for CCP leaders that sought to establish a centralized and sedentary participation framework rivaling that at Labrang. Defining Tibetans as "Zangzu" was an important part of efforts to delineate and to curtail the terms of especially Tibetan men's' translocal net-working mobility (see chapter 6). But this process was not without unforeseen effects for Tibetans: new administrative divisions could allow for new forms of strategic misrecognition—that is, translocal ethnic solidarities not necessarily in line with CCP interests (cf. Gladney 1991). Denoting one of the few groups seen to fit all the criteria for a distinct minzu in the CCP investigations of the 1950s, the label "Zangzu" recognized the cultural, linguistic, and historical links among peoples scattered across a wide territory, even as they were divided among five separate provinces and various "Zangzu autonomous" districts and counties. Yet, historically in regions like Labrang, local phayul could be more important identities for people, depending on the type of interaction they were engaged in, than a broader notion of Tibetanness. By the early twentieth century, while Tibetans in Labrang recognized broad connections with others across the plateau as "insiders" (Tib. *nang pa*), meaning Buddhists, they most often referred to themselves as Amdowa in contrast to Bopa, people from central Tibet under the Dalai Lama's jurisdiction, or as farmers (Tib. *rong pa*) in contrast to nomads (Tib. *'brog pa*), or as members of particular monastic communities under certain trulkus (cf. Ekvall 1960, Tsering Shakya 1993).

Thus CCP recognition as Zangzu lent state administrative weight to a reified translocal identity that had arguably never existed among Tibetans. Indeed, the 1990 national census refers to Zangzu as a monolithic group numbering 4.6 million, and less than half of those people were registered as living in the Xizang Zangzu Autonomous Region (commonly referred to as "Tibet" or "the TAR").[4] The Labrang region was incorporated into PRC state territory when Tawa town was administratively separated from the monastery's subject populations west of the valley. The whole region was then subsumed under Gannan Zangzu Autonomous Prefecture, subordinate to Gansu provincial authorities northeast in Lanzhou. In the mid-1990s, I found that local Tibetans' everyday references to themselves indexed their recontextualization in this new spatial framework, but in ways that varied according to their orientations to urban or rural residence. Tibetans in the urbanizing valley, who tended to be bilingual in local dialects of Chinese and Amdo Tibetan, widely and proudly referred to themselves as Zangzu in Chinese, or when speaking Tibetan they used its gloss, Worik (*bod rigs*, lit. "Tibetan lineage" or "kind").[5] In either language, most referred to themselves as residents of Gansu province and distinguished themselves thereby from Tibetans living in Qinghai especially. By contrast, rural Tibetans (still mostly self-identified nomads), who spoke only Tibetan dialects, rarely used such terminology to describe themselves. Instead for them the term "Bod" (pronounced *wol*) had taken on new meaning as an essential, translocal Tibetanness (like the term "Zangzu") in contradistinction especially to the equally essentialized categories of Chinese (Tib. rgya), Hui (Tib. he *or* herigs), and foreigners—terms that people nonetheless used relative to the assumed existence of PRC national boundaries.

Thus, in the light of the discussion here and in the previous chapter of the complexity and violence of national incorporation in the Labrang region, we can appreciate the great historical process and social *work*—the marshaling of economic resources, personnel, and "thought work"—required to bring off the recontextualization in 1996 of the terrible protector deity Chegyal and his Cham Chen in Labrang. That day, Chegyal appeared under joint monastic and CCP state auspices, for an unprecedented variety of spectators (including television audiences and Minzu Bureau propagandists) whose privileged view now rivaled that of trulkus. This perspective, I would argue, is particularly important for understanding the exigencies of everyday life for Tibetans in post-Mao China because, as I will emphasize in this chapter, the very thrust of public life there worked against such a historical awareness.

Thus, as Louisa Schein (2000) and others have argued, minzu was a crucial category of subjecthood in the context of post-Mao reforms because, as we will see, it was a key medium for *statist forgetting* after the traumas of Maoist socialist transformation (cf. Bulag 2002). Prasenjit Duara, in his analysis of historiography and early nationalism in China, characterized modern nationalism globally as a unique form of state-sponsored forgetting, a way of organizing the past that located new national communities in posited oppositions between "tradition" and "modernity" (1995: 4; cf. Anderson 1990; Dirks 1992: 14; Anagnost 1997). Post-Mao minzu citizenship was supposed to erase the assimilationist traumas of the Maoist years, reemphasize the timeless categorical equality of the democratic ideal, and highlight national unity in the future-oriented quest for development and modernity. Thus events at Labrang like the Cham Chen in 1996 must be seen as instances of potentially clashing participation frameworks for authority and affiliation: trulku tantric prowess and Geluk remandalization versus—as our student Gompo discovered dancing at the ethnic park in Shenzhen around the same time—benign and traditional Zangzu custom limited to (lucrative) colorful displays indexing national unity.

But in this chapter I explore further the *politics of time* in national incorporation processes that such events sought to elide. In this way, we can better understand the tragic historical irony that was "Democratic Reforms" in the Labrang region beginning in 1958—in the face of Tibetan men's guerrilla resistance, PRC national democracy was implemented only through brutal state violence and mandatory participation frameworks for self-recognition. Further, I expand on Schein's notion of the "feminine hinge" (2000: 285) between the static past and advancing national modernity in the PRC to argue that appeals to a new kind of feminine subject operated as key frameworks for ideally domesticated *and* loyally productive minzu citizens. Here I expand on my previous analyses of the spatial politics of contextualization to consider gendered historiography in post-Mao Labrang—especially forms of oral narrative—as an ongoing temporal politics of contextualization that played out in the face of state officials' persistent efforts to shape and delimit memory and forgetting among Tibetans in order to arbitrate proper (minority) minzu citizenship.

AMA DROLMA'S REFUSAL: GENDER, NARRATIVE, AND MNEMONIC RECONTEXTUALIZATION

For a variety of reasons, I had been in Labrang for many months before I began to grasp how much, and in what ways, the past was a heavy and often hidden burden for locals. Most importantly, in the ferment of economic reforms, the bustling public market activities in town and in monastic tourist spaces seemed to displace the past for the present- and future-oriented consumption and development trajectories of locals, tourists, and state officials (cf. Dai 1996, 1999). Gradually I came to realize that for a Tibetan population living with unsanctioned memories of the traumatic ruptures of the Chinese Communist–led revolution beginning in 1949, the "unsaid" of history spoke loudly in *implication*—in implied dialogue with multimedia official histories, in the gaps in written and oral chronologies of events, in the revived performance of the lay and monastic ritual calendars, and in the dodges and silences of my variously positioned Tibetan interlocutors during our many conversations about their pasts:

> FROM FIELD NOTES: "I don't know anything! I'm too young, you know!" (Tib. *ngas shes ni ma red, nga lo chung gi mo*). Ama Drolma, a village matriarch in her late fifties, adamantly repeated this to me after I and my Tibetan woman assistant asked her for a taped interview about local "history" (Tib. *lo rgyus*). She would hear none of our explanations about my interest in people's personal histories and insisted that I seek out the old village patriarchs she listed. Only they, she argued, would know about "early, early, early times" (Tib. *sngan na sngan na sngan na*).

FIGURE 8.
New shops on Labrang's main street, including the Snowland
Internet Bar and a dance hall, summer 2002.

That awkward encounter occurred in the spring of 1995, only a few months into my stay in Labrang, and during an early attempt at "collecting" residents' "oral histories" based on a brief interview schedule. At the time, I thought I had understood Ama Drolma's metamessage to me: as an uneducated lay village woman, she did not consider herself a legitimate narrator of "history." It was not until much later, when I tried to write about the life stories I eventually heard from some sixty Tibetan men and women who had lived through socialist transformation, that I realized Ama Drolma was also pointing up the category of "history" itself as a crucial aspect of the gendered violence of liberation she and her peers had experienced under the CCP.

In this chapter, I rethink "history" as fundamentally a gendered "practice of time" (Mueggler 2001: 7), one that unfolds as situated persons work to remember within a variety of hierarchically arranged discourse genres, under the press of relations of power. This perspective will elucidate local Tibetans' active relationship to the state under CCP rule as most essentially a struggle with the scope and consequences of forms of *metalanguage,* or people's capacities for communicating (explicitly or implicitly) about the nature of discourses and speech events, thereby (explicitly or implicitly) positioning themselves with regard to them (cf. Bateson 1972, Silverstein 1976, Jakobson 1990). If we start from the fundamentally metalinguistic nature of language and meaning production, then we cannot conceptualize "history" as an objective story abstracted from the contexts of the telling. Instead, we have to consider history making as a situated politics of memory. That is, memories are made into stories only through contemporary, context-specific selections or metalinguistic framings that foreground some things and repress others (White 1981: 10; Scott 1991; Marcus 1992; Watson 1994a: 2; Hall 1998: 440; Kansteiner 2002).

In the Labrang region, I found that for Tibetans, the most salient aspect of this process in socialist transformation was the unprecedented state-mandated pressure for all residents, regardless of social position, to publicly perform *explicit* and highly stylized official forms of metacommunication about the past—initially to politicize public spaces as sites for the production of new, self-conscious minzu citizens, and then to *de*politicize them in the wake of the catastrophic consequences of the Maoist years. Thus, in this context, a crucial component of the "micro-physics of power" (Foucault 1984) sustaining CCP rule into the 1980s reform years in Labrang was the ongoing capacity of state officials, despite the great atrocities and acknowledged failings of CCP rule in the previous decades, to arbitrate (public) silence—that is, to effectively push Tibetans' explicit metalinguistic commentary about "history" to carefully guarded private spaces—even as locals appropriated the very terms of that metalanguage from the (Maoist) state. Indeed, unlike Han Chinese individuals and groups who in the 1980s and 1990s participated in a range of public memorializing activities,[6] it was particularly dangerous for Tibetans, as members of a problematic "minority minzu" group, to publicly remember the Maoist years. From the perspective of the Chinese state, their participation in the nation's history has always already been in doubt.

From this angle, we will be better positioned to appreciate the vital reconfiguration of private or household spaces in post-Mao Labrang, as well as the heightened importance and dangers for Tibetans of the subtle practices of implication, or *implicit* metacommunication, in a variety of ritual and everyday contexts—processes that I argue were significantly gendered. Here I address these issues by considering the Tibetans' stories I heard not as reified individual memories of a repressed "history" in Labrang, but as interactions in which we all participated in the ongoing construction of both an alternative historiography of socialist transformation *and* a tension-fraught contemporary scene there. I draw on the work of linguistic anthropologists and literary theorists who treat narrative as a fundamental speech genre in which people work together to order relationships between selves and others in space and time by placing them in the unfolding plot of a story (Bakhtin 1981, Ricoeur 1981, White 1981, Volosinov 1986, Hanks 1989, Tedlock 1995, Ochs and Capps 1996).[7] Narratives are participation frameworks that offer particularly powerful metalinguistic possibilities for speakers to imply stances or "footings" vis-à-vis topics and other people in time and space, as well as vis-à-vis their own current and past selves (cf. Goffman 1981: 147).

By taking narratives to be dialogic speech events framed in particular discourse genres and sociohistorical contexts, we also have tools for analyzing their dynamic and embodied *co-construction:* "narratives situate narrators, protagonists, and listener/readers at the nexus of morally organized, past, present, and possible experiences" (Ochs and Capps 1996: 22; cf. Schwarcz 1996). In this way, we can understand "history" as another important aspect of a dynamic cultural politics of recognition in Labrang—that is, as ongoing negotiations of notions of human agencies contextualized within competing cultural logics of time and space (cf. Bakhtin 1981: 84; Keane 1997)—and we can begin to grasp historians' own constitutive role in any "historicization process" (Daniel 1996: 58) shaping local situations.

My own status in Labrang, including my femaleness, could not but be implicated in this process. In fact, I argue that in Tibetans' stories about the past, gender was both a crucial frame for contemporary subject positions and an *unavoidable index* of past traumatic ruptures in experiences of Tibetan personhood. As we have begun to see, with the violent clash between competing frameworks for masculine authorities after CCP intervention in Labrang, gender difference was objectified, or brought to metalinguistic awareness, in unprecedented ways. This chapter's analysis will allow us to better understand how gendered footings in interactions, especially those of "woman/female" (Tib. *byis mo* or *a yas*), could also index for Tibetans painful memories of state-imposed loyalties to newly self-conscious forms of metalanguage as indexes of minzu citizenship that deeply divided the community in new ways.

Here, then, for the first time we turn to considering in more detail the contested role of Tibetan *femininities* in the emasculating process of national incorporation in Labrang. I argue that Tibetans' alternative historiography in the 1990s was most importantly a dialogue with Maoist "socialist androgyny," a new participation framework especially marked for locals by the emergence of Tibetan (as "Zangzu") women state cadres. In this light, Ama Drolma's refusal to be interviewed did not index her womanly sense of incompetence to narrate a fixed but hidden "history." Instead, she was positioning herself in a variety of ways vis-à-vis recent collective experiences of radically transformed gender relations. For one, she took a very similar stance as did men who refused my initial overtures. That is, like them, she was also denying some of the crucial historiographic assumptions embedded in the terms of the discourse my assistant and I used and in the interview genre of inter-action that I had proposed. And those assumptions were inextricably linked to the ascendance of the CCP over the patrifilial and mandalic participation frameworks in Labrang that had been intact when she was born there.

Even though in other long conversations Ama Drolma had readily talked with me about being born and raised in a Labrang dewa, about her family and dewa affairs, here she refused the requirements of being the subject of *testimony*. As Charles Briggs has argued, the ubiquitous and unexamined nature of interview practices in contemporary societies both contributes to and masks the crucial role of this discourse genre in recruiting people to produce objective, and there-fore authoritative, knowledge. In his view, interviewers attempt to control the type of narrative elicited from interviewees by asking for metalinguistic state-ments in which selves must explicitly stand apart from experience and report, describe, and evaluate (Briggs 1986: 2). Further, in the case of eliciting histori-cal knowledge, interviews most often ask for first-person narratives providing valued "real history" (White 1981: 5)—that is, a subject's experiences only as they pertain to historical events in a particular chronology of calendrical time (cf. Gyatso 1998: 109).

Acting as a foreign social science researcher seeking an "objective" story of the recent past in Labrang, I had not fully realized the particular historicizing power of the interview (nor my status as a female imposing it) in that milieu. In the con-text of the overwhelming might of the Chinese Communist state since 1949 in those regions, and the state's foundational narrative of a traumatic, revolutionary rupture between past and present, interviews have been associated for Tibetans with both the obligation and the felt need to provide testimony about their own relationships to pasts and presents. Testimony could thus be seen to be a now transnational type of first-person narrative that takes on powerful legal and moral weight in the context of a perceived crisis of truth related to past, often traumatic events and the legal agencies of nation-states; it requires narrators to self-present as national subjects (cf. Felman and Laub 1992: 6; McLagan 2003).

It is perhaps not surprising then that in decades of international contests over the national status of Tibet, Chinese state agents and dissidents abroad have all presented memories elicited from Tibetans, most often in the form of first-person narratives, as authentic historical evidence in opposition to what are considered to be the politically motivated silences of opponents' histories of the Maoist years in

Tibetan regions.[8] Yet in all such narratives, speakers are required to take a particularly marked stance toward their stories—they must (implicitly or explicitly) evaluate the past events and agencies they describe, and they must promise to authorities that their speech is material evidence for the truth (Felman and Laub 1992: 5). Ama Drolma's expectation that this was the type of speech genre in which she was being asked to participate perhaps explains why she immediately assumed, when I tried to explain that I was interested in what had changed in Labrang, that I wanted her opinion on which was better, life "before" or life "nowadays" (Tib. *sngan na gi tsho ba sra gi deng sang gi tsho ba sra gi*). In effect, narrators of testimony must present as self-conscious individual selves, and then publicly attest to the "autobiographical pact": that the narrating self (or selves) and narrated self(or selves) are one and the same (Crapanzano 1996: 109; Gyatso 1998: 107), all the while anticipating potentially serious consequences for their speech acts.

Collecting testimonies from Tibetans about Chinese state repression has been a role widely assumed among Westerners, and the appeal of such a stance was, perhaps, not lost on me. In the transnational participation framework of the genre, one can style oneself a seeker of the truth, and assume that this will produce an alliance with Tibetans. But the danger is that any provisional cooperation achieved within the genre can obscure crucial differences in participants' assumed frameworks, and turn foreigners' attention from the importance for locals of *other* (multimedia) forms of metacommunication about the past (Briggs 1986: 2; Hall 1998: 440; cf. Germano 1998). Ama Drolma's refusal (and those of many others) made it clear to me that Tibetans in the PRC do not necessarily share Westerners' faith in the moralizing historiography of testimonials (cf. White 1981: 11). Meanwhile, as we will see, her advocacy for the narrative authority of Tibetan patriarchs over her own, when faced with such a politically weighty form of explicit metalanguage, reasserted the implicit naturalness of a local sex-gender hierarchy that many felt had been radically upended in some of the worst of Maoist state violence.

SPEAKING BITTERNESS: THE GENDERED
VIOLENCE OF STATIST REMEMBERING

The national incorporation of Labrang under the auspices of Maoist historical materialism centered on state-sponsored narrative practices that asserted the superiority of certain genres of explicit metalanguage as indexes of a "modern" and rational minzu self-awareness, awake to the possibility for a radical, *class*-based equality. Meanwhile, Tibetan genres of metacommunication were reduced to evidence of locals' extremely benighted state under Buddhist monastic rule. Hence, during successive social reform and antirebellion campaigns beginning in 1958, Chinese and Tibetan cadres cast state violence directed at Tibetans in the valley as a moral battle for their self-consciousness as participants in the nation's linear historical trajectory—now under the proper, scientifically informed guidance of the Communist Party (cf. Dreyer 1976, W. Chang 1989, Watson 1994a, Duara 1995, J. Chang 1997, Cheek 1997).[9] As I noted in chapter 1, in CCP practice a notion of patient "thought work" was crucial in creating for cadres a sense of the *voluntary* and natural participation of the people (Ch. *renmin*) in the revolution (cf. F. Yu 1964, Whyte 1979, Unger 1993, W. Smith 1996). In Tibetan areas, this process of "socialist education" (Ch. *shehui zhuyi jiaoyu*), grounded in the narrative plot of socialist advance, centered from the beginning on the quotidian obligation for locals to "speak [or to remember] bitterness" (Ch. *suku*, Tib. *sdug ngal bshad pa* or *dran pa*).

In interviews with state agents, and later at compulsory group meetings, Tibetans were required to produce and listen to testimonials of their participation in the Communist-led revolution—that is, life stories attesting to their consciousness of past class-based oppression in the "Old Society" (Ch. *jiu shehui*, Tib. *'jig rten rnying pa*) and their present "liberation" (Ch. *jiefang*) in the "New Society" (Ch. *xin shehui*, Tib. *'jig rten gsar pa*). By the time they were implemented widely in the Labrang region, these discourse practices were rote components of Maoist mass movements; they were in many ways the narrative core of revolutionary praxis throughout the Maoist years (cf. Anagnost 1994, Kansteiner 2002).[10] Conventions for their performance hinged on the narrators' presentation of their brutally victimized bodies under past exploitation, thus supposedly eliciting audiences' empathetic tears and angry solidarity. As Ann Anagnost and others have recently argued, this was the method par excellence for Han work teams to constitute rural villagers as minzu citizens and as eager members of "the masses" (Ch. *qunzhong*, Tib. *mi dmangs*), the new collective political subject nonetheless dependent on the guidance of state cadres on the road to socialism (Anagnost 1989, 1994, 1997; Jacka and Petkovic 1998; Rofel 1999; Hershatter 2001).

But I argue that if we consider the fundamentally gendered nature of this new participation framework as it was implemented in Labrang, we can more clearly discern some of the particular parameters and consequences of socialist transformation for Tibetans, the complex legacies of which continued to play out in the 1990s:

FROM FIELD NOTES: On a fall day in 1995, I had been on the hillside opposite the monastery taking pictures with Ama Tshelo, an older Tibetan village woman and acquaintance of mine from the circumambulation path, who had decked herself out in a newly purchased Tibetan felt robe for the occasion. Ama Lhamo, another friend of mine, had accompanied us at the last minute, even though she told me she did not know the other woman. She was the gravel-voiced, chain-smoking, and vivacious retired Party cadre in a leather fedora and an old Mao jacket Cain and I had spent some time with. She was living alone in a guesthouse run by the estate of the beloved trulku Gongtang in order to complete daily circumambulations at the monastery. After she left us, I walked down with Ama Tshelo and asked her if she knew Ama Lhamo. She looked at me sideways and, in a conspiratorial tone tinged with disapproval, said she did, and that people gossiped about her because they said she was like a "man and woman combined" (Tib. *rgan po ayas gnyis ka*).

The troublesome recognition of Ama Lhamo's androgynous gender status in Labrang as visibly and morally Other (even though as far as I could tell most of her many friends and acquaintances had assigned her to femaleness) seems to me to index the particularly marked nature of shifting femininities in the enduring trauma of socialist transformation for Tibetans there.[11] Indeed, I would argue that, as they were implemented in the Labrang region, speaking-bitterness narratives were the key participation frameworks utilized by CCP cadres to finally directly attack Geluk patrifilial mandalization. This was true not only because the narratives professed to lay bare feudal class relations masked by "religion," but most saliently because they mandated the public performance of a *newly abstract* notion of gender (as a social construction of class relations). This statist gender supposedly offered the metalinguistic consciousness of a truly "modern" PRC subject, a subject who was liberated from the obligations of local kin-based ties and thus empowered to publicly accuse Tibetan superiors of exploitation on behalf of the state.

Most importantly, as against the unremarked categorical abjectness of the female among Tibetans—which, as I argued, had underpinned the restricted spaces and times of masculine authorities in Geluk mandalization efforts—speaking-bitterness practices from 1958 on featured "liberated" Zangzu women "serfs" as emblematic revolutionary agents. Such women "activists" were refigured as *funu*, or modern women in service not to households but to the state (cf. Barlow 1994), and they all eventually sported the mandatory gender-neutral pants and jacket of the ideal socialist subject, (seemingly) participating on equal footing with men (cf.

Zong 1956, Long Rangxiong 1959, Strong 1959, Dhondup Choedon 1978, Ama Adhe 1997). In effect then, these narrative practices positioned Tibetan femininities as particularly marked pivots in the transformation of Amdo fatherlands into subordinate districts of the Chinese Fatherland (cf. Barlow 1994: 269). For Tibetans in Labrang, speaking-bitterness practices were the paradigmatic points at which the traumatic consequences of the "feminine hinge" between "tradition" and "modernity" under CCP rule were first laid out.

As theorists analyzing a wide range of contexts have recently pointed out, because of the overwhelmingly masculinist cultural politics of nationalist struggles, women and feminine embodiment very often come to be disproportionately metonymic as representations of the state of the nation vis-à-vis perceived opponents or the elusive goal of modernity (cf. Enloe 1989, Parker et al. 1992, Yuval-Davis 1997). In China, early CCP leaders drew on the strong link between notions of women's liberation and signs of modernity that had been forged in the nationalist discourses of the early twentieth century. Thus they advocated the liberation of funu from feudal gender hierarchies and their broadened participation in both politics and productive labor as integral parts of the revolution. But CCP leaders and cadres all along were also heirs to the long legacy of profound ambivalence among nationalist elites as to the properly metonymic nature of femininity on the linear road to national modernity—as the sign of a progressive vanguard or of a passive repository of timeless national or ethnic virtue (Duara 1998).

Thus, as many analysts have noted, women could be foregrounded as revolutionary minzu subjects in Maoist mass media such as speaking-bitterness narratives or propaganda posters in order to most strikingly index a national distance from the past, yet in practice they continued to be subordinated in male-dominated state and local contexts (Stacey 1983; Wolf 1985; Diamond 1988; Anagnost 1989; Evans 1998, 1999; Chen Xiaomei 1999; M. Yang 1999). Liberated funu, indexed so strikingly during the Cultural Revolution by the masculinizing socialist androgyny of their Mao uniforms and short hair, were not in actuality signs of radically altered gender hierarchy. Instead, they most importantly embodied a new iconicity of *class* subjectivity that was supposed to usurp local, ethnic, and kin ties and obligations and index the paternal authority of the Maoist state: "In Maoist state discourse," writes Mayfair Yang, ". . . we find a . . . narrative of a family-state of degendered revolutionary subjects led by a wise father" (1999: 45; cf. Chen Xiaomei 1999: 107).

As Han cadres and work teams brought the revolution to the frontier, they brought with them the emerging infrastructure for training and employing the vast majority of women cadres—the All-China Women's Federation (Zhongguo

Funu Lianhe Hui *or* Fulian). This CCP organization and its grassroots bureaus, to the present, have been the main avenues through which Han urban women advocated both socialist education for rural women (including minorities) and domestic reform for urban and rural households (cf. Croll 2001, Hsiung et al. 2001). In Labrang, the first Xiahe county women's association, with Apa Alo's wife Tshering Lhamo as chair, had been established before the CCP victory in 1944 (GZZ 1999: 1155). It is not surprising then that Labrang was one of the first places in the region to establish a branch of the Fulian after 1949, with a Han woman CCP operative as chair and Tshering Lhamo as deputy chair (XDZ 1991: 16).[12]

In the transition years of the early 1950s, young Tibetan women, participating in "women's training classes" (Ch. *fuxunban*), were among the few Tibetan elites and commoners who were recruited for cadre training and political education at new institutes for minority minzu cadres in Lanzhou.[13] In most cases, that was the first time Tibetan women had encountered institutionalized education. Ama Drolkar, a fifty-eight-year-old native of a Labrang dewa, proudly showed me her photograph at the age of seventeen, dressed in Labrang robes and rubbing shoulders with the aristocratic young daughter of Apa Alo himself, in their 1955 graduation portrait at the Lanzhou school. She drily added that they had studied very little "culture and literature" (Tib. *rig gnas*), focusing only on "politics" (Tib. *chab srid*), and she had never learned to read. She never got to do anything with her education, she said, because her mother insisted that since her younger brother was a monk, she was needed at home and could not become a cadre. By contrast, my retired cadre friend Ama Lhamo proudly told me she was from a poor nomad family southwest of Labrang when she divorced and became a Party member and translation cadre in 1953, and she *had* learned to read both Chinese and Tibetan during her cadre training in Lanzhou and Beijing. Of six Tibetans who returned to Labrang to study Tibetan in 1958, she had been the only woman. Tibetan women were thus important objects for recruitment to revolutionary activity, yet early Fulian efforts in the region were more successful in Han-dominated counties.

Indeed, after the Gannan prefecture Fulian was established in 1953, that bureau coordinated intensifying efforts to recruit women as key *grassroots* support for state land and domestic reform projects. Thus in the next two years, when the eastern counties of Zhuoni, Lintan, and Zhouqu (the ones with the highest concentrations of Han residents) first underwent land reform and established Han agricultural "mutual aid groups" (Ch. *huzhu zu*), over seven hundred women became mutual aid group leaders. Meanwhile, only a handful took on leadership posts at higher levels (GGK 1987, GZZ 1999). This was also the very time during which Fulian cadres were in charge of the (short-lived) Marriage Law education campaign, in which women especially were told, following Mao's famous dictum, that they should be free of the fourfold oppression of the (feudal) state, the clan, husbands, and the divine in order to better serve the "new democracy" (Chang Chih-jang 1959). Speaking-bitterness narratives were the framework par excellence for women to publicly demonstrate that new awareness (cf. Anagnost 1994, Rofel 1999, Hershatter 2001). Thus, at least in Han regions, there was perhaps some truth to the GZZ editors' exuberant claim that at this time in Gannan prefecture "there surged forth a group of women activists" (Ch. *funu jijifenzi*; GZZ 1999: 1155).

In Tibetan regions, the Maoist social constructionism of cadres and intellectuals asserted the irrelevance for women of Tibetan notions of kin-based sex difference. At the same time, cadres relied on "scientific" discourses about biological sex and sexuality both to retain male privilege in service to the state and to categorize Zangzu women, along with children, as inherently associated with the hard work of households and most in need of state protection (cf. C. Yang 1959, Dikotter 1995, Evans 1997). State "women's work" (Ch. *funu gongzuo*) in Tibetan regions in the early 1950s thus largely consisted of Fulian-trained Han women cadres attempting to bring a "new life" to rural Tibetan women. They did this by demonstrating the modern socialist possibilities of feminine hygiene, freely chosen marriage, education, and (limited) social mobility, and urging poor women especially, like Ama Lhamo, to "stand up" and publicly liberate themselves by deprioritizing obligations to households and affines and taking on supporting roles to government and Party leaderships. Thus, as far as I know, while some Tibetan women in most Labrang village dewa became government cadres and a handful became Party members, none took on upper-level leadership roles outside Fulian auspices.

As many have noted, Maoist "women's liberation" throughout the PRC was always precariously situated with regard to central authorities' efforts to ally with and domesticate local men in the new participation frameworks of state bureaucracies. However, most rural Tibetans in Labrang experienced Maoist women's liberation quite differently than did neighboring Han communities, or even the few local Tibetans receiving cadre training in the early 1950s. For rural Tibetans, "women's liberation" was conspicuously embodied only later, in the extreme terms with which they first widely experienced speaking-bitterness testimony—that is, in public "struggle meetings" (Ch. *pidou hui*, Tib. *'thab 'dzing*) during the "Antifeudalism" and "Democratic Reform" campaigns in the spring and summer of 1958. As Tibetan men's guerrilla resistance to collectivization efforts along the Sino-Tibetan frontier spread from the mid-1950s on, cadres' patience with United Front policies calling for the gradual reconfiguration of monastic rule and uplift of minority minzu wore out. At the beginning of 1958, then, the few newly "trained" Zangzu men and women cadres were called upon to support PLA troops and to help justify the arrests of local Tibetan lay leaders, monks, and lamas (cf. Dreyer 1976: 159; GGK 1987: 114). Importantly, the great pageantry of the regional struggle meetings that summer worked to *counter* the centripetal force of such monastic mandalizing pageants as the annual Cham Chen, by massing Tibetan laity in the secularized space of the Sangkok grasslands under state auspices (cf. Strong 1959).

Those meetings were held to denounce Tibetan leaders and (finally) initiate "Democratic Reforms" after the last of Tibetan laymen's and monks' hastily mustered guerrilla brigades had been brutally rooted out of the surrounding mountains by PLA troops (cf. Strong 1959: 96; Tenzin Palbar 1994).[14] The meetings thus served as the performative pivot between Tibetan men's defiant mobility and violent resistance on the one hand and the radical displacement of the participation frameworks that grounded their regional authority on the other—the moment when Maoist metalanguage of class-gender liberation finally took on brutal illocutionary force. In this context, we can better appreciate the performative impact for locals of the first public speaking-bitterness narratives delivered by the few Tibetan women identified as poor serfs, and especially by women activists who were dressed in the military-style uniforms issued them by Han superiors (cf. Ama Adhe 1997: 69). When those women took center stage to scream their bitterness at trulkus especially, their testimonies, more than those of Tibetan men, would have indexed sex and gender (for Han and Tibetan listeners alike) as framing categories for a new metapragmatics of radically competing ethnic and class loyalties. Indeed, Tibetans' accounts of this process throughout the frontier zone suggest that in urging (Han and Tibetan) women especially to publicly humiliate lamas, cadres utilized the sex and gender status of women activists to displace the indexical grounds of Tibetan divine masculine authority for that of rational and ordinary biological sex difference instead (Jurists 1960: 26, 222; Dhondup Choedon 1978: 57; Ama Adhe 1997: 69).

Thus in speaking-bitterness narratives, the figure of the Zangzu woman revolutionary agent was particularly suited for the ritualized exposure of monks' and lamas' illegitimate claims to Tibetans' patrifiliation, and for demonstrating the legitimate ascendance of state-empowered Zangzu cadres in their stead—she embodied the culmination of national incorporation as emasculation.[15]

FIGURE 9.
Detail, life-size clay sculpture exhibit "Wrath of the Serfs,"
picting a Tibetan serf woman about to be executed for leading
a serf uprising against estate holders. (Exhibition catalogue,
Lhasa Museum of Revolution, 1976)

By the fall of 1958 in Labrang, the monastery was looted and closed, most Tibetan guerrillas had been captured or killed, and almost two-thirds of the thirty-five hundred resident monks were imprisoned or in labor camps (W. Smith 1996: 482; cf. Tenzin Palbar 1994). The rest of the monks were returned to lay life; worship was forbidden, and rural regions were reorganized into communes (Jurists 1960: 35; W. Smith 1996: 442). Further, the ten-year-old sixth Jamyang Shepa was separated from his tutor and detained. For the first time in the history of Labrang's ruling lineage of trulkus, the sixth incarnation never studied in the great monasteries of Lhasa. With such a blow to the very foundations of local Tibetans' lifeworlds, perhaps the characterization of 1958 by the authors of the first post-Mao official history of the monastery was closer to the perspective of locals than they would have acknowledged: "From this time forth," they assert, "Labrang monastery entered a new historical era" (Luo 1987: 176).

OPPOSITIONAL PRACTICES OF TIME

Of course, traumatic rupture notwithstanding, socialist transformation in Labrang was not a case of an unself-conscious people finally acquiring a metalanguage of history and personhood and thus entering (voluntarily or not) the "modern" world (*pace*, e.g., Nora 1989; cf. Kansteiner 2002: 183). Tibetologists have noted the centuries-old avid interest of Tibetan scholars in a wide variety of historio-graphic genres, a preoccupation that distinguishes them from their models in Indian Buddhist literary traditions (Van der Kuijp 1996: 40; cf. Gyatso 1996, Robinson 1996).[16] Further, as Janet Gyatso argues, Tibetans across regions have long been particularly fascinated with forms of individual life-writing and life-storytelling, including biography (Tib. *rnam thar*) and autobiography (Tib. *rang rnam*), or accounts of exemplary individuals presenting a retrospective process of the development of an enlightened self (Gyatso 1998: 109).

In fact, Tibetans' reverence for life stories, especially since the rise of Geluk hegemony, exemplifies a fundamental orientation of selves and agencies to time and space that was operative among Tibetans in Labrang, and that, I argue, crucially structured their alternative "mnemonic communities" (Kansteiner 2002: 189) under Chinese rule. Tibetan accounts described the lives of individuals presented almost exclusively as acting according to Mahāyāna Buddhist principles of altruism, and, as fully enlightened persons, their lives were meant to be models for others (Gyatso 1998: 103). The pervasiveness of these stories (written, oral, or dramatized) in a variety of ritual and everyday contexts past and present is, as Gyatso argues, "striking evidence of the popularity of the charismatic individual in Tibetan society" (ibid. 102).

As we saw in the introduction, in Labrang the most exemplary of individuals were men recognized as incarnate lamas or trulkus. As such, the metalinguistic effect of locals' avid storytelling about trulkus' lives was the ongoing embodiment both of trulkus as quintessential Tibetan historical agents *and* of reverent narrators and listeners as their faithful subjects. Framed by trulkus' status as enlightened beings, their life stories *in the telling* were another crucial means by which subjects indexically linked particular trulkus to local and transcendent spaces and times. Importantly, as I argued earlier, this altruistic positioning between relative and absolute time and space is what lent incarnate lamas awesome and ultimately *unintentioned* or intrinsic power over the mundane world of karmic causation (Tib. *'jig rten*), and hence it was the basis of their charisma for locals and of their authority to guide and to teach (cf. Keane 1997: 11). Storytelling about trulku lives in a variety of contexts thus positioned Tibetan selves as grounded in *dapa*, or "faith"— that is as situated within the patrifilial mandalic sphere of trulkus' benevolent and powerful protection (see chapter 3). Ama Luji, a Labrang dewa native in her mid-sixties who told me she grew up eagerly listening to stories about the miraculous powers of Jamyang Shepa and Gongtang, perhaps put it the most succinctly: "If [those stories] weren't told," she said, "people wouldn't have faith" (Tib. *bshad rgyu med na dad pa skyes rgyu ma red*).

As we saw in chapter 1, the last of Labrang's ruling trulkus who reached adulthood before CCP intervention was the fifth Jamyang Shepa (see fig. 5). The main Tibetan biography for him, written by the lama-scholar Shabdrong Tshang (1896–1960) in the early 1950s,[17] is framed in Dharma time by the use of prophecies (Tib. *lung bstan*) about the lama's life and lineage, those of others as well as his own. It is punctuated throughout by accounts of temporal and spatial miracles—appearances of rainbows and omens at his birth, the imprint of his foot on a rock, and, as Jamyang Shepa's dream indicated, his visions of Labrang's future. Notably, Shabdrong frames his narrative as a story not of an individual self limited to biographical time, but as a story of *the lineage*—that is, of the enduring self of the enlightened lama across lifetimes. He does not frame the fifth Jamyang Shepa's death of smallpox in 1947 as untimely, but, as does Apa Alo in his later memoir, he presents the trulku choosing to leave and predicting his reincarnation, and he ends the biography with an account of the enthronement in 1952 of the sixth Jamyang Shepa (cf. Huang 1989; and see below, fig. 11). In the process, he *never mentions* the Chinese Communist victory and occupation of Labrang three years earlier in 1949.

Shabdrong's erasure of such a pivotal event for Chinese state historiography in his life story of Labrang's sorely missed central lama exemplifies the "oppositional practice of time" (Mueggler 2001: 7) embedded in Geluk mandalization efforts.[18] Crucially, such life stories were not presented as "myth." Instead, they often lent the narrative force of an eyewitness to strong claims to historical truth; their practical efficacy for local Tibetan readers or listeners depended on this historicity (Gyatso 1998: 9).[19] In practice, then, for most Tibetan men and women in Labrang, trulkus were what Bakhtin (1981: 251) would call essential "chronotopes" in the ongoing narrativization of people's own lives: that is they functioned as organizing and orienting representational centers for fundamental events in space and time. They embodied, and thus rendered alive and substantial, representations that locals, during the Maoist years especially, were increasingly compelled to identify as exclusively and quintessentially Tibetan (or Zangzu).

In mid-1990s Labrang, these interpretive politics and the violence that constituted them just a few decades earlier heavily structured both the said and the unsaid—in everyday interactions, as well as in dealings with foreign researchers like myself. Under reforms, the official media of memory in Tibetan regions still insisted, under pain of arrest and interrogation, on the basic historiographic parameters laid out in Maoist speaking-bitterness narratives. Official history was presented in Tibetan regions in such multimedia forums as National Day celebrations, various anniversary ceremonies, and television shows commemorating the glory of the early CCP and its modern state-building efforts (cf. Schwarcz 1992, Rofel 1999). Official written histories of the Labrang region and Gannan Tibetan Autonomous Prefecture have been rife since the late 1980s. These accounts, usually in the context of encyclopedic "local gazetteers" (Ch. *difang zhi* or *gaikuang*) compiled by multiethnic committees, emphatically make the PRC the subject of a national history (cf. Duara 1995), posing 1949 as the pivotal point at which both men and women were liberated, and erasing almost anything about the suffering of ordinary Tibetans in the 1950s and 1960s especially. Further, speaking-bitterness narratives were post-Mao state officials' response of choice in the face of Tibetans' oppositional practices in public spaces through the 1990s—even when much of the country had moved to repudiate such an orientation in the rush to benefit from the post-Mao market economy (cf. Rofel 1999: 97).

Older men and women I spoke to thus could not avail themselves, in public or as a community, of the therapeutic possibilities of narrative to assert interpretive agency over traumatic past experiences that were inassimilable to the glory of Maoist class-gender "liberation" in 1949 (cf. Laub 1992; Daniel 1996; Ochs and

Capps 1996: 29). As a middle-aged lay trulku scholar and his young lay male student put it to me, ironic smiles revealing their displeasure and resignation: "You
won't find that history anywhere—we have no way to write it" (Ch. *women wufa
xie zhexie*). The Otherness of my feminine presence was also an important frame in
this regard. Many of these conversations included Tibetans' efforts to make sense
of me as an educated, world-traveling woman without children. Many seemed to
read my hyperliberated status as particularly iconic of the unattainable utopia of
American "democracy," and thus my presence widely elicited from Tibetans a
sense of contrastive lack in the face of the realities of "Democratic Reforms" in the
Labrang region—a deeply painful sense of personal disjuncture between emotional memories stored in the mind (Tib. *sems gi nang*) or in the "heart" (Tib. *khog
pa nang*) and the ability to metalinguistically express or narrate them. As Apa
Gyalo, a seventy-five-year-old retired trader, put it, referring to his unspoken traumatic experiences of the Maoist years in Labrang: "We old folks know these things
in our minds [pointing to his head] and in our hearts [pointing to his chest]."

In effect, the violent shift to Maoist metalanguage wielded by women as well as
by men had radically reframed the pleasurable agency Tibetans found through
participation in hierarchically arranged gendered speech genres in general and in
narrative genres in particular, an essential human capacity many contrasted with
the inferiority of mute animals (cf. Lichter and Epstein 1983; Gal 1991: 182).
Tibetans in the Labrang region, where important exchanges in that mandalic
regime of value were often orally transacted, had always recognized the great
power of speech to change or to influence social realities (cf. Ekvall 1952: 30;
Stubel 1958). Indeed in the Buddhist idiom that had become pervasive among
Tibetans, speech, often represented metonymically as "mouth" (Tib. *kha*), was
considered to be an essential component of personhood, one element in the com-
bination of body, speech, and mind that constitutes an individual (cf. Ekvall 1979,
Desjarlais 1992). In such a "speech-conscious culture" (Ekvall 1964a: 1141), great
prestige was attached to authoritative speech genres dominated by monastic and
lay male leaders. The clarity and topical scope of such men's speech was then seen
to be a direct reflection of the advanced state of their minds or intellects. In fact,
in conversations with me about someone's motivations or personality, Tibetans
widely linked speech and mind or "heart" as pairs in compounds like *kha sems*
(mouth-mind) or *kha khog* (mouth-"heart")—grounding the recognition of gendered persons in the causative and semiotic link between (outer) speech and
(inner) thoughts and emotions. In post-Mao Labrang, the unspeakable was thus
fraught with emotional and existential as well as political danger.

In this light, the full import and gendered nature of Ama Drolma's temporal opposition to my request for an "oral history" interview in 1995 becomes clearer. She insisted that she was too young to "know history," yet she was born in the early 1940s, several years before the PLA marched in and "liberated" Labrang. She lived her adult life under Chinese rule and came of age at precisely the time when Tibetan women were increasingly exhorted to liberate themselves as Zangzu funu and to downplay obligations of married women to their households and affines in support of the state. She herself had participated in women's "productive labor" by working, along with her mostly women peers on the shop floor, in a state-run local factory. Thus in the interview, against our use of the Tibetan term for "history" (Tib. *lo rgyus*, which recalled its recent redefinition as a gloss for the statist category of the Chinese *lishi*), Ama Drolma implicitly insisted on referring history to a time, emphasized in her repetition of the time word "early, early, early" (Tib. *sngan na sngan na snganna*), well *before* Chinese Communist intervention in Labrang, when the region was governed through patrifilial alliances between Tibetan lamas and lay male leaders. That was the mandalic regime centered on the monastery that she and others often referred to metonymically as *lama hwonpo* (Tib. *bla ma dpon po*, lit. "lamas and lay male leaders"). In this way, she erased the Maoist years as narratable "history," and, even though several of the men she listed as potential narrators were the same age as herself, she avoided the danger of testifying to her personal experiences therein by referring narrative agency to household patriarchs, those previously charged with transmitting local and household lore.

Indeed, when I finally abandoned such early efforts to interview people and began to participate in conversations on Tibetans' terms, I was able to appreciate not an objective flow of events to which Tibetans were mere witnesses, but the particularly gendered ways in which differently positioned locals actively imagined, and thereby helped to constitute, the structuring power of the state in their lives past and present, even as some explicitly resisted it (cf. Mueggler 2001: 4). Importantly, the main elements of these processes were pervasive among Tibetans, regardless of their gender status or positioning vis-à-vis the new regime in the transition years. As I myself began to partake of the categories structuring the life stories Tibetans offered, I shared in an ongoing process by which both Tibetan men and Tibetan women appropriated the narrative forms and historiographic premises of the CCP's speaking-bitterness genre to participate in an alternative metalanguage about the past. That is, they constructed arrangements of gendered selves, agencies, and moralities in space and time different from those presumed in ideal minzu citizenship, often doing this even if their accounts were not posed in conscious opposition to official histories.

Thus in striking contrast to older Han urban women interviewed by Lisa Rofel (1994) for example, most Labrang Tibetan women like Ama Drolma, in their accounts of the Maoist years, implicitly and explicitly *erased* state discourse of women's liberation in favor of presenting themselves, along with men, as invested in Tibetan patrifiliality. In so doing, and in conjunction with their disproportionate return to wearing local Tibetan robes under reforms,[20] older women participated importantly in repudiating socialist gender-neutrality as an icon of "the people's" (vs. the state's) initiative in achieving modern class and minzu equality. Instead, as we will see, Tibetan men's and women's conscious and unconscious collaboration in alternative historiography reframed the public performativity of socialist androgyny beginning in 1958 as essentially a participation framework for *ethnic assimilation* under Han-dominated state expropriation.

Ama Drolma and other elders who refused in similar ways to be interviewed about recent history no doubt had a range of personal motives for doing so. But I argue that older Tibetans' moves to deny to me the narratability of almost three decades of their own lives both foregrounded ethnicity as the most salient rupture in Tibetan personhood, and highlighted abstract gender as relevant largely to the imposed shape of CCP rule in Labrang. That is, Tibetan men's and women's denials of recent history as *lo rgyus* implied a widespread perception of the consequences for them of the temporal contradiction inherent to (minority) minzu citizenship: the fundamental displacement of the legitimate ethnic subject of historiography, a sense that Tibetan history, or the agency of Tibetan selves in historical time, ended with their recognition as Zangzu and the incorporation of Labrang into the PRC Fatherland. Indeed, the accounts of their pasts I eventually heard from elder men and women across the community in a variety of ways overwhelmingly narrated the Maoist years as a story of the (gendered) Chinese state.[21]

FATHER STATE AND
THE MAOIST QUANDARY OF AGENCY

Marxist historiography in Maoist practice required people to express themselves as radically social. They were to see themselves as constituted not by relationships to divine masculine authorities, nor by CCP state discipline, but exclusively by local historical forces immanent to socioeconomic structure (Dirlik 1978: 9; Unger 1993: 2; Watson 1994a). Their representations of self-process were thus expected to strictly imitate observable, "material" changes in local social relations (i.e., class conflict) that inevitably moved forward toward socialism.

It was arguably through mandatory participation in speaking-bitterness narratives for both men and women that Tibetans were expected to become newly self-conscious in a radically embodied and unprecedentedly public way. Gender-neutral participation in that mandated metalanguage was supposed to recontextualize public space as the modern democratic space of the liberated people, operating all the while under the *unmarked* or absent, yet all-pervasive authority of CCP central state leaders: "One after another, these [speaking-bitterness] accusations in blood and tears coalesced into a billowing rage that buried the decadent feudal system and washed away the muddy, turbid water of the grasslands" (GGK 1987: 114). Thus, as against how some older Tibetans later remembered them, the new androgynous terms of speaking-bitterness participation were most importantly supposed to index the ideally disembodied or abstract nature of translocal state authority.

But the stark polarities of subjects and agencies generated by the use of such stories and resistance to them could obscure for locals and observers alike the painfully subtle mutual constitution of state and local subjectivities that actually shaped socialist transformation in Labrang, as well as Tibetans' memories of it decades later. For one thing, by the 1990s Tibetan men and women across generations widely assumed the (limited) validity of a social-scientific time-space posited in Marxist historiography. The almost exclusive focus among Tibetans on life stories of enlightened trulkus and lamas had given ground to widespread acceptance of the idea that ordinary people's lives, including those of women, revealed important information about the nature of society, especially since local Tibetan "customs" (Tib. *bca' srol las srol*) had become fetishized as markers of ethnic pride.[22] In the Labrang region, there were many educated Tibetans (mostly laymen) proudly researching the "social history" (Ch. *shehui lishi*) of their minority minzu localities (cf. Stoddard 1993). Thus even illiterate village women were not surprised at my expressed interest in their lives. For another, I found that the subtle processes of language choice between Tibetan and Chinese in conversations could imply speakers' experiential distance from Chinese state authority, at the same time as their frequent use of Chinese loanwords and Communist concepts indexed the intimate pervasion of state ideologies.

Traces of the alternative histories embedded in unconscious language choice could be encountered throughout public spaces in post-Mao Labrang. But conscious oppositional historiography was relegated to "private" frameworks (Tib. *sger*), refigured, as we will see, in contradistinction to the state-mediated public spaces first imposed in the 1950s (cf. Watson 1994a). This largely meant conversations were kept within a network of trusted familiars in the informal gathering places of households and monks' quarters. The most intense (and dangerous) of my conversations in these spaces were those in which certain elders took the opportunity of an apparently well-meaning foreign listener to offer bitter stories of the suffering they experienced and witnessed during the Maoist years. The powerful expectations of, and almost compulsive need for, oppositional testimony hit home for me when both men and women would launch with great emotion, even tears, into such stories upon learning I spoke Tibetan, and with little introduction to me, sometimes before I had even expressed an interest in local history at all.[23] These were the stories that most directly opposed the premises of the state's speaking-bitterness genre. And in so doing, I argue, they most starkly recontextualized gender not as a framework for personal liberation but as an iconic index of central Chinese authorities' *unacknowledged pretensions to power*. In their oppositional stories, both men and women appropriated and upended the narrative elements of the genre by recasting the agents, spaces, and times so that they depicted the paternalist Chinese state, and not local Tibetan "class enemies," as the exploiter responsible for the historical breach leading to their unmerited suffering.

Our encounters, as I discovered, were not at all a matter of a simple "liberation" of a repressed, monolithic "Tibetan" voice. Instead, as narrators recruited me to participate in their narratives, knowing that I moved through the community talking with a variety of people, I found myself awkwardly caught up in a bitter class politics among Tibetans. This, I would argue, was the most profound of the hidden legacies of the Maoist years in Labrang, differentiating Tibetans in the 1990s in ways not accounted for in speaking-bitterness depictions of class struggle. As Ann Anagnost and others have pointed out, in the 1950s and 1960s those narratives in Han regions sought to constitute villagers as first and foremost class subjects; they were part and parcel of the class-labeling process that simultaneously marked locals' most important social status in the new regime and posited it as the locus of deepest inherent conflict (1994: 263; cf. Hershatter 2001). Indeed, one of the tasks of the Gannan minority minzu social history research group in the early 1950s was to investigate the capital holdings of Labrang's monastic elite in order to construe them as class exploiters. According to their statistics, the finance minister of the monastery controlled some 5 million yuan in capital, while 10 percent of monks held some 500,000 yuan each, and trulkus and elite monks had the vast majority of gold, silver, and luxury goods (XXZ 1997: 525). Yet for Tibetans in Labrang, "class struggle" was as alien a concept as it was for most Han villagers, expressed by an awkward neologism that directly follows the Chinese, *gral rim 'thab rtsol* for *jieji douzheng*, itself a neologism directly glossing the English "class struggle" (Tsering Shakya 1994: 160).

Mao of course radically reworked Marx's notion of class in his efforts to apply it to rural China (cf. Dirlik 1978, Anagnost 1994). When the rote forms of class struggle were angrily implemented in the Labrang region, this meant not delineating the owners of the means of production, but subsuming the intricacies of gendered ethnic difference under a schema of economic difference by associating all forms of lay and monastic wealth and prestige with the feudal exploitation of "serfs" (Tib. *mi ser*). In this framework, all types of high social status, such as that of lamas, or anti-state resistance, such as that of local Tibetan men who took to the hills in 1958, could be assimilated to an economic model of exploitation regardless of actual personal wealth, and locals found themselves interacting as members of "classes," from serf-owning landlords and their agents, to rich and middle-class traders, farmers, and nomads, to the small percentage identified as poor serfs, those whom, as we saw above, were among the first Tibetan men and women to "speak bitterness," voluntarily or not, against local Tibetan lamas and leaders identified as "class enemies" (cf. Dhondup Choedon 1978: 32).

The elders who risked the political dangers and chose to narrate to me dissenting testimonials of that time, twenty-five of a total sixty, were those who felt themselves to have been grievously victimized in this process, targeted either as class enemies or as farmers and nomads at the time when they found themselves at the bottom of a practical chain of command that left them powerless to resist change.[24] In the 1990s, most were eldest members of struggling village households, and, crucially, their narratives of the Maoist years for my benefit posited causal links between the traumatic events of that time and their perceptions of the gross inequities and social chaos impinging on them in the present.

Thus, in the very regular forms such narratives took, in the patterns discernible in both the said and the unsaid, I could glimpse the emotional toll such unresolved violence had taken on the entire Tibetan community. That is, the burden of the Maoist years in Labrang was fundamentally an ongoing quandary of agency, an inter- and intrasubjective contest over the nature of human agency and morality. I came to realize that the unspeakable among Tibetans was not just the product of state repression; it was also a marker of locals' grapplings with the nature of their own and other Tibetans' agency in (and responsibility for) the unprecedented shape and scope of violence beginning in 1958. Bolstered by public evidence of their contemporary Buddhist piety,[25] these elders could testify to me their moral distance from the devastation of the Maoist years. And they could thereby differentiate themselves from the few (named or unnamed) Tibetans in the community (in many cases friends, neighbors, and relatives past and present) who were said to have directly victimized Tibetans then, and who now lived quietly among them as ordinary citizens.

In this light, perhaps the loudest silences within these oppositional testimonies make more sense. Of all these accounts, only a very few came close to describing the actual content of public struggle meetings or speaking-bitterness accusations, and neither men nor women mentioned the Chinese names or goals of campaigns associated with them nor explicitly reiterated any fragment of Marxist ideology. On one hand, given the massive quantities of Marxist media (in Chinese and in Tibetan translation) imposed on the valley beginning in the 1950s,[26] this narrative absence can be seen as narrators' repudiation of the validity or relevance of state ideology in structuring their memories. On the other, by avoiding description of struggle meetings in particular, narrators also avoided what was perhaps most painful to recount and thus to face in the sight of a foreigner—not only the extreme violence they experienced or witnessed there but also the fact that all Tibetans' public participation in speaking-bitterness meetings potentially placed in radical question the very nature of their contemporary moral and ethnic selves (cf. Humphrey 1994: 24).[27]

Instead, elders' dissenting accounts dialogued by implication with those of speaking-bitterness class-struggle meetings. They did this by asserting a very different chronology of pivotal events that reversed the moral consequences of revolution, ignoring 1949 and making 1958, the very year speaking-bitterness meetings were introduced, the point of historical rupture leading to unprecedented fear and suffering. Ama Tsholo, along with her husband, Apa Jikmay, the last remaining heir of a prominent line of local lay leaders, expressed this notion of rupture in a phrase repeated throughout their co-constructed story: "Nineteen fifty-eight, the year [we] had to be afraid" (Tib. *lnga brgyad lo skrag dgos dus*). That year, not 1949, nor the state-sanctioned beginning of the Cultural Revolution in 1966, was for them and many others the real end of the "Old Society" and the beginning of the new. In the valley, the temporal terms of this alternative historiography were so widespread that Tibetans tended to define "old people" (Tib. *lo lon, rgan po* or *mo*) as those born before 1958. Indeed, my friend Drolma, an educated woman my age, explained this to me explicitly, and perhaps for good reason. Bodies themselves revealed hidden history in Labrang. Those who had lived through the hard labor and deprivation of the collectives had aged extremely quickly, so that, for example, of two sisters who together ran a small shop in town, one aged sixty, the other in her mid-fifties, the older looked ten years younger than her sister because she had fled to India in 1958 and had returned only in 1984.

In striking contrast to official historiography and to the accounts of many old Han villagers expressing in interviews a kind of "socialist nostalgia" for the early CCP years (cf. Rofel 1999), the discursive power of 1958 in Tibetan elders' oppositional accounts was such that events prior to that time under Communist rule were obscured, barely mentioned at all. Thus, their chronology repudiated the retrospective posited in speaking-bitterness stories they heard that year that claimed the benevolent and merely facilitating nature of the state's intervention in the valley since 1949. Instead, these elders tended to associate the arrival of the Chinese state with the emasculating overthrow of monastic rule under lamas and lay leaders and the consequent forced reorganization of their lives in 1958.

Indeed, in these conversations, Tibetan men and women had most striking recourse to a particular narrative device for implicit metacommunication about the (gendered) state, one that I found to be pervasive among Tibetans across the community. In their stories, they cast the Chinese state as the protagonist in the persona of Apa Gongjia, or Father State—a unitary, radically alien, and uncannily powerful paternal agent. As Eric Mueggler has recently argued, understanding the process by which locals imagine their relationships to state agents, especially in the case of ethnic Others within the PRC, is essential for grasping the practical efficacy of state projects locally—despite the actually fragmentary and variable nature of state institutions and their capacities to control subjects over space and time (Mueggler 2001: 4; cf. Anagnost 1994, 1997; Watson 1994a).

These elders' stories, like all other stories I heard of the past, were structured by the binary temporal categories of revolution first introduced in speaking-bitterness stories. But here, the arrival of Apa Gongjia as a fearsome colonizing agent was the threshold to which all narrators' uses of the contrasting time words "before" (Tib. *sngan na, sngon chad*) or "in the past" (Tib. *nyin dus*) versus "now" (Tib. *da*) or "nowadays" (Tib. *deng seng*) referred. The dignified Apa Denzin, seventy-seven years old and a former monk servant of a high-status trulku, had traveled widely as a trader then and after he left monkhood in 1945 upon his lama's death. Despite all the change this cosmopolitan man had seen during his adult years before CCP intervention, his stories over several conversations were always punctuated with the stark temporal contrasts of "before" versus "now." He would eventually tell me about being labeled a wealthy trader and brutally targeted as a class enemy in his village, but he framed our first conversation by asserting that nothing changed until

Apa Gongjia came (Tib. Apa Gongjia *thon dang*), and, switching to the first person plural, he insisted on explicitly teaching me this phrase for the Chinese Communist state: "*We* say 'Apa Gongjia.'" By then, though, I had been routinely and unconsciously referring to Father State in casual conversation for months.

As a protagonist in elders' oppositional testimonies, Apa Gongjia actively "arrives" (from elsewhere) in exactly the same way Chinese Communist campaigns do. Ama Deji (aged 54) and her husband, Apa Dondrup (aged 50), were farmers in one of the main villages. "When Apa Gongjia arrived," said Ama Deji, describing events that did not occur until 1958, "we had to cut off our headdresses, or else we were accused of clinging to old ways of thinking [Tib. *bsam pa rnying pa*]". Narrators referred to Apa Gongjia as both a subject of actions and as an object of local sentiments. As a subject, he was most often an active agent of transitive verbs, emphasized in speech with a particle marking him as such (cf. Agha 1993, Duranti 1994, Ahearn 2001).[28] Akhu Jamyang, a seventy-year-old monk-scholar in the monastery who told me his life story only under conditions of great secrecy, told me how in 1958 Buddhist texts and images were destroyed. When I asked who did the destroying, he replied, "the Chinese," and his young lay male student clarified, "Apa Gongjia destroyed them" (Tib. Apa Gongjia *gis bshigs dang*).

Thus, the hybrid form of the phrase "Apa Gongjia" for the Chinese Communist state encapsulates well local Tibetans' struggles to account for the radically altered time-space introduced in the 1958 campaigns, as well as for the new gendered premises for human agency that transformation entailed. By attaching "Apa," the local Tibetan term of respectful address for lay male familiars of one's father's generation, to the Chinese loanword for public property and hence the CCP party-state (*gongjia*), elders effectively condensed powerful yet abstract and dispersed disciplinary forces into one agent, anthropomorphizing and gendering them so as to recognize both their Chinese origins and their appropriation by Tibetans. To make Father State the main protagonist of their narratives beginning in 1958 was thus to simultaneously reduce and amplify the efficacy of the Chinese state in their lives past and present. And this in turn allowed for vital narrative efforts to interpret and to make claims to agencies and responsibilities for the horrible outcomes of the events of those years.

In the context of oppositional accounts told in private spaces, the persona of Apa Gongjia referred, through safer forms of implication, to a scathing critique of Chinese state policies and officials. By anthropomorphizing the state in this gendered way, elders countered the erasure of state disciplinary agency common in speaking-bitterness historiography and effectively foregrounded the unmarked politics of competing masculinities in Labrang's socialist transformation (cf. Jamyang Norbu 1992). That is, the subject of Father State in their narratives clearly indexed these older men's and women's shared recognition of CCP projects in Labrang as violent efforts to supplant and recontextualize Amdo fatherlands in a process of national incorporation. This in turn, as we will see, worked to solidify elders' collaboration in reproducing a vision of an ideal Tibetan gender complementarity as the ontological ground of an oppositional and morally superior time-space.

I would argue that the metacommunicative effect of the name Apa Gongjia in these accounts derived from its particularly dialogic nature in the Sino-Tibetan frontier zone. For one thing, the disyllabic structure and homonymic pun of the Chinese loanword *gongjia* recalls the Tibetan epithet *gongma* (lit. "high one") for the distant yet powerful Qing emperors and their governments, a term that was still common in this region in the early twentieth century (cf. Ekvall 1939: 51). Thus in a way we could see elders' use of the similar-sounding name Gongjia for the CCP state as a recognition of its commensurate status in the legacy of powerful masculine authorities impinging on Labrang. As against the CCP's claims to be a modern democratic nation-state, Tibetan accounts cast it as an ethnically Other, nonlocal hierarchy of rule.[29] Yet the referential content of the term in this context, and its gendered status as "Father," also mark the CCP as a radically different and morally suspect type of masculine authority. Tibetans' pervasive use of the Chinese loanword for the state here, supplanting the Tibetan term for Qing emperors in use throughout the post-Qing KMT era, iconically indexes the unprecedented pervasion of CCP intervention into their everyday lives. From this angle, we can appreciate the crucial significance of gender in these accounts— gendering the Chinese state as *Father* State not only recognizes state agency and responsibility in Maoist violence by anthropomorphizing it, but it also sarcastically diminishes it as a moral agent by radically *relativizing* it.

Elders' use of the name Apa Gongjia did this on many levels at once. By relativizing the CCP state in the inappropriately intimate terms of a familiar father figure and head of a lay household, elders both sarcastically denied CCP leaders' unspoken claims to absolute and unmarked authority and recognized their radically secularizing attempts to usurp patrifilial alliances between local household heads and the monastery. "Now," said Apa Denzin, using a word for "rules" (Tib. *sgrig lam*) that had been most widely used for monastic discipline, "it is Father State's rules" (Tib. *da* Gongjia *gi sgrig lam red*). Thus as against the older Tibetan term "gongma," which located Buddhas, trulkus, and worldly (patron) sovereigns in the mandalic time-spaces of legitimating lineage and vertical deference,[30] the name Apa Gongjia diminishes the indexical scope and hence legitimacy of the CCP's claims to authority over Tibetans. In this, elders simultaneously mocked state claims to paternal benevolence toward minority minzu especially (cf. Dreyer 1976: 155; Herberer 2001: 126), claims that had been asserted throughout the Maoist years and arguably into the reform era with state rhetoric about the new regime as "the great multiethnic family of the nation" (Ch. *duo minzu guojia*). Elders' exclusive use of the name Apa Gongjia for the state (instead of Ch. *zuguo* or Tib. *mes rgyal*) thus indexes their refusal to be incorporated into the stateless nation of the Chinese Fatherland. That is, it marks their denial of the fictive kinship of "state fatherhood" as either an effective cover for brutal state violence or as a legitimate stand-in for local patrifilial alliances and obligations (cf. Heng and Devan 1992).

In this light, we can better appreciate the "double-voiced" (Bakhtin 1981) nature of the Chinese term *gongjia* (lit. "public property") as used by Tibetan elders here. Contrary to claims made in speaking-bitterness narratives that the ordinary "masses" were the primary subjects of the revolution and owners of communal property, elders' choice of the word "public property" as an epithet for the state in their accounts of "Democratic Reforms" in Labrang sarcastically reduced the Party's main goals to the will to confiscate Tibetans' private wealth, and thus the main markers of their ethnic difference. Indeed, as we will see, throughout these accounts elders depict Chinese state fatherhood as fundamentally illegitimate, because they experienced collectivization not as a moral economy of reciprocal kin-based generosity and obligation but as involuntary and violent expropriation on behalf of far-distant ethnic Others.

Outside the moral grounding of patrifilial alliance and exchange, Apa Gongjia's incomprehensible motives reduce to arbitrary and amoral social domination and impart impunity to his agents for outrageous violence. Ama Dorje, the seventy-one-year-old wife of Apa Denzin who told me she returned from Lhasa in 1959 to find their household and all their possessions confiscated, said that before she returned, one of her younger brothers was among the many Tibetan laymen who were executed by firing squad (as a Chinese loanword, *qiangbi*) for resisting land reforms. I asked why he was executed, and she ventured only: "I don't know; it was Apa Gongjia, you know" (Tib. *mi shes gi* Apa Gongjia *red mo*). Here we come to perhaps the most important rhetorical role of gender in these accounts. As we will see, Father State, as the explicitly gendered protagonist in both men's and women's narratives, exposed Maoist socialist androgyny as in fact a participation framework for an unprecedented shift in the dominant *regime of value*, one that, backed by military might and state terror, reoriented all exchange away from trulkus and the monastery and toward the centralizing Chinese state.

Thus, most generally, the name "Apa Gongjia" allowed Tibetan men and women to construct a certain type of powerful agent in relation to themselves in the past and the present. By persistently referring to Father State as a conscious, active agent in the virtual absence of any other named protagonists, elders implicitly asserted that the ultimate responsibility for the trauma they experienced lay far away from the Labrang locality, with the (male) central Party leaders sending policies down to local cadres. And crucially, as Apa Denzin's remark above makes clear, for elder narrators of oppositional stories of the Maoist years, Father State as an actively dominating and expropriating agent persisted throughout the Maoist years and *to their presents*. Against contemporary official historiography that relegated "mistakes" of the past to the actions of a few named Party leaders or misguided youthful Red Guards during the circumscribed period of the Cultural Revolution, the name Apa Gongjia indexes a refusal to name specific leaders. Instead, he represented for these Tibetan elders a focused masculine will to domination that, from the beginning of Chinese Communist rule, transcended the vicissitudes of Party regimes and remained responsible for the difficulties of their contemporary situations—unlike the ideal Tibetan patriarch, Father State does not reciprocate with benevolent protection, nor does he hand down wealth and authority to lineage sons and daughters. He is a timelessly avaricious agent, refusing to pass on. Indeed, in the summer of 2002, I entered into a long afternoon of listening to Apa Jikmay and Ama Tsholo's angry testimonials about the Maoist years after I had met Apa Jikmay on a village road and he had lamented that Apa Gongjia was destroying village homes to make way for the new highway.

In Tibetan men's and women's oppositional narratives of Maoist violence, the might of Apa Gongjia as an agent also emptied local Tibetans of agency. Thus as against the gross embodiment of class victims described in speaking-bitterness narratives, the vast majority of elders' dissenting accounts focused on violations of their embodied selves under Father State. Both men and women tended to enumerate such events, emphasizing numbers of times their property was confiscated, or they or relatives were arrested or targeted for struggle.

Finally, most narrators who had been villagers at the time focused on the pervasive physical victimization of the majority of Tibetan locals in the unprecedented famine that accompanied confiscations and collectivization in the early 1960s. One of the most widespread narrative elements in these stories was the weed broth (Tib. *ldum bu*) that Tibetans had to eat in communal kitchens in the absence of any other food. Ama Gazang, a sixty-eight-year-old village woman and wife of a retired Tibetan Party cadre, and her friend and age-mate Ama Dukar began their account of the collectives established in 1958 with the common observation that there was no food at that time. When I asked why, Ama Gazang replied matter-of-factly: "Because Apa Gongjia confiscated all [the produce]" (Tib. *ha ne bo* Apa Gongjia *gis moshui byas dang*). She demonstrated how the soup was made from scraps of vegetable leaves and barely edible wild weeds, looking to Ama Dukar for confirmation. She insisted that then "everyone was hungry," and she repeated again and again that many, many people died. Ama Dukar emphasized how many children died as well, and described how everyone's face swelled with malnutrition. All this, they insisted, and they also had to work incessantly in the fields.

CONSTRUCTING GENDERED
SPACES OF MEMORY

Apa Jikmay, the distinguished old village man I met on the road in 2002, was one of the most eager of my interlocutors to provide oppositional testimony of the Maoist years, despite the heightened dangers of public metalanguage since the late 1990s in Labrang (see the epilogue).

Inside the walls of their packed-mud courtyard, I sat comfortably on their newly glassed-in porch and listened for hours as he and his wife, Ama Tsholo, angrily described their experiences of socialist transformation. Apa Jikmay did most of the talking, telling me how, unlike Ama Tsholo, he had been labeled a wealthy landlord and repeatedly targeted ("hatted" as a class enemy, Tib. *zhwa gon dang*) up through the Cultural Revolution in Labrang (1966–68). He never related the contents of accusations against him, nor the details of the beatings and humiliations he suffered. He and Ama Tsholo were most interested in commenting on what was to them the grossly unjust transformation of their gendered social world. Their narratives tacked erratically back and forth in time, framed nonetheless by Apa Jikmay's repeated laments at the loss of his patriline's great local prestige as erstwhile regional lay leaders. He said that nowadays, only old men knew his status and raised their hats as he passed, while (the size and quality of) newly built houses mattered much more as a sign of local prestige: "At that time houses weren't important," he insisted; "now they are" (Tib. *de dus khang pa gal che ma red; da khang pa gal che red*).

Apa Jikmay's struggles with the transformed parameters of gender and class recognition in contemporary Labrang were thus inextricably linked both for him and Ama Tsholo to what they saw as the invalid narrative premises of Maoist campaigns in Labrang. For them, those campaigns had usurped local patriarchs' roles as proper arbiters of transhousehold and lay-monastic communication and exchanges, and replaced them with illegitimate agents of Apa Gongjia arbitrating newly "public" spaces (Tib. *gzhung*). Thus, in this and many other conversations with elder men and women, I could discern how the extreme terms of the gendered respatialization of Labrang beginning in 1958 had also set in motion a radical retemporalization of the region. For them, the physical, spatial, and metalinguistic erasure of the authority of Tibetan fathers and grandfathers (Tib. *a pa, rgan po, a mes*)—those whom, as we saw, were considered responsible for transmitting household and lineage knowledge (cf. Briggs 1986: 83)—threatened to erase local Tibetan historicity altogether. This process, which elders understood largely as young Tibetans' lack of respect and interest in listening to them (Tib. *kha mi nyan gi*), to many was the basis of a widening generation gap they did not know how to bridge. This was particularly so because they saw their experiences of the great changes of the Maoist years most effectively erased in their own children's' ignorance. Ama Dorje, the seventy-one-year-old wife of Apa Denzin and matriarch of their struggling village household, lamented to me that "today's young people have no idea what that time was like." In the context of our conversation about both the "Old Society" and her suffering during the Maoist years, the phrase "that time" (Tib. *de dus*) referred to both periods, the majority of her lifetime.

Thus as a foreign and female sounding-board for oppositional testimony in these conversations, I was precariously situated in the painful collective gap between mouth or speech and mind/heart that the Maoist subjugation of Tibetan patriarchs had produced. As in other single-party states, official efforts in Maoist and post-Mao Labrang to curtail public metalanguage in the face of widely acknowledged Party failings had politicized and rendered more insular Tibetans' private household spaces (cf. Watson 1994a). By participating in private explicit metalanguage across these spaces, I was thus also participating in some Tibetans' ongoing efforts to both retemporalize and respatialize Labrang in gendered ways. I found that for these elders, in the face of the emasculating gap between public speech and private mind/heart in the 1990s, an alternative vision of a Tibetan public had to be constantly reimagined through calculations of, on the one hand, past and present reciprocity and, on the other, relative distance from Apa Gongjia and the bankrupt moral premises of socialist androgyny. For them, this seemed to consist of an imagined network of "honest" or "straightforward" (Tib. *drang mo*, lit. "straight," indexing a straight line between mouth or speech and mind/heart) Tibetan households working hard in ideal gender complementarity to revitalize reciprocal and patrifilial lay-monastic relations, even as interhousehold competition had intensified in the reform-era market economy. This alternative Tibetan public contrasted sharply with the wily and calculating cadres, merchants, and thieves they saw as dominating public spaces in post-Mao Labrang. And crucially, elders implicitly and explicitly attributed the emergence of these dishonest and selfish agents (a hand-wiggle gesture frequently serving as an icon of tortuous lines between their speech and mind/heart) to the social upheavals concomitant with the arrival of Apa Gongjia in 1958.

These men and women narrated that period as a time when state and local agents suddenly acted according to motives inexplicable at the time, a time when all villagers knew that survival in the face of public pressure to reconstitute themselves on narrative premises they did not understand required a drastic split between narrating (in mind/heart) and narrated (in speech) selves (cf. Dhondup Choedon 1978, Palden Gyatso 1997, Panchen Lama 1997). I would argue that the increasingly conventional requirement to publicly perform such testimony under Chinese state auspices eventually led to the widespread delegitimation of civic spaces and associated motives for action, even among those whose original participation in the new regime was sincere. For elders like Akhu Gyaltshan, a monk in his mid-fifties who told me proudly of his boyhood as a monk at Labrang in the 1940s, a crisis of truth in public interactions after 1958 was generalizable enough to characterize the rupture that relegated the "Old Society" to the past. Akhu Gyaltshan insisted that in the "Old Society" (Tib. *'jig rten rnying pa*) people trusted each other, whereas "nowadays" (Tib. *deng seng*) no one does.

We can better appreciate the vital importance for these elders of imagining an alternative, "honest" Tibetan public structured by ideal gender complementarity if we consider that, for most of these narrators, this sudden epistemological rupture was socially and physically manifested in wide-reaching and violently imposed *gender reversals* among Tibetans themselves. Thus in our conversations, both men and women constructed an alternative public consciously by instructing me on to· whom to talk and how. But unconsciously, they reconstructed ideal gender complementarity by involving me in eyewitness counternarratives during which women deferred to men as the authorities representing transhousehold historicity, either by participating as subordinate or supporting narrators in co-constructed stories, or in their own narratives by representing their experiences as purely individual or personal ones.

This was strikingly apparent in my conversations with Apa Dondrup (aged 50) and his wife, Ama Deji (aged 54), farmers in one of Labrang's Lhade or main village dewa, both of them from old Labrang lines. They did not tell me detailed stories of their experiences of the Maoist years until many months into our friendship. Then, while we sat comfortably next to their stove and ate one day, Apa Dondrup held forth with Ama Deji chiming in over the next few hours. Their narrative began with their adamant commentary about the radical transformation they had seen in Tibetans' gendered dress and hairstyles. This unwelcome change in public gender performativity was for Apa Dondrup directly linked to the disturbing forms of contemporary hybrid and gender-blurring behavior he observed in Labrang. Like many other patriarchs in their oppositional testimonies (women did not comment on this explicitly), he found this to be especially indexed by pants-clad women in public spaces (see chapters 3 and 4). This development he (unconsciously) summed up iconically with an uncharacteristic code switch to Chinese in midsentence: "Now you can't tell men from women!" (Tib. and Ch. *da byis lu byis mo* bu zhidao).

Importantly, for them this state of affairs originated in the fall of 1958, during the collectivization campaign that followed closely after the great regional speaking-bitterness meetings on the Sangkok grasslands that summer. At this time state cadres especially, insisted Apa Dondrup, were pressured to leave behind Tibetan clothes for modern uniforms. Here, Ama Deji's contributions increased as they emphasized how the first mandatory public meetings in their village dewa were held in their dewa's *manikhang*, the small temple and communal space devoted to the invocation and propitiation of the dewa's *zhidak* (Tib. *gzhi bdag*, lit. "Foundation [or "Ground"] Lord"). Originally tamed to the service of Buddhism by Jamyang Shepa, zhidak in Labrang were the fierce worldly protector deities who reside in the surrounding mountains.

They were most often imaged as military commanders or warriors and addressed, not coincidentally, as "Amnye" (grandfathers). As the alternative abodes of mountain deities in Labrang Lhade, village temples were jealously guarded sites for dewas' annual communal rites, and in the enclaved spaces of the deities' shrines (Tib. *mgon khang*) within, they were protected from the polluting presence of females. Key acts of prayerful exchange with them on behalf of the dewa were the exclusive purview of dewa patriarchs. In their subsequent description of the 1958 meetings, both Apa Dondrup and Ama Deji used only the new label given to those spaces at that time—*zhungkhang* (Tib. *gzhung khang*) state or public meeting halls. Before they were all destroyed during the Cultural Revolution, the manikhang-turned-zhungkhang were focal points for state-local encounters during "Democratic Reforms" in the 1950s, centers for the rapid respatialization of the valley's population into militarily loyal collectives (i.e., "production teams," *shengchan dui*, and "production brigades," *shengchan dadui*) working state-arbitrated public property for the public and communal good (Ch. *gongshe*) under the ultimate guidance of central Party leaders in Beijing.[31]

But Apa Dondrup and Ama Deji's narrative fundamentally framed these spaces as sites of state terror. For them, they were the central locus for their first terrifying experiences of collectivization as the unprecedented confiscation (a term widely expressed in Chinese, *moshui*) of private household property by *lishaypa*, state cadres (Tib. *las byed pa*, lit. "one who does things," associated with nonmanual labor). That term is a Tibetan neologism glossing the Chinese *ganbu*, and widely among Tibetans it seemed to gloss all persons (including Tibetans) whose public activities were recognized to be primarily on behalf of and remunerated by Apa Gongjia; from the lowliest grassroots cadre to government and Party officials, they were the vanguards of state performativity. For local Tibetans, lishaypa was thus another category of active subject that belied speaking-bitterness efforts to erase state disciplinary agency in favor of "the people." In the wake of the military crackdown on Tibetan men's armed resistance to such efforts begun elsewhere, we could see the appropriation of local temples under the auspices of state-trained young Zangzu men and women grassroots cadres in this way as culminating the conquest of local Tibetan patrifilial authority—the triumph of public over private in Labrang meant the unprecedented extension of state discipline and interpersonal surveillance into the gendered core of Lhade life. Apa Dondrup insisted that "everyone was terrified of the cadres" during the confiscations, and at the zhungkhang meetings people would inform on others suspected of exploiting locals and hiding wealth. In this way, Labrang villagers' speaking-bitterness stories throughout the valley in 1958 narrativized cadres' confiscations as state-mediated class justice.

Just as struggle sessions against trulkus and lamas had done that summer, the Lhade zhungkhang meetings followed upon military violence against Tibetan men with new participation frameworks for secularization via gendered desecration. This after all was the very time, as my retired cadre friend Ama Lhamo told me, when she was first led with her cadre training group on a tour of the empty monastery. She described how terrified she had been in that unfamiliar, dark space. In terms of the zhungkhang meetings, we need to appreciate that the gendered ritual division of labor in Lhade mountain-deity worship underpinned the historicity of patrifilial links between the mandalic order of the monastery, the settled dewa households in the valley, and the land as authoritative locality itself. Most of the Lhade patriarchs I spoke to (women knew very little about this) proudly narrated the history of the relationship between Jamyang Shepa and their dewas' *lha* or god. It seems that the Lhade took on their special status vis-à-vis the monastery, became "God Dewa," when Jamyang Shepa identified and tamed the local mountain deity linked to a settled village's territory (cf. hor gtsang 'jigs med 2000). As we saw in chapter 1, the fourth Jamyang Shepa, as part of his broad efforts to consolidate monastic control, established an administrative district of patron villages in the valley called the Four Lhade Tribes. An important part of that effort was his initiative in founding the annual communal worship of an overarching dedicated mountain deity for the Four Lhade Tribes on the mountain behind the monastery (cf. Li Anzhai 1982, 1989; Ma Denghun and Wanma 1994). That move illustrates how mountain-deity worship was an important part of Geluk efforts to mandalize and sedentarize *both* laymen and worldly deities, thus turning their support to the defense of local monastic interests. It is the trulku's exclusive power, through consecration—or, better, vivification rituals (Tib. *rab gnas*)—to emplace deities in particular material receptacles (Tib. *rten*). In this way, he makes them subject to powerful exchanges with humans, grounding and localizing his masculine authority. The material receptacles of protector deities in the mountains and in village temples, and the material receptacles of protector deities and Buddhas in the monastery, were supposed to link all local land and exchange under the tantric prowess of Jamyang Shepa (cf. Bentor 1993, 1997).[32]

In this light, we can better understand how my interlocutors would consider Apa Gongjia's intervention in 1958 to be encapsulated in profoundly threatening gender reversals. Indeed, the vast majority of Tibetan women cadres and Party members took on that (mostly low-level) secular status after 1958, including the only woman trulku in the region, the twenty-two-year-old Alak Gungru Tshang, who returned her nun vows, joined a minority minzu cadre training class in Lanzhou, and became chair of the Gannan Fulian (cf. Zhao 1965; KHBG 1993: 14; GZZ 1999: 1155). In fact then, in a variety of ways, the "liberation" of Tibetan women as Zangzu funu under Apa Gongjia was directly linked to the violent pacification of Tibetan men and the subsequent expropriation of the region.

When I asked Apa Sangye, a seventy-one-year-old retired trader in another dewa, if the cadres who enforced the 1958 confiscations were all Chinese, he scoffed and said: "No! There were a lot of Tibetans!" And for him, the most emblematic among them was Apa Alo's own daughter, a scion of Labrang's ruling patriline. Much of our conversation had revolved around Apa Sangye's account of his and his monk brother's lifelong devotion and service to that family in Labrang. Unlike Apa Jikmay, he said he had not gone to "join the bandits" in the mountains, but had stayed in town along with many other men, whereas men in surrounding nomad dewa like Sangkok, Amchok, and Gangya had all gone. But Apa Sangye, as did many other men and women, expressed great resentment that virtually all adult men in town who were not cadres were arrested during the crackdown, whether they had been "rebels" or not.[33] He himself was imprisoned for three years, and it was during that time, he said, when he and most other men were gone, that most of the first confiscations of household property were done. When his wife invoked their patrifilial ties and begged Apa Alo's daughter not to take their things, he recounted: "She would hear none of it. She had become an activist [Ch. *jijifenzi*]."[34]

Thus, of all the Tibetan activists (the majority of whom were most likely male), the figure of Apa Alo's daughter, a female cadre who had seemingly turned on her own ruling lineage and directly denied the historicity of patrifilial alliance, stood out for Apa Sangye as encapsulating the literal and figurative conquest of local Tibetan men. Indeed, Tibetan women cadres in Labrang emerged at precisely the time when upper-echelon Han county and prefecture officials needed Tibetan women *in general* as both model minority citizens and as literal surrogates for absent Tibetan men. Gazetteer statistics for Xiahe county record greatly decreased numbers of adult men relative to women during the Maoist years (XXZ 1997: 214–19), at the same time as an influx of Han and Hui settlers decreased the overall percentage of Tibetans by 25 percent,[35] and upper-level government and Party positions were overwhelmingly dominated by Han men (XXZ 1997: 674; GZZ 1999: 1131). In this context, we would have to see the emergence of Tibetan women state agents in Labrang, clad at that time in military-style uniforms, to be disproportionately metonymic of a particularly cataclysmic and emasculating regime of value shift for Tibetans, one that relied on military violence to incorporate them into the PRC nation-state by finally bringing to bear the radical time-spaces of Mao's Great Leap Forward policies.

In contrast to Han communities across the country, where accounts abounded of locals' frenetically eager nationalist participation in the Great Leap Forward, for Tibetans, national-level military discipline enforced the mass militarization of local *labor* that underpinned Mao's Great Leap drive to maximize rural production and channel all extractable value to the rapid industrialization of the country (cf. MacFarquhar 1983: 100; Harding 1987; Watson 1994a; W. Smith 1996). In the 1990s then, older Tibetan men's and women's gendered collaboration in oppositional testimony countered the Maoist crisis of truth they experienced in 1958 by unveiling the performative lie of speaking-bitterness socialist androgyny. Far from indexing modern democratic "liberation," the performance of Maoist gender neutrality for them actually indexed the violent transition to a new "mode of commodification" (Appadurai 1986: 16) in which persons, as laboring bodies, were subject to unprecedented *standardization* as extractable units of labor value. The spectacles of speaking-bitterness performances, as they evolved over time, could thus be seen as oppositional "tournaments of value" in a new Maoist status economy. In them, narratives themselves came to be commodities, and narrators vied to recruit locals to labor by making performances of loyal labor for state-guided progress the main media of transvaluation (cf. Dhondup Choedon 1978: 30; Watson 1994a; Rofel 1999). Thus, in Apa Dondrup and Ama Deji's narrative, as well as in those of Ama Luji and others, they tended to distill down to this essence what many scholars have argued were actually complicated and shifting systems of remuneration in the collectives. Faces registering indignant disbelief, they described how, under the supervision of cadres, people were compensated for their work in "work points" (Ch. *gongfen*, Tib. *skar ma*) that not only registered their (perceived) daily amount of manual labor but also classed them as workers on a scale of sheer physical ability (thus children could earn only half, and the old and infirm nothing) and marked the propriety of their daily "attitudes" toward collective labor, all within state-set quotas for remuneration that were to provide virtuous subsistence only (cf. Dhondup Choedon 1978: 29; Harding 1987; Tenzin Palbar 1994: 193).

In effect, elders' critiques implicitly asserted that Apa Gongjia in this way illegitimately expanded upon the long-term, yet relatively fruitless, efforts of various authorities in the Labrang region to appropriate lucrative resources from local Tibetan labor.[36] Thus in August 1958, at the same time as it decreed the launching of the "Antifeudalism Campaign," Gannan prefecture's three-year-old People's Congress declared that all prefecture resources of mines, rivers, grasslands, and forests now belonged to the "nation." And by winter, after the great ceremony in Hezuo congratulating the prefecture on its struggle with feudalism and its successes in establishing communes, major state-run raw-materials processing plants and livestock farms began to open, including later the factory in which Ama Drolma and her women peers had worked (GGK 1987: 259; GZZ 1999: 622; cf. Dreyer 1976: 164).

In this light, we can better appreciate the gendered ways in which elders linked the state terror of confiscation with the social and spatial upheavals of collectivization in their narratives. Of all the personal items and property confiscated after the zhungkhang meetings, Apa Dondrup and Ama Deji, as did many other elders, were most pressed to describe the confiscation of Tibetan women's *rawa* or headdresses, the elaborate pieces of colorful cloth ornamented with coral and silver coins (depending on the wealth of their households) that young women first had braided into their long hair when they underwent, in their late teens, the coming-of-age rite held annually at the new year (cf. Tenzin Palbar 1994: 187–88). At that time, as Apa Dondrup told me, length of hair for both women and men indexed their progress through gendered life cycles, but "no older woman," he emphasized, "would ever be seen with her hair short." During girls' coming-of-age festivities in the 1930s and 1940s, referred to as "letting down the hair" (Tib. *skra phab*), households gathered dewa donations for the property their daughters would eventually take with them into marriage (Tib. *rdzong ba*, lit. "parting gift"; cf. Yu Shiyu 1990b, 1990c; Zhang Keji 1993).[37] Thus, with the relative absence of men during the 1958 campaigns, women's headdresses would have been particularly marked signs of both households' (private) patrimony *and* the vital exchangeability of women as reproductive labor among them—they indexed Tibetan gender relations and labor obligations as crucially kin-based.

Apa Dondrup and Ama Deji were most adamant, then, when they described the meager compensation, in CCP paper money at prices way below market value, that households received for the silver and coral on the headdresses. And Apa Dondrup's only "performative breakthrough" (Hymes 1975) into actually dramatizing the terror of the zhungkhang meetings was when he animated a cadre accusing a woman of hiding a headdress: "You!" he said sharply, pointing at me, "You have a headdress! Where is it!?" Thus, as various Buddhist images were being taken from the monastery and sold in Chinese urban centers (cf. Tenzin Palbar 1994: 185), and women gathered under the auspices of uniformed cadres in the once sex-segregated spaces that had protected the deities' image-receptacles in village temples, the confiscation of their headdresses marked the transition to a new standard for proper gendered subjectivity—from local Tibetan patrifiliality to (voluntary) labor for the translocal agent of Apa Gongjia. As June Dreyer notes, a 1958 article in the Party journal *Minzu Unite* reported that Tibetan women in Gansu had agreed to discard their headdresses because they finally realized that their weight slowed down their work in the fields and that the materials they took up could be used to more practical ends (1976: 161; cf. Panchen Lama 1997: 103). Elders' critiques, however, asserted that this process was more about *recommodifying* both women and the household wealth they carried to benefit Apa Gongjia.

Indeed, after Apa Dondrup's brief performance, Ama Deji immediately noted that "in those days, we all had to eat together in the zhungkhang," and Apa

FIGURE 10.
Young women who have just undergone the "letting down the hair" (Tib. *skra phab*) rite show off their new headdresses during the New Year festivities, 1949. (Photo by Wayne Persons)

Dondrup insisted, as did others, that "we weren't allowed to start a fire in our stoves." In the Labrang region, the vaunted "communal kitchens" (Tib. *thun mong ʐa khang*), serving up to several hundred people between 1958 and 1961 (cf. Tenzin Palbar 1994: 191), meant turning the restricted spaces of Tibetan sex-gender divisions of labor inside out: it displaced men's exclusive transhousehold ritual authority with the functionality at the core of women's erstwhile (ritualized) household domain, the stove (Tib. *thab*).[38] In fact, as Roderick MacFarquhar and others have argued, with the massive demands for rural labor that Great Leap policies produced under the slogan "More, Better, Faster, Cheaper," the primary reason for communal kitchens and collective child care was to convert female reproductive labor value to "productive" labor for the state. A 1958 *People's Daily* article cited by MacFarquhar says this explicitly: touting successes in Henan province, it argues that with communal kitchens, "6 million units of female labor power had been released from domestic chores" (1983:103; cf. Wolf 1985).

I would argue that "women's liberation" during the Great Leap Forward set the stage for the unprecedented state exploitation of female labor throughout the

Maoist years in the PRC. Mao's famous dictum "Women Hold Up Half the Sky" could be read then as grounded in a new vision of binary sex difference that evoked science to expediently remove social barriers to women's "productive" work. As we have seen, in the Labrang region, this was particularly important—as Apa Jikmay indignantly put it, with all the Tibetan men gone in the valley, women actually did the plowing![39] Contrary to the vaunted sex-gender and minzu egalitarianism of socialist androgyny, in Labrang, as in other Tibetan regions, state officials appealed to the supposed intrinsic nature of Tibetan females to provide badly needed social stability and productive labor.

This perspective, then, sheds light on the portrayal of Tibetan women in the Fulian journal *China's Women* between 1956 and 1964. In those accounts of liberated Zangzu women, published for what Harriet Evans estimates was a "potentially enormous" audience of Han women (1997: 17), Tibetan women are depicted as model workers on the Sino-Tibetan frontier whose intrinsic racial and sexed nature particularly incline them to cheerful and self-sacrificing work (Ch. *wusi dagong*). Even though in many cases rural Tibetan women and Tibetan women cadres were arguably working hard to support their own communities and relatives, their grassroots work liaising with nomad collectives or supporting state development projects is depicted as always on behalf of the state. Thus, during the construction of the massive Kang-Zang highway between Sichuan province and the TAR, Zong Zidu depicts Zangzu women doggedly and voluntarily bringing supplies across mountainous terrain to unspecified state workers, even though many of those workers were local Tibetan men conscripted to work on such projects in the 1950s: "At the time," Zong exclaims, "our Han workers all frequently said that Zangzu women were amazing and that such indomitable spirit was truly worth studying!" (1956: 9; cf. Karan 1976: 47).

Thus for Tibetans, the "feminine hinge" of socialist transformation was not far from what they would eventually encounter under post-Mao market reforms—in the face of Tibetan men's violent resistance, the push to develop state infrastructure in Tibetan regions, and the disastrous economic consequences of the Great Leap Forward, Tibetan females were supposed to embody ideally docile and voluntary (i.e., unremunerated or cheap) Communist labor. This perspective helps explain the very different treatment Ama Dorje said she received when she and her husband, Apa Denzin, were arrested along with other Amdowas in Lhasa after the uprising there in 1959. They were separated, she said, and while he spent several years in jail, she and about two hundred other Amdo women were detained only a few months before being trucked back to their home regions in order to work in the new communes. It also elucidates the very harsh punishments meted out to Tibetan women suspected of turning their supply-line support to Tibetan rebels (cf. Ama Adhe 1997). The only time Ama Lhamo's rapid-fire sarcasm abruptly stopped in our many conversations was when she described her terror that she would be executed along with others after she had been imprisoned in 1958 on suspicion of using her cadre status to take supplies to rebels. She had been accused, she said, by two other Tibetan women cadres who were trying (in vain) to deflect attention from themselves.

This was the time, then, to which Ama Gazang and Ama Dukar were referring in their tale of incessant hard work and famine in Labrang under Apa Gongjia's confiscations. During our long conversation that day, it was only after Apa Thamki, Ama Gazang's retired Party-cadre husband, had left for his office that the two women began to recount the extent of the suffering they experienced after their Labrang Lhade had been incorporated into a commune. Far from feeling liberated in the newly expanded public spaces of socialist androgyny, they depicted themselves as only passive experiencers of actions, bereft of even the ability to feed their hungry children. Ama Dukar described how as young women, minus their headdresses, they were forbidden to worship at the empty monastery and had to do farm work all day long, opening up "wastelands" (in Chinese, *kaihuang*) by plowing new fields on high grassland plateau, all for harvests over which they had no control. Here then, as with other elder men and women I spoke to (and Ama Gazang herself had introduced me to several of them), the women's private oppositional speaking-bitterness narrative of the Maoist years positioned me as a medium for the construction of an alternative Tibetan public, one that collectively belied CCP stories of gender-neutral class liberation and acknowledged the consequences of the state's own quandary of agency during the Maoist years—that the "feminine hinge" allowed state officials to simultaneously claim "the people" as owners and initiators of a "democratic" revolution, while usurping masculine disciplinary agency for Apa Gongjia.

ORDINARY FOLKS AND STATE CADRES: RECONSTITUTING GENDERED CLASS

Older Tibetan women's participation in such counternarratives implicitly worked to reconstitute Tibetan patrifiliality as the proper gendered social order. In contrast to previously widespread practices of "complementary filiation" among Tibetans in the Labrang region, in which women in certain contexts were supposed to *tem-*

porarily stand in for absent men within a patrilineal framework, such narratives critiqued CCP efforts to inappropriately replace recalcitrant Tibetan men and masculinity with women and femininity in major exchanges under brutal state expropriation. And yet, I found that men's and women's narrative collaboration in focusing on the physical suffering of "everyone" (Tib. *hanebo*) during the Maoist years, and the narrative clarity afforded by the figure of Apa Gongjia as the conscious agent responsible for it, was not enough to remedy elders' deep ambivalence in accounting for new divisions among Tibetans then, and the consequent moral dilemmas that that period still raised. Ama Gazang's situation particularly illustrated this. Her embittered stories of the famine were framed by persistent remarks about her fear and anger about being old, isolated by her relatives, and uncertain in what she considered to be the social chaos and moral flux of newly market-oriented Labrang. She was always lamenting that she and Apa Thamki had no children and survived only on the small pension he received as a retired Party cadre. But she never admitted that her present anxieties were fundamentally shaped by the moral predicament produced by Apa Thamki's participation as a cadre in Maoist violence *and* by his ongoing impunity.

As we have seen, how to account for local Tibetans' own involvement in state violence was a quandary that faced all elders. In many stories, the figure of Apa Gongjia allowed for a therapeutic polarization of state versus local subjectivities in the violence. Apa Sangye, the retired trader who had proudly told me of his close relationship to the family of Jamyang Shepa, described for me with great disgust the day he and his wife were secretly circumambulating the monastery during the Cultural Revolution in the late 1960s and watched as Tibetan villagers "happily" tore down monastic buildings. He sardonically imitated them by raising his open hands in the air and dancing around as he sat. But he was also careful to say that such ordinary folks, the *wesang*, were not responsible for those actions (Tib. *khag med gi*); they had to do what Apa Gongjia and the cadres said. Apa Denzin, who had participated in the demolition along with his dewa, said that of course he had been sad that day but they had to pretend to be happy (Tib. *skyid po byed dgos*), and with a sour look on his face he said that nowadays the government claims that the wesang themselves did the destroying. "But we had no choice," he said, "or the cadres would struggle you" (i.e., make you the target of a criticism meeting or "struggle session," Ch. *pidou hui*).

Thus, despite rhetorical recourse to Apa Gongjia as primary agent, these men and women were acutely aware of the role of Tibetan cadres as agents of Chinese state-constituted violence during the Maoist years. Importantly, their depictions of such cadres posited a deep, binary social division among Tibetans that amounted to a gendered oppositional class politics in contemporary Labrang. Contrary to the expedient class labels that were given to a wide variety of Tibetan male leaders as "exploiters" of the "serfs," and then deployed in accusatory speaking-bitterness narratives, these elders reclassified subjects of the narratives, inverting the moral roles of accuser and accused and asserting a fundamentally hierarchical relationship between exploiting lishaypa (state cadres) and exploited wesang (local "ordinary"—that is, non-state-affiliated—Tibetan laymen and laywomen, across farming and nomad regions and *regardless* of previous economic status).[40] Even though at various points in their stories of the Maoist years both men and women would qualify their statements about a particular person, most condemned the local Tibetan cadres categorically as exclusively venal agents, those who used the work of the state to enrich themselves. As Apa Denzin carefully explained, to become a cadre at that time was to agree to do bad things (Tib. *a ha ma byed dgos*), to do the work of the Chinese (Tib. *rgya gi bya ba byed dgos*). He insisted that before 1958 he himself had been asked to be one but he had refused.

In both men's and women's narratives, the term *wesang* (not *mi dmangs*, the Tibetan neologism for the Chinese word *renmin* designating ideal minzu citizens) emerged in opposition to *lishaypa* as the name for an imagined alternative Tibetan public in Labrang, one that consisted in a patrifilial moral economy structured by ideal gender complementarity. In constructing this categorical dichotomy, elders metalinguistically distanced themselves from both gender and class as social constructions relevant to their "liberation" under the CCP, foregrounding (gendered) ethnicity instead. In so doing, I argue, they revalorized the unmarked politics of Tibetan masculinities and further emphasized the nature of state-local relations as a contest of ethnic masculinities. In this alternative vision, class exploitation, just like abstract gender, is relevant only to the competing, Chinese masculine authority of Apa Gongjia and to the cadres (men or women) who chose to be masculinized in that new way. Thus, in contrast to state rhetoric about "women's liberation," and the expedient emphasis on Tibetan women as state agents in the revolution, both men and women narrators overwhelmingly focused on the fateful agency of Tibetan men during the Maoist years. This to them was the epistemological ground for the ongoing revitalization in 1990s Labrang Lhade of what I would call a patrifilial Tibetan "shadow world" of the ordinary folks.

Apa Denzin's insistence on the conscious nature of his choice of (masculine) loyalties in the 1950s illustrates how much that choice had come to be a benchmark for elders' judgments about the moral authority of Tibetan men's subjectivities in particular. When the elders referred to Apa Gongjia as an object in their sentences, it was most often for this purpose, as a measure of men's conscious, *contemporary* loyalties.

FROM FIELD NOTES: One winter afternoon, I went for a return visit to Ama Luji's small home in one of Labrang's village Lhade. I met her as she returned from her daily circumambulation, and I ended up perched next to her stove, drinking tea and listening to her characteristic tumble of stories and opinions. Soon her old husband, Apa Cheka, came in to tell her that some *ganpo* (Tib. *rgan po,* male elders) had requested his presence at the village manikhang to help choose the next village head (Ch. *duizhang,* lit. "team leader"). When I asked them about that system, they immediately contrasted contemporary village heads (chosen every 3–4 years) with Party members (Ch. *dangyuan*), who are such for life. Even though the majority of village Party members they listed were old women, both angrily focused only on Gyaplo, the past and present Tibetan Party secretary and head of their district, a man Ama Luji bitterly insisted was not like other "real" *ganpo* (Tib. *rgan po ngo ma*). Real *ganpo,* she said, took up guns against the Chinese and fled to the hills. "And," Apa Cheka added, "most of them were killed by PLA troops." In their subsequent co-constructed narrative, they said that Gyaplo by contrast had joined the People's Militia (Tib. *dmangs dmag*) in the early 1950s and had helped to guide Chinese troops to Tibetan guerrillas in the mountains around Labrang. From that time on, Ama Luji argued, his family went from poor to the most powerful in their village. He was the one who ultimately adjudicated their work points in the collectives and during campaigns paraded class enemies around the village carrying a PRC flag. In a sentence whose temporal frame was left ambiguous, she insisted that "he really liked [or "likes"] Apa Gongjia" (Tib. Apa Gongjia *a hon da dga' gi*).

Here, Ama Luji and Apa Cheka's narrative juxtaposed the atemporality and contemporary presence of Gyaplo's state loyalty to those of "real" Tibetan male elders, the men who somehow survived the Maoist years with their Tibetan masculinity untainted.

In conjunction with the reform-era revitalization of both trulku and mountain-deity worship throughout the Lhade, these men (and with Apa Cheka present, Ama Luji was implying her husband was one of them) and their sons again publicly presided over dewa affairs from the rebuilt spaces of dewa temples, networking across dewa through marriages and annual ritual obligations at monastic pageants. These were the patrilines from which sons tended to be chosen as *dehwon*

(Tib. *sde dpon,* dewa leaders) or *duizhang* ("team leaders"), exclusively charged with coordinating the ritualized patrifilial obligations within and among dewa, and between dewa and the monastery. As Ama Luji and Apa Cheka's casual use of the commune-era Chinese loanword *duizhang* as a gloss for the old Tibetan term *dehwon* illustrates, in this and many other narratives, men and women depicted the patrifilial reciprocity of this ideal masculinity as *timelessly present,* implying no actual rupture during the Maoist years and reclaiming the categorical space at the bottom of the CCP chain of command for "real" Tibetan masculine authority.[41]

Indeed, Apa Dondrup, in the midst of our long conversation about dewa history, resorted to the most common form of characterizing statement among Tibetans (linking a subject to an attribute with the copula *yin* or *red,* "to be," uninflected for tense) to describe the timeless reciprocity between, and common goals of, Lhade male elders on the one hand and, on the other, trulkus and monks in the monastery: "The road of male elders and that of the monastery are one and the same" (Tib. *rgan po cho ra dgon pa 'gro lam gcig red*). He proudly listed some of the ritual obligations his dewa's male elders once again annually fulfilled for the monastery, likening them to past obligations to provide transport and militia, and depicting Labrang's village Lhade as thus superior to nomad pilgrims who could claim no such intimate connection to the monastery. The dewa male elders who maintained this alliance were and remained for him the core of the Tibetan ordinary folks, those who now rightfully represented the dewa in village elections.

Importantly, across men's and women's narratives, appeals to the ideal timelessness of complementary gender roles worked to transform nostalgic visions of the mandalic order of lamas and lay leaders into some form of contemporary reality. Amnye Gompo, a well-respected village patriarch and former monk in his seventies, agreed to tape an interview with me (one of only two elders, both men, who did) largely because of his great pride in being asked to talk about local history or *lorji* (Tib. *lo rgyus*), associated for him, as it was for Ama Drolma, with a time safely prior to Chinese intervention. Perched in the place of honor on the household warming platform, he regaled us—his son and daughter-in-law, my assistant, and I—for hours with stories about his experiences in pre- and, eventually, post-CCP Labrang, framing his narratives by situating himself at the outset as a *makwa* or surrogate son to the household, heir to the history of "our" household patriline (Tib. *rus pa*). Yet, in opposition to the historicity of both the household's legacy and socialist transformation in his narratives, when we asked him about contemporary ritual roles, he resorted to characterizing statements with the reassuring timelessness of future tense to describe the three main gender categories (see chapter 5) as arrayed in a complementary division of labor: "Monks [Tib. *grwa pa*] will do whatever monks have to do; men [Tib. *byis lu*] will do whatever men have to do; and women [Tib. *byis mo*] will do . . . whatever women have to do."

Relatedly, for Apa Sangye, the old man who had so lamented to me Apa Alo's daughter's betrayal, this ideal gender complementarity, as it had been for Apa Dondrup, was most importantly indexed by the public performativity of gendered Tibetan dress. After hours of narrating his lifetime of serving Jamyang Shepa and Apa Alo's family, his experiences as a "class enemy" during socialist transformation, and his criticisms about contemporary life in Labrang, he took me up to his private, well-appointed quarters on the second floor of his household to show me some photographs. Proudly leafing through a scrapbook he kept, he showed me hundreds of photographs not only of his clan back in his rural home region, but also many documenting Apa Alo's aristocratic line as well. He particularly pointed out a precious, creased old photograph of Apa Alo in the mid-1930s, flanked on either side by his son and his daughter (the eventual activist), all decked out in full Tibetan regalia. The next sequence of recently taken photographs depicted young women from his clan at home, showing off the splendor of their new headdresses. He pointed to these proudly and said, "See, we are real Tibetans" (Tib. *nga cho bod kho thag red*), explaining that they had just undergone the coming-of-age rite making them eligible to marry into others' households.

This he contrasted with the state of affairs in post-Mao Labrang, where a gendered person's patrifilial status in relation to households could not be always be read from their body or behavior. In effect then, patrifilial gender complementarity, previously indexed by the material wealth one carried in gendered ornaments, grounded for people a moral economy in which individuals, as members of households, could legitimately accumulate wealth within participation frameworks that regularly displayed and fulfilled reciprocal obligations. Ama Dorje remembered gendered roles in trade on behalf of households in the "Old Society," in which men like her husband accumulated capital by engaging in translocal wholesale and women by engaging in local retail trade, as the epitome of gender-neutral freedom, *not* class exploitation: "That was *such* a happy time!" (Tib. *skyid po mi nyan gi*) she exclaimed.

For these elders in the 1990s, the honesty or straightforwardness of this imagined community of reciprocally bound households of ordinary folks was historically grounded across the Maoist years in what they saw as most men's heroic, unequivocal decision to violently resist Apa Gongjia. Thus, in stark contrast to this vision, elders depicted Maoist cadres like Gyaplo as recruits to Apa Gongjia's rapacious exploitation—the real and *ongoing* local class enemies. In effect, in our conversations, elders appropriated the terms of the Marxist socioeconomic analysis first introduced in speaking-bitterness narratives and, in both explicit and implicit ways, asserted perhaps the most damning of their criticisms: that the impunity provided by the brute might of Apa Gongjia allowed certain Tibetan male cadres, as *illegitimate patriarchs* cynically operating under the moral and temporal justifications of a degendered and depoliticized minzu democracy, to continue to enrich their households based on the expropriation of the ordinary folks that had begun in 1958.

Indeed, as many analysts of Maoist state violence across the PRC have argued, perhaps the main site of locals' participation was the People's Militia, a national grassroots organization that worked, in the wake of increasing international tensions, to militarize the populace in 1958 (MacFarquhar 1983: 101). In practice, this was an alternative participation framework for local young men especially, who sought social mobility to bypass their male elders. In a sense, then, we could see the Communist revolution locally as a coup of masculinities, in which some of the worst violence was perpetrated by People's Militia toughs, young men who were often from the poorest households; they were the ones who enforced the new class order locally (cf. Dhondup Choedon 1978, Nee 1983, Chan et al. 1984, Friedman et al. 1991, Tenzin Palbar 1994). Evidence suggests that Labrang was no exception to this. Tibetan cadres like Gyaplo and Apa Thamki rose in Party and government ranks after their decision as young men in 1958 to join the People's Militia against the rebels. As Apa Thamki told me, he had renounced his monk vows as a teenager to join the Party in 1953. In 1958, he was called back to Labrang from his minority minzu cadre-training classes in Lanzhou to help put down the rebellion. His account then skipped the next decade completely. But many of the older men and women I spoke to depicted such men during subsequent "Democratic Reforms" gleefully dividing amongst themselves confiscated clothing, money, and jewelry, avoiding manual labor, and eating well during the famine by beating starving villagers and confiscating their produce for the "commune": "Don't be friends with him!" spat Ama Tsholo in 2002, after I told her and Apa Jikmay about my friendship with Apa Thamki and Ama Gazang.

For such elders, these accounts resonated strongly with their perception that those who had served the state well then continued to live well in the present, while they themselves struggled to afford butter. In urbanizing Labrang of the mid-1990s, where high inflation and the market economy required cash income for the purchase of everyday necessities, not to mention newly available luxury commodities, elders like Ama Luji consistently framed their stories of the Maoist years with angry assertions about how rich cadres were now, while the ordinary folks had no recourse at all (Tib. *bkod pa med*). Indeed at that time, some of the nicest homes I had ever been in were those built by Tibetan Party cadres after the reforms. But by 2002, Lhade elders' estimates of the huge cash salaries and pensions given to local Tibetan cadre men did not reflect the diminishing economic power of older Tibetan state cadres relative to private businessmen. By then, older men's and women's angry stories of binary class exploitation worked to simplify and to make sense of an increasingly complex situation, in which once again they felt the nature of human agents and their moral responsibilities to be greatly in flux.

The wives of Gyaplo and Apa Thamki, both of whom I came to know, were then in particularly difficult positions vis-à-vis the past and the present; they had situated themselves in gendered roles complementing men others deemed to be illegitimate patriarchs. I spoke with Ama Karma, Gyaplo's earnest and histrionic sixty-four-year-old wife, for an afternoon in their extremely well-appointed and newly renovated home in a village Lhade. As a former "liberated woman" who, as others told me, had joined the Party with her husband in 1958, cooking for PLA troops sent to put down Tibetan rebels, she had apparently taken up the ideal supporting role of a socialist minority woman and had benefited from her husband's salary and connections over time. Thus the terms of Ama Karma's narratives contrasted sharply with those of other elders I spoke to. She was most concerned by the (to her) inexplicable breakdown of trust and social order in contemporary Labrang, and unlike others did not link this situation to the disingenuous agency of Apa Gongjia during the Maoist years. Instead, she tended to situate ultimate responsibility at the local level, thus metalinguistically aligning herself with the new (masculine) PRC order. She proudly asserted that her husband was not arrested in 1958, while only those men who became "bandits" (Ch. and Tib. tufei *byas dang*) were arrested. And she situated responsibility for adjudicating work points in their collective not, as had Ama Luji, with her own husband, Gyaplo, the production-brigade Party secretary, but with the lowest-level woman cadre at that time, the production group head (Ch. *zuzhang*).

Ama Gazang was also awkwardly positioned. As a village woman who never became a cadre, she had, for reasons I never knew, married Apa Thamki later, after the worst of the state violence, but she had benefited from his salary and Party networks during his long career after the Cultural Revolution. Thus her own angry and very detailed stories about witnessing "bad" Tibetan cadres after 1958 could have been indirectly condemning her own husband. She wavered, then, between vilifying such men for their conscious actions on one hand and asserting that they weren't really responsible (Tib. *khag med gi*) on the other, since everyone was terrified and every level of cadre had to answer to superiors. When I asked if any of those cadres were still alive, she quickly insisted no, they had all died. But others insisted otherwise. Apa Denzin was perhaps most direct. After he had described how during the famine the ordinary folks like himself were reduced to hiding food from the cadres in the pockets of their robes, he declared that there were still many of those former Tibetan activists around. "They are retired now," he said. Then, switching to a first-person-plural subject, he said: "Outwardly [Tib. *kha nang na*] we are nice to them, but inwardly [Tib. *khog na*] no one likes them. We don't forget."

CONCLUSION: ALTARING TIME-SPACE: BUDDHIST HISTORICITY AND KARMIC JUSTICE

FROM FIELD NOTES: As our four-hour-long conversation finally wound down, Apa Jikmay, Ama Tsholo, and I were all emotionally drained. But they still felt compelled to extend their metalanguage about the past from the spoken frameworks of their narratives to the unspoken communication of beloved enclaved objects. In awed succession, they showed me objects they had hidden during the Maoist years: the water-stained book documenting the fourteenth Dalai Lama's trip with the Panchen Lama to Beijing in 1955 to meet Mao, an old Swiss pocket watch, and a precious *zhi* stone Ama Tsholo swore the tenth Panchen Lama had given her uncle. But their most reverent display was saved for last—they ushered me over to see their new household altar or shrine (Tib. *mchod khang*). Filling the whole wall, it was rendered in hand-carved wood and nicely painted. Ama Tsholo lovingly pointed out each item. Unlike other altars I had seen, there was only one Buddha image, a small golden statue of the historical Buddha Śākyamuni, given pride of place in the center. Ama Tsholo explained that her own older sister, who had fled to India in 1958 and returned to visit for the first time after reforms, had brought them the image along with the offering implements of small cups and butter lamps. The main items in the altar, however, were photographs of beloved trulkus—the tenth Panchen Lama, the fourteenth Dalai Lama, and a recent portrait of the four contemporary "golden throne" trulkus at Labrang, including Gongtang.

As we have seen, Tibetans in Labrang in the mid-1990s were variously positioned vis-à-vis the revitalized monastic community and state institutions amidst the rapid flux and intensifying inequity of a market economy. As they gradually recruited me to participate in the structures of their everyday lives, I came to realize how certain elders' dissenting narratives of the Maoist years were an important part of a much larger Tibetan oppositional practice of time in which Tibetans across the community *and* across generations were engaged. I was not the only one hearing oppositional testimonials in the Labrang region. Such stories circulated widely among Tibetans as second- and thirdhand accounts told by children and grandchildren, or as unsourced legend. But older men's and women's choice to narrate versions to me in the midst of our broad-ranging conversations about their lives highlighted the persistently antagonistic dialogue between gendered discourses and participation frameworks that were premised on clashing moralizing logics of space and time, despite official historiography's threatening dominance in public spaces.

In the context of great political danger associated with speaking to a foreigner, men's and women's alternative speaking-bitterness testimony powerfully worked to disclaim the "autobiographical pact" to which they had all presumably testified during Maoist class struggle, replacing it with the conviction of their contemporary narrating selves. As we have seen, this was not a process of mere substitutions of narrative elements. Instead, the shared gendered terms of their oppositional testimony worked to circumscribe the efficacy of the Chinese state and effectively distanced their contemporary selves from its narrative premises. Unlike the vast majority of my interactions with local Tibetans, elders' dissenting first-person testimonials about the interventions of Apa Gongjia were limited, like Maoist speaking-bitterness narratives and the minzu subjectivity they sought to produce, to social and thus radically secular spatiotemporal terms. In this, these stories were distinguished from and subordinated, often in the same conversation, to other, more predominant discourse genres in which space and time expanded to include other possibilities for efficacious power that overwhelmed state-sponsored socialist realism with its own realness and encompassing morality.

In fact, the truth claims of both men's and women's oppositional testimony about the Maoist years were fundamentally linked to the performativity of their own and others' faith in the opposing gendered historicity of the Buddha Dharma, as manifest especially in the heroic power of local trulkus. Indexing the failure of cadres' attempts in the 1950s and 1960s to substitute the charisma of Mao Zedong for that of Tibetan lamas, as far as I know there are no stories among Tibetans about the supernatural (or, better, supersocial) powers of Apa Gongjia (cf. Mueggler 2001). As against the highly intentioned and thus arbitrary coercive force of Apa Gongjia, elders were much more interested in registering their awed amazement (Tib. *ya mtshar*) in recounting local lore about the fundamentally unintentioned and thus objectively transcendent power of Tibetan lamas over time and space. In those accounts, even those about their own lifetimes, women tended to defer to men, and both men and women marked time not with calendrical years but with a central trulku's position as a particular incarnation in a lineage (e.g., *sku sngan ma* or *sku 'di*, the previous incarnation or this incarnation). Thus, despite new forms of self-expression in first-person narratives of ordinary men's *and* women's social lives, these elders still reverently maintained a gendered hierarchy of discourse genres by subordinating and orienting their own stories to those of paternal masculine authorities. In this way, they accomplished in speech what they also embodied in revitalized ritual practices—men and women collaborated to reconstruct an alternative patrifilial Tibetan public, one that rehierarchized registers of exchange to reassert altruistic trulkus as the main media of transvaluation.

In the newly insulated spaces of private households in reform-era Labrang, we could see household altars like that of Apa Jikmay and Ama Tsholo to be key forms of multimedia metacommunication about the past. Almost every Tibetan household I visited had an altar, enclaved in a special cabinet and adorned as lavishly as the household could muster. The nicest of these were referred to as *kunga rawa*, literally meaning "pleasure grove" but referring to shrines or temples and thus beautifully ornamented enclaved spaces for the transmission of the Dharma. In post-Mao Labrang, such altars could cost several thousands of yuan, and the various offering implements of butter lamps and bowls could cost hundreds more. For these households, the altar was the ritual and moral center of gravity. It was the site of daily and special annual offering exchanges with deities animated in the receptacle-images and statues by lamas' vivification rites, in which various pleasing offerings were exchanged for both this-worldly blessings and karmic merit. Those exchanges were often coordinated with exchanges made in Lhade manikhang and were keyed especially to the monastic ritual calendar culminating in the lunar new year (Losar, Tib. lo gsar) and the Great Prayer Festival.[42]

Importantly, though, the size and elaborateness of the household altar, ideally arranged under the stewardship of men alone, not only indexed a household's contemporary economic status amidst heightened competition and increasing socioeconomic difference among Tibetans, but it also *iconically situated* the household patrimony in an intimate and idiosyncratic history and hoped-for future of patrifilial links to particular trulkus' mandalic orders—offerings made there indexed the dedication of commercial value to Buddhist monastic authority. Hence, in Labrang the largest photographs, and those placed highest, in household altars tended to be the current Jamyang Shepa and Gongtang, but each had smaller old and new photos of other favorite trulkus, including boy trulkus who had reincarnated those who had died during the Maoist years—in this revitalized moral economy, trulkus and deities were again important agents *and* objects of exchanges that transformed capital into the higher Buddhist values of blessings and karmic merit.

When trulkus reinhabited Labrang monastery in the early 1980s, most villagers and nomads quickly reoriented themselves to them as their supporting Lhade, even before the collectives were completely disbanded. And one of the very first acts of restoration that monastic officials oversaw was the repair of the five reliquary stupas of the previous Jamyang Shepas (GGK 1987). I argue that the massive appeal of this move for Tibetan men and women, despite the ongoing salience and oftentimes gross inequities of a gender hierarchy among them, was the opportunity to publicly relocate moral agencies and exchange in the knowable space and time of a Buddhist cosmology. Thus in the gendered division of ritual labor in household altar practice enabled by and dedicated to personal trulkus, both men and women reasserted an ideal hierarchical gender complementarity that located them in the ongoing, unbroken historicity of a Geluk mandalic framework.[43] It was after all through the medium of their household altar under Apa Jikmay's stewardship that Ama Tsholo and her sister were reunited in that framework after the Maoist years.

But for Tibetans it was arguably trulkus' exclusive transcendent power to relink speech and mind/heart in post-Mao Labrang that grounded the unmarked nature of their masculine authority at the top of this hierarchy. As enlightened beings and community leaders centered in the monastery, lamas animated and arbitrated the karmic historical world of moral justice. Elders like Apa Dondrup most often referred to this concept with the compound *jundray* (Tib. *rgyu 'bras*), which constructed individuals' actions as causes (*rgyu*) that inevitably produced just effects (*'bras*) within and across lifetimes. For him, the split between the "Old Society" and the new under Chinese rule was characterized by a fundamental loss of *jundray* in the legal arbitrations of authorities. Further, as people nearing the ends of their lives, I found that older men's and women's stories of Maoist violence were framed in their ongoing karmic preparations for death and transmigration through the accumulation of merit (Tib. *dge ba*). As Ama Luji explained, proudly showing me their household's elaborate altar lined with offerings placed in front of images of deities, the Dalai Lama, Jamyang Shepa, and Gongtang: "In Buddhism you must do good things like this, or else after you die your soul [Tib. *rnam shes*] has no place to go."

For those who lived with the impunity of Apa Gongjia and Tibetan cadres for the violence of socialist transformation in Labrang, the inevitability of death was

FIGURE 11.
Images of local trulkus and deities for sale in a Labrang street
market during the summer of 1993. Largest photos: *left,* Gongtang
Tshang; *right,* current (sixth) Jamyang Shepa, a layman.

associated with the inevitability of karmic justice. Crucially, trulkus were not necessarily direct and conscious arbiters of this justice, but in their capacity as embodiments of the Dharma, they could see, and thus witness to, the unerasable karmic
fruits of any individuals' good or bad deeds in the past, and provide guidance for
future moral action before one died. As Ama Luji explained: "When you go to
worship Jamyang Shepa, you cannot tell lies, because he knows your mind" (Tib.
sems la shes gi). In a way then, trulkus' very presence in the Tibetan community
laid bare hidden histories of unspoken conscience, representing always the potential to distinguish those whose choices remained "straightforward" during the
Maoist years from those whose choices did not. Thus, like several others who told
oppositional stories about that time, Ama Luji's smile was both satisfied and sarcastic when she noted that many old Tibetan Party members, like Apa Thamki,
now quietly sought the karmic guidance of trulkus and worked hard to accumulate good merit. Even Ama Karma and Gyaplo had a gorgeous altar in their home.

But such ironic observations of cadres' public and private piety were not enough
to assuage community rage about Maoist state violence that circulated in stories
about trulkus. "Most of the Tibetan activists have died," insisted Apa Gyalo, the old
retired trader who told me that he had been horribly struggled throughout the
Maoist years, and, he continued, switching to the first person plural, "we say that
was *jundray* [karmic justice]. We say that for doing such things you will die [Tib. *shi
'gro dgos*]." I had heard, in other conversations, stories passionately told about the

circumstances of their deaths. According to my lay male friend Kazang and his young monk nephew, neither of whom personally experienced Maoist violence, when the great trulku Gongtang was finally released from prison in 1979 and returned to Labrang the following year, locals responsible for violence against the monastery and its monks and lamas began to die horrible deaths, which Kazang and his nephew described in gory detail as the slow torture of unexplained illnesses. This they interpreted as due to the wrath of Gongtang.

Such stories of karmic retribution in the presence of trulkus most vividly pitted the locally grounded yet transcendent masculine empowerment of Tibetan trulkus against the alien and arbitrary masculine authority of Apa Gongjia. The graphic terms of unmerited bodily violence introduced in Maoist speaking-bitterness stories are here reworked to describe the inevitable karmically wrought sufferings of a Buddhist hell. In the tense political environment of reform-era Labrang, where state officials hopefully constructed Tibetans as docile Zangzu, and Tibetan Buddhism as a benign aspect of traditional ethnic custom and a profitable tourist spectacle, "history" was anything but a static collective story, for locals and state officials alike. Instead, as my narrative participation both triggered and foreclosed Tibetans' representations of the traumas of socialist transformation, I came to see that alternative historiography among Tibetans was an ongoing and deeply gendered interpretive battle—with themselves as well as with the state. In the face of increasing socioeconomic inequality among Tibetans and a generation gap they feared would erase their memories among the young, older men's and women's private counternarratives of the past vigorously posited a radically different social and moral world from that of Maoist historiography and PRC minzu citizenship, a world in which the Chinese Communist revolution united honest and pious lay Tibetans as a community of exploited "ordinary folks" who were still morally grounded by heroic laymen. Meanwhile, the transcendent witness of trulkus both revealed and adjudicated the truly unspeakable—the unredressed state violence and illegitimate patrimonies of local cadres.

THREE · Mother Home

Circumambulation, Femininities,
and the Ambiguous Mobility of Women

THE GENDERED
TRAJECTORIES OF REFORM

The gap between statist forgetting and local remembering first came to a head in post-Mao Labrang in September 1979, six months before the rehabilitated trulkus Gongtang and the tenth Panchen Lama arrived to make Labrang a national model of Tibetan monastic revitalization (cf. Tian 1991). That was when, with the relative detente in Beijing-Dharamsala relations after the epochal third plenum of the eleventh CCP congress, the first of three fact-finding delegations sent by the Dalai Lama, and led by his older brother Lobsang Samten, made its first stop in Labrang before heading on to Lhasa. In a spontaneous event that was to presage similar ones throughout Tibetan regions, cadres accompanying the delegation were reportedly completely nonplussed when thousands of Tibetan men and women from across the region swamped the delegation on the main road and in the empty space before the remaining monastic buildings with heartfelt worship and sobbing testimony about their sufferings (cf. W. Smith 1996: 566; Tsering Shakya 1999). Lobsang Samten recounted his experience in Labrang, his first encounter with rural Tibetans in the PRC, this way (cited in Avedon 1984: 333):

> We opened our windows, it was unbelievable. Everywhere people were shouting, throwing scarves, apples, and flowers. They were dying to see us. They broke the windows of all the cars. They climbed on the roofs and pushed

inside, stretching out their hands to touch us. The Chinese were screaming, "don't go out! don't go out! they'll kill you! they'll kill you!" All of the Tibetans were weeping, calling, "how is the Dalai Lama? How is his Holiness?" We yelled back, "he is fine. How are you?" Then when we saw how poor they were, it was so sad, we all started crying too.

That event was arguably the first and only occasion since CCP intervention in which Tibetans in Labrang rehistoricized public space with oppositional metalanguage. As such, it starkly embodied locals' repudiation of the egalitarian pretensions of Maoist socialist androgyny, and, as elsewhere in the wake of the delegations' visits over the next two years, it demonstrated to reform-minded CCP leaders the marked status or "special characteristics" of Tibetans' place in the nation's historical trajectory.

As Melvyn Goldstein and others have argued, the CCP regime shift with the rise of Deng Xiaoping and his pragmatist policies in the late 1970s and early 1980s "was one of the most dramatic transformations in 20th century Chinese history" (1998b: 1). And yet, as Tibetans' narrative recourse to the ongoing presence of Apa Gongjia in post-Mao Labrang implied, in Tibetan regions especially, Dengist state leaders merely attempted to *recontextualize* the paternal moral authority of the CCP-led revolution in order to distance themselves from the "leftist mistakes" of the Maoist years and lead the nation back to the proper linear road toward a (still socialist) modernity.

In the early 1980s, this recontextualization of national space and time was perhaps epitomized in Hu Yaobang's efforts as the new Party secretary to hark back to earlier CCP paternalist rhetoric and recast reformist CCP intervention in the TAR as humanitarian aid, only now the Party offered aid in revalorizing the "autonomy" of Zangzu status while "opening up" the region to market forces and expert-led development. As we saw in chapter 2, what I would call a state-sponsored "market-induced amnesia" was particularly important in post-Mao Tibetan regions for redomesticating angry and exhausted locals within this reconfigured PRC nation-space. Attempting to convince the Dalai Lama to return from exile, Hu asserted as much in 1981: "The Dalai Lama should be confident that China has entered a new stage of long-term political stability, steady economic growth and mutual help among all minzu. . . . There should be no more quibbling over the events of 1959" (cited in Goldstein 1997: 68; cf. Jamyang Norbu 1992; W. Smith 1996: 575; Hessler 1999; Tsering Shakya 1999: 381).

As we will see, this new process of reform *and* statist forgetting in post-Mao

Labrang was to rely on promises to locals of the novel pleasures of agentive consumption and mobility in order to reincorporate Labrang into an *ideally segmented* spatial order, one that, like the 1996 Cham Chen, would elide state discipline while containing Labrang monastery as an icon of the past, nonetheless conducive to the forward march of civilizing modernity (cf. PRC State Council 2001). From the perspective I have been developing in the previous chapters, we of course would have to understand this multilayered process as a deeply gendered one. In this light, perhaps the most important change with Deng's reforms was the shift in the locus of valorized masculine agency away from the quotidian spaces and times of the Maoist state infrastructure and toward translocal mobility and the alluring future horizons of private (capitalist) enterprise (cf. Comaroff and Comaroff 2000: 295). But in this chapter I argue that, with post-Mao "stability" and "development" in the locality the highest priorities in the Labrang region, the "feminine hinge" was, as before, a crucial pivot in efforts to effect this historical transition for cadres and ordinary folks alike.

As we began to see at the end of chapter 2, for Tibetans in Labrang by the mid-1990s, this process played out most saliently in the gendered spatial politics of shifting divisions of ritual labor. In this chapter, I turn these considerations to an exploration of perhaps the most broadly quotidian and public of ritual work among Tibetans as a way to explore the gendered nature of both state-sponsored reforms and monastic revitalization in Labrang. During my fieldwork, I spent much of my time walking in circles. From the beginning of my stay, I entered the flow of local Tibetans' lives by joining the near-constant flow of foot traffic along what was arguably the most important course of movement for Tibetans in the entire valley: the newly rebuilt, three-mile-long circumambulation path tracing the perimeter of the monastery grounds. A daily circuit around the monastery was an ideal way to interact with Tibetans, because this particular path, what locals called the *shikor* (Tib. *phyi skor*, lit. "outer circuit"), seemed to be the most open of public spaces connected to the monastery. Indeed, as Robert Ekvall put it decades ago (1964b: 248), this could still be called "the most social of all religious observances" among Tibetans in Labrang, because the path mapped out a participation framework in which worshippers from all walks of life shared the same space and orienting practice.

But I was to realize that historically, and especially in recent years, this was not a space in which differences dissolved, but was one in which the very communal nature of its practices persistently delineated gendered ethnic differences that were foundational to Geluk *re*mandalization efforts after reforms. As the name of the path suggests, circumambulation is, among other things, about boundaries. And I attempted to cross one every time I strode onto the path, turned my right side to the monastery, and got in line to turn the prayer wheels and send the mantra-prayer of *om mani padme hum* into its efficacious spinning. Even though, as I mentioned in the introduction, the path turned out to be the most important public framework for my gradual "regendering" as a knowable feminine subject for locals, I also was occasionally brought up short there by some women who were very aware of my difference from them and what it represented in post-Mao Labrang. Here, I argue that such moments of misrecognition, in which I walked the circumambulation path and yet did not enter into the Tibetan women's' participation frameworks, were most fundamentally shaped by our different assumptions about the parameters and historical legacies of female sexedness.

THE MICROPOLITICS OF SEX AND CONTEXTUALIZATION: EMBODYING SPACES

In this chapter I consider circumambulation (Tib. *skor ba 'gro pa, skor ba byed pa;* lit. "to encircle") as a gendered spatial practice in order to map out some of the processes by which Tibetans in Labrang, especially Lhade residents, worked to reestablish important boundaries after the political economic shifts and personal traumas of socialist transformation. My focus on the contested production of gendered space amidst new "quandaries of agency" in post-Mao Labrang will demonstrate the importance of an emerging oppositional politics of embodiment among Tibetans, in which Tibetan forms of sexedness grounded alternative frameworks for recognizing persons and deities as legitimate agents in local and translocal exchanges. In other words, in such routine spatializing practices as circumambulation, the grounds for a sex-gender hierarchy, locating differently empowered male and female bodies within a reconfigured Tibetan mandalic order and in karmic time, were being relaid in the 1990s, despite ideologies advocating Buddhist or modern feminist forms of gender equality, and in the midst of countervailing practices under the press of the globalizing state and economy.

Here I deepen my analysis of the local dynamics of gender and monastic revitalization in Labrang by exploring further the micropolitics of contextualization embedded in everyday interactions. In the previous three chapters, Erving Goffman's spatial concept of "participation frameworks" has served to conceptualize the indexical links people forged between contemporary selves and events and competing macro spaces and times. In this chapter, I draw on the insights of Goffman and others on the *micro*subtleties and "astonishing flexibility" (Goffman

FIGURE 12.
Tibetan women turn newly rebuilt prayer wheels in the summer of
1992. Shikor circumambulation path, east side, Labrang monastery.

1981: 147) of situated talk to emphasize the fundamentally intersubjective and often
unconscious nature of meaning production among gendered subjects in post-Mao
Labrang (cf. M. Goodwin 1990, Mannheim and Tedlock 1995, McDermott and
Tylbor 1995, Hanks 1996, Irvine 1996, Keane 1997, Silverstein 1997).

From this perspective, we consider the ways interlocutors constantly negotiate
relevant participation frameworks by deploying locally salient linguistic and bodily
cues to signal their alignments, or "footings," with respect to their utterances and
to each other, as well as to a range of other social contexts and agencies (Goffman
1981: 128). We could thus see participants' footing shifts in interactions as a most
elemental level of cultural politics, a process in which interlocutors, in shifting participant roles, dialogically construct a metapragmatics of meaning and action in
unequal social fields (cf. Mannheim and Tedlock 1995, Duranti 1997). Recalling my
arguments about gender, space, and contextualization in chapter 1, this, then, is
another avenue through which to grasp the subtle simultaneity of space-time in
post-Mao Labrang—the ongoing and often mundane cultural work by which people marked off and constructed arrangements of gendered subjects, places, and
nations amidst the actually messy and recently intensifying interconnectedness of
people and spaces in the valley.

Perhaps the most charged of participation frameworks were those produced through the state-local politics accompanying the development of the tourism industry focused on the revitalizing monastery. Since the mid-1980s, tourism had drawn tens of thousands of foreign and domestic visitors, the vast majority of whom were Han Chinese urbanites (Yang Ming 1992: 14).[1] In this shifting milieu, I found that in my conversations with Tibetan locals across generations, their metalinguistic assertions about Tibetan sexedness (the nature of [Tibetan] males versus females) helped them to identify local relationships between body and mind, household and monastery, and to reorient bodies and projected futures to the essential *centricity* of the Buddhist values produced by trulkus and their monastic assemblies in the monastery.

As a key activity for the reproduction of such mandalic spaces of exchange, circumambulation practice offered frameworks for the assertion of Tibetan sexedness in new ways, thus forming a moving boundary that constructed gendered spaces vital to the Tibetan community within great spatial and political economic transformations that rendered them more precarious than ever before. As we will see, femaleness for Tibetans was, as before, marked as a relatively impure and karmically undeveloped state of human personhood. But I argue that, in the ferment of economic reforms touting the allure and national benefits of intensified translocality, locals' claims to Tibetan femaleness repudiated the expanded public spaces of Maoist socialist androgyny and grounded instead the cyclic reproductive labor of newly insulated Tibetan households. Women were thus positioned as disproportionately responsible for the maintenance of Labrang as a Tibetan *locality*. Importantly, this played out in an idiom of women's maternal nurturance that nostalgically positioned Tibetan *nay* or lay "homes" (Tib. *gnas*) as sites for the ideal absence of the translocal motives of Apa Gongjia, and thus as vital substitutes for the lost hegemony of lay-monastic masculine alliances across the phayul. In this context, then, in contrast to the romantic presumption among some foreigners that tourism journeys somehow essentially shared the spatial orientations of locals' pilgrimages, the presumptive translocal mobility my feminine presence indexed on the circumambulation path sharply distinguished me from the village women I encountered there.[2]

THE DILEMMAS OF DEVELOPMENT:
MODERNITY AND MOBILITY

In 1985, the year provincial officials opened Labrang to foreign tourism, Labrang monastery had revitalized with state support to become the figurehead Tibetan

Buddhist monastery in Gannan prefecture and in Amdo Tibetan regions generally.[3] That very year, a Tibetan layman named Phakwa Gyab published "The Magnificence of My Phayul," a poem of praise to his fatherland, Labrang, in Gannan's popular Tibetan-language literary journal *Daser* (Tib. *ʒla ʒer*, lit. "Moonlight").[4] As a lay male friend told me, that journal was part of the boom in secular Tibetan-language literature of the early 1980s, and he fondly remembered how he used to avidly acquire and circulate every issue among his lay male and monk friends learning to read and write Tibetan in those early reform years. In a distinctly hybrid poem of sixteen four-line stanzas, combining formal and semantic elements of popular songs and Buddhist praise poetry, Phakwa Gyab carefully constructs an optimistic vision of his phayul as thriving after the reopening of both the monastery and the market under the *now* enlightened policies of the CCP. Importantly, his veiled critique of the disastrous policies of Maoist Party regimes takes the form of a poem that iconically reproduces crucial aspects of the spatiotemporal pretensions of Dengist state claims to Labrang.

With characteristic Buddhist hyperbole and metaphor, Phakwa Gyab devotes the first eight stanzas to framing Labrang monastery as the center and "ornament" of his fatherland, ending up by positioning it above the world of humans as the source and *abode* of the highest possible values embodied in Buddhist image-receptacles and teaching lineages:

der bzhugs rten dang brten pa
rin thang gzhal du med pa
'dzam gling yongs gyi gces nor
bsdus kyang 'gran par mi bzod

'dzam gling gtsug gi rgyan gcig
mdo smad bkra shis gyas 'khyil
chos rgyud 'byung pa'i *gnas mchog*
mkhas mang 'byung ba'i zhing yin

The divine objects and temples there
are precious beyond measure [so that]
even if all the cherished wealth in the world
were gathered together, it still would not compare.

An ornament on top of the world,
Amdo's Tashi Khyil is
the supreme abode from which come the lineages of teachings
and the heavenly realm from which come the multitudes of scholars.

Then, with an abrupt footing shift that (unintentionally?) emphasizes the inapt nature of the juxtaposition, Phakwa Gyab devotes the final eight stanzas to hyperbolic praise for modernizing secular development in Labrang, enumerating, as in this stanza, the valley's natural resources and praising the availability of consumer goods:[5]

'ur 'ur sgra yis gnon pa'i
yangs pa'i tshong ra'i khrod du
tshong zog rin chen sna tshogs
klu rgyal mdzod la 'gran 'dug

In the midst of the vast marketplace
Pressed in by the noisy [bustle]
Various precious consumer goods
Contend with the storehouses of the Naga king.

Appealing to the awkwardly double-voiced metaphor of the sun,[6] the final stanza attributes this praiseworthy state of affairs to the "sun" of the Party in the (newly clear) sky of reform policies:

bsngags 'os pha yul ljongs 'dir
'gyur bzhi'i pad tsal rgyas phyir
tang gi jus mchog nyi ma
dwangs gsal mkha' nas shar song//

In order to cultivate the lotus grove of the Four Modernizations
In this praiseworthy fatherland,
The sun of the Party's excellent policies
Has risen in the clear sky.

From the perspective I have been developing in the previous chapters, we could see Phakwa Gyab's praise poem for his fatherland as a layman's early reform-era effort at strategic misrecognition in order to rehierarchize Labrang under the masculine authority of the monastery as a supreme and divine *nay* or "abode" (Tib. *gnas*), a stance representing in poetry a process that, as we are beginning to see, was embodied in everyday and ritual practice among Tibetans across the valley after reforms. That is, structurally and semantically, he orients the phayul first to the higher and centered ground of the monastery, effectively reversing the implied spatial order of the Dengist state's vision of the segmented coexistence iconically expressed in the slogan *aiguo aijiao* (Love Your Country; Love Your Religion). But the poem also indexes the difficult dilemmas posed by younger Tibetans' hopeful compromises with the new regime: both structurally and semantically, it reproduces the ideal containment of the monastery as a discrete and domesticated local realm of picturesque objects and rationalized knowledge production benignly complementing modernization. In Phakwa Gyab's vision of linear progress in the valley, there are no recalcitrant and mobile nomad tribes, only individually motivated, hardworking, frugal local residents; there are no trulkus, not to mention their translocal masculine tantric prowess, and there is no socioeconomic or patrifilial link between the subjects of the first and second halves of the poem.

I would argue that, in the optimistic "first blush" of the reform years in Labrang, Phakwa Gyab's reiteration of a new statist spatiotemporal order, even as he reclaimed his Tibetan phayul, was not just due to his prudence in the face of state limits on public metalanguage. Instead, his poem indexes the legitimacy, especially for younger Tibetans at that time, of a capitalist modernization telos, a utopic aspiration that provided locals with both new grounds for strategic misrecognition *and* new dilemmas under CCP rule. Indeed, as attested in policy papers and Han economists' writings, in Labrang the discursive grounds for liberalizing or "opening" both monastery and market within a radically reconfigured "socialism" was the claim to a new moral economy with a nationalist future. As many have pointed out, Deng's call for citizens to participate in the "Four Modernizations" (Ch. *si ge xiandaihua*) drew on earlier CCP debates in order to reconstitute ideal PRC subjects—his reforms were to liberate citizens so they could pursue their progressive natures as both hardworking producers and unselfish household consumers (cf. Ma Guangrong 1990, Teng 1990). This bottom-up process, fueled by measures to cut investment in heavy industry and increase household incomes and consumption by investing in agriculture and commodity production, would then inevitably spur modernization and development on a national scale (cf. Dutton 1998; Hunter and Sexton 1999: 73). Thus, in a stunning reversal of Maoist policies that was made official only with the fourteenth CCP congress in 1992, Dengist state leaders in many ways effectively joined a global trend in touting the efficacy of (capitalist) market economics as a stateless, national moral order (cf. Comaroff and Comaroff 2000: 294).

Yet in post-Mao Labrang, the contradictions endemic to capitalism in centralized states were arguably particularly acute. That is, the specter of ethnic conflict in the frontier zone underscored the inherent dilemma facing Chinese state-sponsored capitalists: the need for citizens' flexible or mobile labor and consumptive agency on one hand and the need for state control of their labor loyalties and aspirational mobility on the other (cf. Dutton 1998: 10). Indeed, the Han social scientist Gong Xikui, in a 1989 article advocating the moral superiority of capitalist opening up, argues that the CCP household-registration system (Ch. *hukou dengji*) linking household members across generations to rural or urban residence needed to be reformed because it cast a "thick feudal cloud" over China's economy, fixing citizens in hierarchical rural-urban spatial relationships that did not allow for vertical sociospatial mobility. Instead, he asserts, the new market economy should promise the personal liberation of choice of work and abode according to levels of skill in enterprise (translated in Dutton 1998: 85).

But as the Han economist Teng Pingwen put it, describing the ideal reform process in Gansu minority regions as a studied balance between opening up and ongoing state regulation: "Reforms must promote both invigoration at the micro level and control at the macro level in order to maintain and encourage the stability and the development of the whole economy" (1990: 12). Yet the vision of regional development for the frontier zone advocated by Han and Tibetan economists and social scientists imagined an invigorated market economy replacing a "long-term, selfish, closed natural economy that shackled the farmers and nomads and rigidified their thinking" (Ma Guangrong 1990: 165; cf. Gesang Daji 1993). This new form of (state-guided) development would then finally rid the region of its *self*-imposed "historical" and infrastructural handicaps, bringing the time-space compression of modernization to bear in order to fully integrate the frontier with the national economy and community.

As I mentioned in my introduction, I found that Tibetans in Labrang had oriented themselves to the dilemmas raised by their precarious position on this linear road to development. Tibetans frequently seemed to assume that all non-Tibetans, Han, Hui, and foreign visitors, were agents of change, while they themselves were not. Many, especially younger generations, had assimilated an impression that Tibetan culture was somehow inferior and "backward" or "left behind" (Ch. *luohou*, Tib. *rje ldos*), even as "modernizing" change was associated with an intergenerational loss of Tibetan ethnic and moral humanity. I was frequently told by Tibetans young and old, from the valley as well as from other regions, that Labrang was the wealthiest and most "open" (Ch. *kaifang*), and hence morally lax, town in Gannan.

In this, local Tibetans were grappling not only with their relationships to the past, but also with their ongoing structural disadvantages under reforms. That is, under economic policies privileging the "opening up" of urban centers to the east, by 1995, when I was in Labrang, the great benefits of relatively easy social and geographic mobility, professional careers, and leisurely consumption were still largely accessible to Han urbanites. In fact, the thrust of development efforts in the Labrang region was arguably toward keeping Tibetans *rooted locally* as either primary producing households (the vast majority of Lhade residents outside Labrang town were farmers and nomads) or, under the slogan *litu bu lixiang* (Leave the Land, but Don't Leave the Township), as local entrepreneur households leaving primary production while living and investing locally in "township enterprises " (cf. GGK 1987: 119; Gesang Daji 1993: 58).

The massive provincial investment in bridges and highways in the early 1980s culminated in the completion of the Lanzhou-Gannan national highway(cf. Yi 1993). Han and foreign tourists thereafter made a five-hour trip to Labrang across mountainous terrain that until the 1950s had taken caravans of pack animals and their armed escorts a week or more one way. Those journeys regularly compressed the complex spaces and times separating Lanzhou from Labrang into weekend or even day trips.[7] But this time-space compression of the post-Mao "opening up" process did not eradicate the unequal spatial relationship between the frontier zone and the Chinese "interior" that had emerged in the early twentieth century and intensified during the Maoist years.[8]

Instead, urban tourists' translocal mobility both relied on and constituted the ideal *immobility* of local Tibetans in time and space. That is, their journeys traced the course of the intensifying assimilation and exploitation over time of the Tibetan frontier by Chinese state regimes. Indeed, tourists' efforts to extract value from Tibetans in the form of images and experiences positioned Tibetans again as primary producers at the bottom of a national regime of value. As Marshall and Cooke (1997) state, natural resources in the prefecture were still all state-owned; apparatuses to extract them were dominated by Han, and processing plants were outside the prefecture in urban areas.[9] Further, the "responsibility system," in which households, now the main units of production, were responsible for remitting to the state annual "quotas" of their products at below-market prices, was still in place in nomad regions, effectively allowing for state extraction of the products of Tibetan primary industry (especially meat, leather, and dairy products) for use elsewhere.[10] And Hui merchant families had taken up their previous niche as mediators between Tibetan products and Han and foreign buyers, competing with state bureaus for Tibetan pastoralist products, opening tourist shops, and reviving neighboring Linxia as a regional market hub for processing and resale of raw goods from pastoralism, forestry, and mining. According to Gesang Daji (1993: 54), except for villages along public highways, by the early 1990s 80 percent of the villages in

Gannan were not accessible by car, and half the townships did not have paved roads. It would seem then that highways in Gannan were primarily built to facilitate the continuing exploitation and control of the frontier, not to expedite local travel (cf. Karan 1976, GGK 1987, Ma Guangrong 1990).

As Tibetan elders' complaints about emerging class politics and urbanization among Tibetans in the valley made clear, the great allure of consumption, touted by Deng Xiaoping as the main driver of modernization, was particularly problematic for locals. Indeed, the relative scarcity of tillable land was one of the main things villagers complained to me about, and it heightened the sense, especially among the older generations, that they were increasingly vulnerable to the vagaries of inflation in the marketplace, on which many now relied for the cash purchase of subsistence goods. In fact, when Ama Drolma so adamantly refused to talk about the past with us that day, the change she *did* want to talk about was recent frightening inflation. The collectives finally broke up in 1982, and with the implementation of the "household responsibility system" in the narrow valley, households were allocated only one-half mu per person. In the 1990s, very few households had more than one or two mu of land, while many had lost theirs because of development in the urbanizing valley. By 1990, statistics for numbers of people in Labrang town registered as belonging to "nonagricultural" households ranged from 71 percent to 89 percent of residents (cf. XXZ 1997). Meanwhile, the complaints of development officials about nomads' lack of "commodity consciousness" after the dissolution of collectives arguably derived from their frustrated efforts to encourage nomads to orient their production to export sale because nomads' relative self-sufficience and interhousehold barter reduced their dependency on consumer goods and cash (e.g., Ma Guangrong 1990: 156; Ma Jiang 1993; cf. Goldstein 1989, Escobar 1995). Thus especially for Lhade households in town, the process of "becoming consumers" (Carrier and Heyman 1997), at the same time as market liberalization brought a decline in state funds and services, meant new exigencies for ordinary folks to compete for income on unequal footing with better-connected Hui or cadre households.[11]

As we saw, Tibetans across generations both implicitly and explicitly expressed their awareness that economic reforms in post-Mao Labrang still represented the will of Apa Gongjia—that is, in practice for many Tibetan households reforms did not constitute linear progress. Instead, reform policies relied on Maoist state infrastructure to *return* to the aspirations of KMT policies to domesticate the frontier through markets, not militaries. I would argue that, like the short-lived KMT campaign in the 1930s and 1940s to "develop the Northwest" (Ch. *kaifa* Xibei), the

Dengist regime in fact sought to extract value from the domesticated frontier without the costs of state violence. In this light, then, we can make more sense of the contrasting gendered representations of mobility relative to native place I found among Tibetans in the 1990s.

In Phakwa Gyab's optimistic portrait of his fatherland, the harmonious self-sufficience of both monastery and residents relies on the vigorous local market in consumer goods and services. But in his poem the hegemony of translocal masculine alliances across the grasslands and centered on the monastery has been reduced to individuated consumption under CCP auspices in the valley alone. By contrast, consider another vision of (feminized) Tibetan home that I argue was particularly prominent in the Labrang region by the 1990s. This vision was epitomized in the popular "Nostalgia Songs for Mothers" (Tib. *ama dran glu*) written and sung by young laymen especially. Amidst the personal dilemmas and structural constraints of the reform years in Labrang, those songs countered the arbitrary and illegitimate discipline and expropriation of Father State by emphasizing an ideal of what I call "Mother Home": a perduring and intensely intimate household space shaped by a Tibetan mother's unconditional nurturance yet compassionate ability to *let her grown sons leave*.

MOTHER HOME: FEMININE CYCLICITY AND FIXING THE LOCALITY

mgo yar bkyags mig gis mthong sa na
sprin dkar po lding ba'i shar phyogs na
du nag po lang long 'phyur sa na
ma drin mo che yi dur *gnas* yod
de mthong ba re la a ma dran
bu mos gus zhan rung mjal snying 'dod
mig khra ril mchi ma 'khor nas byung
ngag dal mos a ma lan gsum pos
sems skyo ba'i lag pas brang la brdungs
ngas bsam shing a ma snying nas dran

Before my upturned eyes,
To the east where the white clouds float,
And where thin black smoke billows,
There is the *home* of my kind mother.
All those visions remind me of mother.

Even though I never showed my devotion much, I so want to see her.
Tears fall in round drops from my eyes,
And I slowly call mother three times.
With melancholy heart I beat my breast with my fist.
I miss mother from the core of my heart.

In many ways this Nostalgia Song by Gangjan Oser published in 1987 in *Daser* is formulaic; yet it is also intensely personal.[12] In sixty-three lines he sketches the emotional memories a glimpse of household smoke triggers of his late mother and his natal home far away. The poem, punctuated by the formulaic refrain of missing mother from the core of his heart, traces the shape of his life cycle under her constant nurturance, and after he reaches adulthood and leaves home, she stoically declines in health, expresses her enduring love for her son at her deathbed, and dies. He ends up with heartfelt longing for the return of her nurturance and support:

tshig snyan mo thos na skyid pa la
thugs brtse bas skyong na bzang ba la

How happy [I] would be to hear her sweet words;
How good it would be to be under the care of her loving heart.

In the early reform years, at the same time as young Tibetan laymen and monks, along with rehabilitated lamas and trulkus, enthusiastically reconstituted the masculine historiography of their phayul by publishing articles in *Daser* and elsewhere about the lives of great Tibetan trulkus and lama-scholars (e.g., Lhamo skyabs 1986), "Nostalgia Songs for Mothers" (there is no counterpart genre for fathers) expressed men's aspirations for the return of the enduring cyclicity of a feminine Tibetan home. Importantly, in a trend that only intensified into the 1990s and 2000s, images of Tibetan feminine cyclicity pervaded the writings, art, videos, and music of foreigners, Han, and Tibetans alike, visions perhaps epitomized in slow-motion video montages juxtaposing images of women working at churning butter or spinning yarn with clips of women spinning handheld prayer wheels or circumambulating. Such visual tropes linked essential female sexedness to the local reproductive cycles of child rearing, household subsistence labor, *and* quotidian Buddhist ritual practice (cf. Mills 2003: 158).[13] I argue that the vision of Tibetan women as mothers or quintessential nurturers in post-Mao Labrang encapsulated an emerging spatial politics of embodiment in which femaleness grounded and substantialized *both lay and monastic* Tibetan *nay* or "abodes" amidst unprece-

母 爱   吉美 作

FIGURE 13.
"Mother Love" (Ch. *Mu Ai*), by Ji Mei
(Tib. 'jigs med). Line drawing of a
Tibetan nomad woman nursing her child
in their tent. Back cover of journal *Daser*
("Moonlight"), vol. 4 (1983).

dented ethnic heterogeneity and Chinese state hegemony (cf. Yuval-Davis 1997:
22–23). This was, then, a specifically pan-Tibetan vision of female-sexed motherly nurturance, one that countered both Father State *and* the depoliticizing thrust
of post-Mao popular and state representations of the "colonizing love" of the
Tang dynasty Chinese princess Wencheng (Bulag 2002: 94; Powers 2004: 31–38).
In those recent representations, Princess Wencheng marries the Tibetan king
Songtsan Gampo and literally mothers the Tibetan people to (relative) civilization.
In this way, I would argue, Wencheng is recontextualized in reform-era rhetoric as
a *national* mother for Tibetans, a feminine figure representing the ideally stateless
and democratic multiethnic nation under Han Chinese guidance that post-Mao
CCP leaders offered Tibetans.[14]

As Charles Keyes and others have argued, the role of mothers in Buddhist contexts cross-culturally has been overdetermined (1984: 227; cf. Ortner 1983, D. Paul
1985, Aziz 1988, Cabezón 1992, Sponberg 1992, Faure 2002). In monastic settings
like Labrang, the circumscribed nature of femaleness as feminine nurturance was
metonymic of the ideal role of local lay communities as patron supporters at the
peripheries of the central, masculine ritual work of monks and lamas. Importantly
then, appeals to femaleness both grounded a sex-gender polarity that had underwritten Geluk monastic hegemony in the frontier zone and worked to resolve the
inherent tensions that that polarity produced. As we saw in chapter 1, Geluk mandalization efforts relied on a gendered liberation path emphasizing male renunciation in monastic fraternities (ostensibly) separate from the distractions and temptations of household contexts.

Thus in the Labrang region, the great prestige and potential benefits of a monastic career based on an ideal of lifelong celibacy resulted in an ethic of "mass monasticism," which, as Melvyn Goldstein (1998a: 15) emphasizes, was unique to Tibetan contexts in the relatively large percentage of men it drew to life in monastic communities.[15] The situation at Labrang was the same as that described by Goldstein for the huge monastery of Drepung in Lhasa: the size of the monastic community, at over thirty-four hundred monks by 1949, was taken as an index of the success of Geluk mandalization locally (Pu 1990: 508). Based on figures from censuses taken in the decades before 1949, monks in the region now roughly equivalent to Gannan prefecture were about 17 percent of the Tibetan male population, while monks in Labrang monastery represented about 15 percent of the Tibetan male population in Xiahe county (Pu 1990, Li Anzhai 1992a, Zhang Tianlu 1993).[16]

As I mentioned in chapter 1, Chinese scholars and Western missionary observers in the early twentieth century were horrified at the peculiarity of the sex-gender system that consequently developed in the region and complained about the social "chaos" apparent in the juxtaposition of celibate monasticism in Labrang with the relatively open sexuality in the teeming market town next to the monastery (Gu and Lu 1938, Yu Xiangwen 1943; cf. Makley 1997; and see below, chapter 4). Indeed, as many observers have noted, there are inherent tensions in the symbiotic exchange relationship between Buddhist celibate monasticism and lay communities (Goldstein 1964, 1998a, 1998b; Tambiah 1968; Spiro 1970; Aziz 1978a; Keyes 1983, 1986; Ortner 1989; Samuel 1993). Labrang monastery, as the vital local base for Geluk mandalization in the region, relied on the laity for economic support even as its transcendent status depended on denying any polluting influence from that relationship. And the laity relied on the monastic community's taming performance of virtue as an efficacious "field of merit"—that is, to generate both this-worldly blessings and merit for better rebirths through practices of offering and homage. Hence the predicament at the heart of the Buddhist sex-gender ideal operative in Labrang: celibate monasticism posited a polarity of male- and female-sexed bodies and required their separation in a denial of (hetero)sexuality, yet it critically depended on their relations for the reproduction of its own numbers and the lay economy that supported it (cf. Miller 1980, Aziz 1988, Sponberg 1992, Gyatso 2005).

However, as we will see in this and the next chapter, historically the juxtaposition of asceticism and sexuality represented neither ludic chaos nor disingenuous monastic exploitation. Instead, what most fundamentally constructed the boundary between lay and monastic worlds were practices that produced a basic and grounding *gendered body-space* vis-à-vis the monastery—that was the gendered essence of

FIGURE 14.
View of Labrang monastery from the southeast in the winter of
1949. Marion Griebenow's Christian Missionary Alliance headquarters is the large building in the foreground. (Photo by
Wayne Persons)

mandalization across social contexts. The ongoing coherence and efficacy of this
body-space relied on the practical links locals forged between ritual and everyday
activities and discourses that placed patrifilial sexed bodies relative to spaces
reflecting a gendered social hierarchy vis-à-vis ritual power and bodily (and hence
moral) purity, with trulkus at its pinnacle and laywomen at its base (cf. Huber 1994a,
1999). I argue that in post-Mao Labrang, this process of gendered embodiment was
most importantly played out in the recognition of sexed bodies and their appropriate mobilities vis-à-vis reconstituted Tibetan *nay*. A well-known proverb in the
region succinctly expresses the ideally disciplined and complementary mobility of
males and females, gendered career trajectories that underpinned the reproduction
of the lay-monastic relationship:[17]

ban de 'gro sa sgar red/
byis mo 'gro sa *gnas* red/

The place where a young boy goes is a monastery;
The place where a young girl goes is her [new husband's] *home.*

The terminology used in the proverb reflects spatial categories in everyday use in the Labrang region. Significantly, in lay contexts Tibetans used the word *nay* to refer almost exclusively to the natal home of a *man*, so that the phrase used to refer to the preferred and still most widespread type of marriage was *nay la ndro*, literally "to go home" or "to go to a husband's natal home." Amidst the vigorous revival of the networking and exchange practices of Tibetan marriages in the Lhade under reforms, "home" for Tibetans was paradigmatically patrilocal, and men's and women's mobilities and labor obligations were evaluated relative to their spatial relationships to that ideal household.

In my conversations with Tibetans across the community, the gendered division of household labor in the valley was one of the topics that aroused the most adamant metalanguage about the essential differences between men and women. Importantly, regardless of their personal stances on it, monks, nuns, laymen, and laywomen all tended to cite a timeless notion of a sexual-karmic polarity of males and females to explain a spatialized division of labor that associated women with affairs "inside" (Tib. *nang*) the household and men with prestigious ritual and political affairs "outside" it (Tib. *phyi*).[18] In the framework of those discussions, my interlocutors, with varying degrees of explicitness, tended to argue that the male body was the result of greater stores of merit (Tib. *bsod nams*) from past lifetimes, and this underlay men's relative ability to transcend bodily and household limitations and to succeed in pursuits of the mind.

Meanwhile, the female body was marked as a lower rebirth (Tib. *skye dman*), with fewer stores of merit, and thus was more hampered by physiological processes and suited to the cyclic labor of nurturing both the members of Tibetan *nay* and their agricultural or pastoralist patrimonies.[19] None of my interlocutors explicitly emphasized the categorical psychophysical *uncleanness* (Tib. *mi gtsang ma*) of females; that notion emerged in other, implicit, ways, as people in jokes, in offhand comments, or in didactic instructions to me asserted commonsense links between uncleanness and mundane work, corporality, bad deeds, and the lack of merit. Hence, my laywoman friend Drolma castigated me when she saw a sweater on the floor in our apartment. Assuming the sweater was Cain's, she informed me, with great solemnity and knitted brow, of my error in putting his clothing on the dirty floor. Her comments linked verticality, purity, maleness, and merit as against an implied female Other: "We do not put men's clothes on the floor; men have great[er] stores of merit! We Tibetans take this extremely seriously!" Thus as against the "egalitarian" or "androgynous" Buddhism recently advocated by some foreign feminists (e.g., Gross 1993), the inferior karmic status of a female body, perhaps the most pervasive explanation for gender asymmetry in Indian and Tibetan Buddhist traditions, was highly salient in post-Mao Labrang (cf. D. Paul 1985: 170; Huber 1994a: 358; Gyatso 2003).

However, as Gangjan Oser's heartfelt sentiments illustrate, and contrary to Maoist Fulian rhetoric, this sexual-karmic polarity did *not* amount to pervasive discourses and practices of misogyny in Labrang. In part, this was due to Tibetans' resolute tendency, despite Maoist socialist realism, to construct personhood in general as the temporary outcome of ontologically continuous mental, spatial, temporal, divine or demonic, *and* corporeal factors—for Tibetans like Drolma, concerned that unclean contact would affect Cain's stored merit, the biological body did not exist as a fixed isolate but was in some ways an emergent entity subject to intentioned and unintentioned interventions (cf. Adams 1992, 1999; Huber 1994b). In theory then, as Akhu Sherap, our student Gompo's old lama, explained to me, if somatic outcomes of stores of merit were the result of a complex configuration of past actions and contemporary situations, then both sex transformation (as in female to male, male to female, or a mixture of the two) and liberative gender transformation (as in monkhood, nunhood, or lamahood) are human possibilities in this and subsequent lifetimes, regardless of the "bodily base" (Tib. *lus rten*) one is born with (cf. Huber 1999, Gyatso 2003, 2005; and see below, chapter 5). Thus I argue in this and the next two chapters that in actuality, a sexual-karmic polarity among Tibetans grounded a certain flexibility in the sex-gender system that was foundational to Geluk mandalization.

In addition, in a trend that I do not think was solely for my benefit, men and women tended to downplay notions of female uncleanness and figure females' relative inferiority in the positive terms of mothers' complementary support and labor. Thus, in practice, female inferiority served mainly to mark women as expediently positioned, *entailed Others* for male reproductivity—that is, men's' capacities to pursue, embody, and transmit the transcendent in male-exclusive lay and monastic contexts (cf. Campbell 1996: 90). In fact, I argue that amidst the exigencies of reforms, women, as potential matriarchs of patrilocal *nay*, took on heightened importance as crucial conduits and reproductive support for the revitalization of patrifilial ties among households *and* between households and the divine mandalic *nay* of deities and trulkus in the monastery.

In this, we also have to see the revitalizing lay-monastic relationship in post-Mao Labrang as a gendered politics of *deity* recognition and embodiment. Tibetologists have often remarked on Tibetans' intensely ritualized relationships with natural or constructed environments—relationships that do not always accord with Buddhist doctrine (cf. Bishop 1989, Karmay 1994, Germano 1998). In his insightful work on Tibetan pilgrimage practices, Toni Huber (1994b: 25; 1999: 10) argues that ordinary Tibetans' sense of efficacious space is shaped by intimate relationships between humans and deities that are seen to inhabit matter and bodies as well as space. As we saw in the poems and proverb cited above, in places like Labrang, the term *nay* in Tibetan, meaning "place" or "abode," or as an involuntary verb, "to be" or "to abide," was used to refer not only to patrilocal lay homes but also to Buddhist deities' mandalic abodes.

These layers of connotations point to a pervasive everyday ontology, operative among Tibetans across regions and social statuses, that emphasized the substantial or embodied nature of locals' relationships with powerful, transcendent agencies, and they foreground *contiguity* as the principal means for individuals or collectives to interact with them (cf. Huber 1999: 10). Thus in Labrang, the concept of *nay* in practice substantialized and rendered efficacious the trulku-established receptacles of Buddha images and structures, embodying practitioners in turn as participants in a mandalic order under trulku auspices. Indeed, just as Bentor (1993: 111) found among Tibetans in Nepal, in Labrang, Tibetans rarely hung images of relatively abstract mandalas in their homes, preferring consecrated deity images like statues and thangkas (scroll paintings). As elsewhere, practitioners entered into beneficial relationships with deities' *nay* primarily through rituals of "worshipful encounter" (Tib. *mjal ba*) focused on bringing the body into close contact with them. In places subject to mandalization under the tantric prowess of trulkus, such *nay* were considered to be particularly empowered places that could, in the idiom of Buddhist texts, clear away defilements hindering individuals' progress on the path to enlightenment.

Thus, as I found in Labrang, part of the wide appeal of Buddhism for monastics and laity alike was this emphasis on the efficacy of a *nay* as a function of embodied moral purity (Tib. *dag pa*). As many of my interlocutors insisted, committed contact with them could cleanse (Tib. *sel ba*) the "psychophysical person" (Huber 1999: 16) of his or her accumulated bad deeds (intentional or not)—deeds indexed by the unclean state of the ordinary body—and clear the way to desired outcomes in this or future lifetimes. Importantly, such purifying "power places" were constructed spatially along mandalic lines, having, in Huber's words, "a central focus at which resides the . . . deity of a *nay;* the closer or more directly oriented one is to this center the stronger the empowerment and more intimate the encounter" (1994b: 46). Thus, under Geluk mandalization both before and after CCP intervention, everyday and ritual interactions among Tibetans in Labrang worked to reproduce a mandalic social geography, one characterized by the priority given to (purified) centrality over (impure) periphery.

In the mid-1990s, circumambulation, in which the worshipper performed circuits around a mandalized place, object, or person, was still the practice par excellence for bringing the body into sustained and close contact with a central abode, providing the means for any faithful subject to absorb some of the very physical benefits of its power (cf. Ekvall 1964b). Yet as we will see, the exigencies of capitalist reforms effectively heightened the importance of the reproductive labor of *female* cyclic mobility vis-à-vis lay and monastic Tibetan *nay* in the valley.

REMANDALIZING LABRANG: CONTESTED CIRCUITS

Robert Ekvall (1964b: 253), in his discussion of ritual practices among Tibetans, remarked that the importance of circumambulation often went unnoticed by foreign travelers. I found this to be the case in Labrang, where the unceasing flow of Tibetans turning the prayer wheels around the monastery seemed to get lost in the bustle of state-sponsored tourism and commercial activity focused on the great monastic buildings and festivals. I argue however that it was this quotidian activity, at the peripheries of the tourist lens and the state gaze, that was most important for the reconstruction of the monastery as a center of Tibetan community. The analysis in chapter 2 gives us some grounds for understanding that for local Tibetans, the resumption of circumambulation during this "recovery" period was not just a return to tradition; the practice had new meanings in a radically transformed society. Under the ongoing authority of Apa Gongjia, circumambulation could be experienced as a form of resistance (cf. Schwartz 1994). Yet in our conversations, Tibetans also expressed the awareness that the monastic center it outlined had a changed relationship to the community, one that was both more threatening to the state in recent years and more precarious as a Tibetan power place or *nay*.

Historically, the outer circuit or shikor had special importance as a transitional space between monastic and lay worlds. As such, it was both a boundary that separated ritually restricted spaces for the reproduction of the Buddha Dharma (Tib. *chos*) from the mundane world (Tib. *'jig rten*), and it was a public space in which all Buddhist practitioners—men and women, young and old, lay and monastic— shared a practice and orientation toward the monastic center. Importantly, as Ekvall (1964b: 239) points out, such outer circuits were not actually circular, but followed the ground plan of particular monastic complexes. Hence at Labrang, the path outlined a historicized and localized center that included all monastic buildings and their associated constituencies. It formed the perimeter within which monastic spatial regulations were in effect—past the prayer-wheel sheds monks could not freely go, women could not enter, and laymen had to dismount and disarm. At the same time, the huge oval traced by the path was considered to be the most efficacious for the laity, because it encircled all the monastic buildings, monk assemblies, deities, and lamas, thereby combining the efficacy of the various *nay* within its confines (ibid.: 244; and see above, figs. 7 and 13).

Thus practitioners' encompassing circumambulation on the shikor reiterated the ideally symmetrical circularity of Jamyang Shepa's mandalic field of action, even as they oriented themselves to the particular historicity of his and others' incarnations—all along shikor circumambulation was instrumental in *remandalizing* Labrang monastery writ large as a *supreme* or overarching *nay* (Tib. *gnas mchog;* cf. Huber 1994b, Schrempf 1994). In this regard, the shape of the mural depicting Labrang monastery in its heyday, painted in the 1980s and displayed in the monastery's "museum" room for tourists, becomes significant. In contrast to the photograph of the monastery in figure 7 above, the bird's-eye-view perspective of the painted mural mandalizes the monastery by rendering it circular and isolating it from all nonmonastic references. The maṇḍala is then lent three-dimensionality by the great detail given to monastic buildings, and the mountains and river encircle it as if bending geography to the shape of the complex. As I discovered from several monk guides' exegesis of it, in the context of the museum display, the mural was meant to depict the timeless wholeness of the monastery prior to CCP intervention, despite the historicity of the complex—the front hall of the great assembly hall depicted there was not added until the mid-1940s.

Further, shikor circumambulation around the monastery, as a key mnemonic or historicizing practice pervading everyday life, was perhaps the most important *publicizing framework* for a wide range of personal and collective orientations to the centripetal forces of monastic exchange. Circular movement on the outer circuit allowed for the public display of levels of bodily commitment to a personal Buddhist time frame of desired gains in relation to past deeds, through publicized seriation or through displays of relative bodily or oral work (e.g., walking quickly, reciting prayers, turning all the heavy prayer wheels,[20] doing extra circuits, and making incense offerings inside intermittent temples, or tracing the circuit with full-length prostrations). All the major public festivals on the monastic calendar by the nineteenth century included shikor circumambulation, either formally or informally. The most important collective circuits were the annual monastic processions around the shikor, like the procession of the future Buddha Shampa (Skt. Maitreya) on the final day of the Great Prayer Festival, or the Sertreng, the annual second-month procession of Labrang monastery's collection of sacra (precious objects exhibited as offerings to protector deities). Those formal processions allowed jostling crowds of laity to seek benefit from contact with some of the most important and enclaved image-receptacles and sacra, thus very publicly reproducing the supreme value of Buddhist *nay* under monastic auspices (see chapter 5).

Hence, back in the summer of 1936, when the KMT official Ma Haotian climbed the mountain opposite the monastery and looked down on it, he described it in centripetal terms. He saw a huge, oval-shaped monastic complex, its perimeters literally revolving with the flow of circumambulators. From his vantage point, Ma described it as surrounded by green cultivated fields along the banks of the river, with villages "scattered like stars around it" (1942–47: 59).

As we saw in the previous chapter, since the overthrow of the monastic leadership in 1958, inhabitants of the valley experienced a fundamental reorientation of social space that saw the center of power shift to the secularized spaces outside the monastery. By desecrating the monastery and establishing the Weixing People's Commune in Tawa, the town formerly referred to in Tibetan as the "Edge" of the monastery, CCP leaders constructed a newly ascendant center with extraordinary power to regulate people's everyday lives. After collectivization, the moving boundary of circumambulation that continually constructed the monastery as a mandalic center was forcibly disintegrated. For those who could remember, the image of the empty monastery, its outer circuit motionless, encapsulated the ascendance of the state's secular power over the region (even though, as Apa Sangye and others told me, people continued to circumambulate secretly throughout the Maoist years).

In the 1990s, the impress of state power could still be felt in the ways the monastery was spatially organized as a circumscribed tourist museum nonetheless breachable by translocal interests and state authority. Under the 1978 provincial policy of "monastic self-sufficiency" (Ch. *yisi yangsi*, Tib. *rang kha rang gso*) for reopened Tibetan monasteries, formulated even before Gongtang was released from prison, Labrang monastery was allowed to reopen only if its newly appointed leaders renounced so-called feudal exploitation of the masses by engaging self-sufficiently in the new moral economy of market exchange in order to construct a peaceful and "pleasing" environment. And in doing so, monastic officials were supposed to rationalize their finances by making them transparent to county and provincial authorities in annual reports (KZC 1978; cf. Tian 1991).

Thus, the 1982 State Council decisions to name Labrang a national center for the preservation of "cultural relics" and to allocate eight hundred thousand yuan to rebuild its library to hold such "relics" worked to institutionalize the monastery's national containment in the reform years. But at the same time, Labrang's leaders were permitted to establish tourism businesses and other enterprises employing monk workers, enterprises from which monastic accountants were reporting annual income of six hundred thousand yuan by the early 1990s (cf. Tian 1991; Suo Dai 1992: 125; Yang Ming 1992: 13). This altered national political economic framework was then reflected geographically and kinetically in rebuilt monastic spaces. Whereas before 1958, all traffic up and down the valley had been routed around the monastery on the shikor (cf. Wulsin, cited in M. Alonso 1979: 96), in the 1990s the Lanzhou-Gannan national highway cut straight through the monastic grounds, bifurcating the original oval-shaped complex and taking all manner of secular traffic through.

Further, with the arrival of the Panchen Lama and his appointment of Gongtang as chair in 1980, monastic leadership had been drastically reorganized under the (ostensible) authority of the state-supervised Democratic Management Committee that convened in the former estate mansion of a prominent trulku (see chapter 5). But the gamble the state chose to take at Labrang in supporting its revitalization as a policy model and tourist site resulted in a newly dangerous situation. Since the mid-1980s, there were two competing centers at opposite ends of the valley—at one end, the rapidly revitalizing monastery, which had the highest concentration of lama-scholars in the Amdo region and was attracting hundreds of young monastics and lay worshippers from afar, and at the other, the headquarters of the Party and government of Xiahe county, whose buildings by the 1990s were rivaled in size only by the large new tourist hotels that had been erected between them and the monastery (see fig. 1).

The revitalization of the lay-monastic relationship among Tibetans critically involved the reassertion of the relationship between the transcendent power generated by the monastic community and the space it formerly occupied. Since open worship was once again permitted, Tibetan circumambulators immediately reclaimed the boundaries of the monastic center by persistently tracing the original shikor. With the establishment of the new state-supervised monastic leadership, the provincial and county governments formally agreed to return all land originally occupied by monastic buildings to the monastery. The upheaval and resources involved in such a move and in reconstructing buildings to match as closely as possible their original appearances evidenced the (perhaps unique) clout of Labrang with state authorities and, as some disgruntled cadres and ordinary folks put it, the steadfast conservatism of monastic authorities. It was indeed, as Marshall and Cooke (1997: 1430) reported, one of the "great success stories" of Tibetan Buddhist revival under the CCP. By the early 1990s, the space within the shikor "almost seethed with animation" (ibid.: 1457) as monastic life resumed and reconstruction progressed at a rapid pace. From the mountains above the valley, the perimeters of the monastic complex could be seen to revolve once more.

THE TOUR: FEAR AND LOATHING IN THE MONASTERY'S CENTER

When I arrived at Labrang for my third stay in March 1995, I took the standard tour of the monastery to get a sense of what had changed. As a foreigner, I had to buy a ticket (at 21 yuan or around 3 dollars each for foreigners, up from 8 yuan in 1992) at the "reception hall" in the newly paved main courtyard of the monastery. The escalating ticket prices indexed the intensifying recommodification of the region and the monastery under reforms. Tourist commodification of rural regions in Gansu had begun very early; already in 1982 the first Gansu tourism guidebook geared to Han urbanites touted Labrang's new national status as a state-protected cultural unit and lauded the "minzu color" of Labrang's remaining monastic buildings (Duan et al. 1982: 20).

It was only after Deng Xiaoping's famous "southern tour," in which he called on Chinese citizens to step up the market economy, that provincial authorities began in earnest to exploit local color as a way to compete for mobile global capital (cf. Oakes 2000). Labrang, marketed domestically and internationally as a more accessible "Little Tibet," figured importantly in national and provincial state officials' efforts to invigorate "tertiary industry" through tourism development.[21] The profound spatial recontextualization this entailed is evident in Geng Fu's 1993 discussion of "tourism resources" in Labrang. Like others, Geng structures his description of the region from the spatial perspective of a tourist arriving in the valley. There, he finds an array of immobile objects, from landscapes to livestock to Tibetan lay homes and monastic buildings, and implicitly, to local laypeople, monks, and trulkus, all available to him as commensurate tourist values—experiences exchangeable for cash: "All of these tourist sites," Geng insists, "are things domestic and foreign tourists are most interested in; thus opening and developing Xiahe's tourism resources is an urgent task in reform and opening up" (1993: 212; cf. Duozang Caidan 1992).

Along with the few Han tourists at the monastery that cold day, I followed our nineteen-year-old monk tour guide toward the great whitewashed walls and gold-plated bronze rooftop of the monastery's main assembly hall. Tibetans historically considered this hall to be the center of the monastery. It was the largest building and the seat of the Thisamlang college, to which the bulk of the monastery's inmates belonged. It was also the meeting place of the monastic councils that, under the ultimate authority of Jamyang Shepa, governed the monastery and the surrounding region. As we saw in chapter 1, its main front courtyard was the site of the annual Cham Chen, and the main roads inside the monastery all emptied into it (see fig. 6).

Our tour guide, who had been casually telling me in Tibetan that he hated tour guiding and especially disliked Han tourists, marched us to the side door of the assembly hall. I was struck by the careless ease with which he moved his body and openly talked Sino-Tibetan politics with me as we walked. Just outside the door of the hall, he paused and turned to address two young Tibetan women acquaintances in local Tibetan dress who had been on their way to circumambulate one of the temples. Calling to them in Tibetan, he invited them to come along and take the opportunity to worship. The two women seemed surprised and embarrassed, as this was not a festival period, in which women were traditionally allowed to worship inside monastic buildings. Hesitating for a moment, they finally shuffled forward, eyes down and giggling as they said again and again, *ngo tsha gi, ngo tsha gi!* ("We're embarrassed," lit. "[Our] Faces are hot").

I stayed at the back of the group with them as our monk guide led us into the dim interior of the huge hall and began his tour in Chinese. We slowly moved along the periphery of the hall while the monks seated on cushions in the middle chanted the morning assembly. The only light came from the open doors, a few small windows high above, and the butter lamps burning in front of the Buddha images on the altar at the front of the hall. The younger monks on the edges of the assembly eyed us with amusement and curiosity as our guide described the two scarf-laden thrones in which Jamyang Shepa and the abbot of the college sat above the assembly for important meetings. The Han men and women whispered to each other, exclaiming that they couldn't stand the smell of the butter lamps.

Meanwhile, my Tibetan women companions could barely contain their fear and embarrassment. Their bodies registering all the ways Tibetans display respect and status inferiority: hats off, shoulders hunched and forward, eyes down, they touched their foreheads at the feet of every deity depicted on the walls. They would not speak, except when one of them, sweating profusely, whispered to me that she was afraid. Their fear and discomfort visibly increased when our guide led us into the posterior temple, where the higher ceiling and narrower space made one feel small in front of the huge, five-meter-high bronze statue of the future Buddha Shampa and the gold and silver reliquary stupas of the five previous incarnations of Jamyang Shepa. While the Han tourists watched at the door and our guide introduced the images, the Tibetan women hurriedly did several prostrations in front of Shampa and backed out. The monk's brief monologue never mentioned the side room accessible only through a closed door from Shampa's chamber. We were ushered out without seeing the weapon-adorned *nay* or shrine of Damjen Chegyal, Gompo, and Jikshay, who, as we saw in chapter 1, were the fierce protector deities charged with guarding the Geluk teaching lineage in general and the internal affairs of the college in particular.

Finally, moving clockwise around the chanting monks in the center, we made our way around to the side door on the east side of the hall and left the dim interior for the main courtyard of the monastery. As we emerged, the two Tibetan women seemed pleased and relieved, and one wiped her brow and pointed to her chest, telling me that her heart was still beating very fast. They hurried off then to continue their circumambulation, leaving us and the Han tourists, who, laughing and chatting amongst themselves, followed the monk guide to the next temple on the itinerary.

DAPA: GENDERED BODILY COMMITMENTS

I chose to describe this brief encounter, among hundreds like it occurring every day in Labrang, because the complex array of participation frameworks produced during it encapsulated so well both the collaboration of Tibetan men and women in reproducing gendered ritual spaces at the very core of the Labrang Tibetan community, and the unequal possibilities for their social mobility in relation to them. Drawing on the insights of Goffman, theorists now increasingly recognize the complexity of participation frameworks *within* speech events, in that different roles and responsibilities of interlocutors vis-à-vis the contexts and agents they project can be embodied concurrently by one person, or shift quickly with minute changes in linguistic and bodily cues. Hanks argues that the best way to capture this complexity is to consider the ways in which multiple participation frameworks are *embedded* in an encounter as participants position themselves, within the cultural constraints of locally salient discourse genres, as speakers or addressees at degrees of distance from an assumed original interaction or framework (1996: 169; cf. Goffman 1981, Irvine 1996).

In this encounter, all of us negotiated the newly emergent cultural politics at Labrang, in which the basic framework of Tibetan ritual efficacy requiring bodily proximity to an empowered abode had been, under monastic auspices, dangerously interwoven with that produced in Chinese state-sponsored tourism—tourists' "romance of proximity" (Schein 2000: 123) to authentically ethnic sites staged and sold for their viewing pleasure. Thus the monk guide's simultaneous interaction with the Tibetan women asserted the moral priority of the central sources of Tibetan Buddhist value over the state-sponsored authorities and market forces that had brought the tourists there. The monk's gesture to include the Tibetan women in the group of ticket-buying tourists, and the women's acceptance of his authority to do so, as well as their very visceral sense of fear and awe at finding themselves in that most restricted center of the monastery, worked to reanimate and reempower the images of deities and lamas and the assembly of chanting monks as autonomous agents of exchange in the face of their recommodification and categorical leveling as commensurate objects of exchange—representations of a "Zangzu" exotic available for extractable value (cf. Mitchell 1992: 310).

By allowing the women to perform the most basic of Buddhist devotional practices amidst the tourists, the monk guide, together with the women, implied that the assumed *original* participation framework at issue, the one within which all others were embedded, was that of worshipful encounter, not the tour. In so doing, they reasserted the three-dimensional nature of that space and its occupants, their hierarchical locations at the center of a patrifilial mandalic order extending horizontally through this world and vertically to worlds beyond. In this way, they mutually produced *dapa* (Tib. *dad pa*), or faith, that very physical orientation of submission, devotion, homage, and offering to transcendent Buddhist masculine authorities that had become the "line in the sand" for identification with Tibetan-ness in the face of threatening social change (cf. Ekvall 1960: 46; Nowak 1984). In the light of this chapter's analysis, we could see dapa historically as the personal orientation that publicly embodied both practitioner and residents of Buddhist *nay* as participants in hierarchical exchange, positioning Buddhist agents as transcendent media of transvaluation as against the allure of competing media and values that, as we saw in chapter 1, had already intensified since especially the early twentieth century in Labrang.

With the intensification of tourist commodification in the 1990s, the performance of dapa was the measure by which pilgrims to the monastery (of any ethnicity) were recognized and distinguished from tourists, and it was so closely associated with Tibetanness that often merely speaking (any dialect of) Tibetan was enough to gain entrance to (appropriate) monastic buildings *sans* ticket and tour. I witnessed and experienced this on many occasions, and many monk tour guides I met over the years, including our guide that day in March 1995, told me this explicitly. Apparently, the proactive function of ticketing and restricted guided tours in supporting Tibetan monasteries financially, as well as in preserving Tibetan *nay* as sites for transcendent exchanges, is lost on many foreign observers, who often depict such practices as foisted upon Tibetans by the Chinese state (e.g., Buffetrille 1989, Marshall and Cooke 1997).[22] However, as this encounter illustrates, even in the face of such unprecedented intrusions, dapa was not a primordial orientation uniformly shared among Tibetans. Instead, as we have seen, Tibetan men and women were at base differently positioned vis-à-vis Buddhist authority; dapa in practice was defined by the gendered body-space orienting sexed participants to mandalic frameworks.

From this angle, we can go back and better understand the significance of shikor circumambulation after reforms. As my encounter with the old woman at the beginning of this chapter indicated, during my circuits of the monastery every day for a year, I found on the shikor the most Tibetan of public spaces in town. Life on the path was an essential element of the continuing cohesiveness of inter-dewa and interregional Tibetan community. Unlike the streets and markets, or even the courtyards of the great monastic buildings, the shikor was essentially a monolingual space, and all practitioners were united by a corporeal orientation to the monastic center as an efficacious *nay*. The core group of circumambulators were adult men and women, married household members in village Lhade who met there caught up on family news, conducted business, and gossiped while walking.

Importantly, in my conversations and debates in other contexts with locals of every stripe, one of the main ways my interlocutors, like Akhu Sherap, argued for the essential gender equality of Buddhist personhood was to say that the mechanisms underlying the ritual efficacy of such "meritorious work" (Tib. *dge las*) as circumambulation were the same for everyone. As my discussion in chapter 2 illustrated, after decades of Maoist state violence and expropriation, and the circulation of stories about those experiences across generations, locals had much invested in finding this merit work to be broadly agentive or empowering, and they widely insisted that anyone could participate in the potential "justice and optimism" (Lichter and Epstein 1983: 254) of individual karmic agency by choosing to work hard at worship practices that expressed pure dapa in the power of the *nay* in question.

Individual dapa was most essentially performed through the public display of bodily commitment to the completion of circuits. Many insisted there is no efficacy to half a circuit of the monastery. And the most determined of practitioners, the ones who walked so rapidly that they passed everyone else many times, were those who had ritual obligations or *jawa* (Tib. *bca' ba*) given them by a lama, most often a trulku with a particularly close relationship to their households, whom they had approached for help with a particular problem, usually physical ailments, but also household difficulties. Serious practitioners conceived of their "merit work" as efforts toward the achievement of a "circumambulation standard" (Tib. *skor tshad*), which was set at a daunting ten thousand circuits (for any monastic building) and most often formed the basic numerical unit of lamas' ritual prescriptions. As one old man insisted to me, using his fingers for emphasis as he walked the path, "the circumambulation standard is not one hundred circuits, not one thousand circuits, but *ten thousand* circuits!" People I walked with were often making elaborate calculations of time needed to complete such tasks and comparing their numbers of accumulated circuits or the types of ritual tasks they had taken on. The shikor at average walking speed took an hour to complete, and thus several years were required to finish ten thousand circuits. The sheer amount of time and physical energy necessary to bring about sought-for benefits required quite a bodily commitment for practitioners, and some of the most serious, usually the elderly, devoted hours every day for several years to their tasks.[23]

Thus, through the publicizing frameworks of circumambulation after reforms, locals could make their bodily performance iconic of the relative depth of their dapa, not only as a general orientation to the once attacked mandalic order of the monastery, but more specifically as evidence of their committed "straightforwardness," their capacities to fulfill past vows and trulkus' prescriptions, or to labor on behalf of patrifilial households. Ama Lhamo, whose androgynous state-cadre look had, as we saw, rendered ambiguous her local recognition as a Tibetan subject, was one of the most ostentatious of shikor circumambulators, tracing the path several times a day with full-length prostrations, and letting people know she often got up at 4:00 A.M. to do so.

However, as we have seen, circumambulation in the 1990s formed a moving "bulwark" against unprecedented and increasing intrusions into the restricted spaces of Buddhist masculine authority. Instead of encircling a center whose transcendent power and worldly authority derived from its ritual separation in space and time from the mundane world, Tibetan circumambulators had to elbow through and cut across the secular and state spaces that not only extended right up to the former "walls" of the monastery, but that also penetrated the center itself, threatening its status as a supreme power place and rendering its worldly authority ambiguous. For the first time in its history, the monastery's central trulku did not inhabit the residence for which it was named. As a married layman and Chinese-educated cadre, the sixth Jamyang Shepa resided for the most part in Lanzhou, the provincial capital. The status of the monastery as the seat (and maṇḍala palace) of the central Jamyang Shepa trulku was thus strangely compromised (see fig. 1; compare with fig. 13).

The daily multiethnic traffic of the urbanizing valley cut a straight line through the monastery and connected it directly with state headquarters, thereby tracing the channels of authority that now supposedly sanctioned monastic officials and trulkus like Jamyang Shepa, and drawing the lines of translocal market exchanges upon which the monastic community increasingly depended. Tourism brought Han Chinese and foreign visitors as well as Muslim merchants, including women, onto monastic grounds in movements and at times that disrupted the cycles of ritual life.[24] And Tibetans themselves were caught up in the transformations breaching the shikor, as women vendors and worshippers came and went, and young monks, because of the diminished ability of the monastic leaders to discipline them, regularly left the monastery to indulge in the increasingly available worldly pleasures in town (see chapter 5).

THE CORPORALITY OF A FEMALE

Thus in post-Mao Labrang, we have to appreciate that despite the communal nature of shikor circumambulation, gender difference was highly significant—in both the maintenance of the moving "bulwark" and in the processes that threatened it with disintegration. As before, the majority of circumambulators were women, including younger adult women, married or not. And most of the men on the path were elderly, working for a better rebirth in their waning years.[25]

This difference is striking when it is considered that historically and under reforms, nomad, farmer, or urban Tibetan women had far less leisure time than men because, in all those contexts, they were responsible for the vast majority of reproductive household labor (including most farm work, dairy production, and care of livestock in both natal and affinal households). In this, I suspect that Akhu Konchok, in the explanation he gave me for women's disproportionate participation in quotidian worship practices like circumambulation and ritual fasting (Tib. *smyung gnas*), was citing long-standing cultural logic that magnified men's contributions relative to the prestige associated with masculine, "outside" tasks. Contrary to overwhelming evidence indicating the opposite, Akhu Konchok insisted to me that more laywomen participate because they have less to do than laymen, and their tasks in the household require less energy since laymen do all the major, "heavy" (Tib. *ljid mo*, with connotations of "weighty" or "important") work.

I would argue that Akhu Konchok's appeal to the dichotomous terms of a specifically Tibetan sex-gender division of household and ritual labor was part of a larger oppositional effort among Tibetans to reclaim the local weightiness of Tibetan masculine authority in the face of intensifying, yet in important ways *newly unmarked*, emasculation under Apa Gongjia. That is, his metalinguistic denial of a starkly practical fact (to which he himself had attested in other conversations) was a microcosm of a larger process in reform-era Labrang: the allure of capitalist modernization, in contrast to Maoist socialist androgyny, allowed for the unremarked convergence of state-local and interethnic androcentric interests (of men *and* women) on an unprecedented scale. In other words, the emerging spatial and political economic order in the 1990s was structured by a new politics of complementary filiation among Tibetans, in which both state officials and local households increasingly relied on women's unmarked reproductive labor, idealized and naturalized as the intrinsically altruistic labor of Tibetan mothers, to shore up competing yet precariously interdependent masculine social orders. In this context, I argue, the reconstitution of the participation frameworks of circumambulation allowed for the performance of an oppositional and remedial Tibetan-marked sexedness that had particularly difficult effects for young Tibetan women.

As we saw in chapter 2, since the CCP takeover, the pressures and allures of alternative discourses about the proclivities of sexed bodies were one of the main factors contributing to "strategic hybridity" (cf. Schein 2000) among Tibetans, as well as a crucial avenue through which the Maoist state expanded its reach across the frontier zone and into Tibetans' daily lives and labor. With reforms, Tibetans in Labrang were subject to nationwide shifts in which state and popular media appeals to biological explanations for male dominance worked to naturalize the increasingly interconnected and capitalist market economy (cf. Honig and Hershatter 1988, Anagnost 1989, Evans 1997, M. Yang 1999). As Emily Chao (2003) has pointed out, the masculinization of the burgeoning private sector in China, embodied in the new national heroic figure of the bold, risk-taking urban entrepreneur, also feminized state and service work as passive and static, and, as we will see in the next chapter, hypersexualized young women's bodies and motives if they appeared in commercial spaces. I argued in chapter 2, using Louisa Schein's phrase, that this process in China was part of a newly expanded global capitalist emphasis on "the feminine hinge," in which translocal capitalists sought cheap and docile labor in labor forces increasingly segmented along rural, ethnic, and, most widely, gendered lines.

Here, and in the remaining chapters of this book, I argue that this reconfigured "feminine hinge" under reforms had very different consequences for the mobility of Tibetan men versus women in the Labrang region. As we have seen, the continued hegemony of Apa Gongjia had rendered monastic leadership tenuous and emasculated male secular authority in the Lhade. These changes, combined with state limits on numbers of monks and the decline of rural secular schools (cf. Bass 1998) in the 1990s, left a "vacuum" in which young Tibetan men literally had no place to go locally (see chapter 5). Young men in the valley thus increasingly shored up threatened masculinities by pursuing opportunities for "modern," urban work and pleasure outside household and monastic life. Meanwhile, young women with such aspirations found themselves squeezed between broadened participation frameworks for their gender-appropriate public agency inherited from the Maoist years and intensifying demands that their mobility remain narrower relative to men.

Nonetheless, in a trend that further intensified the processes of increasing population densities, sedentarization, and ethnic heterogeneity in the frontier zone since the founding of the monastery, Labrang by the mid-1990s had become a vital node in a regional movement to urbanity, a gathering place for young aspiring Tibetan men *and* women (cf. Sperling 1990, Ya 1991, Sun 1993, Schein 2000). Such rapid demographic shifts associated with state violence in locals' living memory contributed to the strong sense many Lhade residents had that their valley was under siege by unprecedented numbers of non-Tibetan outsiders.

As Amnye Gompo told me regretfully while explaining the contemporary system of village Lhade governance, in the past, their Tawa Lhade was all Tibetan, but now it was divided into Tibetan (Tib. *bod rwa*) and Hui (Tib. *he rwa*) sections, with elder male representatives from each handling their affairs separately. And much to the consternation of Tibetans in other village Lhade, by the mid-1990s Han and Hui households had begun to move into the historically all-Tibetan villages up the valley. Indeed, the 1990 and 2000 census figures for Labrang town (vs. the more rural Jiujia township) recorded growth rates far higher than reported natural rates of population increase—from 9,164 in 1982 to 12,868 in 2000.[26]

Importantly, perhaps because for the first time the 2000 census included data for persons in Labrang without household registration, by 2000 Tibetans in town are recorded as *48 percent* of the town's total population, more than double the percentage reported in the 1982 census, in which Han and Hui, just as was reported in the 1930s and 1940s, far outnumbered Tibetan residents in town (cf. Li Shijin 1948; Zhang Qiyun 1969; Li Anzhai 1982, 1992a). Allowing for inevitable errors, this drastic increase of Tibetans counted in town may index the status of Labrang town as a site for the intensification of rural-to-urban regional migration *among Tibetans themselves,* including monks, nuns, and nomad households (cf. Schein 2001: 236). Such a process then would seem to contravene many locals' strong views that Han and Hui immigration was the greatest demographic pressure.[27]

In this context, evidence suggests that young Tibetan women seeking social and economic opportunity were translocally mobile to an unprecedented extent by the mid-1990s. Indeed, while according to KMT statistics gathered in 1941 (numbers that are not broken down by ethnicity), except for 1,220 women counted as engaging in local "commerce" (Ch. *shangye*) in town, the vast majority of people engaged in nonprimary production were men, and the vast majority of immigrants counted in town were men (XXZ 1997). That general situation would seem to corroborate the written sources and Tibetan elders' stories I heard in which long-distance trade in Labrang is portrayed as largely the purview of local Tibetan men, and the majority of immigrants were Hui merchants and Han state workers. Yet under CCP reforms by the 1990s, significant numbers of young Tibetan women residents of Labrang, including Ama Drolma's divorced daughter-in-law, sought work in larger cities, sending part of their incomes back to their households in Labrang. In a 1995 four-part series on "women's development" (Ch. *funu fazhan*) in the *Gannan Bao,* Gannan's Chinese-language government newspaper, Guo Lu praises Gannan's women for bravely entering "commodity economics" and cites as an example the more than seven hundred women from the largely Tibetan Jiujia township who helped support their households back home by living and working year-round in Lhasa or Shenzhen (Sept. 21, 1995; cf. Iredale and Fei 2003: 19; and see below, chapter 4).[28]

Thus, like young men, young Tibetan women were increasingly drawn to the expanded horizons promised by Deng's call to modernizing progress and agentive consumption, yet their aspirations could confront them with particularly painful dilemmas. Young urban laywomen I came to know often idealized the gender equality mobile Han and foreign women tourists seemed to enjoy, while envying the fashions and beauty products they saw modeled by cosmopolitan women on television. My friends Drolma and Tshomo, both low-level cadres in their late twenties who lived in our small apartment building with their husbands and small children, expressed pride in their (albeit meager) independent incomes and in their ability to establish households separate from their in-laws in the Lhade villages— a practice that contravened renewed pressures for patrilocal residence. The pressure on Drolma and her husband, Tsonji, was especially great, since he was the only son of his household who had remained in the valley. But both Drolma and Tshomo also chafed at the added time and effort it took them to run between the duties they, as mothers and daughters-in-law, still shouldered in their in-laws' households some distance uphill, and those of their work units and their own households in town.

In this, Drolma and Tshomo came up against multifaceted and intensifying pressures to *mother* in appropriate ways—that is, to define their feminine personhood most fundamentally through the cyclic performance of altruistic support of households and communities. As we saw in chapter 2, elders' narrative recourse to the reassuring timelessness of gender roles worked to counteract the stark historicity of Maoist social change and ethnic assimilation. Importantly, in those and other conversations with Tibetans across generations, Tibetans' recourse to the ideal *cyclicity* of gendered life trajectories asserted the moral rightness of human movement within the Tibetan temporality of year cycles (Tib. *lo 'khor*), keyed to the ritual cycles of household and monastic calendars—after all, the terms for "circle" or "circuit" in Tibetan (*skor ba, 'khor ba*), when used as verbs, also connote moving or traveling.

Further, as evidenced by Lhade Tibetans' disproportionate focus, both before the Maoist years *and* after reforms, on girls' coming-of-age rites as preparation for patrilocal marriages, Tibetan femininity in particular was metonymic of this ideally patrifilial personhood. When I was there, Lhade households in urbanizing villages were enthusiastically reviving the "letting down the hair" rites for girls, preferring to borrow old headdresses that had been successfully hidden during the Maoist years (see fig. 10). Thus, during the new year festivities, while Tibetan matriarchs like Drolma and Tshomo feverishly worked to clean and purify their households and to prepare heaps of festive foods for guests, teenage girls, most of whom usually wore pants and shirts, and many of whom were in school, had their hair *temporarily* braided and dressed, and proudly made the rounds of neighbors collecting donations of cash, shiny store-bought blouses, and jewelry for their eventual marriages, donations that were then displayed next to household altars as their fathers hosted feasts on their behalf.

This practice thus not only repositioned women as crucial social and biological conduits for maintaining the patrilineal household as the ideal, abiding social unit over time, but it also embodied Tibetan men's and women's collaborative efforts to *recommodify* formerly state-appropriated female productive labor as again reproductive labor for private households. This process was so important to locals, I argue, because it countered the stark emasculation embodied in the figure of the revolutionary Tibetan woman dedicated to progress under alien auspices, and grounded the privatization of household spaces and kin-based affiliations that gave Tibetans a vital sense of relative liberation from Apa Gongjia under reforms.

But the new focus on Tibetan mothering was not at all a simple return to "tradition" in a conservative community somehow left behind by "modernity." Instead, the unremarked disproportionate focus on female reproductive labor made possible especially men's aspirations to modernize, mitigating or eliding their ongoing emasculation as marginalized subjects under reform-era state efforts to extract value from the frontiers. Hence, in my conversations with Lhade residents, as well as in secular writings and performances, a Tibetan mother's unselfish labor was depicted as grounding a post-Mao vision of *civilized* Tibetan households, ones in which a matriarch's hard work and frugal consumption brings the rationality of cleanliness and order to household relationships and activities (see AKS 1993: 77–78).

Importantly, Tibetans' focus on the modernizing role of Tibetan mothering under reforms coincided with intensified state development efforts, endorsed by local Fulian cadres, to cultivate rural Tibetan women as low-level state cadres and as the "main troops" (Ch. *zhuli jun*) for developing primary production for export-oriented sale of consumer goods (Jia 1995). As Guo Lu's four-part series indicates, the Gannan newspapers in the mid-1990s were full of articles lauding Tibetan women's labors in local state work, in commercializing pastoralist production, or in setting up local enterprises "suitable to the special characteristics of females" (Ch. *shihe nuxing tedian;* Guo 1995), such as beauty salons, or food and social welfare services. Thus, just as state leaders relied on Tibetan women's labor in the absence of men during the Maoist years, under reforms, in the face of young Tibetan men's persistent translocal mobility and recalcitrance to state development goals by the 1990s, state bureaus looked to rural Tibetan women to embody the *litu bu lixiang* (Leave the Land, but Don't Leave the Township) ideal of state-controlled capitalist development, shoring up much-needed local production for extractable value. Only now, I argue, reform-era modernization discourse allowed for the unremarked *convergence* of state and Tibetan local interests in this project.

Thus, as Lhamo mtsho (1995) implies in a rare Tibetan feminist critique that nonetheless echoes reform-era Fulian rhetoric, and as my friends Drolma and Tshomo discovered after they had set up their new households, state-sponsored "women's work" did not address the basic gender asymmetries that still so severely limited Tibetan women's social mobility—the difficulties of arranged patrilocal marriage, divorce laws that favored husbands, "birth planning" policies that targeted married women only, and the division of labor that kept women and girls working longer and harder in the household than men and boys (cf. Wolf 1985, Gilmartin 1990, Barlow 1994, Judd 1994, Evans 1997, M. Yang 1999).

As I discussed above, for Tibetans in this region, a basic polarity of sexed bodies enabled what was in practice a relatively flexible sex-gender system underpinning Geluk hegemony. In post-Mao Labrang then, the terms and conditions under which bodies were sexed became key sites for the reproduction and maintenance of Tibetan *nay* under masculine authorities. Amidst all the contestations around gender occurring in the valley past and present, spatial practices vis-à-vis Buddhist *nay* most clearly embodied a basic hierarchy that was not at all ambiguous to Tibetans: the exclusion of females, as humans with lesser stores of merit, from the most powerful of *nay*, regardless of age, status, or ethnicity, emphasized a polar opposition of hierarchically arranged sexed bodies over all other social distinctions.

In striking contrast to confident exegeses of the egalitarian nature of Buddhism, or to discreetly phrased criticisms of gender asymmetry among Tibetans, the topic of female exclusion from Buddhist *nay* elicited, among laity and monastics alike, exclamations of ready agreement and an embarrassed lack of exegesis about the reasons for such exclusions. I discovered this when I asked my lay male friend Wande the reasons for women's exclusion from the protector deity Naychung's newly rebuilt abode, the important *nay* just west of the monastery that Ma Haotian had described in 1936 as bristling inside with images of fierce deities, arrows, and swords(1942–47: 96). Wande's quick response was to explain gender difference in terms of a commonsense tautology: "Men are men, and women are women" (Tib. *byis lu byis lu red byis mo byis mo red*). When I posed the same question to the young monk Akhu Gyamtsho, his sheepish reply was to attribute the exclusion of women to sheer physical difference, *outside* any Buddhist teachings. Males and females, he asserted, are just built differently (Tib. *chag srod mi gcig gi*). And even Drolma, one of the most overtly feminist of my urban women friends, endorsed the notion of their basic sex difference in relation to Buddhist *nay:* "Males and females are equal!" she insisted, citing Fulian discourse. Yet, she added, "the only difference between them is stored merit" (Tib. *pho mo 'dra nyams, bsod nams cig gi khyad par yod gi*).

Unlike other forms of pollution that could apply to both men's and women's bodies, the pollution associated with female bodies in Buddhist *nay* was not subject to purification efforts (in this lifetime). It was instead a kind of negative power that adhered to a female body and derived from its opposition to male bodies as more determined by *corporality* than males. Tibetans I spoke to, both lay and monastic, did not talk about females in Buddhist *nay* in terms of "pollution" (Tib. *grib* or *sgrib*). Instead, they focused on the dangers of contiguity with the female body to the efficacy of both lay and monastic ritual contexts. In practice then, the pollution of female bodies in Buddhist *nay* was essentially the congenital capacity to drain the intentioned male power (Tib. *stobs*) to transcend and tame or control, the power that I have argued was the basis of Geluk mandalization efforts in the region. Thus, unlike other forms of pollution (such as the presence of bodily fluids), for which avoidance practices were not necessarily enforced or universal, but that were open to a range of individual decisions for action, people were very clear that female avoidance of certain Buddhist *nay* was mandatory and enforced (Tib. *mi 'jug gi;* cf. Ortner 1983: 109).

Tibetan women in post-Mao Labrang, as absence and presence, respectively, were thus crucial to the reconstruction of the main sites of Tibetan masculine authority, both Buddhist power places and the ideal patrilocal household—to both monastic and lay *nay,* the abiding foundations of the Tibetan community. And, at the very time when opportunities for translocal mobility were greater than ever before, the Tibetan community and Chinese state policies together narrowed the parameters for the performance of proper Tibetan femininity, requiring Tibetan females to mother—to embody and fix, to reproduce and maintain the continuity of basic social units (within competing social orders) in time and space. Under reforms, for cadres and ordinary folks alike, females ideally fixed locality, while males embodied the possibility, and the dangers, of translocality. The presence of women within the shikor in Labrang corresponded to the attenuation of monastic authority to regulate both lay and monastic bodies. And, as many young men were adrift in the absence of previous routes to male social mobility and power, what *women* chose to do with regard to Buddhist *nay* was particularly important.

Most significantly perhaps, Tibetans collaborated, within new spatial practices that allowed wider parameters for individual choice, to establish "inner sanctums" of ritual fixity in which the exclusion of females was both deeply assumed and consciously enforced. These inner sanctums were, not surprisingly, the *nay* at the core of the monastery—the abodes of the fierce protector deities whose task it was to defend the internal and external interests of Geluk mandalization against human and supramundane enemies. In the 1990s, those deities and their cult under the auspices of monastic lamas and trulkus represented the last bastion of a militaristic Tibetan power at the core of the maṇḍala—the Geluk violence of liberation or the transcendent tantric masculine power to stave off, attack, or tame intruders. As such, these spaces were also the last bastion of the mandatory exclusion of females. These were the spaces that for my interlocutors, men and women, lay and monastic, were immediately and emphatically associated with the most basic difference between men and women—the presence of a female body in such places was so unimaginable that most could not speculate about what would happen if a woman were to enter them.

On my daily circuits on the shikor, and in interactions I had in and around monastic space, I found that Tibetan women self-regulated to avoid the most restricted of spaces and times. However, their avoidance was *not* disempowered absence—women performed their absence from powerful *nay* by actively engaging with them from the ritually demarcated peripheries. In fact, under reforms, circumambulation as an opportunity for individual and collective agency was particularly appealing to Tibetan women. This was so not only because karmic agency was one of the most compelling forms of individual agency available to women under intensifying pressures, but also because the juxtaposition in recent years of alternative logics of sexedness amidst the high stakes of interethnic and state-local politics had *feminized* the participation frameworks of such ritual work producing dapa, or faith, among Tibetans.

Perhaps the best indicator of this process was the transformation I found occurring in the meanings people attributed to a famous series of folktales about Arik Lenpa, "the Simpleton from Arik." These well-known narratives, related to me by Tibetans across the community as true stories, tell of the pilgrimages of a nomad man from Arik south of Labrang to the Jokhang temple in Lhasa, and of the miraculous effects of his deeply sincere and naive faith in the living reality of the deities there. In one tale, his faith is so honest that when he enters the temple to worship and asks the protector deity on the wall to hold his staff for him, the deity complies. In another, the barefoot image of Shampa dutifully lifts his foot so that Arik Lenpa can put on the shoe he made for him. However, as my lay male friend

Kazang, a successful businessman in town, insisted, previously the stories were taken to indicate the great benefits of pure dapa—in that such an unobscured mental state actually brought to life the deities and bent them to one's will.

But in recent years, he explained, the stories were often interpreted as evidence of the naive stupidity and hopeless parochialism of the nomad pilgrim. That was how, he said, his hard-driving entrepreneurial father-in-law invoked the stories, as an object lesson for Kazang when he felt his son-in-law was being too altruistic. In effect, the current context called into question the masculinity of Arik Lenpa, his faithful pilgrimage focused on the main *nay* of the central city contrasting sharply with the wily and cosmopolitan masculinity of the urban entrepreneur. Indeed, it was perhaps widespread yet unarticulated fears of such emasculation under reforms that explain a spate of local stories I heard about from Akhu Sherap, Drolma, and others in which male infants and young adult men without warning transform into females—the structural marginalization of Tibetans under Apa Gongjia actually threatened males' somatic stores of merit in one lifetime, and I heard no counterpart stories for female-to-male transformation (cf. Aziz 1988; Gyatso 2003, 2005).

Thus, on an ordinary day in Labrang in the mid-1990s, village women could be seen rushing about on errands, working in fields, or hurrying to do a few circuits of the monastery while crowds of young men gathered at pool tables set up in the streets. And on holidays, when the merit-making power of the monastery was said to increase a thousandfold, women still outnumbered men on the path by two-thirds.[29] For young and old women I spoke to, circumambulation was the most important avenue for empowered action aimed at self-improvement in a rapidly changing world with few opportunities for women's social mobility and education. With little access to resources necessary to reap benefits from the corrupt, globalizing marketplace, at the same time as demands on them from state and household had increased, many Tibetan women took what little time and energy they could find and invested it in the efficacy they sought from lamas and deities in the monastery.

I was struck by the wide range of strategies to benefit from their "merit work" that I found among women on the path, benefits they conceived of as sometimes very individual or as including their loved ones. And, even though Tibetan women had unprecedented year-long access to monastic space in recent years, the vast majority of those within the shikor at any one time were performing daily circumambulations of temples in order to bring about specific benefits associated with them. Significantly, women circumambulators across regions, statuses, and generations shared an overwhelmingly this-worldly and corporeal orientation to the gains they sought. The majority I found to be resolutely strategizing for relief from physical illnesses or for help with influencing their reproductive futures. Thus most circumambulators of the monastery's medical college (for relief from illnesses) and Drolma temple (for influencing childbirth) were women, while the largest number of lay male and monk circumambulators on ordinary days could be found at the massive Shampa temple, which was thought to bring about better rebirths. Finally, for hard-pressed women, circumambulation was "working leisure" time—the shikor especially was a noncommercial public space outside the household where women could legitimately relax and interact across village and region while simultaneously performing virtuous work (see chapter 4).[30] Thus, in the face of intensifying pressures on women to embody the altruism of collective agency, the publicizing frameworks of circumambulation allowed them to both strategize for individual benefits and display their (motherly) labors to reproduce lay and monastic *nay*.[31]

CONCLUSION: THE TOUR REVISITED AND THE BURDEN OF ENCIRCLING

If we return to our tour of the main assembly hall and look at it in the light of this analysis, the crucial role of gender in the cultural work engaged in by the Tibetan participants becomes even clearer. In this encounter, in which monk guide, Han and foreign tourists, Tibetan women worshippers, and the chanting monk assembly interacted at the center of the monastery, the assertion of a basic Tibetan sex-gender hierarchy structured the complex embedding of participation frameworks involved, and enabled the negotiations among them that, for the Tibetans, reestablished the masculine authority of lamas, monks, and deities. And this was accomplished in the interaction in the same way I have argued gender difference generally operated among Tibetans in post-Mao Labrang—by allowing the Tibetan women to worship during the tour, the monk guide used the women's embodied alienation from the authoritative contexts indexed by the presence of Han tourists, foreign "Tibet supporters," and chanting monks to powerfully augment his status as an authoritative broker between the main sets of participation frameworks those varied people and interests created.

In the face of such an unprecedented intermingling of bodies and motivations in that space, the presence of the Tibetan women brought clear difference into play: they understood neither the Chinese-language tour nor the texts chanted by the monks. Their awkward, timid, and deferential behavior and limited participant roles contrasted sharply with the casual ease with which the monk guide negotiated the various participation frameworks in the encounter, and simultaneously inhabited different participant roles within them. After inviting the Tibetan women along, the monk guide never addressed them again. Their hushed "side play" talk to me about their fear and embarrassment both recognized their subordination to the participation frameworks of the tour and the monk assembly, and since their comments were still loud enough for the monk guide to hear (yet unintelligible to the Han tourists), they constructed a participation framework that included the monk guide as authoritative listener.

In this encounter and others like it, the masculine authority of monks and trulkus was challenged by the presence of Han and foreign men and women, whose bodies in that space indexed both the superior power of the Chinese state *and* monastic acquiescence to it, in addition to the privilege of access to the globalizing marketplace under the press of new state and local efforts to produce and accumulate capital—in the 1990s, competing regimes of value faced off at the center of the monastery itself. The monk guide countered that intrusion by allying with me in Tibetan-language talk the Han tourists did not understand, and by limiting tourist access to certain spaces, but his inclusion of the Tibetan women brought the visceral power of their sincere corporality into play. In contrast to the casual metalanguage of Han tourists' blasé observations, my talk of politics, or the monk's Chinese-language exegeses, the Tibetan women's comments were limited to exclamations about the state of their bodies. Thus, as a vital counterpart to trulkus' ritual efforts to revivify Tibetan deities after reforms, the women's performance of dapa as an involuntary physical response of bodily shame, fear, and awe powerfully manifested that basic sex-gender hierarchy that established Tibetan Buddhist masculine authority as unquestionably transcendent (cf. Rappaport 1979). During the tour, while everyone in the group was kept out of the protector-deity shrine, the Tibetan women embodied the fear and awe that established the protector deities inside as terrifyingly powerful to Tibetans. Thus, the Tibetan women's worshipful performance did for the encounter what women's circumambulation practice was doing for the community in general: contrary to the "exhibitionary order" (Mitchell 1992) of the tour for tourists, their (feminine) worship restored the reciprocal bodily contiguity that grounded patrifilial ritual efficacy for Tibetans, thereby reasserting the abiding *co-presence* of deities, and by extension the benevolent trulkus and monks empowered to invoke and tame them, as supreme agents of higher Buddhist exchanges.

By very publicly granting the Tibetan women access to that *nay* without tickets, the monk guide declared to his audience of Han and foreign tourists the moral superiority of such a bodily orientation. But he was also implicitly calling upon the women to counter the emasculating acquiescence indexed by his own and monastic leaders' participation in state-supervised monastic reconfiguration and tourist commodification. In effect, the most vital reproductive labor manifested in women's visceral worship was to help stave off the defanging of Geluk Buddhism in Tibetans' reform-era remandalization efforts, which was a real danger for trulkus too closely accommodating both global capital and the state. Contrary to the segmented-off and transparent monastic order portrayed in the "monastic self-sufficiency" ideal and in Phakwa Gyab's portrait of the phayul, such feminine (or feminized) worship contributed to the rebuilding of a patrifilial mandalic order that, in the 1990s, was bringing in resources from far outside the valley and in amounts far exceeding those dutifully reported to the state (see chapter 5).

That day then, the women came from the ritual peripheries (the shikor) into the monastic center on the monk's authority, and returned to the peripheries to continue their circumambulation after the encounter. The Tibetan women's committed circular movement thus counteracted the linear, alienated movement of the tourists into the monastery on state authority and away—reducing Labrang to an inferior periphery serving a Chinese center. From this angle then, we can see the increase of women's access to monastic space in Labrang in the 1990s in the way Akhu Konchok described it to me—as an effort among Tibetans to "expand" or "raise up the Buddha Dharma" (Tib. *chos gong 'phel gtong ba*) in the midst of intense assimilation pressures.

Thus, amidst unprecedented gender mingling within the shikor, spatial practices that excluded all female bodies from Buddhist power centers reestablished a particularly Tibetan sex-gender hierarchy that both grounded and empowered the Tibetan community in Labrang. Yet the irony is that the sex-gender hierarchy that was so foundationally empowering in these ways to the Tibetan community vis-à-vis outsiders was taking a heavy toll on Tibetan women especially. While women viewed their circuits of the monastery as a way to exercise a form of (karmic) agency, many of my laywomen and nun interlocutors expressed weary resignation about the prospect of ever being able to escape either the seasonal cycles of household life or the rebirth cycles of *saṃsāra*. I found that for Tibetan women, especially the younger generations, the potential "justice and optimism" of karmic agency were muted by the limitations of sex. As Charles Keyes (1983) argues, relative to the various ways people in Buddhist communities explain and ameliorate misfortunes, karmic causation is often associated with a *lack* of agency; among Tibetans, it was most generally invoked to explain those basic social inequities that cannot be changed. People spoke of relative stores of merit most often to account for those whose seemingly intrinsic social privilege vis-à-vis others (e.g., men, the wealthy, and foreigners such as myself) could be read from their bodies and behavior.

In post-Mao Labrang, aspiring Tibetan women were increasingly aware of the "catch-22" in which the karmic explanation of gender difference placed them relative to Tibetan men and foreign women: if men's inherently superior accumulation of merit allowed them access to social and ritual resources necessary for upward mobility, women's inferior merit kept them both excluded from access to highest ritual powers and encompassed by the affairs of the household, with little time for the virtuous work or scholarship that leads to Buddhist advancement or the self-improvement required for social mobility. As a young nun who had persevered against great household opposition to become a nun at age twenty-one so emphatically put it: "Women must have children . . . and work and work very hard, so that one has no merit accumulated toward one's next life, no merit at all, none at all!"— mothering for her represented not a paramount achievement but a barrier to individual advancement. In all my discussions and interviews with Tibetan men and women about gender difference, the embarrassed silences, the various explanations, the emphatic denials were all attempts to deal with the dilemma posed by this practical fixity of sex among Tibetans, despite beliefs in the possibility for sex or gender transformation. Indeed, as we have seen, the spatial practices constructing the most essential places to the Tibetan community fixed Buddhist *nay* by turning on the expediently static nature of sex.

But what aspiring women (such as nuns or educated laywomen) especially recognized was that the responsibility for and consequences of the relative immutability of sex among Tibetans were largely laid on women's shoulders. As quintessential mothers, Tibetan women's enclosure by the household, as well as spatial practices that excluded them from the most powerful of ritual contexts, ensured that they did not have the opportunities for "maximum bodily contact" (Huber 1994b) with a *nay* that aspiring men did. And their importance to the household economy kept most close to home while some young men pursued new opportunities for secular education and advancement, either in local Chinese state bureaucracies or in private enterprise.

As we saw, laywomen *were* moving, to empower themselves and to take care of their households; but within an ideology and emergent social effect (i.e., through the division of labor and social space) of fixity, their movement was ultimately circular. In this context, women's encircling was movement-in-stasis; they encircled the monastery (Tib. *skor ba 'gro pa*) and yet had few prospects but to keep making the rounds of rebirths (Tib. *'khor bar 'khor ba*), in which the highest life form they could realistically expect to achieve was again a female body. Thus, at a time when local memories of an unprecedented attack on the very foundations of the Tibetan community were still fresh, and great assimilation pressures threatened the reconstruction of local Tibetan institutions, Tibetan women were disproportionately charged with maintaining the stability, the "abidingness" in time and space, of both monastic and lay *nay,* at the same time as that great burden was increasingly devalorized under the new gendered terms of CCP-sponsored "commodity economics."

FOUR

Consuming Women

Consumption, Sexual Politics,
and the Dangers of Mixing

A PICNIC

On a rainy July day in 1995, my husband and I joined Drolma's in-laws for a picnic in their tent pitched high on a peak above the valley. This was the time of year, the much-awaited *shinglong* season, when the village Lhade surrounding the monastery celebrated household and community harmony and prosperity in communal offering rites to Lhade mountain deities (Tib. *gzhi bdag*) at the deities' abodes in the mountains, followed by all-day picnicking, songfests, and games. But during that long, damp day of our visit, I was reminded of the ways in which the practice of such a local and Tibetan-marked unity critically relied on the maintenance of hierarchical differences in gendered sexuality, differences that, as we began to see in the previous chapter, could produce seemingly stark contradictions (to an outsider) as well as greatly unequal moral and physical burdens for men and women.

The tent that day was set up as most Tibetan domestic space was—with the stove and utensils associated with women's cooking and cleaning on one side, and the ornate cushions, table, and festive foods associated with men's hosting and recreation on the other. My friend Drolma was the daughter-in-law of the family, having married in from a neighboring region some four years earlier. She bustled about helping her mother-in-law cook and serve refreshments. Meanwhile, her father-in-law, her husband, Tsonji, and Tsonji's closest male friend affectionately lounged against each other on the cushions, keeping each other warm under wool blankets, and intermittently napping, telling jokes, and playing cards. Cain and I, as guests, perched on the cushions opposite the men. But as the day wore on, we became increasingly uncomfortable, not because of any major change in the situation, but because we could not get warm! To rely, as did the men, on each other's body heat to do so would have been extremely inappropriate because in the Labrang region, any public behavior suggestive of desirous heterosexual contact was considered improper—especially in the presence of parents.

When, in desperation, Cain tried to put a blanket across the two of us, we immediately encountered the standard reprimand—Drolma's urgent glance in the direction of her sleeping father-in-law and the quick, discreet brush of her index finger across her cheek. That gesture was widely used among Tibetans to remind one of the shameful or "face-warming" (Tib. *ngo tsha*) nature of certain behavior. We got the point and quickly, miserably, removed the blanket. In my cold discomfort I bitterly noted the irony that while such seemingly innocent behavior (to us) was deemed so dangerously sexual, the cards with which the men casually played were adorned with photos of Chinese women in tiny string bikinis, posed to display as much as possible of the material assets offered by reform-era modernity—ample breasts, curvaceous buttocks, glittering televisions and motorcycles. In the context of post-Mao Labrang, where even women selling sex would not publicly bare their ankles, such images of nearly naked female bodies seemed to me strikingly obscene; yet they circulated among the men with little notice from anyone in the tent that day.

THE MICROPOLITICS OF SEX AND CONTEXTUALIZATION: CONSUMING SEXUALITY

Sex sells. So goes the oft-repeated maxim that conveys the inevitability of both biological imperatives and capitalist profit motives. But as many social theorists have recently argued, recourse to this seemingly explanatory phrase elides the historicity of the relationship between sexuality and consumption, as well as the particularity of its local operations. To stop there would be to foreclose an exploration of such questions as, Why and what does it sell? How? And with what consequences? Foucault's groundbreaking work provided the seminal insight that the power of the erotic to attract (and repel) lies not in universally experienced biological drives but in the uniquely compelling ways it links bodily processes with the social within a specific, gendered cultural politics (Foucault 1978). This then is the starting point for my analysis of the shifting cultural politics of sexuality, or beliefs and practices associated with reproduction, as well as erotic desire, pleasure, and prohibition, and their differential impacts on Tibetan men and women in post-Mao Labrang.

In this chapter, I focus on sexuality as a way to further explore reform-era national incorporation in the Labrang region. That process, I have argued, must be seen as an extension of the asymmetric local-translocal socioeconomic articulations that had accompanied the intensifying encroachments of competing outsiders in the frontier zone since the turn of the twentieth century. A focus on sexuality in this process can reveal particularly dynamic relationships among sex, gender, ethnic or national identity, and power because the (dangerous) capacity of sexuality to titillate or even to liberate is premised upon the simultaneous construction and transgression of foundational social and biological differences. Here, I continue my analysis of the micropolitics of sex and contextualization within larger political economic participation frameworks by considering shifting premises for sexuality and consumption under "modernization" in Labrang as another important aspect of an emerging cultural politics of embodiment and recognition in the valley. That is, types of sexed bodies, as well as gendered moral subjects, spaces, and ethnic identities, were recognized or resisted as locals negotiated newly competing participation frameworks for gendered sexual discretion amidst the rising allure of commodity voyeurism. This perspective then directs our attention beyond essentializing discourses locating sexual impulses in (sexed) bodies and sumptuary pleasures, and instead focuses on the ways people interactively negotiate access to the sexual within shifting time-spaces.

In that predominantly rural and pastoralist region, the peculiar status of Labrang before and after CCP intervention makes it a particularly compelling place to examine the role of sexuality in such processes. As a Tibetan Buddhist "power place," the political and economic efficacy of the Jamyang Shepas' Geluk mandalization efforts was premised in large part on the huge monastic fraternity's corporate claim to lifelong celibacy, and yet as we saw, by the late nineteenth century the valley was also the site of urban, transgressive liminality in Tawa, the market town that developed in the Lhade villages alongside it. Thus, as I argued in the previous chapter, the situation at Labrang just prior to the CCP takeover actually epitomized a gendered cultural politics of the body that ran throughout Tibetan regions but was particularly marked in Geluk practices: the (often elided) symbiotic relationship between asceticism and sexuality.[1] As Janet Gyatso recently put it, "sex [i.e., sexuality] epitomizes the central problematic of Buddhism" (2005: 274). Here, I emphasize that lay and monastic efforts to negotiate this predicament at the heart of Geluk monasticism relied on reproducing the perceived link between a patrifilial moral economy under corporate monastic auspices and the monks' categorical bodily or sexual purity. Thus in the economic ferment of broadening markets in the early twentieth century, gendered frameworks for public sexual discretion were particularly important for keeping the lay-monastic relationship safely moral and socially vital. This is because (a certain form of) celibacy was arguably the foundational idiom and index of the manly moral will of monks and lamas to avoid inappropriate mixing or exchange, even as notions of compulsive masculine (hetero)sexuality grounded the transcendent efficacy of tantric Buddhist ritual.

However, as we have seen in previous chapters, the ambiguous nature of rehabilitated Tibetan monastic authorities under state-imposed regulations on lay-monastic exchange, and the demands of competing visions of modernity during and after the Maoist years, had opened up new possibilities for locals' participation in frameworks of mobility, work, and leisure, reconfiguring gendered spaces and thus rendering newly problematic that historically interdependent relationship between ritually powerful asceticism and sexuality. I argued in chapter 3 that after Deng's reforms, and especially since he and his Party regime put their official stamp of approval on these processes in 1992, the great allure of commercialized consumption was, on the one hand, a key means for post-Mao state efforts to reincorporate national subjects and channel their privatized labor loyalties. On the other hand, it promised citizens ways to seek forms of social mobility in increasingly heterogeneous processes that eluded the CCP's pretensions to regulate them (cf. Honig and Hershatter 1988, Dai 1996, Dutton 1998, Davis 1999, M. Yang 1999, N. Chen et al. 2001).

In line with trends in other urban centers in the PRC by the mid-1990s, including in Lhasa, I found in Labrang that a new form of commodified sexuality worked to sell not only bodies and products but also the sparkling future visions of a capitalist modernity (cf. Schein 1997, Dutton 1998, TIN 1999, M. Yang 1999, Hyde 2001). That is, against still potent memories of the extremities of Maoist sumptuary restrictions in the name of collective progress, commodified sexuality sold citizens the immediate lure of opportunities to participate in a new form of private agency. Under Deng's reforms, consumption to "live comfortably" (Ch. xiaokang) was figured as modern agency par excellence. This was a capitalist vision of personhood attainable via objects and the availability of easy or labor-free value that served also to heighten China's appeal to coveted foreign investors (cf. Appadurai 1986; Anagnost 1995: 30; Davis 1999: 17; Comaroff and Comaroff 2000: 298). In this context, a new commercialized erotics, depicted in expanding mass media, drew Tibetans in through the fantasy appeal of the spectacular sexuality of foreigners and Han Chinese urbanites.

And yet, as I argued in chapter 3, Dengist visions of modern consumption amounted to a particularly problematic sleight of hand in the Sino-Tibetan frontier zone, because they promised experiences of mobility and agency to precisely those subjects who were relatively immobilized as primary producers *and* as (sexualized) tourist products: "By evoking in the consumer the desire to consume," asserts Michael Dutton, "the consumers are themselves consumed" (1998: 4). But contrary to the arguments of some Tibetologists, who tend to recontain Tibetans rhetorically by depicting their post-Mao consumption practices as passive and culturally adulterating acquiescence (see Kvaerne 1994), I argue that among Tibetans in Labrang, as elsewhere, commercialized consumption was "eminently social, relational and active" (Appadurai 1986: 13). It was a crucial means, as we saw with the practices of rebuilding elaborate household altars or reviving girls' rites of passage, through which locals were remaking patrifilial networks within and among households and between households and the monastery.

However, in Labrang I found that, as elsewhere, this active process played out most importantly as gendered "consumption struggles" (Carrier and Heyman 1997: 364), in which the new exigencies of commodity voyeurism in town intensified public scrutiny of men and women as different types of locally and morally based consumers. Thus in this chapter, I expand on chapter 3 to flesh out my analysis of the disproportionate burdens placed on Tibetan women and femininities in post-Mao Labrang by considering the ways in which Tibetan femininities, as marked Others for newly valorized forms of privatized masculine agency, were positioned not only as ideally maternal subjectivities for shoring up local production and reproduction, but also as quintessential and hypervisible *icons* of ideally accessible commodities. In a process that reiterated throughout the PRC what is now a global pattern, what young Tibetan women especially faced was that the problematic nature of feminine sexuality after reforms positioned them as pivots between ongoing state and local needs for devalorized and labor-intensive (re)production on the one hand and, on the other, intensified efforts to elide, through consumption practices, the realities of increasing social stratification.

As Bourdieu famously argued, "the eye" or the capacity to see and thus consume in certain ways is not innate but is the product of particular histories and is reproduced through forms of education (1984: 3; cf. Mulvey 1975, de Lauretis

1999). In Labrang, consumerist "training in desire" (Dutton 1998: 4) constructed sexualized female bodies as both hypervisible and hyperpassive —the ultimate commodity fetish. Thus representations of "easy women" simultaneously embodied the dream of the easy accessibility of capital under reforms and helped to render *in*visible the ongoing structural emasculation of Tibetans as a group by constructing leisurely consumption as the purview of active, masculine entrepreneurs. The unfortunate consequence for Tibetan women in town was that, even as more women (including nuns) than ever before sought opportunities in social and geographic mobility, state and local interests converged on both containing or regulating *and* objectifying female sexuality above all.

SEXUALITY ON THE FRONTIER: BOUNDARY AND TRANSGRESSION

Since sexuality cross-culturally is so often intimately linked to notions of foundational social and biological differences, constructions of sexual license or excess are common tropes for alluring or threatening Otherness (cf. Manderson and Jolly 1997: 6). Images of the transgressive, eroticized mingling of sexed bodies and gendered spaces are perhaps one of the most powerful metaphors for the danger of social disorder or for the fantasy of individual freedom, depending on the inclinations of the author. Many theorists have explored these issues in European and American colonial discourses (e.g., Enloe 1989, Stoler 1991, McClintock 1995, Comaroff 1997, Grimshaw 1997). In the Chinese context, writers for centuries have depicted the frontiers of empires as spaces outside the civil propriety of a Chinese cultural order emanating from imperial courts, as peripheries populated by carnal, barbarian Others and the criminal dregs of Chinese populations (cf. Harrell 1995).

These themes figured importantly by the early twentieth century as the KMT regime attempted to construct a modern nation and assimilate the frontiers to a new order based in part on a proper marital sexuality and the elimination of (a refigured notion of) "prostitution" (cf. Hershatter 1997: 9). Thus the increasing numbers of Chinese state agents who made it to the Labrang region during that time, and the foreign travelers and missionaries who came on their coattails, shared a broad perspective vis-à-vis the sexual practices of Tibetans there. The description of Tawa town by Frederic Wulsin, the Harvard anthropologist and explorer who visited Labrang during the short-lived Muslim occupation in 1923, sketches the general shape of this vision of the town (cited in M. Alonso 1979: 96):

The village is a dirty little place, half Chinese, and half Tibetan. Its architecture has no charm but its population has: a medley of lamas, wild tribesmen, Chinese fur buyers, Mohammedan soldiers and richly dressed Tibetan women with magnificent straight figures and white sheepskin hats. Many [women] live by their charms.

For such travelers (the vast majority of whom were men), the large number of Tibetan men in monasteries, and Tibetans' seemingly indiscriminate sexual and marital practices, opposed their own understandings of proper gender practices based on the restriction of women to domestic spaces, and male control of household property through, in the Chinese case, the maintenance of patrilineal clans. Against such ethnocentric gender assumptions, Tibetan sexuality and monastic practices could be seen to be "absolutely free" (Ch. *wanquan ziyou*) or grossly debauched and chaotic (Ch. *hunluan;* Gu and Lu 1938). Observers like Li Anzhai and Robert Ekvall in the 1930s and 1940s considered Tibetan celibate monasticism to be extremely abnormal, resulting in such "deviance" as homosexuality and incest (Ekvall 1939, Li Anzhai 1992b; cf. Rijnhart 1901; Gao Changzhu 1942; Bray 2001: 37).

Yet significantly, as Wulsin's description above suggests, these writers tended to focus on Tibetan women's bodies as markers of the peculiar sexual license and therefore the disarray and vulnerability of Tibetan societies vis-à-vis encroaching modernity (cf. Schein 1997: 60). For them, the greater visibility and apparent freedom of movement of Tibetan women relative to neighboring Hui or Han communities was striking. Foreign and Chinese travelers to Labrang in the early twentieth century invariably remarked on the absence among Tibetans of highly visible practices for controlling women's bodies and sexualities such as foot-binding and forms of veiling that could be seen among the Chinese and Muslim Chinese communities just east of the valley (e.g., Teichman 1921, Gu and Lu 1938, Ma Haotian 1942–47). As did Wulsin, visitors thus often remarked, with simultaneous disapproval and lust, on the proud beauty of Labrang women parading their heavily adorned bodies during festivals, or on the unabashed toplessness of nomad and farming women in the fields or circumambulating the monastery. Many visitors, like Zhang Qiyun in the 1930s, attributed this abnormal state of affairs to the "sex imbalance" caused by large numbers of men in the monastery (1969; cf. Yu Shiyu 1990a, Li Anzhai 1992b, Lhamo mtsho 1995). Zhang opined that this was the reason he saw unusual numbers of Tibetan women in town engaged in low-paid manual wage labor.[2]

As the contest over shaping a Chinese nation heated up in the 1930s and 1940s, notions of feminine respectability came to be one of the main measures of a strong, civil, modern nation-state among Han nationalists. As Prasenjit Duara has pointed out, KMT nationalists and reformers expanded on the patriarchal legacy of the late Qing emphasis on female virtue and sacrifice, and expressed "heightened concern with preserving female virtues . . . when the increasing integration of China into global capitalism produced rapid change in gender relations among urban families" (1998: 298). This emphasis on female virtue was expressed not only in the brutal massacre of "Communist" women, but also in Chiang Kai-shek's so-called New Life Movement, under which "virtuous and chaste" girls' schools proliferated and "prostitution" was constructed as a social evil detrimental to social order (Fairbank and Feurerwerker 1986: 146; Hershatter 1997: 260; Duara 1998: 300).

This context, then, sheds light on the portrayal of Labrang Tibetan women in a Tibetan male student's essay (in Chinese) on local customs written at the recently opened KMT elementary school in Labrang in the mid-1930s, and cited approvingly by the KMT education official Ma Haotian. In the process of listing Tibetans' "bad customs," including the "superstitious" belief in "lamaism" and sending sons to the monastery, the student turns to Tibetan laywomen (cited in Ma Haotian 1942–47: 33):

> Tamen zhexie funu de da ban shi jinu. Zhe shi bu hao de fengsu. Jianglai woman yao gaige fuzhuang. Suo yi yao gailiang de yijian, yinwei Jiang Weiyuanzhang qiannian tichang Xin Shenghuo . . . fei gailiang bu ke.

> Those women are mostly prostitutes. This is a bad custom. In the future we must reform clothing in order to improve [our] thinking because Committee Leader Jiang the year before last advocated the New Life Movement. [We] must improve [ourselves] no matter what.

Duly mimicking the rhetoric of the Nanjing government in elementary Chinese, the student asserts that the majority of audaciously bedecked women in Labrang were "prostitutes" (Ch. *jinu*), and he makes them iconic of backward and thus debauched Tibetan custom. Here, instead of reading female nakedness as wanton, the Tibetan student appropriates KMT discourse to read feminine ethnic dress as debauched visibility. The rhetoric he reproduces here encodes the dream of assimilation and ethnic homogeneity within the masculine order of a new modern Chinese nation that would encompass and incorporate the defiantly promiscuous frontiers. Yet, the student's dutiful echo of KMT disapproval of Tibetan women's seeming audacity also points to KMT officials' struggles, noted above in chapter 1, with the frustrating capacity of the Geluk mandalic regime in Labrang to withstand encroachments and remain hegemonic among Tibetans, thus greatly limiting Chinese state efforts to both domesticate and exploit the frontier.

In this light, we can also appreciate how Gu Zhizhong and Lu Yi (1938: 79), two Chinese men who passed through Labrang on a KMT-sponsored inspection tour during the same period, eroticized the place itself as a feminine object of (still thwarted) colonial longing amidst competing outside interests. In a travel account written in very colloquial language designed to entice and thrill Chinese readers, and describing Tibetans as exotic yet dirty and backward "Fanmin" (barbarians), they summarize their findings in gendered terms:[3]

> Labuleng hao bi shi yi ge hen mei de chunu, yijing you ren xiang ta [fem. pronoun] juezhu le, shangshi zhege chunu, bu neng qinfen zili, ta [fem. pronoun] biding yao duoluo.

> Labrang is just like a beautiful virgin; there are already rivals for her. If this virgin cannot become diligent and establish herself, then she will inevitably degenerate.

Here, they liken the status of the Labrang region to the inherent vulnerability of a beautiful virgin, who must be very judicious in choosing the best among her many suitors—that is, one who would protect her reputation in a proper marriage and keep her from falling into otherwise inevitable moral debauchery (i.e., prostitution). As Duara points out, the feminization of land, territory, or nation in this way was prevalent in Chinese nationalist writings during the Japanese invasion especially, utilizing images of a raped woman to represent the "defiled purity of an invaded nation"—and to simultaneously posit a radically feminine lack of agency defended by a vengeful masculine agency (1998: 297; cf. Bulag 2002).

In Gu and Lu's portrayal, then, a vision of the vulnerability of feminine sexuality serves to heighten a sense of urgency in the face of the actual tenacity of Tibetan rule, and to locate Labrang in the spatiotemporal order of a sought-for Chinese nation. The trope of an ideal civil marriage headed by a responsible male in charge of a properly moral economy serves thus as both explanation and justification for KMT expansionist aspirations in competition with other outside interests.

LAMAS AND LOVERS: GENDER, ASCETICISM, AND SEXUALITY IN LABRANG

One day, during a conversation in my apartment, Drolma cited a well-known proverb that, to her, summed up the nature of the Labrang region:

bla brang nga bla ma mjal sa red/
de zhor gi rogs pa btsal sa red

Labrang is the place to meet and worship lamas;
In the meantime it is the place to look for lovers.

This proverb, and Drolma's citation of it, express well both the particularly intense situation at Labrang and the "ironic detachment" (Lichter and Epstein 1983: 249) that has widely characterized the lay relationship to monasticism in Tibetan communities. The parallelism here sarcastically recognizes the simultaneity of the transcendent power of celibate lamas in the monastery and the relatively open sexuality in town. It conveys as well the assumed normality of laity pursuing both Buddhist and sexual exchanges there. However, as I argued in chapter 3, contrary to the portrayals of Chinese and foreign observers in Labrang prior to 1949, the juxtaposition of celibate asceticism and sexuality referred to in the proverb did not amount to a ludic or lewd chaos. Instead, just as the proverb's structure keeps the two realms of activity separate and grants primacy to the worship of lamas, so gendered practices vis-à-vis households and the monastery generated hierarchical distinctions among bodies and spaces, thereby reconstructing foundational boundaries for the Tibetan community in the midst of intensifying pressures from competing social orders.

What outsiders found so alarmingly chaotic in the Labrang region was the relative flexibility in the Tibetan sex-gender system that developed because of the particularities of Tibetan kinship and Buddhist monasticism there. As we saw in chapter 1, by the nineteenth century, the main social and property-holding unit (for urbanites, farmers, and nomads) was the household, *not* the lineage (cf. Mills 2003). Thus relative to most Chinese and Hui communities, among Tibetans there was less structural necessity for, or moral weight on, female chastity as a guarantee of paternity, and a variety of marital arrangements were possible in order to preserve a household's holdings across generations. Further, as we have seen, local men's translocal mobility made women responsible for the majority of household affairs. Thus, Tibetan women in the Labrang region generally had a wider range of spatial mobility (that is, outside the actual confines of a household courtyard) than their Han, Hui, or even foreign missionary counterparts.[4]

But we have also seen that spatial mobility does not necessarily translate to social mobility. As many theorists have recently pointed out, one of the main ways social spaces are gendered is through the differential control of sexualities (cf. Colomina 1992, Spain 1992, N. Duncan 1996, Ross and Rapp 1997). In androcentric communities, where power and resources are dominated by men, domestic spaces often work to enclose "proper" sexuality that serves the ultimate interests of masculine authorities. Female bodies outside those spaces can be the most immediately visible markers of social disorder, because their presence so viscerally disrupts the performative concealment of sexuality, thus dangerously sexualizing both their bodies and the spaces they inappropriately traverse. Despite the horrified disapproval of outsiders at the apparent visibility of Tibetan women in the early twentieth century, Tibetans in Labrang (and elsewhere) were no exception to this sexualized androcentrism. Such observers missed the particular cultural parameters on gendered bodily comportment that maintained the boundaries of Tibetan male authority in the region—the basic "set of orientations" (Huber 1999: 11) I began to lay out in chapter 3 that, in everyday and ritual practices, posited a particular sexual-karmic ontology linking sexed bodies to spaces and types of human and nonhuman agency in order to valorize Buddhist exchanges and concomitant values.

We need to understand then the particular performativity of sexuality for Tibetans past and present. That is, amidst intersecting discourses on ideal or moral sexual behavior and its transgression, what mattered "on the ground," in interactions, were specific behaviors that came to index especially dangerous transgression. I found that for Tibetans in post-Mao Labrang, that meant behaviors that *shamed* oneself and others, engendering public disrespect or disapproval. *Ngo tsha,* literally "warm face," the term most often used throughout Tibetan regions to express this sense of embarrassment vis-à-vis others, refers to an involuntary, visceral response, and therefore implies the depth of one's unconscious knowledge of proper comportment. Shameful actions were those seen to threaten key social institutions like household, monastery, or village by exposing the irreality of stated ideals. Importantly, as I gathered from elders' vehement narratives about the 1930s and 1940s in Labrang, which behaviors took on those meanings depended on historical and interactional contexts.

In other words, the cultural politics of the body operative in Labrang allowed for a wide range of sexual behavior, even in that center of celibate monasticism, if it was kept discreet—that is, socially hidden—in particularly Tibetan ways. Still, as the community negotiated intensifying capitalist exchanges during the KMT years, that basic sex-gender hierarchy kept the parameters of sexual discretion narrower for women than for men. And as we saw in the previous chapter, amidst the social flux and moral ambiguity of life under Dengist rule, the essential terms of that hierarchy had powerfully converged with those promulgated in Chinese state and global media discourses in efforts to narrow those parameters even further for Tibetan women.

I argued in chapter 1 that Geluk monastic mandalization was not incompatible with burgeoning forms of capitalist exchange before and after CCP intervention. In fact, the expanding export market and trade opportunities in town allowed lay and monastic Tibetans alike to invest in the mandalic order at Labrang in ways the fourth and fifth Jamyang Shepas especially attempted to regulate (see chapter 5). Indeed, the famous iconoclast scholar and former monk Gendun Chopel, in his critical works written after he was banished from Labrang monastery in 1927 for his irreverent ways, echoed Buddhist temporal themes of the continuous degradation of the Dharma and lamented that purely intentioned celibate asceticism among Tibetans was increasingly rare in the ferment of expanding commerce (dge 'dun chos 'phel 1990: 389; cf. dge 'dun chos 'phel 1992: 126). By the early 1950s, the Gannan social history research group asserted that fully 20 to 25 percent of adult monks engaged in commerce (XXZ 1997: 525).

Thus, as Chinese state agents and development projects began to press in on Labrang with the founding of the KMT county of Xiahe there in 1928, the negotiation of gendered sexualities became a key site of contention between Buddhist and non-Buddhist regimes of value. I argue that this conflict turned on differential efforts to recommodify Tibetan women not only as providers of services or forms of reproductive labor, but also as types of sexual objects exchangeable for other desired values. KMT reformers, just as would their CCP counterparts, associated bedecked young Tibetan women with prostitutes and advocated desexualizing them and modernizing their labor by encouraging their adoption of Han-style pants. Meanwhile, local Tibetans and monastic officials associated women in pants with dangerously independent, "modern" female agency—and perhaps with female bodies that would thereby be more revealed out from under long robes. As Apa Dondrup, himself a young monk on the eve of the Communist takeover, told me, Tibetan women then would never wear pants or be seen in the town's restaurants. If they did, he insisted, brushing his cheek with his finger, people would talk, and they would be very embarrassed (Tib. *ngo res tsha rgyu red*).

In such a context, the report of Li Anzhai, a Han anthropologist and social reformer who lived in Labrang with his wife, Yu Shiyu, between 1938 and 1941, of an informal economy among certain monastic officials of differentially *fining* laymen and laywomen takes on added significance (1982: 6).[5] According to Li, the practice of fining laity for unfulfilled labor obligations to the monastery *and* for transgressive conspicuous consumption was commonplace at the height of Labrang's regional status as a commercial center. And, asserts Li, monk officials could thereby become wealthy by the end of their three-year terms. Monk officials thus had individual incentives to channel inappropriately utilized value back to auspices of the mandalic order by enforcing sumptuary restrictions, and importantly this played out in gendered terms. While lay patriarchs were fined if they displayed their household wealth and prestige by ornamenting houses in ways too closely approximating monastic buildings, some Tibetan women, reports Li, were fined for "imitating" Chinese and donning pants. This was, not surprisingly, precisely the time when Apa Alo and his wife were collaborating with Li and Yu, among others, to establish secular schools in town separate from monastic authority, including a first-ever school for girls (cf. Tuttle 2005).[6]

In this light, we can appreciate that the relative flexibility of Tibetan gender practices vis-à-vis monasticism that was so concerning to outside observers during that period in actuality played out within dynamic articulations of particular socioeconomic processes *and* basic understandings of the body. That was a nexus of practices and ideologies that for Tibetans I spoke to mapped continuities across the radical disjunctures of the Maoist years. As we have seen in previous chapters, historically Tibetans widely considered the body to be the contingent outcome of multiple corporeal and mental forces, extending beyond the space-times of an individual's agency or lifetime. On Buddhist liberation paths, body and mind were thus precariously interdependent even as they were radically opposed.[7] Here, I argue that it was constructions of hierarchical gendered sexuality that provided important ways to regulate and channel such dangerous mixing in valorized exchanges within monastic and nonmonastic contexts.

I argued in chapter 3 that among Tibetans in Labrang the body-mind opposition expressed in notions of corporeal hindrances to intentioned Buddhist striving was broadly embodied in perceived fundamental differences between females and males. And we saw that relative moral or ritualized propriety was most generally evaluated in an idiom of corporeal cleanliness and filth (Tib. *gtsang ma*, *mi gtsang ma*). Thus ritual and everyday efforts to control dangerously contagious corporeal pollution indexed the vital categorical boundaries of the community (cf. Douglas 1966, Diamond 1988). Not surprisingly, the most potent of substances, the most potentially offensive to deities and other humans, were the effluvia associated with the lowest, grossest bodily functions—urine, feces, gas, saliva, bad breath, menstrual blood, semen (cf. Nebesky-Wojkowitz 1956). For Tibetans then, the body was inherently unclean, and both men and women could be polluted and polluting through inappropriate, bad deeds, contagion, or even descent (in the case of unclean lineages into which no one from a "clean" lineage would marry).

Yet, the very possibility for ritual and social efficacy throughout the community critically depended on the sexual-karmic polarity of male and female bodies *and*, I argue, on an assumption of the natural, compulsive sexual attraction between them. I found strong parallels between local understandings of the workings of sexuality, as expressed in lay rituals, folklore, love songs, and drama, and those exported to Tibet in Indic tantric and monastic cults. That is, lay and Buddhist elite understandings of sexuality converged on a notion of compulsive heterosexuality from a masculine point of view—the primary sex act was intercourse, and the primary sexual agent or subject was male, and his essential object female. In fact, as Janet Gyatso argues in her recent analyses of medieval Tibetan tantric and medical texts, despite various attempts by foreign feminists to recuperate "feminine" experience in Indian and Tibetan Buddhist tantric texts, tantric yoga techniques for liberation were structured on male physiology and sexual experience (i.e., the flow and retention of semen, ejaculation, etc.: 2000, 2003; vs., e.g., Allione 1984, Shaw 1994).

As the active sexual agent, male lust was seen to be most physically compulsive, a key source of vitality that needed (proper) outlets for physical and mental well-being—hence the great ritual and moral power associated with denying or controlling it. Importantly, in Buddhist liberation technologies, the relatively impure female body was necessary as the stimulating source of this "natural energy"—as a vessel or an aid (in tantric yoga) or as a constant threat (in celibate asceticism). As sexual object, ideal female sexuality was analogous to the assumed physiological role of the vagina in intercourse—relatively passive or compliant, not compulsively desirous but requiring males for arousal. Thus, despite powerful Buddhist discourses that posited the inherent emptiness of such this-worldly and material attributes as sex, in the tantric idiom that structured Geluk mandalization at Labrang, the grounding sexual polarity (Tib. *yab yum*) constructed male adepts and deities as "Buddha-subjects" in contradistinction to female consorts (Campbell 1996: 182). Essentially then, females in the mandala were positioned as crucial conduits and *commodities* in exchanges between practitioners and (incarnated) deities. Hence in such mandalizing rituals as the "Offerings to the Lama" practice, which as I mentioned in chapter

1 was widespread among monks in Labrang, the practitioner visualizes his lama as a Buddha in union with his consort, and among the visualized offerings to the lama are divine (female) consorts of "pleasing youth" (cf. Makransky 1996; Lopez 1997: 377).

Without this gendered economy of heterosexual compulsion in Labrang, there would have been no particular value or virtue in a male (vs. a female) asserting his will over the body's treacherous attraction and need for the other. This then underlay the great prestige and power of celibate monkhood (vs. nunhood) as a superior masculine gender status (see chapter 5). I argue that in Labrang both before and after CCP intervention, a monk's shaved head and maroon robes did not mark the desexing of his body (he was not thereby "neutered" or "feminized"), but they most essentially marked the ideal *desexualization* of his body. In other words, a monk's performative transformation indexed the corporate monastic claim to a steadfast intention to be purified of the greatest pollution or hindrance to male subjectivity and striving: the (sexualized) female body. As many theorists have pointed out for a variety of Buddhist cultures, and as I found in post-Mao Labrang, the most salient aspect of Buddhist monasticism in the monastic codes of conduct (Skt. Vinaya, Tib. *'dul pa*) as well as in popular consciousness, what most basically distinguished a monk (Tib. *a khu, grwa pa*) from a layman (Tib. *khyim pa*, lit. "householder"; *byis lu* or *gsar bu*, lit. "boy"; or *rgan po*, lit. "old man," "patriarch"), was the corporate performative claim to heterosexual celibacy and thus bodily purity (cf. Keyes 1986; Zwilling 1992; Gyatso 2003, 2005; and see below, chapter 5).[8]

From this angle, we can further our understanding of the enabling nature of the sexual-karmic polarity among Tibetans in Labrang. Intentionality, desire, and the possibility for social and karmic mobility or transcendence was associated with the masculine. Meanwhile, the feminine was associated with that which is immanent to the body, to place, to households and the mundane. Contrasted to the male standard, the adult female body was more corporeal and thus more impure precisely because of its "extra" physiological features indexing sexuality—vagina, breasts, menstruation, pregnancy. Celibate asceticism then was intimately bound up with manliness—through it, a practitioner supposedly demonstrated the strength of his will to control heterosexuality and to keep potential feminization at bay. A story my lay male friend Kazang laughingly told me in English seems to epitomize this masculine ethic. He said it was widely known in Labrang, but I had heard only allusions to it when friends cited the proverb "Monks are pure, but their speech is impure" (Tib. *a khu gtsang rung kha mi gtsang*):

FROM FIELD NOTES: According to legend, the beautiful wife of the Mongolian prince, the scion of Labrang monastery's main lay patron family, was living with her husband very near the monastery. In her comings and goings, she often heard monks saying sexually teasing things to her. When she told her husband about it, he assured her they didn't really mean those things. But she didn't believe him and said she would try a test. Adorning herself in a very sexy way, she propositioned a monk, saying, "Can I go with you?" He agreed and took her in bed with him. But the entire night he slept far apart from her. In the morning, he said, "You think I am impotent," and he took her hand and showed her his erection. He told her, "Jamyang Shepa has stamped on my penis, and I will not have sex!" She felt very guilty for her lack of faith and decided to build something for the monastery.

Thus here, even when a beautiful female body comes in closest proximity to a monk, he is able to stoically deny her as an expression of his commitment to Jamyang Shepa's mandalic order. Since the female protagonist takes her monk target as metonymic for the entire monastic community, the narrative in the telling reasserts the monastery's corporate claim to manly celibacy and hence its appropriate status as a field of merit for patrons' exchanges. In this sense, despite centuries of tension between them in Tibet (especially since the rise of the reformist Geluk sect), tantric sexual yoga and celibate monasticism were not that far apart. Both traditions of liberative practice were based on the manly control of compulsive heterosexual attraction and thus provided males with techniques to avoid the draining effects of intercourse with a female body and to gain the Buddhist values of ritual efficacy and power from it instead.

The intertextual nature of this gendered discourse on sexuality by the first half of the twentieth century was perhaps best expressed in Gendun Chopel's 1938 *Treatise on Passion,* an exposition on "sexual arts" written after his wide travels took him finally to India (dge 'dun chos 'phel 1992). In it, he draws on a variety of sources to appropriate themes that had been circulating in Indian and Tibetan tantric and medical discourses for centuries, asserting that frequent copulation consumes the male body while it does no harm to a female. And early sexual intercourse, around age sixteen, matures a female body and keeps it youthful while it wears out males, who should more properly wait until age twenty-four (dge 'dun chos 'phel 1992: 158):

If at a young age men do it with women, they will lose their power and will age quickly. However, if women meet with men at a young age, it is said they thereby forestall aging. This is not something that I made up; I am explaining what has been proven by the experience of old men and women.

Gendun Chopel's defensiveness here, duly noted by his translator Jeffrey Hopkins, seems to indicate that, despite his antinomian feminist leanings as expressed in this work, this assertion is less about condoning female sexual desire and more about justifying the widespread male desire for young—that is, relatively pure and attractive—female bodies. This concern is reflected past and present in the great categorical significance in Tibetan lay and tantric ritual of premenstrual virgins—that is, those girls whose sexual virtue and relative corporeal purity can be socially attested. In the context of otherwise exclusively male ritual practices, they have stood for the most desirable consorts and stand-ins for ḍākinīs (Tib. *mkha' 'gro ma*, divine consorts) to make offerings to lamas and local deities—as a category, they were the quintessential tantric commodity, their ritual service paralleling the service labor provided by laywomen in everyday contexts.

SPATIALIZED GENDER POLARITIES: CONTAINING AND TAMING SEXUALITIES

Tibetans in the Labrang region did have practices for the relative enclosure and control of female corporality and sexuality, practices that had taken on heightened significance under reforms. This emphasis most generally played out (across farming and nomad regions) in the widespread insistence on the spatialized gender polarity of woman/inside::man/outside that I discussed in chapter 3. Here, I argue that Tibetan sexual discretion focused on maintaining the ongoing *appearance* of this distinction at junctures that were particularly salient for locals, thereby protecting the grounds of masculine ritual and social authority. Negotiations and judgments of behavior occurred with reference to prescriptions for ideally gendered bodily performance so that public judgment of illicit or lewd behavior (Tib. *'dod log* or *log g'yem*) could be avoided or duly brought to bear. In that context, the most important grounds for sexual discretion were not frequent punishment or complete confinement for transgressors, but the everyday bodily disciplines of monasticism and marriage under public scrutiny and gossip in the narrow valley.

As Melvyn Goldstein has pointed out, the ethic of "mass monasticism" in regions supporting huge Geluk establishments meant that only a small minority of monks approximated the monkly ideal (1998a: 15). Only the most advanced of scholar-monks could gain initiation into secret lineages of yoga tantra.[9] As we will see in chapter 5, the system actually allowed for a wide range of masculine proclivities as long as they appeared to serve the order and did not emerge publicly to threaten its transcendent authority. As Ellen Ross and Rayna Rapp argue, "celibacy" must be seen not as a universal denial of sexuality per se but as a historically specific set of practices for performing different types of moral behavior vis-à-vis particular notions of sexuality. They argue then that cross-culturally celibates are distinguished from others in particular cultural settings more by their "array of alternative sexual practices" (Ross and Rapp 1997: 157; cf. Castelli 1991, Faure 1998, S. Bell and Sobo 2001, Khandelwal 2001). In fact, contrary to the insistent narrative above, monks and lamas did have secret liaisons with women; some returned to lay life and married; many had close homoerotic friendships not necessarily marked as "sexual," and private homosexual practices among monks were tolerated, in part because they were viewed as a practical release for the frustrated heterosexual drives of monks of lesser ability.[10]

In lay life as well, practices of bodily and linguistic avoidance focused on maintaining the invisibility of inappropriate heterosexuality, keeping males and females at a certain physical distance in public, especially those of the same generation or of improper kinship relation,[11] and proscribing explicit talk about sexuality with members of the opposite sex. Close public affection and touching, and private frank talk about sexuality was reserved for same-sex age-mates, and not marked as problematically sexual. And, as I discovered in more than one lay home I visited, lay households often manifested the distinction between unclean and desirous bodies and pure Buddhist minds by diligently maintaining a spatial divide between mundane spaces, but especially bedrooms, and rebuilt household altars and Buddha images. Drolma, whose small apartment in town, like mine, made this difficult, scolded me for hanging an image of Donpa (Śākyamuni Buddha) at the foot of our bed and cited the Tibetan practice of hanging cloth covers in front of their images. "You can't do it in front of a Buddha!" she counseled, raising this as an example of the concept of lok yem (lewd behavior); "it will bring much suffering in your next life!" (Tib. tshe phyi ma a nyos pa hon da che rgyu red). Thus, contrary to early Victorian Western observers, who assumed covers over Tibetan thangkas were meant to hide the obscenity of the deities' embrace, for Drolma, such covers were necessary "so they can't see us doing bad things!"

Importantly, the enclosure of female sexuality occurred through practices that rejected, in certain ways, female intrusion into male domains of intentionality outside the household. This meant, as we saw in the previous chapter, excluding female bodies from certain monastic spaces and from lay offering rites to mountain deities. And it meant curbing the public performance of female sexual desire independent of the household. For example, as the narrative about the princess and the monk illustrates, men, even monks, had much more leeway for the appropriate expression of heterosexual desire in public. They could tease each other and women friends using sexual euphemisms and innuendo, while women were expected to be much more circumspect, displaying their shyness and embarrassment even as they laughed at men's jibes. This basic difference can also be seen in the widespread avoidance behaviors associated with the performance of *layi* or popular Tibetan love songs.

These songs tell stories of ideal romances between brave stalwart warriors and beautiful loyal women. In village and nomad communities, they were most often performed at particular courtship gatherings in alternating male-female paired-response form. They could produce the greatest embarrassment in women especially if they were caught singing them outside those ritualized contexts by male friends or relatives, parents, or within earshot of the monastery. For example, one day when I was working with my laywomen friends Droko, who had grown up as a nomad, and Tshomo, who grew up in town, to write down a common *layi* sung in nomad regions around Labrang, the two of them went to great, shrieking lengths to keep the paper from the eyes of Kazang, my lay male friend who happened along. He immediately surmised what they were doing and made a big show of grabbing the paper. The verses of the song we had written so far said nothing overtly sexual. Instead, they expressed the courtship hopes of both male and female protagonists for a faithful, honest lover, using common metaphors to swear a strong, unwavering commitment despite the disapproval of parents.

In this context then, women whose public comportment was deemed too independently desirous or instrumental risked being associated with negative agencies by the community—bad mothers, unclean housekeepers, gossips, and prostitutes—that is, those women who came to embody the draining effects of female intentionality or desire out of control, and thereby gave vent to the impure and socially destructive agencies of demons (cf. Ardussi and Epstein 1973, Lichter and Epstein 1983, Kapstein 1997). In the Labrang region, the most important practices for enclosing female agency were the coming-of-age and marriage rites aimed at publicly appropriating a woman's sexuality to the interests of the (ideally) male-headed household, thereby making her reproductive future one of the important values obtained with her exchange between households.[12] Despite the diversity of practices that scandalized outside observers, Tibetan androcentrism meant that the ideal forms of inheritance and marriage exchange were not that far from local Chinese practices. Indeed, Akhu Konchok explicitly made this analogy in our conversation one day, and he cited as emphasis the Chinese saying that plays on the different gender connotations of the Chinese homophones *jia1* and *jia4*, *nande dang jia, nude gei jia* (lit. "Men bear up the household [over time], while women are married into it).

As we have seen, Tibetans widely valorized sons and arranged, patrilocal, monogamous marriages that kept the household patrimony intact and established beneficial alliances by bringing in a daughter-in-law. From this angle, we would have to see "letting down the hair" maturation rites for girls (Tib. *skra phab*) as community efforts not only to channel their labor but also to channel their sexualities. At precisely the life stage when lay and tantric ritual asserted girls' ideal sexual desirability, households publicly asserted a daughter's sexual maturity and her status as a good prospect for a patrilocal marriage.[13] Thus, since a marriage was paradigmatically accomplished through the rites of negotiation and feasting between households that brought the bride into the purview of her new husband's home, it legitimized their sexual relations and subsequent children as belonging to that household. In post-Mao Labrang, I found that the expression *Tonmo yed* (Tib. *ston mo byed,* lit. "to throw a feast party), and in addition the phrase *nay la ndro* (Tib. *gnas la 'gro,* lit. "to go home" or "to go to a husband's natal home"), which I discussed in chapter 3, were widely used to refer to marriage in general, yet they specifically connoted this type of union. In this light, we can better assess what some foreign missionaries before CCP intervention disapprovingly called the "sexual hospitality" of Tibetans in border regions (e.g., Edgar 1924; Ekvall 1960: 379). In communities structured through the translocal movements of men and their hosting activities that cemented and maintained alliances, the coming-of-age rite for girls authorized the (discreet) sexual activity of unmarried daughters as under the auspices of their natal households. In some cases then, especially in nomad regions, a father could grant a male guest sexual access to a daughter—a liaison in which she may or may not have already willingly participated (cf. Li Anzhai 1982, Hermanns 1953).

This perspective then helps to flesh out the discussion of marriage and kinship practices I began in chapter 1. A focus on the cultural politics of sexuality among Tibetans illuminates how alternative marital practices in the region operated in part as strategies, in the face of an actual shortage of marriageable men, to maintain the performative hierarchy between virtuous, relatively pure women inside the household domain and improperly sexualized, impure women outside it. In actuality, there was a gradient of more or less ideal marriages, which nonetheless in practice did very similar things for women. Drawing on the symbolic resources of the paradigmatic marriage rite, these practices, from "taking in a son-in-law"

(Tib. *mag pa 'jog*), to arranging a "temporary" (Tib. *gnas skabs*) marriage, to "marrying a daughter to heaven," all in fact married a daughter into her natal household, thereby publicly legitimizing her sexuality and claiming her children as heirs.[14]

These practices allowed women and their families to assert the gender-appropriateness of their own or their daughters' activities that seemed to be carried out independently of men in this center of monasticism and itinerant trade. As we have seen, the reality was that monasticism and long-distance trade took men out of local households for long periods. Indeed, the Chinese social scientists Li Shijin (1948) and Li Anzhai (1992a), who separately conducted research among Tibetans in the 1930s and 1940s, expressed surprise and concern at the relatively high percentage of women-headed households in both farming and nomad communities in the Labrang region. Finally, alternative marriage practices allowed Labrang locals to distinguish between the relative purity and virtue of female sexual behavior that was motivated by altruistically maternal or reproductive feminine agency—that is, sexual behavior that brought offspring and income to the household—from that of "prostitutes" (Tib. *smad 'tshong ma*), "unmarried," unattached women who were seen to "sell" sexual intercourse for personal gain and lust. That term, which I heard often in Labrang as a gloss for the Chinese *jinu*, literally means "woman who sells the lower [body parts]."[15]

As numerous oral and written accounts I collected attest, Labrang as a commercial center was renowned among male travelers throughout Tibetan regions for the beautiful, sexually available women of Tawa town (Tib. *mtha' ba mdza' ma, bla brang mtha' mo*). But such women did not necessarily think of themselves as "prostitutes." Instead, in many cases they competed for lovers and called their unions "temporary marriages," living all the while in their natal households and contributing their own and their children's labor, as well as the monetary or in-kind "gifts" of their lovers, to the household's income.[16] Reports on Labrang's commercial economy prior to CCP intervention never list sex as a commodity, nor do they give any indication of how much commercial value could be redirected to households this way. But in part through engaging in this sector of an informal economy of women's local trade, such women could be locally powerful and proud—they were real locals after all, surrounded by friends and relatives in their natal households and Lhade villages versus the *nama* (Tib. *mna' ma*), or daughters-in-law, who had more ideally married in. Having undergone the "letting down the hair" rite, their bodies were adorned as adult laywomen, and thus displayed their association with a household. They went about usual daily activities of married women, tending the household's fields and livestock, worshipping appropriately at and supporting the monastery. In this way, I would argue, they were not dangerously different from nama, because they were still discreet by Tibetan standards—that is, they did not performatively disrupt key gendered boundaries by making inappropriate heterosexuality socially visible.

The ritual and social propriety or "cleanliness" of such women could, then, be contrasted with the relatively chaotic and morally impure sexuality of unattached women seen to be taking multiple lovers for money. This, as many elders in village Lhade told me, was associated not with their own community in the valley but with the liminal times and spaces of the great monastic festivals, when the town's population swelled several-fold with the influx of men and women pilgrims from nomad regions especially.

I found in Labrang as elsewhere, Tibetans, just like Chinese, could attribute civilized sexual respectability to themselves as a way to distinguish themselves from regional or ethnic Others they considered more primitive and thus more sexually promiscuous. (cf. Huber 1999). Indeed, in a conversation about nomads with Tashi Ji, the cosmopolitan daughter of one of the wealthiest Tibetan business families in town, she emphasized her distaste for nomads' uncivilized ways by citing the many stories her old mother told her about nomads "copulating like animals" in tents. Against such elders' anxious perceptions of increasing social "chaos" and their own market vulnerability in the valley, the specter of the increasingly visible, unfettered sexuality of nomad men and especially women in town, not only during festival periods but also with the increasing immigration of nomad households in recent years, was particularly repugnant.

POST-MAO CONTESTS: A SEXUAL MISRECOGNITION

My friend Drolma, as it turned out, was not an ideal nama or daughter-in-law. In fact, she had eloped with Tsonji, the eldest son of that prominent Labrang village family. The two had met in college in the provincial capital, and Drolma often nostalgically told me how she had been swayed by his romantic persistence in courting her. At the time, she was convinced of the "modern" virtue touted in state and popular media of choosing her own mate based on *tsedung*, mutual "love" or "feelings," a word that among the educated was often replaced in otherwise Tibetan conversation with a Chinese gloss—*ganqing* or *aiqing*. Drolma persevered against her own prominent family's pressure to marry a local man and stay in her home region, forgoing a proper wedding feast and moving instead to Labrang to live with her new husband.

In the early days of our friendship, she would compare her own relationship favorably with the ideal "modern" marriage she felt Cain and I embodied. In one early conversation, she asserted that the usual Tibetan terms for "husband" and "wife" (*makwa* and *nakmo*) did not apply to her and Tsonji, because they had an independent relationship. And yet as we saw in chapter 3, Drolma discovered in Labrang that she still had to negotiate a delicate balance between her separate household in town and her duties as a nama in her husband's natal household in the village.

In this context, I came to see the stories Drolma often told me in the privacy of my apartment as important moves in her own micropolitics of contextualization as she actively recruited me to witness her upstanding and moral footings vis-à-vis her narratives of sexual misbehavior in the valley. In the course of lamenting the increasingly immoral sexuality she saw among young people in the valley, Drolma told me of the time she had been walking down the main market street one afternoon in Labrang. A young Tibetan man she didn't recognize approached her, grabbed her arm, and entreated her to stop, telling her, "Girl, I'll pay whatever you ask!" (Tib. *byi mo khyod sgormo du ster dgos na nga ster ra*). Throughout her long and emphatically repeated narrative, Drolma was increasingly adamant that I see, in her tone, expression, and gestures, her righteous indignation at the man's presumption—even though her initial embarrassed laughs did not completely conceal her pride at being deemed so desirable.

Significantly, her first move was to insist, to the man in the story and to me as listener, on the man's misrecognition of her as a "prostitute" (a group of women in town she had just labeled using the Chinese word *jinu*). And despite her ambiguous status as a daughter who had defied the obligations of arranged patrilocal marriage, Drolma said she did this by repeatedly telling him, "I am a daughter-in-law!" (Tib. *nga mna' ma ʒig yin*). This, she explained, was her way of telling him that she had married out (Tib. *gnas song sdod gi*), and thus that she was not the kind of person who did that (Tib. *nga da demo de byed go no mi ma red*).

Perhaps her increasingly vehement indignation and almost obsessive repetition of her responses to him in her narration of the story for me was compensation for the fact that that assertion was not enough to safely distinguish herself from a woman whose body was for sale. According to her, on that and another occasion in which she ran into him outside a pool hall, he ignored her and continued to pull her arm and ask her price. She said only when she recognized him as the married son of a local family and scolded him for running around on his poor wife did his face warm up with embarrassment, and he tried to appease her by saying, "No harm done! That's just how young guys are nowadays!" (Tib. *pha med gi da de ring nang kha gsar bu cho red mo*).

NEW SEXUAL REGIMES

As this interaction and Drolma's framing of it indicate, the transformed social and political economic context under Chinese rule had greatly altered the gendered participation frameworks for sexual discretion in Labrang. Thus, in a newly emergent cultural politics of sexual recognition, the meanings attached to sexed bodies and gendered spaces had dangerously shifted, thereby threatening the enclosure of heterosexuality and especially female sexuality that had underwritten the participation frameworks of Geluk mandalization in the region. Commentary in international news media and pro-Tibet activist writings beginning in the late 1990s tended to depict these developments throughout Tibetan regions as emanating exclusively from the outside in.

Such writings portrayed the apparent breakdown of sexual morality among Tibetans as the direct result of Chinese colonization efforts, the intentional "sexual degradation" (Jamyang Norbu 1999: 4) of the people in order to demoralize and thus better control them. Significantly, they focused on the increasing numbers of "prostitutes" as the main indicators of these "social evils," enumerating them, debating their motivations, methods, and places of origin.[17] (Some argued they were mostly Han Chinese migrants.) As one exiled Tibetan interviewed for the 1999 Tibet Information Network Briefing Paper on prostitution in Lhasa put it (TIN 1999: 22): "Earlier our society was a conservative society, with a lot of influence from traditional values. Earlier there was no space for pre-marital and extra-marital sex. But now society has changed. I think it is largely because of the bad influence that the Chinese have brought. . . . Now sex is relatively open in our society in Lhasa."

As I found in my fieldwork, such portrayals could resonate strongly with local Tibetans' views about the spatial and temporal structure of change. As we saw in chapter 2, within the culture of nostalgia and resistance that emerged around local historical memories of the radical disjunctures of the Maoist years, Tibetans were hard pressed to view themselves as anything but the victims of outside forces and agents of change embodied in the figure of Apa Gongjia.[18] But as I have argued in previous chapters, such constructions of self and Other can hamper an understanding of the vigorous, yet ambivalent, agencies of differently positioned Tibetans past and present as they negotiated modernities on their own terms—negotiations that had differential effects for men and women.

As I mentioned above, these processes were already in motion before the PLA marched into Labrang in the fall of 1949. But it was not until the CCP's violent overthrow of the monastery in 1958 that Chinese state agents were able to eradicate forcibly the gendered spatial practices that had kept the crucial symbiotic relationship between Tibetan celibate asceticism and sexuality socially invisible. At the same time as local cadres closed the monastery, returned monks to lay life, and organized Tibetan dewa into communes, a crucial part of state efforts to dismantle the local patrifilial moral economy centered on the monastery and to channel all value to the state was the attempt to shift the economic center of gravity to monogamous couples devoted to the collective. Hence in 1958 Labrang's town government and rural commune cadres attempted to widely enforce the "modern" marriage and gender relations first mandated in the 1950 marriage law in efforts to register all marriages as monogamous, freely chosen unions (XXZ 1997:700). Thus, as indexed by the frequent changes in the national marriage and other domestic-relations laws made by subsequent Party regimes through the 2000s, efforts to regulate new forms of sexual discretion in Labrang, as elsewhere, were an important part of the ongoing process of national incorporation.

In this light, we could see the mandatory public performativity of socialist androgyny in Labrang after 1958 as the outcome of CCP efforts to incorporate Labrang into the PRC nation by imposing a new regime of sexual discretion posited on an ideal of the nearly complete visibility and service of the biological body to the public body politic (Ch. *gong*). In actuality though, such efforts to mandate a new sexual regime among Tibetans had only limited effects by the mid-1960s (XXZ 1997: 700). Thus, at the height of the Cultural Revolution, socialist androgyny amounted in practice to a pitched politics of recognition in which bodies indexed a Communist sexual puritanism. That is, despite the actual practices of individuals and collectivities, the (supposedly) gender-neutral drab pants and shirts indicated one's renunciation of all the bourgeois, private distractions of ethnic pride, personal pleasure, and erotic desire; the consignment of sexuality to the "scientific" context of state-regulated reproduction within monogamous marriage; and the dedication of all household members, including women, to "productive labor" on behalf of the collective.

Zealous Chinese and Tibetan cadres, in 1958 and again during the Cultural Revolution, drew on the righteousness of this "true" renunciation to reject the cultural provisions that had kept Tibetan monastic renunciation prestigious and powerful—attempting to desacralize it by casting once discreet sexual practices as perverse sexual crimes. As one ex-monk asserted in a now infamous article written several months after the crackdown at Labrang and echoing the extreme terms of speaking-bitterness narratives, "[Monks and lamas are] more ferocious than wild animals. There is not one who has not violated a woman, and not one who has not violated the young monks. They are all like beasts" (Anonymous 1958). And among the "activist" Tibetan women participating in public struggle sessions were "liberated" women, whom cadres had labeled "prostitutes" and encouraged to accuse monks and lamas of sexual exploitation (cf. Jurists 1960: 222; Hershatter 1997: 322). As we saw in chapter 2, it took the brute imposition of an unprecedented state-sponsored feminism to get Tibetan women into pants—to dispense with some of the Tibetan limits on their social mobility and promote the virtue of their taking some leadership roles as citizens of a modern Chinese nation.

Yet as many recent theorists have argued, there is much to suggest that this Communist regime of sexual discretion based on an ideal of a gender-egalitarian sexual purity never eradicated deeply held assumptions in Chinese discourses, codified in KMT-era scientific sexology, that associated normal sexuality with "naturally compulsive" male desire for female objects (cf. Dikotter 1995, Evans 1997, Hershatter 1997). In fact, the new regime merely substituted different bodily practices for maintaining the social invisibility of sexuality, while retaining the close link between male sociopolitical power and the ability to choose multiple female sex partners. The ongoing exploitation of women in this fashion was one of the main ways Han state officials allied with local and non-Han men, drawing on compelling points of overlap in different androcentric systems to make social reforms more palatable by allowing local men to exercise power at certain junctures. This deep androcentrism would then shed light on the adamant narratives I heard from several older former monks at Labrang, a similar account of which the Panchen Lama tells in his 1962 report on CCP atrocities in Amdo regions (1997: 50). They told me that when monks who had not been arrested at Labrang were forced to marry, they were lined up along with unmarried laywomen in a room with cadres looking on. But according to them, it was the men who were allowed to "choose" their wives among the women assembled there.

This was the source of much disgust and shock among Tibetans and Chinese who witnessed the disparity between Communist moral ideals and the actual behavior of some cadres. As Zhang Qingyou reports, CCP officials in Linxia (just east of Labrang) attempted to appease Tibetans protesting the Communist occupation of

Labrang in the early 1950s by punishing scores of Han cadres sent there to set up the government for flagrant "corruption" and "whoring" (Ch. *suji piaochang*) with local Tibetan women. The cadres protested they were merely respecting local customs as they had been instructed to do, and that refusing Tibetans' "gifts" would have been insulting (Zhang Qingyou 1991: 50). And the Panchen Lama disgustedly reports that Tibetan monastic officials appointed to the new "Democratic Management Committees" were openly wearing lay clothes, seeking prostitutes (Ch. *suji*) and having sex with women on monastic grounds (Ch. *sinei jielian funu*; Panchen Lama 1997: 55).

Effectively, the forced assimilation of Tibetans to a new moral order under Communist rule was accomplished through the radical collapse of those gendered proscriptions on corporeal discretion that had kept Tibetan celibate asceticism and sexuality socially separate and mutually beneficial. The remarkable regulatory power of the so-called modern socialist morality thus worked to open unprecedented spaces for some Tibetans to experience liberating agency. Yet at the same time the relentless promulgation of such a socialist morality in state discourse served to underscore the obscenity of state officials' attacks on Tibetan gender practices.

CONVERGING GAZES AND DISPROPORTIONATE BURDENS

This perspective sheds further light on the precarious nature of Geluk remandalization efforts after reforms, efforts that relied on reconstituting the ritual and political economic efficacy of male celibacy within fundamentally altered participation frameworks that were increasingly mediated by state and global agents and exchanges. This process, as we have seen, produced the everyday dilemmas facing young Tibetans, especially young women, who were caught between urgent conservative pressures and passionate aspirations for modernity. As I argued in the previous chapter, the transition to post-Mao reforms under Deng's new Party regime was accomplished in large part through the powerful convergence of state and local androcentrisms, in which Tibetan men took leadership roles in monastic and secular governments, and the patriarchal bias of marriage and property law was carried forward in reconfigured legislation. And yet, the increasing numbers of young men moving to Labrang as monks in the 1980s came up against state efforts to contain the monastery as a tourist site and as a circumscribed educational institute, to which admission was supposed to be limited to the most virtuous, scholarly elite (see chapter 5).

In post-Mao Labrang, then, nostalgic efforts throughout the Tibetan community to rebuild the monastery "exactly as it was" (Tib. *a na ma na red*), and thereby protect the virtue and ritual power of male celibacy, ultimately held monks to a *higher standard* for bodily performance than ever before, foregrounding celibacy as the main measure of a monk. In fact, as we have seen, the exigencies of "reform and opening up" had broadened the frameworks for the local recognition of persons to an unprecedented extent. As many Tibetans told me, nowadays shameful behavior on the part of Tibetan monks or laity was not just a matter of individual sin or weakness. Instead, as my earnest young lay male friend and schoolteacher Dargye put it, such behavior brought disgrace on the whole minzu group (Tib. *mi rigs gi ʒhabs 'den*). As he used the term, "minzu" referred to a panregional community, now defined in contradistinction to the audience of "modern" Others descending on the town in increasing numbers—the foreign and Han Chinese tourists who were informed by their own romantic assumptions about the ideal sexual morality of "real" Tibetan monks in contradistinction to the relatively unfettered sexuality of the lay Tibetan folk.

Yet as we have seen, the shifted political economic frameworks for profitable exchange under reforms meant that neither local Tibetans' defensive conservatism in revitalizing monasticism nor state regulations and development projects could fully contain the expanding aspirational mobilities of young Tibetan men and women. In this local context, we can better appreciate the now global role of sexuality as another crucial aspect of the "feminine hinge" so fundamental to capitalist modernization efforts. That is, a particular vision of hypereroticized heterosexuality constructs a polarized hierarchical vision of sex difference, and it adds the powerful pull of experiences of biological arousal to the naturalization and elision of emerging social stratification vis-à-vis access to capital and the fruits of modernization (cf. Lin 1999). And yet, especially in places like Labrang, visions of gendered sexuality could operate for ordinary folks and cadres alike as master tropes for the promiscuous *mixing* manifest in selfish or asocial exchange—that is in forms of exchange perceived to be ultimately consumptive (extracting value) rather than reproductive (channeling value into key, sometimes competing, social units: i.e., households, "the Tibetan community," the county, or the nation; cf. Anagnost 1995).

I found that in the 1990s local Tibetans' efforts to control sexuality in this transformed context, and thus reestablish powerful Tibetan difference, ironically brought them onto shared ground with the Chinese state and popular media. This is so because the weight of public scrutiny and negative social consequences came down not on transgressing males (robed or not) but on publicly visible female bodies (those of both laywomen and nuns) as iconic of both inappropriate, disruptive sexual agency in particular *and* asocial capitalist exchange in general. In fact, Tibetans' struggles to both maintain an authentic Tibetanness linked to the past and to participate in the juggernaut of global modernities were premised on deeply assumed correspondences between, on the one hand, their own notions of privileged male sexual agents pursuing female objects and, on the other, those they saw in the proliferating discourses of the media. Thus, as I argued above, in post-Mao Labrang, Tibetan women and femininities bore the brunt of the disciplinary burden of state and local interests in reproductive labor and consumption while simultaneously embodying the sexualized fetish of easily obtained capital. Yet, despite the intense personal dilemmas these seemingly contradictory pressures posed for young Tibetan laywomen and nuns in town, such pressures were ultimately linked in state-local efforts to fix localities while channeling and domesticating the translocal aspirations of *young men*.

Thus, as young Tibetan laymen and monks sought ways to stave off the emasculating effects of their participation in refigured career frameworks under Chinese state auspices and reclaim masculine mobility—out of households and across public spaces—young women found their movements curtailed by increasing demands that they simultaneously shore up the household economy and exhibit a Tibetan feminine respectability and bodily purity that would maintain the inviolability of male celibacy. Aspiring laywomen like Drolma, Deji, and Tashi Ji were thus pulled between such local demands, their own newly possible aspirations for social mobility and independent sexual agency, and the profound sexism of the market and the state that in the 1990s increasingly collaborated to commodify women categorically as sexual objects to be consumed.

As we saw in chapters 2 and 3, for many young women (of any minzu) who had grown up since the Communist takeover, the radical period had broadened the participation frameworks for public female agency. Yet Fulian feminist criticisms of old "feudal" controls on female sexuality and the enforced androgyny and sexual prudery of the Maoist years meant that young women throughout China widely experienced the reform period as a time for asserting what felt like a liberating feminine difference and sexuality modeled after the kind they associated with a "Western" modernity (cf. Honig and Hershatter 1988, Evans 1997, X. Li 1998). In the Labrang region, this meant that an unprecedented number of young Tibetan laywomen, many with the support of their natal households, acted on their aspirations for social mobility and sought higher education. And many experimented with Western fashion and makeup, or left home regions against household opposition looking for ways to participate in the modern forms of work and egalitarian, freely chosen love and household relationships widely extolled in state and popular discourses. Meanwhile, as I have argued elsewhere, Labrang had also become a regional center for unprecedented numbers of young rural Tibetan women seeking to join the three nunneries being rebuilt there.[19]

By the early 1990s, Labrang, with its unique opportunities for secular and monastic education, wage work, and contacts with cosmopolitan Others, had become a gathering place not only for young monks and nuns but also for unmarried ambitious Tibetan laywomen and laymen from surrounding rural Lhade as well from rural regions of Qinghai and Sichuan provinces. In the midst of this onslaught, Tibetan residents of village Lhade across generations often characterized the change to the town as the extraordinarily promiscuous intermingling of males and females in public spaces. I found that they tended to express their anger and disgust in terms mirroring those set down in state discourses. Echoing late-1980s state anxiety about the "spiritual pollution" let into China with the "opening up" process, locals, especially the older generations, were appalled and perplexed by the moral ambiguity and social "chaos" (often expressed using the Chinese loanword *luan*) they felt came in from the outside, despite the increase in young Tibetan men's and women's monasticism. Ama Metok was an opinionated and cosmopolitan shopkeeper in her late forties who came to Labrang in 1984 when her husband, a local, returned to Labrang from exile in India. As I sat with her behind the counter of their small shop where they sold the miscellaneous small goods and snacks pilgrims and tourists preferred, she would hold forth, in bitter and sarcastic tones, on her low view of the town: "So many young people just marry for a short time, have kids, and then go their separate ways," she insisted; "so many kids around here have this father or that mother. They have no feeling [in Chinese, *ganqing*] for each other. Like me and Gonday: we have been married twenty-four years. That's the way it should be. But these young people, all they look for is money!" (Tib. *sgor mo lta rgyu red*).

As many observers have recently pointed out, despite the relative lenience of the reform years, Chinese state policy and propaganda continued to emphasize the evils of premarital sex and the great virtues of sex for reproduction within a well-regulated monogamous marriage. In fact, for beleaguered state officials confronting the Janus-faced consequences of opening the country to international trade, regulated sexuality had again become a key barometer of enlightened modern civilization and national health. For example, as Dutton notes, some of the harshest policing policies of the late 1980s and early 1990s were reserved for those involved in prostitution and pornography (1998: 13). And by July 2000, as reported in *China News Digest*, rising perceptions of a national phenomenon of "family disintegration," due to widening national awareness of practices of bigamy, concubinage, and domestic violence by new elite businessmen, had garnered unprecedented bureaucratic cooperation in efforts to amend the marriage law to legislate them. Finally, Ann Anagnost argues that it was precisely the modernist goals of the Dengist state's birth-planning policies (Ch. *jihua shengyu*) that offered the best possibilities for "restor[ing] the statist ambitions of the party leadership" after the debacles of the Maoist years (1995: 23; cf. Scharping 2003). Yet the birth-planning emphasis on later marriages, and the greater openness of the popular media about sexuality and romance, meant that youth sexuality was both highly problematized and greatly evident. And state prudery had not yet been overcome enough to implement widespread sex-education programs, or to make contraception widely available before marriage.

Instead, local Tibetan and state gazes converged on "sexually saturated" female bodies as the simultaneous objects of lust and social controls. Chinese discourses about "scientific" sexuality since the early twentieth century had focused on "naturally" compulsive male sex drives and the need to control "deviant" females pursuing sexual encounters—for the good of society and of the women themselves. As Harriet Evans argues, in CCP rhetoric for decades, the female "third party" (Ch. *di sanzhe*) was "constructed as the single most important—and dangerous—threat to marital and familial stability" (1997: 200). The female "third party" thus serves to fetishize the ultimate danger of the asocial consuming woman, she who seeks selfish pleasure and thus consumes or destroys key social relationships. Thus since the 1980s, "cautionary tales" aimed at curbing extramarital sexuality were widely circulated in newspapers, youth magazines, and local rumors. These tales had different messages for men and women (cf. Honig and Hershatter 1988). For men, they emphasized the great danger of being duped and drained (of vital physical energy and money) by wily oversexed women. For women, they emphasized their vulnerability to being exploited by men and discarded, their reputations ruined forever. I found that this gendered construction of sexuality resonated strongly with Tibetans in Labrang, who lamented what they saw as young males' precarious hold on vows of marriage or celibacy. "Now," said Ama Metok, leaning forward confidentially, "many monks can be seen going to the movie houses around here. Gonday gets very angry when he sees them going." But I argue that the ironic consequence of this was a confluence of conscious and unconscious responses that together worked to narrow the participation frameworks for sexual discretion for Tibetan women in town.

1) A manager at a conference goes to an elegant bar...

1.某实业有限公司经理肖斌为参加商品交易会来到某市,住进了豪华的酒店最高级房间。

2) The bait: a beautiful woman...

2.他刚进房间,一个妙龄少女随之而来。1.70米的个头,婷玉立,凤眉樱唇,加上两个迷人的小酒窝,肖斌看呆了。

3) The hook: sex for a price...

3.对眼前的少女,肖斌自然是知道她是干什么职业的。"多少钱?开个价吧!"他爽快地说,少女含笑不语,伸出了两个五指,肖斌二话没讲,留少女住下了。

4) The trap: she demands more... 5) The threats: 5 thugs outside...

2000元钱,但他不为所动,提出要两万元,少一分都不付,否则告他强奸。

走,却见四、五个凶形大汉守在门口,他横恶又凌地转。在他们的逼迫下,只好拿出两万元钱。

6) Words spreads. His family broken, he dies of a heart attack.

开了爱不了解此大的打击,肖斌终因心脏两突复而命归黄泉了。

身败名裂赴黄泉
为还一夜风流债

丁振济 作

To Pay for One Night of Romance, He Ends His Life in Disgrace!

FIGURE 15.
Cautionary tale cartoon in *Tibet Daily* newspaper (Lhasa),
May 1995

By the early 1990s, Tibetans in Labrang widely accepted the state's discourse on prostitution as a social evil and a crime that gave inappropriate sexual and commercial license to unattached women. Thus, indignant men and women in our conversations tended to blame the increasing divorce rate and flagging monk discipline on unmarried women in town they now labeled "prostitutes." And pervasive gossip about young nuns in town emphasized their supposed frequent sexual liaisons with monks (see Makley 2004). Indeed, Ama Metok offered no other causal explanation for young monks' unprecedented public consumption practices except for her quick leap to lamenting the presence of prostitutes in town. Leaning forward again, she whispered that "around here it is only this [pointing toward her crotch] and this [rubbing thumb and fingers together, meaning money]." And Drolma, during another of our long conversations, explicitly equated unmarried women seeking sexual encounters in town with prostitutes *and*, switching to Chinese to make the point, with "third parties," the ones, "just like in the movies," who were responsible for breaking up households. In these examples of the micropolitics of sexual contextualization, in addition to the newly problematized category of "nuns" (Tib.

jo mo, a ne), we find the emergence of "prostitution" as a new general category for dangerous sexual exchanges with any unattached women, despite, as we will see, the actual diversity of sexualized exchanges in the valley. In Labrang by the mid-1990s, even though many Tibetan women taking money for sexual services gave a cut of their earnings to dance-hall managers, most worked independently. Thus in such conversations, locals explicitly associated "prostitutes" with unproductive illegitimate entrepreneurship, those whose asocial commercial activities as "third parties" selfishly built careers outside patrifilial household exchanges and thus literally consumed upstanding lay households. In contradistinction to the disciplined mobilities associated with nama, "prostitutes" (and, ironically, nuns) stood for undisciplined consuming bodies (cf. Anagnost 1995).

This type of entrepreneurship then contrasted sharply with the state-touted masculine ideal of bold capitalist enterprise for producing jobs and consumer goods that was supposed to productively modernize both localities and the nation. And it flew in the face of state development efforts to recruit women to sex-appropriate forms of productive local enterprise, such as retail marketing and services. Indeed, when I first traveled to Labrang in the early 1990s, there were very few local Tibetan merchants on the streets, but by 1995, Lhade village matriarchs, like Ama Metok, had taken up their former niche of retailing to visiting nomads and pilgrims cheap goods and secondhand clothing imported by husbands and sons, literally cornering the streetside intersection market opposite the monastery. The cleverest among them could bring in much income for their households *and* receive state recognition for it. I was amazed when one of the leading street vendors, Ama Damdrin, a woman in her fifties with a quick smile and a flashing gold tooth, took me home for dinner. Their house, all from commerce, she proudly told me, had been built five years earlier and was huge, including space for a planned altar. Proudly displayed on the wall of their guest room was her 1981 award from the county government: "progressive producer Comrade Damdrin" (Ch. *xianjin shengchanzhe* Damdrin Tongzhi).

In effect, in contrast to this locally rooted and state-encouraged female commerce emerging among decollectivized Lhade residents, the presence in the valley of foreign and urban Han women tourists, as well as of rural Tibetan laywomen and nuns, exhibited an unprecedented translocal mobility of female bodies. This had dangerously sexualized and desacralized public spaces in and outside the monastery. It thus had become paramount for local women to distinguish themselves from the unrestrained sexuality associated with tourist women, nuns, and prostitutes—even though for many young laywomen in town who sought to distance themselves from commercial sex their own aspirations for independent social mobility and their desire to postpone the disproportionate burdens of marriage were precisely the motivations that were increasingly leading young women of every stripe to accept money for sex, not only in Labrang, but across the country.[20] In the Lhade villages, this process took the form of the simultaneous vilification of "prostitutes" as exclusively selfish lowbrow merchants financing illegitimate consumption on one hand, and on the other an intensifying insistence on the correctness of an ideally Tibetan feminine respectability, along with the progressive devaluation of forms of marriage other than ideally negotiated patrilocal unions.

From this angle, we would have to see the revival I discussed in chapter 3 of girls' coming-of-age rites in the Lhade villages as frameworks for the public demonstration of girls' *ideally corporate* agency—that is, by manifesting the "indebtedness engineering" of time-delayed reciprocal gifting among household members and between households, the rites were hopeful corporate efforts to earmark the mobilities and sexual careers of daughters, whose activities had often expanded outside the household, for future trajectories of proper consumption for the reproduction of patrifilial household networks (cf. Appadurai 1986: 12). Further, as Ama Karma complained to me one day while describing her efforts to find a husband for her granddaughter, it had become much harder for a household without sons to find a man willing to take on the labor and residential requirements of marrying in and becoming a *makwa* or surrogate son. And I found that the perceived public chaos of the market town heightened elders' sense that women's sexual liaisons while living in natal households were illegitimate—that is, participating in no lasting commitment to a household's patrimony. Thus across the community people tended to equate the practice of "temporary husbands" with "prostitution" and disgustedly echo the sentiment that in Labrang, kids didn't know their fathers, only their mothers. Apa Sangye for example grimaced when I mentioned the phrase "temporary husbands." He immediately distinguished the practice from married couples (Tib. *bza' ba*). Temporary marriages, he said, are when two people who have not had a feast just live together or have regular trysts. He said that that practice was common here in Labrang but would never occur in his rural home region. "Here in Labrang," he insisted, "they have no shame" (Tib. *ngo tsha rgyu med gi*).

The performative burden of bodily shame and ritualized purity thus disproportionately fell on young women, even when their robed bodies and shaved heads as nuns rendered them almost indistinguishable from young monks and publicly asserted their commitments to altruistic lifelong celibacy (see Makley 2004). Respectably feminine adult women were expected to publicly index their potentially altruistic motherhood by demonstrating their distance from inappropriate heterosexuality and commercial exchanges in their discreet speech, dress, and physical distance from laymen and monastic bodies and spaces. Against the shameless public visibility of young women and men in town, the demure embarrassment of naive young girls or wives, devoted to the work of their households, served to shore up the moral superiority of discreet sexuality as reproductive exchange. Hence in everyday conversation, the phrase most widely used to characterize the behavior of brazenly public women was the Tibetan idiom *nyak gi nyok gi*, which locals often interchanged with the Chinese idiom *qi da ba da*. Both carry connotations of extraordinary disorder, but the Tibetan adds the sense of *corporeal filth*—due to indiscriminate and polluting intermingling. Drolma often used that Tibetan trope to describe "prostitutes" in town, and in our talk, she sought my acknowledgment of her difference from them: "We two are correct, aren't we? We found husbands and got married!" (Tib. *da 'u gnyis ka rang gis bza' tshang zig gi btsal las de byas dang na, nga cho 'grigs bsdad gi e na?*)

Yet, as many of my laywomen and nun friends in Labrang discovered, their efforts to keep their sexuality appropriately invisible could not prevent the increasing visibility adhering to all young female bodies concomitant with the broadening "scopophilia" (cf. Mulvey 1975) of consumer capitalism in the PRC. As elsewhere in China, one of the most compelling attractions of a cosmopolitan modernity for young Tibetans was the vision of open, erotic heterosexuality premised on the heightened pleasures of a hyperempowered man possessing a hypersexualized woman (cf. Lin 1999, Hyde 2001). Since the 1980s in China, the promise of such pleasure had been coded on the naked or seminaked bodies of Western and, increasingly, Chinese or other Asian women models, who were then posed and framed to sell everything from playing cards to state-sponsored scholarly journals. These, as elsewhere, were the marketing practices that directly associated the erotic thrill of passive, compliant femininity with the easy accessibility of the pleasures produced by capital. In the Labrang region, where realist images and photographs of ordinary people had been widely introduced only during the Maoist years, the hyperrealism of photographs of ideal sexualized Others thus offered Tibetan consumers (men *and* women) the pleasures and power of a new form of decontextualized looking, a kind of voyeurism based on a refigured aesthetics of gendered bodies as objects to be desired and envied (cf. Goffman 1979, Kuhn 1985, Harris 1999).

In Labrang, monks and laypeople I spoke to often said it was the naturally irresistible lure of such exposed female bodies depicted in smuggled videos that drew the crowds of young men and monks to video halls at night. And in our conversations, young Tibetan men expressed envy and resentment of the tall, muscular bodies and aggressive virility of white men they saw in the media or attributed to male tourists in town. For example, during a party one evening in my room, a well-known Tibetan folksinger, who hailed from a nomad region and always emphasized his nomadic masculinity in dress and demeanor, got very drunk. Inhibitions gone, he expressed his sadness at the fate of Tibetans under Chinese rule and in the same breath told me how much he wanted to exchange his five-foot-five body for the over-six-foot-tall blonde one of the young German tourist man sitting opposite him. Meanwhile, rumors abounded of the easy sexual availability of white women in town and elsewhere, and I was asked more than once by Tibetan men and women if it was true that we Americans could have several spouses, keeping wives or husbands in all the different places we visited.

Contrary to concerned pronouncements in pro-Tibet activist discourse in the late 1980s and the 1990s about the pervasive and increasing "apathy" and despair of young Tibetan men in China, I found that many young men in the Labrang region were extremely vigorous in their pursuit of possible "modern" futures and lifestyles held out for them in the globalizing media. In the context of the state's relentless surveillance of and crackdown on any sign of Tibetan dissident activity, and the increasing education gap separating urban Han youth from minorities (cf. Bass 1998), newly available commodities offered a particularly appealing way for many young Tibetan men to avoid state violence while shoring up their (Tibetan) masculinities and participating in modernity. As I argued in previous chapters, under CCP rule the realm of the private in the valley had become increasingly elaborated and valorized, associated with both secret spaces or aspirations for resistance to Chinese state hegemony, and for fantasies of transcendence—of the limitations of the state and the now intensely feminized local and domestic order. In this context, forms of communal consumption and voyeurism as masculine *networking* emerged as the most accessible avenues for youthful masculine translocal agency, thereby constructing a bifurcated feminine Other that marked the refigured boundary between public/translocal and private/local: the female sexual commodity outside and the respectable feminine (ethnic) reproducer inside.

In fact, as I discovered from many Tibetan lay male friends and acquaintances, communal masculine consumption—of alcohol, food, travel funds, and cigarettes—was considered to be an essential means for building and reproducing the vital masculine networks across generations and regions that in post-Mao China provided any opportunities for social mobility or participation in commercial entrepreneurship. The strong sense that this was an *unavoidable* aspect of masculine personhood was perhaps expressed most starkly by Thupten, a young cosmo-politan hotel manager who had returned to Labrang from exile. At an afternoon party at the home of his friend, a well-known Tibetan Public Security Bureau (PSB) cadre, he matched his friend's rapid succession of drinks while explaining to me in English that even though female maids at the hotel made less than he did: "It's better for women [gesturing toward the two young women in the room], because they don't smoke or drink. For us men it's hard, because we have to smoke and drink. Whenever a friend comes to town, we have to shell out money to enter-tain them. When a festival like Losar comes around, all we do is drink, going to different friends' houses all day." He summed up by emphasizing that his monthly tab at the hotel bar was often more than his monthly salary.

In this context then, the shared practice among young men of consuming hypersexualized women as quintessentially available commodities worked to mas-culinize their broader consumption practices as valorized and important forms of entrepreneurship—that is, as canny, wishful investments in a potentially profitable future. Meanwhile, they could retain the propriety of their Tibetan households by insisting on the relative stasis and respectability of Tibetan women. As the wealthy Tibetan businessman visiting Labrang who had just propositioned me sheepishly said, when I indignantly asked him about his wife at home: "Tibetan women have it hard. But we Tibetans have too many rules for them" (Ch. Zangzu *funu hen xinku. Women* Zangzu *guiju tai duo*).

In contrast to Chinese urban centers, in Labrang during the mid-1990s the pub-lic exposure of young women's bodies was still strikingly Other, signaling to many locals I spoke with an almost completely unfettered sexuality. Tibetan women never appeared in public or in images with their bodies bared.[21] In fact, I never saw a Tibetan woman there wearing a Western-style dress. Instead, the most fashion-able of young women in town preferred to feminize pants and long-sleeved shirts—wearing high heels, large earrings, and baseball caps. My nun friends in particular were meticulous about properly covering their bodies in public. Mean-while, Western and Chinese women tourists who walked through town in shorts and sandals sent ripples through Tibetan onlookers, and one traumatized Chinese woman in a halter top was chased down the main street by a group of Tibetan boys.

But Tibetan women themselves could not escape the ordering power of the new consumerist voyeurism. By the early 1990s in Labrang, Tibetan female bodies in public drew looks—whether it was to scrutinize them for their opposition to the undressed commodity, or to judge them in terms of the new corporeal eroticism. As many observers have noted, since the mid-1980s in state and popular media forums Tibetan women had been represented as icons of exotic, ethnic Tibetanness, representations of the exciting availability of "Tibet" as a service society for Han urbanites (cf. Gladney 1994, Harrell 1995, Lopez 1998). I noted in the introduction that tourism literature about Labrang (produced both locally and elsewhere) featured young Tibetan women in tight-fitting "traditional" dress, as dancers and hotel hostesses. Indeed the turn of the sexualizing gaze to Tibetan women had only intensified since Deng's call to the market in 1992. The first of several "Miss Tibet" contests was held at the Lhasa Holiday Inn in 1992 (Zhambu 1992, Macgranahan 1996), and a decade later such efforts in the PRC were matched by a competing "Shambala Miss Tibet" contest founded by a young Tibetan man in Dharamsala, sparking much controversy among the exiled community (cf. Page 2002, RFA 2002). By 2004, the PRC Xinhua news agency announced that the tourism bureau of the TAR had "launched a two-month-long pageant to select Tibetan beauties to serve as image ambassadors for tourism promotion," and, not to be outdone, the organizers of the "Miss Tibet" pageant in exile claimed that the 2004 TAR pageant was meant to counter theirs, and that the third annual exile pageant already had six "girls" confirmed as contestants.

Fully in line with trends in Chinese regions (cf. Evans 1997: 15; Schein 1997), even the prestigious Amdo Tibetan literary journal *Drangchar* (Tib. *sbrang char*, "Light Rain") from the early 1990s on featured on its covers, with almost monotonous regularity, young, beautiful Tibetan women in traditional dress—even though the journal and the writings it showcases were produced almost exclusively by men. Yet it is perhaps no coincidence that the journal's designers shifted to featuring beautiful, ethnically marked Tibetan women on its covers (versus the highly regarded Tibetan male poets and writers featured in the 1980s) just after state officials in Qinghai and Gansu became concerned about the increasing attention young nationalist Tibetan male writers were garnering among educated youth. By the late 1980s, several prominent poets had been arrested in Amdo, and one of the most promising, the much-hailed Dondrup Gyal, committed suicide in 1985 (Tsering Shakya 2000).

Thus, commodifying ethnic women on journal covers not only sold journals but also signaled assent on the part of Tibetan intellectuals to state-sponsored capitalism, thereby working to divert attention from the journal's function as a major site of Tibetan male cultural production. In these ways, the pressures of a repressive state and a sexist market drew Tibetans themselves into capitalizing on longstanding fantasies among Chinese and Westerners about the exotic sexuality of

Tibetan women. As Gail Hershatter states, in the mid-1990s wealthy Chinese businessmen in the eastern coastal regions were willing to pay as much as five times more for sex with an exotic "minority" woman than with an urban Chinese woman (1997: 348; cf. Hyde 2001).

In places like Labrang, this new kind of eroticized looking was so powerfully insidious because it was so eminently gender-appropriate, and therefore *unmarked or invisible.* As elsewhere, Tibetan women, regardless of their commercial interests, were drawn in as they identified with the power and pleasure of attracting looks and thus exercising public sexuality. Yet, in addition to the rapid increase in numbers of young nuns visible on the streets, one of the things that most angered Labrang locals was the apparently unabashed pride of a group of young women who took money for sex in town. These were women from Lhade villages who identified with the historical reputation of beautiful Labrang women and as before lived at home while competing for clients among Tibetan male pilgrims and traders, and often taking customers to the small guesthouses owned and run by local Tibetan men. As Sodnam, my lay male friend who owned a guesthouse, explained to me, Labrang's Tawa town still had a reputation throughout Tibetan regions and India for beautiful, available Tibetan women, and though he did not allow liaisons on his premises, many of his Tibetan businessmen friends from other regions would book rooms with him for the express purpose of seeking them out. Some, he said, would not return after a few days, staying for the rest of their visit with their chosen lover. In some cases then, part of the very attraction to Labrang was the lure of easy sexual consumption for networking men. Kazang told me of the time he and his friends visited Labrang in the late 1990s, indulging in the services of such women. He jokingly told of the *layi* song his friend had made up: "The easy friends are Tawa women!" (Tib. *rog pa rtsa mo mtha' mo red*)—and the verse went on to advise that you can be very close with them for a night, and the next day they don't know you!

For their part, the women considered themselves to be at the pinnacle of a hierarchy of women selling sex in town. And they considered their high earnings and ability to purchase consumer goods to be direct evidence of their superior beauty *and* marketability.

FROM FIELD NOTES: met one such woman, the beautiful Lumo, gold tooth glinting jauntily, in a small dance hall renowned around town as a pick-up joint. We sat on benches at the edges of the room around which were scattered a few old nomad men and some very drunk young nomad men, some of whom looked to be no more than teen-agers. Lumo flopped down next to me, looking extremely sophisticated in her trench coat and silk scarf, and we struck up a conversation. Leaning in confidentially, she whispered to me in Chinese that all the women here were prostitutes (Ch. *mai pi de*), and she assured me that they, depending on one's "face," could make thousands of yuan a month, especially during festival seasons.

That was several times the average salary of a government cadre in town, and such successful women could then buy the accoutrements of modern femininity—makeup, jewelry, and leather jackets, thus further investing in their competitive value; these women were not just illegitimate consumers, but maverick entrepreneurs in pitched competition for the market in sex. In recent years, the intensification of their corporeal competition was indexed by the nicknames they acquired in town, which ranked them according to their physical beauty: "Number One Body," "Number Two Body," "Number Three Body" . . .

Despite the increasing outrage of some Lhade villagers, these women were elite in some ways, proudly reprising forms of female sexual agency and exchange that had been tolerated in pre-Communist Labrang. Several locals indignantly told me that they were so proud of their success this way that when the police raided guesthouses for prostitutes one summer and paraded the handcuffed couples down the street in an effort to humiliate them, the women instead arrogantly walked along as if it were a badge of honor. In the new cultural politics of sexual recognition in those circles, perhaps the PSB officials had played into their hands—their marketable value being enhanced by the transgressive display of their relative desirability. Further, many continued to contribute income to their natal households, and, it was rumored, some families even collaborated with daughters to host their "temporary husbands" for a fee. Several I knew were very pious supporters of the monastery, worshipping often and donating labor to its reconstruction or to cook and clean for monks. Meanwhile, the lower end of the sex-work hierarchy were the poor and sometimes desperate rural Tibetan women who came to Labrang as pilgrims or wage workers and sold sex for a couple of yuan a night. Locals still tended to associate the most polluting promiscuity with them.[22]

However, the expansion of Tibetan men's gender-appropriate agency into activities and sexual pursuits associated with prestigious modern consumption meant that *all* Tibetan women had to work harder—in household labor and in protecting their bodies and reputations. As I argued in chapter 3, contrary to state feminist rhetoric, in the Labrang region there were still very few opportunities for women's education or participation in market enterprises. And the moral flux of the sexist marketplace had diminished the public spaces and times through which young women could pass with their sexuality unmarked, thus remaining safe from assumptions of easy availability. Even the most elite of the sex workers had to work hard to keep men's advances in forms and in times and spaces they agreed to:

FROM FIELD NOTES: After we switched from Chinese to the more familiar Tibetan, Lumo told me that she had grown up in a nomad family in southern Qinghai, the fourth of seven children, and that she had come to Labrang several years ago. She leaned over then and told me she was dying to go to America (Tib. Meigo *a 'gro na 'dod gi*) and hoped to save enough money for the trip. She was determined in this, even when my lay male friend Sodnam told her that was highly unlikely. With a sour look, she switched back to Chinese: "This place is a dead-end" (Ch. *zher mei yisi*). I added, "especially for women," and she agreed heartily, perhaps hoping to win my help, saying: "Women here have it so hard!" (Ch. *zhege difang de nude tai ku le*). Just before we were to leave, a drunken nomad boy seated on her other side began to flop over her, grabbing her head and shoulders. She tried feebly to pull him off, but he got her in a headlock, and she had to endure it until his friend came and dragged him outside. I left her sitting there, hair a mess, and told her to be careful. She replied: "No problem. I'm used to it."

As for Drolma, she ruefully explained one day that it was essential for a respectable young woman to keep her sexuality discreet and not to be seen with prostitutes, or else her "reputation" (Ch. *mingsheng*) would be lost for good, humiliating her husband and family and exposing her to the advances of strange men. Yet as several of my young unmarried women friends told me, knowledge of sex and use of contraceptives (something widely assumed to be women's exclusive responsibility) were associated with prostitutes. Thus unmarried women who indulged in sex with boyfriends (and there were many!) risked humiliating pregnancies or subjected themselves to multiple abortions in order to protect their reputations.[23]

As Drolma's narrative about her daytime encounter with the young Tibetan man in the street illustrates, the great difficulty for young Tibetan women was that even the diligent performance of devotion to an ideal household was not enough to stave off the insidious reach of the commodifying gaze. After all, the ultimate message of Deng Xiaoping's economic reforms after 1992 was that anything—or quintessentially any female body—could be possessed with money. Drolma's was only one of the many stories I was told by Labrang Tibetan women ranging in age from their teens to their late forties of being accosted on the street and offered money for sex by men young and old—even Ama Metok told me of the old nomad men who asked her to "go in the back" for a couple of yuan. The most dangerous spaces and times, the ones in which women risked men's physical violence, were those most closely associated with the practices of men's modern consumption and networking—nighttimes and the bars and dance halls (several of them Tibetan-owned) like the one I visited where Tibetan men and women performed *layi* songs and dances to hook up for the night. Young Tibetan women on the street at night were fair game—subject to harassment and physical advances.[24] I was told of several such incidents by young women who had attempted to go out at night on errands. Young nuns in town were subject to veiled resentment during the day, but if caught out at night they risked overt harassment and violence. A group of young nuns told me of the time they had had to go out at night to see a nun friend who had gotten ill. They said that they had encountered a group of monks who threw stones and yelled at them. They all agreed that it was very scary to go out at night.

Such gendered encounters in public spaces illustrated the difficulties for both Tibetan men and Tibetan women in negotiating newly demarcated and polarized public and private realms, and in achieving or conforming to the ideal gender roles associated with them, when so many quotidian challenges to such ideals existed. The intensifying cultural politics of gender and sexuality in this still subordinate Tibetan frontier region under Chinese rule meant that young Tibetan men and women were faced with the painful dilemma of increasing state and local demands for idealized Tibetan masculinities and femininities even as they encountered a diminished capacity or willingness to embody them. As I found during my fieldwork, this process could place aspiring men and women consumers at tragic odds with each other—while young men sought to shore up masculinities and transcend the local by feminizing it, young laywomen and nuns in unprecedented numbers sought to participate in modernity by expanding their educational and economic horizons as agents, not commodities, in powerful exchanges.

Such gendered consumption struggles in post-Mao Labrang were perhaps epitomized in the most public form of legitimized male violence against wives or girlfriends. This, as many friends told me, was when women cadres or workers from a Lhade village in town participated as agents in modern leisure by going to a dance hall in the evening with friends. Stories abounded of great public dramas in which husbands and boyfriends in a jealous rage burst in on office parties at restaurants or bars, making a show of roughing their women up and dragging them off home. Sadly, Drolma's life in Labrang perhaps encapsulated the potentially tragic consequences of such a gendered process. Over time, she could do little to keep her husband, Tsonji, an underpaid, low-level cadre, from spiraling down into depression, indolence, and increasingly, beating her.

Over the time of my stay in Labrang, I watched them both struggle mightily, as he made earnest efforts to repent, making offerings and prayers to the peaceful Buddhas in his natal household's altar, but also struggling to shore up his faltering masculinity by drinking with male friends. Importantly, in the context of the Tawa Lhade, the only dewas in the valley or anywhere else in which women household members were allowed to carry their households' annual offering arrows up to the dewas' mountain-deity abodes,[25] perhaps the most significant of Tsonji's efforts to bolster his masculinity were his prayers to strengthen the protection of his deity Amnye Shalak, his personal "warrior deity" or "birth deity" linking him to his home dewa as his place of birth (Tib. *dgra lha, skyes lha*). On the advice of a local diviner, Tsonji was to do this in order to stave off the attacks of the more powerful warrior deity of a male rival. But Drolma eventually gave up hopes for the romantic modern union she had left home for, and instead found herself more and more limited by his jealous anger. As his drinking binges and excursions with male friends increased, so too did his reprimands of her for being out too long, for singing love songs during a party, for being at work. No matter how much Drolma fought back—physically, during his increasingly vicious beatings, and socially, by striving to be an ever more pious wife and daughter-in-law, she could never convince him of her wholehearted commitment to him and his household.[26]

CONCLUSION:
CONSUMPTION FOR POWER?

I have shown that Labrang on the eve of the Communist victory was not the debauched and chaotic community of Chinese and foreigners' colonial fantasies. Instead, by looking at sexuality as people's situated negotiations between embodied moral ideals and the gendered practice of sexual discretion, we could appreciate the complex sociohistorical conditions in which a particularly Tibetan hierarchy of sexed bodies and purified agencies could keep the crucial relationship between celibate asceticism and sexuality in Labrang mutually beneficial and thus ritually powerful. The bodily disciplines of monasticism and marriage marked inappropriate heterosexuality, not homosexuality, as the most dangerous of transgressions to

Tibetans. And ritualized constraints on polluting female sexuality maintained the possibility for transcendent male subjectivity. But Tibetans' forced assimilation to a new socialist moral framework, and the sudden socioeconomic flux of the reform years, had profoundly altered the gendered participation frameworks for sexual discretion in town—resulting in the unprecedented intermingling of male and female bodies and ethnic Others in and around monastic spaces. As we have seen, the master trope of uncontrolled female sexuality among lay and monastic locals in the 1990s linked this sense of expanding, inappropriate mixing to anxieties over the unprecedented loss of control over channels of exchange.

I have tried to demonstrate in this chapter the difficult and differential consequences for men and women of a new eroticism of the frontier—in which state and local gazes converged on Tibetan women's bodies as commodified objects of both sexual desire and efforts to contain it. Under the press of intensifying voyeurism in the valley, the presence of both unmarried female sex workers and female monastics from rural regions most starkly demonstrated that Tibetan women were *not* categorically committed to the spatial and temporal cycles of local patrifilial exchanges, of themselves (in marriage), or of their labor (in subsistence production; cf. Gutschow 2001). In effect then, as Tibetan men's sexual agency expanded in unmarked ways to meet modernity, Tibetan women's sexuality was increasingly marked and curtailed in order to maintain the patrifilial integrity of Tibetan households and masculine power places.

This perspective, then, sheds light on the significance of a story circulating in Labrang in 1995 and 1996. I heard several versions of this narrative from lay and monastic men and women, and it was repeated to me as the oath-swearing truth, always in the context of conversations about chaotic sexuality and commercial exchange in town. In one version, it takes place in a guesthouse, in another in an open field, and in a third in Lhasa. In Drolma's version, a Tibetan woman from a Tawa Lhade accepted several hundred yuan to have sex with a foreign man (Tib. *phyi rgyal pa,* meaning American or European). But her client's huge penis, typical of such men, punctured her, nearly killing her and scarring her for life. Kazang's version was more detailed, and his female protagonist was from another Labrang Lhade. His narrative added that after her disastrous encounter, the woman was forced to go to the state-run hospital, where the doctors refused treatment until she admitted what she had done, and then they required her to pay an exorbitant fee—double the amount, he emphasized, that she had earned in her sexual transaction. She was informed (too late!) by the doctors that it is impossible for Tibetan women to have intercourse with foreign men because such men are too big.

We can see these narratives as local Tibetan versions of a "cautionary tale" for Tibetan women: they single out Tibetan women as the problematic agents in the perilous local encounter with the global. And the tales emphasize their inherent, inescapably physical handicap and vulnerability in the face of the overpowering capitalist lust of the West. Drawing on the authority of "scientific sexuality," the narratives punish the female protagonist for her greedy, independent, and public intercourse with modern commerce not only by condemning her to permanent damage to her body and reputation, but also, in Kazang's version, by saddling her with the consequences of a bad investment. Thus, the rumor encapsulated in narrative form the increasingly disproportionate burdens on local Tibetan women to maintain the moral contours of the community, even as young men and monks' participation in the modern marketplace was increasingly seen to weaken their commitments to households and the monastery (see chapter 5).

To recall the picnic scene with which I began this discussion, Drolma's quick and silent insistence on reminding my husband and me of a Tibetan sense of face-warming shame in that situation illustrates how women in Labrang carried the burden of keeping inappropriate heterosexuality invisible. Meanwhile, Tibetan men's expanding participation in the commodification of women as sexualized objects could be as unmarked and casual as exchanging girlie cards in a game among male friends. However, the danger for all Tibetans, men and women, was that the erotic appeal of a Han-mediated modernity substituted consumption for local autonomy and power, and diverted attention from the ongoing emasculation of *all* Tibetans in intensifying state efforts to exploit the frontier in the drive to capitalist modernization.

FIVE

Monks Are Men Too

Domesticating Monastic Subjects

THE MICROPOLITICS OF SEX AND CONTEXTUALIZATION: NEGOTIATING THE MASCULINITY OF MONKS

In the three previous chapters, we have come to see how a variety of interests and practices converged on maintaining the *marked* and metonymic nature of women and femininities in the frontier zone under CCP rule, even as violent political economic shifts also greatly altered the everyday participation frameworks for men and masculinities. In the preceding chapter, I demonstrated that, as against locals' perceptions of the unprecedented translocal mobility of youthful lay and monastic bodies in the valley under reforms, nunhood, and with it "prostitution," came to be (negatively) marked as ambiguous gender statuses. This process, I argue, served to shore up the categorically *unmarked* nature of monkhood as the moral ground for Geluk remandalization efforts. Yet this occurred at the same time as locals were acutely aware of the heightened problematic visibility of young male monastic bodies in public spaces since the early 1990s especially.

I argued in chapter 3 that Dengist economic reformers relied on Maoist state infrastructure to negotiate the contradictions inherent to the dynamics of statist capitalism. In the frontier zone especially, the profoundly sedentarist vision of a PRC nation comprised of hardworking locally rooted households under a still centralized CCP rule encountered the capitalist need for (channeled) mobility and the controlled yet bold transgression of translocal entrepreneurs. As Lisa Malkki and others have argued, in such contexts—but especially, I would add, in regions and among populations positioned as sites and sources of primary production—any nonstatist mobility can come to be "pathologized" in state discourses as abnormal, immoral, or threatening (Malkki 1997: 62). In the Labrang region we could see this as playing out most generally in a *gendered cultural politics of mobility*. In other words, in refigured visions of Amdo fatherlands versus Father State, the ongoing contestations over locals' proper aspirations and career trajectories under reforms were shaped by competing gendered kinship idioms for persons' naturalized commitments to households under transcendent masculine authorities. In this context, then, it was not just young Tibetan women's mobilities and aspirations that could be pathologized in local discourse and practice, but so too could those of young Tibetan *men*, especially nomad men and monks.

Thus, in this final chapter, I close my exploration of the fundamental roles of sex and gender in the recontextualization processes of national incorporation in the Sino-Tibetan frontier zone by coming full circle to consider again the precarious nature of Tibetan masculinities under CCP rule. Here, I examine the central and contested role of monastic masculinities in the ongoing dialogue, played out now on the (capitalist) road to "modernization," between the paternal authorities of Tibetan masculine divinity and those of the Chinese state. In this, to really get at the ways sex and gender categories operated locally, we have to consider monkhood in Labrang, along with lay man- and womanhood, to be one of three ideal gender statuses articulating in different ways with a male-female sexual-karmic polarity. In that Geluk mandalic order, monkhood gender held out the possibility for disciplined *transcendence* of the polluting attachments of one's sexual-karmic inheritance (cf. Keyes 1986: 85). A monk's transformed body, name, and practices were supposed to index the superiority of that gender status over the desires and aspirations of mere laymen—that was the performative basis of the crucial yet endangered diarchy of Tibetan masculinities in post-Mao Labrang.[1] But as we saw in chapter 3, Amdo Tibetan fatherlands of the reform era were supposed to be defined by the tightly circumscribed trajectories of especially male citizens' rational and unselfish aspirations for progress on behalf of local households—*and* on behalf of a national future to be accessed downriver and to the east. "Labrang" in Phakwa Gyab's praise poem as well as in Xiahe-county tourist maps was to signify only a site of capital accumulation and state administration limited to the narrow valley.

Yet as we have seen, just as in the early republican years, this statist spatiotemporal ideal encountered the political economic reality of the seemingly undisciplined mobilities and interregional networks of young Tibetan laymen and monks amidst the vigorous *re*mandalization efforts of Geluk trulkus based at the rebuild-ing monastery. Thus, by the mid-1990s, another crucial aspect of the micropolitics of sex and contextualization I encountered in Labrang was the convergence of interests, among Tibetan cadres and ordinary folks alike, on recreating and *domes-ticating* male monastic subjects in visions of a "true" or "normal" Tibetan monas-ticism, a process that again called Tibetan masculinities into question.

When the first of the Dalai Lama's post-Mao delegations toured the remaining buildings of Labrang monastery in 1979, that was the first time any exiled Tibetans had been back in a monastery in the PRC. They were greeted at the main assem-bly hall by just eleven elderly monks. According to Lobsang Samten, when dele-gation members asked the cadre in charge where all the monks had gone, they were told that they had all voluntarily left in 1958 and that none now wished to return (Avedon 1984: 336). Yet within a few years, especially after the Panchen Lama's efforts to establish Labrang as a regional center of monastic revitalization, hun-dreds of young men sought Buddhist teachings and ordination there. The influx of young monks swelled the ranks of the monastic community from the four hundred or so older former monks allowed to return in the early 1980s, to more than a thou-sand monks (only 800 of whom were officially recognized as members of assem-blies) living in and around the rebuilt monastery by the mid-1990s. The vast majority of those monks were under the age of thirty-five. Thus, largely because of the draw of the monastery, the valley had developed as an interregional node in which competing aspirations for mobility *and* fixity came to a head.

In this light, recall the tourism brochure I discussed at the beginning of this book, in which images of Tibetan women *and* monks were feminized next to a photograph of the cosmopolitan lay male hotel manager. Here, we could see Tibetan Buddhist monasticism as another important "feminine hinge" on which turned post-Mao state efforts to transition to reforms under a new Party regime. That is, in ways that were much more directly interventionist than the efforts of Qing courts ever were, Dengist state policy-makers attempted to circumscribe the centripetal pull of Labrang monastery and channel the mobilities of young Tibetan men by appropriating the participation frameworks for their ideal *taming* (Tib. *'dul pa*) under monasticism, thereby attempting to both fix and emasculate them vis-à-vis state authority and tourist consumers.

In this chapter then, I expand on my analysis in chapter 1 to emphasize how the dialogue between Tibetan masculine divinity and state authority came down to an emergent cultural politics of recognition around the loyalties and properly disci-plined bodies of monks. As we will see, many young monks, in their efforts to

inhabit a monastic status within the constraints of the transformed political economic situation in Labrang, drew on the relationship between lay and monastic
masculinities in new ways that were threatening the very grounds of post-Mao
Geluk remandalization. This perspective will then serve as a culminating account
of the stakes of national incorporation for the Tibetan community and for the
Chinese state at the turn of the twenty-first century.

THE FIST OF A MONK: MASCULINITY
AND THE MANDALA'S BORDERS

When the burly young monk hauled off and hit the young Chinese cameraman in
the face, so hard that the man's head snapped back in a whiplash motion, no one in
the crowd seemed shocked or surprised except the hapless cameraman himself. It
was early March 1996, the thirteenth day of the lunar new year in Labrang, the festival day on which a huge (roughly 15' × 30') appliqué thangka of a Buddhist deity
(Tib. gos sku) was unfurled to great fanfare on a hillside across the river from the
monastery. Akhu Konchok and I had followed the crowds of Tibetan nomads and
locals dressed in their finest, as well as Chinese and foreign tourists and photographers, pressing in to accompany the procession of young monks, more than thirty
of whom carried the furled image of Opakmay (Skt. Amitābha, the Buddha of
Immeasurable Light) up the monastery's main avenue to the ritual site. As another
of the principal ceremonies (the Cham Chen was held the following day) constituting the fifteen-day Great Prayer Festival, the display of the huge thangka represented one of the peak ritual events of the year. On that day, lay and monastic
communities came together to seek blessings from one of the most important
Buddhist deities and pray to him for peace and prosperity in the coming year.

The creation of such thangkas in the late 1980s and early 1990s, each of which
cost tens of thousands of yuan and required a team of artisans to complete, was
meant to carry forward the previous practice at Labrang of annually alternating
the display of images of peaceful Buddhas such as Donpa (Skt. Śākyamuni),
Tshongkhapa, Opakmay (Skt. Amitābha), and Shampa (Skt. Maitreya; cf. Luo
1987: 59; Li Anzhai 1992a; Suo Dai 1992: 51). The event, in effect, annually disclosed to lay and monastic subjects the most revered *peaceful* Buddhas in Geluk
teaching lineages, their hyperbolized size iconic of their transcendent authority
and splendor. Thus the display and worship of the massive thangkas during the
Great Prayer Festival served as an important performative counterpart to the disclosure of Chegyal's wrathful taming prowess on behalf of the community during

FIGURE 16.
A massive thangka of Donpa (Skt. Śākyamuni) is unfurled in the
spring of 1949 at the last *gos sku* ritual before CCP intervention.
The table of offerings to him stands next to the wall at his feet.
(Photo by Wayne Persons)

the Cham Chen the following day. That is, especially in the case of the image of
Tshongkhapa, the annual great thangka display constructed a communal mandalic
sphere for individual offerings to peaceful Buddhas, whose great wisdom and compassion were to be seen as the fruits of disciplined enlightenment. Those divine
agents were thus supposed to embody another essential aspect of Jamyang Shepa's
overarching masculine agency that linked his authority to the premises of Geluk
monasticism—the human possibility for moral and epistemological transcendence
through institutionalized discipline.

Thus the Great Prayer Festival, as a multimedia forum for the disclosure of
numerous peaceful and wrathful Buddhist deities, worked to construct an overarching mandalic sphere that indexed Geluk monasticism as the ideal participation
framework for the highest value exchanges. And, especially after the fifth Jamyang
Shepa moved to further consolidate monastic power in the early 1940s, the wide
range of Buddha emanation bodies manifest during the Great Prayer Festival
under the auspices of Jamyang Shepa and pressed to his will positioned the central

monk-trulku not only as the ultimate indexical link between the mundane and the absolute on behalf of the polity but also as the paradigmatic embodiment of an *ideally disciplined masculinity* that wielded both peaceful wisdom and (compassionate) violence (cf. Samuel 1994: 68). In this way, the Geluk mandalic order annually asserted in the Great Prayer Festival, and projected into the future with its culminating procession around the monastery of the future Buddha Shampa, worked to reestablish definitive access to and recognition of deities as the exclusive purview of monastic masculine prowess.

Indeed, by the early 1940s, the performative heart of the festival were the rituals and interstitial practices that produced and displayed the properly masculine roles of monks and the complementary yet subordinate, roles of laymen in wielding the manly will to tame—the ideal hierarchical relationship between lamas and lay leaders that Apa Dondrup and other elders had touted to me as a timeless, metonymic characterization of lay-monastic relations in the valley. That diarchy of masculinities was perhaps epitomized during the festival then by the exclusive role of the eight laymen appointed as the Cavalrymen of Namtisay to guard exterior monastic spaces while a corporate assembly of monks from all colleges gathered inside the main assembly hall as guardians of Geluk teaching lineages. In those years, monks attended six assemblies per day during the festival, chanting the most important prayers, listening to lectures on the core monastic curriculum by the head abbot, and watching the testing of candidates for scholarly degrees. Yet the superordinate status of monastic disciplinary power was indexed early on in the festival, when the chief monastic disciplinarian (Tib. *tshogs chen zhal ngo*) lectured in Tawa town to Tibetan, Han, and Hui laity and merchants about the scope of monastic law and their duties to the monastery. And throughout, assistant monk disciplinarians (Tib. *dge g'yog*), their authority lent force and weight by the huge wooden shoulders they wore under their robes, maintained solemn decorum among the monks.

Thus, as we saw in chapter 1, such elaborate mandalizing pageants on the eve of the Communist takeover were a crucial means for constructing patrifilial relations between Tibetan monks and laymen. In 1940, when the twenty-five-year-old Jamyang Shepa returned matured from his studies in Lhasa, where he had been exposed to the progressive ideas of such men as Gendun Chopel, the concentration of diarchic power in his and his brother Apa Alo's hands gave him a strong base from which to advocate for greater monk discipline amidst monks' increasing participation in commercial exchange (cf. Stoddard 1985, Huang 1989). And yet, at the same time, that power base allowed both brothers to establish modernizing institutions of their own, including perhaps the most innovative (and threatening) monastic institution Labrang had ever seen—Jamyang Shepa's controversial Vocational School for Young Monks (Ch. Labuleng Si Qingnian Lama Zhiye Xuexiao), initiated in 1943 with funding from the KMT Education Bureau (cf. Tuttle 2005).[2]

Thus the mandalizing pageants of the Great Prayer Festivals in the years just prior to the Communist victory were especially important as iconic indexes of Jamyang Shepa's flexible masculine agency or worldly "skillful means" afforded him by his lay-monastic power base. As I argued in chapter 1, the contextualizing thrust of mandalization in those events was to recruit monk and lay male subjects to participate in rehierarchizing deity recognition and exchange under the exclusive auspices of the central monk-trulku, even as monastic and lay male leaders increasingly encountered and themselves participated in political economic change. Indeed, with lay pilgrims of every stripe pressing in not only to absorb through bodily contact the great blessings and merit to be had by worshipping at the maṇḍala's center, but also to invest in and consume the potential mundane bounties of those annual "tournaments of value," such events also represented the particularly stark dangers of indiscriminate mixing and undisciplined consumption, threats to the essential hierarchies of the maṇḍala. The great festivals at Labrang thus annually ritualized the appropriate masculinity of monks—recruiting subjects to model both the pinnacle of monastic achievement and ritual power, and the cooperation of monks and laymen in regulating access to divine exchange at the center.

In 1996 then, as I mentioned in chapter 2, the crowds of Tibetan attendees and the extraordinary splendor of the ritual events during the Great Prayer Festival evidenced the success of Geluk mandalization after reforms in reorienting mobility and exchange toward the monastic center. Indeed, during that two-week period, much to some Lhade villagers' dismay, the hotels and guesthouses were packed with pilgrims, and the vast majority of nomads I spoke to were from the regions historically referred to as the "Eight Lhade Tribes" of the monastery, its erstwhile subjects. Most importantly, the great thangka display that day was also particularly significant in post-Mao versions of the festival as a whole, because it served as the most massive and conspicuous index for that diverse audience of disciplined patrifilial consumption on behalf of the revitalizing mandalic order—the vast majority of the funds for the thangkas had been donated by Lhade subjects who, against state policy, had again taken up alternating obligations to support the annual festival (cf. Li Dekuan 1989).

And yet, in 1996, just as in the past, the success of mandalic discipline also produced its Other—the danger of indiscipline and subversion of hierarchy. In fact, the most important line of conflict and site of frenzied commotion during the festival was that between the tantric ritual center at the public ceremonies and the crowds of ordinary laity eager to touch it or make offerings there. The borders of the maṇḍala were thus the "ritual battlefront" on which lay and monastic men joined in the most legitimate use of masculine violence. Historically, at the largest of the ceremonies, such as the unfurling of the huge thangka, young monks, chosen for their physical stature and aggressiveness, had protected objects of worship from the pushing crowds with intimidation and sticks. Meanwhile, a great "tiger" (Tib. *stag*) led a cordon of young and elder laymen armed with poles in policing the environs of the ritual space. In the past, those roles were reserved for teen boys and patriarchs from the oldest Lhade villages. In 1996, most of the lay guards I encountered were from Sakar, one of the oldest Lhade, and the tiger was manned by two young laymen under an orange-striped cloth. The boy in front carried the tiger's huge snarling papier-mâché-and-wooden head on a pole, looking out from under an orange striped blanket attached to it. His partner held onto his waist and bent over to simulate a tiger that towered over the crowd. Aided by lay officials with their sticks, the boys working the tiger delighted in "attacking" the crowd, swinging the huge head to whack errant worshippers, or careening their bodies into people to push them back quickly for the passage of a lama or Buddha image (see fig. 17).

Just as many observers had described it in the past, the tiger's interactions with the crowd could be hilarious. But while I dodged and ran with the crowd on those days, it was quite clear that the lay officials' efforts to discipline the crowd and clear ritual spaces were very serious. Their force augmented by the size and weight of the tiger, and galvanized by the excitement of the moment, the lay officials' "attacks" on crowd members could result in injuries and even fistfights. Indeed, it was the legitimate threat of real violence that made most ordinary laity respect the authority of the tiger and his assistants, and retreat immediately when they approached. In this way, the tiger, animated and assisted by young laymen from Lhade villages, was an effective incarnation of heroic masculine might and potential for violence in the service of Buddhist monasticism. As Akhu Konchok explained it to me, the tiger worked to protect mandalic spaces at ritual events because Tibetans considered tigers to be among the most powerful and ferocious of animals, and their ritual roles demonstrated the power of Buddhism to tame and bend to its purposes even such wild creatures (cf. Li Anzhai 1982).

In fact, the intrinsic wildness of such (male) animals was indexically linked, across participation frameworks, to the intrinsic masculinity of young men. In the Labrang region, young men at the height of their strength and valor (aged between

FIGURE 17.
The crowd-controlling "wild yak," manned by two village boys,
attacks the crowd at the Shampa (Maitreya) Procession ending
the 1996 Great Prayer Festival.

about 15 and 30 years) were called "tigers of the East" (Tib. *stag shar ra*) in
proverbs, folklore, and everyday conversation (cf. Kohn 1997: 68). Further, at the
final public ceremony of the Great Prayer Festival, the procession of the future
Buddha Shampa, the tiger was joined by two other crowd-control animals, the lion
(Tib. *seng ge*) and the wild black yak (Tib. *'brong*). Like the tiger, the lion and the
wild yak are also prominent symbols for masculine strength and heroic violence in
Tibetan folklore and Buddhist iconography (cf. Nebesky-Wojkowitz 1956; Rock
1956: 118; Tucci 1988: 168). Indeed, the three are often depicted as the mounts for
the various protector gods.

And yet, as I argued at the beginning of chapter 2, in contrast to the past, during the 1996 Great Prayer Festival at Labrang, the exigencies of a new, ideally segmented spatial order and a transformed regime of value under Apa Gongjia came
to a head. In those mandalic frames, locals encountered exquisitely close juxtapositions for increasingly high stakes, all under continued state-imposed limitations
on public metalanguage. In fact, in the previous six months, the private frameworks of conversation in the valley had been abuzz with scandalized talk about the

Dalai Lama's decision to recognize the eleventh Panchen Lama without CCP approval. Delegations of Han cadres from the national and provincial Religious Affairs Bureaus had been sent to Lanzhou and Labrang, and all prominent personages in town, including the sixth Jamyang Shepa, the very aged Apa Alo, and Tibetans who had returned from exile, had had to attend mandatory meetings and were pressured to make public statements condemning the Dalai Lama's choice. One young laywoman, having watched television news reports, remarked to me that "only Alak Gongtang Tshang remained honest" (Tib. a lags gung thang tshang *kher re zig drang mo red*), in that he had merely stated that he hoped the two sides could come to an agreement.

That watershed event, in which state loyalties again had to be attested publicly, was to greatly alter state-local relations in the valley, and its ramifications would be felt for years to come. Thus in this context, we can appreciate the heightened tensions that close juxtapositions of bodies and interests at the 1996 Great Prayer Festival could provoke. As we saw with the Cham Chen, during those weeks, the "work permit" (Ch. *gongzuo zheng*) ribbons fluttering on the chests of the Tibetan lay officials had to compete with the "official guest" (Ch. *benke*) ribbons pinned to the lapels of the foreign and Han tourists and state media crews who had descended on the monastery to capture images of the festivities (cf. Makley 1998). The "official guest" permits, as indexes of fees paid to the monastery's Democratic Management Committee, were supposed to allow the wearers better access to ritual spaces during the festival than that given to ordinary laity. Those "guests" (who were mostly Han men), cameras ready and pointing, were everywhere in evidence on the days of the public ceremonies.

This, then, was the context in which the unfurling of Opakmay's thangka became the ritual frame for a culmination of interethnic and state-local hostilities played out in legitimized masculine violence. After the thangka was hung on the hillside, ready to be unfurled, I had stayed among the crowd of lay Tibetans on the edge of the oval-shaped clearing at the foot of the hill while Akhu Konchok used my camera to film the goings-on. As Akhu Konchok and I watched from our separate vantage points on the peripheries of the ritual space, a young Chinese cameraman and his assistant, the name of their work unit, the provincial Bureau of Education, emblazoned on the back of their photographer's vests, worked the edges of the crowd to film the preparations for the thangka's vivification rite to be undertaken by the head abbot of the monastery (Tib. *tshogs chen khri pa*). Monk officials had carefully arranged the space in front of the thangka so that when the abbot arrived, escorted by the Eight Cavalrymen (whose role during the entire festival had been reduced to that function), he could quickly and efficiently set up a purified mandalic space, invite Opakmay, make offerings to him, and return to the monastery through the crowds.

The Chinese cameramen, seeking close-ups of the preparations, carefully avoided eye contact with the lay officials, ignoring their admonitions and dodging their flailing sticks, to film the abbot's throne placed opposite the hill. But their authoritative invisibility (cf. Lakoff 1995: 27) was breached when they finally strode directly to the center of the ritual space to film the offerings to Opakmay set there on small tables. That move was too threatening, because it juxtaposed too closely the objectifying gazes of the camera and its projected alien audiences with the Buddhist goals of the ritual. By audaciously moving to the center and claiming authoritative distance behind their cameras, the Bureau of Education cameramen asserted that the primary value of the offerings, and by extension of the event as a whole, lay in their nature as signs of the correctness of CCP policies after reforms and of the transcendent authority of the state to arbitrate citizens' public participation frameworks—the very move CCP leaders had made with regard to the eleventh Panchen Lama when they rejected the Dalai Lama's choice and organized the choice of another boy. Yet those very implements indexed the Geluk mandalic exchanges exclusively arbitrated by initiated monk-lamas and trulkus. Vivification rites (Tib. *rab gnas*) were the ritual threshold through which lamas intervened in everyday deity recognition and opened the mandala to the substantial co-presence of the central deity for higher Buddhist exchanges. In this way, such practices to transform artifactual representations into the abodes or "supports" of Buddhas could be seen as performative counterparts of high trulkus' practices of recognizing new human trulkus, such as the Dalai Lama's recognition of the eleventh Panchen Lama.

Thus, when the Bureau of Education cameramen ignored the young monk who approached them and asked them to leave, the monk's response was immediate and violent. With a few large steps, he crossed the distance the cameramen imagined insulated them from monastic authority and punched the younger of the two in the face. No one moved to protest, and none in the crowd around me commented. The cameramen, their faces shocked and embarrassed, had no recourse but to move back to the sidelines, and now their lack of eye contact with the monk came off not as the disdain of the superior but as the chagrin of the cowed. The tiger, for good measure, made sure they hurried, chasing them off and whacking their expensive camera. As Akhu Konchok told me later, the cameramen were spitting mad when they reached the edge of the crowd where he stood, and they complained to him that they shouldn't have been hit, because they had an "official guest" pass to collect footage for the Bureau of Education's "propaganda work" (Ch. *xuanchuan gongzuo*). Akhu Konchok said he told them that their passes were meaningless here. In this context, he told them, we (spectators) are all the same.

THE HERO'S BURDEN: NOSTALGIA AND LAY MASCULINITY UNDER NATIONAL INCORPORATION

I began my discussion of the contested nature of monkhood and its relationship to masculinity with a detailed description of this interaction because it illustrates so poignantly the contexts in which the practice of Tibetan masculinities became the last line of defensive contextualization between secular interests under the auspices of the state and divine realities under those of the monastery. In this situation, the young monk's unhesitating move from verbal command to physical assault, the tiger's quick support, the lay onlookers' unconcerned acceptance of the violence, and the cameramen's lack of reprisal combined to recreate an ideally heroic Tibetan masculinity that unequivocally resists intrusion. And yet the apparently clear-cut quality of that participant role, and the unproblematic way the monk seemed to inhabit it at that moment, belied the recently controversial nature of monkhood and masculinity among Tibetans in the frontier zone. Indeed, I argue that in post-Mao Labrang, the ritual frames of such grand monastic pageants were the only contexts left in which ethnic interests appeared to be so purely polarized and violent resistance to Chinese interference on the part of Tibetans could be open and legitimate.

Outside that ritual frame, young Tibetan men (roughly 35 years and younger) who grew up under the Chinese state's unprecedented control of the region had to make their way in a greatly transformed society that had compromised and curtailed masculine routes to social mobility and achievement, throwing into radical question what it meant to be a Tibetan man under Chinese rule. Those who chose to become monks had to do so within a community that was deeply conflicted about the nature and roles of monkhood and monasteries at the same time as local Tibetan lay cadres and intellectuals, like my young lay male friend the schoolteacher Dargye, searched for ways to address great social inequities between Tibetans and Han, and to develop Tibetan regions and educate Tibetan youth on their own terms.

This conundrum was the source of deep anguish for such young men as Tshering Khar, a twenty-five-year-old graduate student I came to know in Lanzhou. Tshering Khar had grown up in a small village in Qinghai hearing stories of valiant Tibetan resistance to PLA military campaigns in the 1950s and Cultural Revolution struggle sessions in the 1960s. During several long conversations, Tshering Khar told me, in his particularly passionate way, about his struggles to find a career that would be most helpful to Tibetans, against the advice of his Chinese professor, who had urged him to do something more "practical." He despaired of being able to help stem the tide of Tibetan assimilation to Chinese habits along the former frontier, and contrasted what he saw as Tibetans' historical readiness to assimilate (Ch. *tonghua*) in those regions with the relative strength of Hui ethnic identity that had kept Hui viable and advancing westward to the present. The frustration and sense of personal impotence Tshering Khar expressed in such contexts contrasted sharply, often in the same conversations, with the rapturous admiration he evinced—drawing out syllables, touching the side of his hand to his forehead, and squinting his eyes in emphatic pain—for the brave Tibetan men who had resisted assimilation under the greatest duress during the Maoist years. In this regard, he related for me the story of the public humiliation and subsequent death of Sherap Gyamtsho (1884–1968), the famous lama-scholar from Labrang, at the hands of Red Guards during the Cultural Revolution.

Citing the oppositional testimony of his own father, who, he said, had been present at Sherap Gyamtsho's struggle session near their village in 1968, Tshering Khar recounted how his father had been forced along with other villagers to watch in silence as the Red Guards screamed and laughed at the old monk. He said his father told him how Sherap Gyamtsho, then nearly eighty-four years old, was made to stand on a platform above the crowd, bent over with tea jars hanging from his neck as his tormenters made him drink urine and yelled in his face, "Which is better: Tibetan Buddhism or the CCP?!" In a powerful performative breakthrough, Tshering Khar then put himself in the role of Sherap Gyamtsho, bending over and rolling his head exhaustedly to reply: "No matter what you say, I will still believe in Buddhism" (Ch. *wulun ni shuo shenme wo haishi xin Fojiao*).

But in his narrative to me, Tshering Khar never mentioned the lama's renown as one of the first Geluk hierarchs to show an interest in the potential for communism to help modernize Tibetans' lifestyles and protect their political autonomy, a predilection that was to make him the most influential Tibetan lama in China in the two decades after the Communist victory (cf. Stoddard 1986: 86; Tuttle 2005). As a robed Buddhist monk in the state positions of Vice-Chair of the Qinghai People's Government (1949–67) and President of the China Buddhist Association (1953–66)—positions he used to champion Buddhist interests and the rights of Tibetans on the one hand, and urge Tibetans to accept communism on the other—Sherap Gyamtsho's life epitomized the kinds of strategic compromises and misrecognitions that, as we saw in chapter 1, Tibetan leadership in the frontier zone had had to make in order to meet intensifying challenges from outside interests even before the Communist victory (cf. Stevenson 1999).

Tshering Khar's emotional enactment of Sherap Gyamtsho's heroic resolve and ethnic loyalty, without reference to his controversial relationships to the Chinese state, illustrates the powerful ways Tibetans constructed contemporary male heroes or *hwawo* (Tib. *dpa' bo*, lit. "brave ones"), even as that very process established impossible role models for young men faced with the dilemmas of everyday life in China. *Hwawo* was a term, both before and after Chinese Communist intervention, for a man without fear, whose strength, ferocity, and intelligence allow him to unhesitatingly face and conquer his enemies. It was thus a master trope for an ideal masculine subjectivity that was applicable to *both* lay and monastic men, a subjectivity that successfully bridges the tamed and untamed poles of ideal manhood (cf. Samuel 1994). Such a man is epitomized in the figure of the lay nomad warrior, depicted in local lore and lay songs and in the cult of the protector deities. In eulogized battles waged on behalf of localities, the "wildness" (Tib. *rgod*) of such a warrior is associated with the proud autonomy and mobility of the open grasslands and with the single-minded ferocity of undomesticated (male) animals (cf. Watkins 1996: 47). And yet, as we saw in chapter 1, the masculine hero in Geluk Buddhist lineages was also historically represented in the figures of enlightened lama-monks, those "heroes in striving for enlightenment" who altruistically left household settings to conquer and tame the enemies of Buddhism—the multiple connotations of the term *duwa*, to "tame" and "conquer," but also to "cultivate" and "discipline," suggest a broad framework among Tibetans for understanding this kind of masculinity as still (and quintessentially) the purview of monks.

But I argue that Tibetans' precarious encounters with competing modernities in the frontier zone from the late nineteenth century on problematized this mandalic framework encompassing a range of heroic masculinities. That is, for locals facing newly objectified notions of Tibetanness and, thus, transformed relationships to their phayul under development and administrative pressures from Chinese regimes, the hierarchical relationship between lay and monastic masculinities came to be increasingly attenuated. This is one way to understand the rise and flourishing of the eclectic or "unbounded" *Rimay* (Tib. *Ris med*, lit. "unbounded") movement among non-Geluk lamas and yogins in eastern Tibetan regions, which in effect, through new syntheses of teachings, *delinked* tantric lineages from Geluk monasticism (cf. Samuel 1993). In particular, this perspective sheds light on the avid interest the great Nyingma scholar and Rimay lama Ju Mipham (1846–1912) took in Gesar, the Tibetan warrior hero and protagonist of epic poetry in Amdo and Kham regions. As many have pointed out, Mipham wrote reams on Tibetan Buddhist philosophy and practice, but he also devoted many works to Gesar, including tantric rituals of offering, akin to the Geluk "Offerings to the Lama" rites, that seek to evoke and appropriate Gesar's unwavering military strength against enemies of the Dharma (cf. Samuel 1993: 540; Samuel 1994; Nalanda Translation Committee 1997: 402). Further, as Robin Kornman notes, it was these works on Gesar that became popular in the 1980s and 1990s among Tibetans in and outside the PRC (1997: 39).

We could perhaps see Mipham's tantric focus on Gesar in the nineteenth-century ferment of political economic pressures in the frontier zone to be an effort to mandalize the mobile and militaristic force of Gesar's lay masculinity *outside* both the parochial interests of monasteries and the radically localized purviews of regional lay protector gods. In the versions of Gesar's life Mipham edited and in the various tantric rites he composed, Gesar is figured in effect not only as a divine general and king for all Tibetan regions, but also as a lay trulku, an emanation of aspects of what Mipham took to be the most essential Tibetan Buddhas. In one of Mipham's incense rites to Gesar for example, the first-person subject positions Gesar as a father (Nalanda Translation Committee 1997: 402–4):

Kye
Lha ki ki ki and *so so so,*
Father Gesar the king, god of war,
At the time when enemies fill the kingdom,
Lord Tamer of Enemies, don't be idle, don't be idle.
I put my hope in no other protector but you.

Then when he has invited Gesar to sit and receive his offerings, he praises him:

If there is a warrior god, it is Gesar.
If there is a divine soldier, it is Gesar.
If there is a lama for the next life, it is Gesar.
If there is a leader for this life, it is Gesar.
Outwardly, he is the mighty general Norbu Tamer of Enemies.
Inwardly, he is Avalokitesvara.
His unchanging mind is Lord Padmasambhava.
I offer and praise the deities—may their wishes be fulfilled.

Here then, Mipham powerfully positions Gesar as an embodied indexical link to all categories of heroic masculinity for Tibetans at the time (cf. Kornman 1997: 43), yet Gesar manifests in human form *not* as a monk but as a lay warrior. I would argue that, when viewed within the historical frameworks of the intensifying press of competing modernities in the frontier zone, we could see Mipham's tantric appropriation and elevation of Gesar as an important index of a newly emergent antisectarian *pan-regionalism* among Tibetans. Mipham and others called on the militaristic lay agency of (Father) Gesar to operate as a decontextualized and eminently mobile masculine authority defending both a newly objectified Tibetanness and a broadened Buddhist fatherland refigured as a modern Tibetan nation (cf. Samuel 1994: 72).[3]

This process, I argue, was significantly manifest in the 1980s and 1990s in a new romance of *lay* masculinity among relatively alienated Tibetan men in exile (e.g., Karmay 1994) or in urban lowlands within the PRC. Importantly, the nostalgia for lay masculinity, both in and outside the PRC, coalesced around a revitalized and refigured cult of *ʒhidak,* the regional lay protector deities most often addressed as "grandfathers" and based in local mountain abodes. I found that among Tibetans throughout the valley, men and women most often referred to their dewas' mountain deities as, on the one hand, "warrior gods" (Tib. *dgra lha*), deities who have special capacities to protect worshippers from enemies in worldly, including economic, pursuits (cf. Nebesky-Wojkowitz 1956: 319; Samuel 1993: 182), and on the other, as "birth gods" (Tib. *skyes lha*), deities who are viscerally linked to males born in their dewas, as their protectors and, in a way, as their personal avatars.[4]

As we saw in chapter 4 with Drolma's husband Tsonji's efforts to strengthen his relationship to his warrior god against that of a rival, men's worship of dewa mountain deities as their birthright warrior gods located emergent Tibetan manhood in ongoing contests with other men. And those hopeful exchanges with such deities sought the sources of masculine power and achievement (Tib. *stobs*) in local topographic and jurisdictional spaces, even as individual men could carry that privileged relationship wherever they went. I would say, then, that collective worship of mountain deities at male-only annual *labtse* rites at the deities' abodes in the mountains took shape in inherent tensions between men's local and translocal, as well as collective and individual, interests and obligations. In effect, in the face of emasculation pressures under CCP rule, the powerful iconicity operating in such gendered deity-recognition practices indexically linked Tibetan male sexedness to individually desired masculine attributes and authority at the same time as it remasculinized localities across both men's socioeconomic differences and disjunctive time.[5] Hence the appeal of such practices among urban Tibetan men especially. By the mid- to late 1990s, Tibetan men's' interest in mountain deities, in research writings and in popular media, belied the relative absence of mountain deities in state and tourism media (see for example hor gtsang 'jigs med 2000). The boom in video compact disc (VCD) production among Amdo Tibetans in the late 1990s especially produced ubiquitous images of the deities' labtse rites, most often as background for male singers' ballads and praise songs in Tibetan or Chinese. In such music videos, the camera invariably lingers, in slow motion, on shots of crowds of laymen (seemingly) acting in accord, but made small next to the huge arrow heaps and incense fires inviting the deity to respond to their individual prayers for worldly "luck" and achievement.

Yet such a focus on ritual exchanges reconstructing a legacy of lay militaristic masculinity threatened again, like Mipham's Gesar, to configure masculine loyalties and aspirations outside the disciplinary purviews of *both* monastery and state—Buddhist monasticism in post-Mao China for some Tibetan men could itself be associated with a feminizing discipline (e.g., Karmay 1994: 113; cf. Lopez 1997, Huber 1999).

THE PRESTIGE OF TAMING: MANHOOD AND MONKHOOD

Thus, amidst the intensifying emasculation pressures of national incorporation in the frontier zone, an emergent nostalgia for visions of lay masculinity, both in and outside the PRC, worked to revalorize Tibetan masculine attributes of competence and translocal authority and mobility as against the increasingly equivocal status of monastic masculinity. Yet, for many Tibetans I spoke to in Labrang, the qualities of a hero (or at least their potential) were seen to timelessly inhere in the male sex (regardless of lay or monastic status), as part of the felicitous karmic legacy of a greater store of merit than females'. Those qualities were perhaps best encapsulated in the ubiquitous use of the Tibetan modifier *ngar gi*, meaning "aggressive," "vigorous," "strong," or "forceful," but operating in practice as a general trope for highly valued assertive competence, something that could apply (with different valences) to both men and women.

But such qualities were also considered to be the basis for men's superior competence in the world outside the household. Becoming a man, for Tibetan boys, as many of my male friends' life stories attested, was most essentially about the ability to move—in daily activities that took them out of the household and into homosocial and patrifilial relationships of blood and friendship.

In the decades before Communist intervention, it was these relationships (and *not* necessarily the close control of women) that secured men's ultimate authority as heads of households (Tib. *bʐa' dpon*) and heads of dewa (Tib. *sde dpon*). In the Labrang region, the elaborate rituals and customs regulating those homosocial relations linking households in translocal networks (such as rituals of fair hunting, safe caravanning, and hosting guests, customs of conflict mediation and patron or tenant responsibilities to monasteries) constituted the "traditional law" that grounded local Tibetan authority in Amdo fatherlands despite the overlordship of various Chinese regimes (cf. Ekvall 1964a: 1110; Wang Zhouta 1996a: 406).

This angle on heroic masculinity both as an inherent karmic legacy of male sexedness relative to females and as a precarious patrilineal gender legacy relative to competing outside regimes then provides us with a way to understand more clearly the complex and shifting relationships between monkhood and lay manhood for Tibetans. I argue that monkhood in the Labrang region was primarily an alternative masculine gender status that was seen to be an indispensable complement to lay manhood. This is because monkhood provided a socially sanctioned and prestigious way for boys to renounce obligations to households altogether and live in the near exclusive company of men devoted to the maintenance of Buddhist institutions deemed vital to the (local and translocal) Tibetan community. Importantly, it was the highly structured nature of everyday ritualized praxis at such powerful and conservative monasteries as Labrang that maintained the performative claim of the monastic community to have *tamed* lay masculinity to the service of Buddhism (cf. Gyatso 2005: 272). And this, rather than strict enforcement of or attention to vows taken, underlay the power and prestige of monks as the moral leadership and field of merit for the laity. If we begin in this way from the perspective of the everyday performativity of gendered monk identities, we can appreciate that the inherent gap between the monk ideal and actual monk behavior that fell far short of it was not *necessarily* experienced as "paradoxical" or "contradictory" for Tibetans (*pace* Keyes 1986; cf. Gyatso 2003, 2005; Mills 2003). We then have a basis for understanding the historically contingent ways that that difference could emerge as a consciously perceived problem threatening the boundaries between lay and monastic worlds.

Most generally, monkhood did not necessarily represent a "sharp division" of the male population either before or after Communist intervention. In actuality, the basic bodily and spatial transformation manifested in the initial move to monkhood provided a set of "performative resources" or participation frameworks within which Tibetans could strategically reinvoke, in different ways and to various degrees, a clear distinction between lay manhood and monkhood construed as an altruistic commitment to celibacy and Buddhist scholarly achievement. The most important way that this distinction was invoked in everyday life was the widespread assumption that the passage to monkhood was an essential means by which the explosive potential of heroic masculinity could be channeled and refined (cf. Goldstein 1964, Keyes 1986). In my observations of and discussions with Tibetans of every stripe, I found that the most basic aspect of heroic masculinity in practice was the assumption that young men were naturally compelled to engage in violent competitions with other young men, and to pursue sexual encounters with women. Indeed in a proverb about drinking that people often cited for me, young men's aspirations for heroic masculinity complement young women's aspirations for beauty:

stag shar ra gis chang 'thung na dpa' bo/
byis mo gis chang 'thung na yag//

When young men drink they want to be heroes.
When young women drink they want to be beautiful.

In the 1990s, heroic masculinity for young laymen was still ideally forged in the display of (the potential for) physical violence, and young nomad men, as before, were especially associated with the capacity for particularly brutal masculine violence.[6] In the Labrang region, frequent fights among young drinking buddies, played out in the context of male-only activities that worked to establish local and translocal networks, was the legitimate behavior of laymen, behavior that was not necessarily interrupted by marriage (cf. Watkins 1996). In fact, I would argue that there was no specific rite of passage, equivalent to those of "letting down the hair" and marriage for girls, aimed at socializing lay boys to responsible adulthood. Instead, boys were expected to learn to channel those masculine inclinations to honorable pursuits demonstrating patrifilial loyalty to friends, kin, and regions through respect for male elders and daily participation in homosocial activities, and men were expected to mellow and become wise and pious with old age. Hence the crucial importance of monkhood: as the only major rite of passage for boys, the passage to monkhood—so clearly marked by a boy's movement out of the household and into the highly structured participation frameworks of monasticism, and by the transformation of his body through shaving the head and donning a monastic costume—invoked the great virtue of the intention to tame the powerful compulsions to physical violence and (heterosexual) desire that were seen to inhere in maleness.

This, I argue, was the basis for the prestige attached to that transformation, a prestige that constructed monkhood, at even the most basic level, as a superior or "higher" gender status than lay manhood in Labrang's mandalic order—monasticism mandalized monks more closely than laymen. In the 1990s, I found that locals still widely used spatialized tropes of vertical deference to construct this hierarchy. Tibetans across the community frequently referred to respect for monkhood as "placing monks up high" (Tib. *grwa pa cho yar ra 'jog pa*), while a monk returning to lay life was referred to as a "fallen monk" (Tib. *grwa log*). Indeed, Tibetan translators originally chose *duwa* as the term for the section of the Buddhist canon dealing with monastic discipline (lit. "The Taming," Skt. Vinaya), emphasizing the intention to tame masculinity to the service of Buddhism as the basis for the heroic status of monks, who ideally use will and intellect instead of weapons to conquer both internal (i.e., mental) and external enemies of the Dharma. Since heterosexual desire and physical violence were considered to be the most compulsive of naturally male attributes, it is not surprising that (a performative claim to) celibacy and nonviolence were the most salient characteristics of monks for Tibetans, and the grounds for their tantric power in the region.

Most importantly, the privileged status of high lamas and trulkus as transcendent paternal disciplinarians and mandalic tamers was evidenced in their roles as the most valued mediators among subordinate masculine authorities—between laymen and mountain deities (zhabs drung 1952: 371.2; cf. hor gtsang 'jigs med 2000) as well as between tribal factions of laymen in interregional conflicts.

Thus, in internecine battles among tribesmen, monk-trulkus were the only ones whose divine authority and moral standing could convince angry parties in the most protracted and vicious of feuds to agree to a compromise solution (cf. Ekvall 1952, 1964a, 1964b). This phenomenon, much to the frustration of Tibetan and Han cadres, continued throughout the early years of the CCP and on into the 1990s. Local CCP histories (e.g., XDZ 1991) boast that the enlightened efforts of early CCP work teams were able to resolve such centuries-old grassland conflicts as that between the nomad groups in Gangya and Gyalwo on the border of Qinghai and Gansu. However, state cadres were never able to effectively resolve such conflicts without the intervention of Tibetan lamas and trulkus (cf. Huang 1989, Zhang Jimin 1993, Wang Zhouta 1996a). In fact, as grassland conflicts increased in the reform years with the overpopulation of the plateau regions, mediation duties were one of the most important functions of rehabilitated Tibetan trulkus such as Gongtang Tshang (Wang Yunfeng 1997: 117).

The participation frameworks of monkhood in Labrang were thus supposed to reestablish an essential gender differentiation within the male population—*not* between saintly, detached scholar-monks and wild laymen, but between all boys and men whose robes and lifestyles marked their dedication (in the sense of being earmarked) to the service of monasticism on the one hand, and all remaining boys and men on the other. And this "performative binary" (i.e., one is or is not a monk), sustained by the whole range of everyday ritualized frameworks of monastic life (and not just by specific rituals aimed at "purifying" vows; cf. Lopez 1996b: 503), grounded the sex-gender system that constructed the monastery as the political economic center of that mandalic order. This was the dynamic, I argue, that allowed for the development of "mass monasticism," in which boys as young as six or seven years old could be dedicated to the monastic life by their parents.

At such powerful Geluk monasteries as Labrang on the eve of the Communist takeover, the incorporation of monastic subjects through daily strictures on dress, spatial movements, deference practices, ritual propriety, and the like most importantly produced monastic bodies as central indexical signs of the acceptance of the mandalic order, *regardless* of individual monks' beliefs or attitudes (cf. Rappaport 1979: 194). In this way, the performativity of monkhood as Labrang monastery rose to power allowed for a wide range of monastic masculinities without disrupting the vital hierarchical distinction between "monk" (Tib. *a khu* or *grwa pa*) and "layman" (Tib. *byis lu* or *gsar bu, rgan po*).

The initial passage to monkhood imposed the monk-layman gender binary on what was actually a continuum of heroic masculinities ritually disciplined to varying degrees for service to the Buddhist order. Thus, levels of vows were just one, and often not the most important, of the ways a person's location on the continuum was noted. Age, trulku status, monastic occupation, and especially, attendance in and progress through assemblies or classes were also important classifiers (cf. Goldstein 1964, 1989; Li Anzhai 1982, 1989; Goldstein and Tsarong 1985; Ellingson 1990; Cabezón 1997). At Labrang, the most significant measure of progress toward a monk ideal was not level of adherence to vows but the level of scholarly achievement in the monastic curricula deemed canonical there. As I noted in chapter 1, the bulk of monastic inmates at Labrang during its heyday belonged to the Thisamlang college for intensive study of Jamyang Shepa's debate manuals. Indeed, the demands of the program of study at Labrang meant that the lifestyles of monk-scholars (Tib. *dpe cha pa*, lit. "book ones") most closely approximated the monk ideal set forth in various monastic disciplinary codes.[7] With little time for anything else, these monk-scholars had to rely on alms distributed by the assembly and the largesse of their families; they were the ones who most consistently devoted themselves as subordinates to lamas—ritually, in daily offering rites, and pedagogically, in daily lessons—and they had relatively little time for interaction with the mundane world outside monastic space. Depending on the level of their success, such scholars could achieve great fame in the monastic community and among the laity, earning recognition as lamas in their own right, or acquiring renown as tantric masters.

For the most part, Tibetans felt that only a small minority of men had the stores of merit, talent, and self-discipline to pursue such a career. In fact, the whole system was set up to maintain the possibility and prestige of refining masculinity through study for those few who chose it, while providing supporting roles for the vast majority of monks, who could not be expected to repress masculine inclinations to that extent. From this angle, levels of vows functioned not so much as markers of increasing commitment to moral discipline but as standard points in the maturation of a young monk at which he was considered able to choose levels of participation in monastic life. As such, they marked progressively greater prestige, and relatively greater moral consequences for the decision to return to lay life. Thus, at Labrang, the youngest boys were distinguished from lay boys only by their robes and residence in monasteries. They "took" only the first five vows (Tib. *dge bsnyen*) and lived with monk teachers (often relatives) while gaining some basic literacy. Akhu Gendun, a twenty-year-old monk studying in Labrang, told me in our formal interview that he had taken up residence at his local monastery at the age of seven, in 1982. He said that while he had donned robes and had his hair shaved when he entered the monastery, he did not take "vows" (Tib. *sdom pa ma blangs*) until he took the "going forth" (Tib. *rab byung*) vows at age twelve.[8]

The "novice" vows (Tib. *dge tshul*), in which a monk pledged to refrain from thirty-three transgressions (Tib. *blangs 'das so gsum*) seen to be subsets of the ten basic vows, were then taken to be a fairly momentous status change. This occurred when a monk was considered to be fully adult, the vows rendered more virtuous because the intentions they represented were seen to be voluntarily assumed by a mature individual. In fact, Akhu Gendun had not yet taken his novice vows at the age of twenty. For him, the transition was a big one, for which he planned to return to his home monastery to undergo the ordination ceremony with his main lama. Fully ordained status (Tib. *dge slong*), in which a monk pledged to uphold 253 detailed vows, was thus in practice the point at which monks with the (at least initial) intention of pursuing the career of a scholar and joining the classes teaching the more advanced texts were distinguished from the rest.

At Labrang, this decision was usually made around the age of twenty, and only a minority of monks chose it. This did not preclude a fully ordained monk from failing at his studies and moving to other monastic occupations or leaving monkhood altogether. Levels of vows corresponded to scholarly progress only inasmuch as they were usually taken at standard ages (cf. Li Anzhai 1982, Ellingson 1990). The reality of monkhood at Labrang was that most ordinary monks differed little from nuns except in the relative prestige attached to the various occupations they undertook to bring in income—most stopped at the novice level of vows and achieved only basic literacy (cf. Goldstein 1998a: 21).

In effect then, during the heyday of the monastery, the graded participation frameworks of monasticism were able to encompass a wide range of dispositions and degrees of personal devotion to refining masculinity in pursuit of the monk ideal. Most generally, the everyday decorum of monastic life, backed up by a monastic judicial system that meted out punishments for monk misdeeds (ranging from fines to corporeal penalties or imprisonment), protected the elaborate mandalic hierarchy of increasingly pure and empowered bodies.[9]

The most expected of ordinary monks was to serve this order in publicly appropriate ways, and barring particularly egregious crimes of murder, embarrassing sexual liaisons, or treason, little they did would result in expulsion from the monastery (cf. Goldstein 1998a: 17). In this context, even a category of hypermasculine monks, popularly called *dapdop*, could flourish.[10] At Labrang, just as in Lhasa, such monks could be said to be those who, as they grew to adulthood, worked to repress masculine compulsions the least. Instead, they developed a culture of "warrior monkhood" that distinguished them from laymen (e.g., adopting distinctive hairstyles, ways of wearing monastic robes, carrying huge "keys" as weapons, since knives and swords were theoretically forbidden to monks—all of which were meant to emphasize their ferocity in frequent fights with other monks and laymen). Huang Mingxin, the Han scholar who was a monk at Labrang in the 1940s and eventually became head teacher at Jamyang Shepa's Vocational School for Young Monks, recalled in our interview that the dapdop at Labrang were the "scariest" of monks there, different from the scholar-monks and ordinary monk workers. He demonstrated with his hands how the sets of keys they wore could be up to a foot long.

Indeed, Gendun Chophel, in his famously scathing "alphabetic poem" sent to his monk critics at Labrang after he was expelled in 1927, sarcastically notes the irony that while his monk critics claimed he had been expelled for his heretical views by the monastery's ferocious protector god, Naychung Trinlay, other monks would seem to have been committing far more serious transgressions against monastic discipline:[11]

> ka ye kho bo gzhan du song rjes su/
> kha nas ci bshad med pa'i a khu 'gas/
> ga yang gnas chung 'phrin las rgyal po yis/
> nga rgyal che bas sdod du ma bcug zer/
>
> ca dag byed pa'i chos skyong shig yod na/
> cha rgyus yod med sa cha kun 'grims nas/
> ja chang skam lug sogs kyi tshong byed pa'i/
>
> nya nyog de tsho sdod du ci la bcugs/
> ta la'i 'dab bzhin sham thabs rdog ga brgyab/
> tha chal lag cha lcags gri ja shing bzung/
> da lta gzhan du bskrad na chog pa la/
> na ning do tshigs je mang je mang red/

Hello! After I went away
Those few monks who can explain nothing said that
Because I am too arrogant,
King Naychong Trinlay did not let me stay.

If there were a Dharma protector to clean up [the monastery],
Why did he allow those to stay who do impure things like
Traveling all over to places familiar and strange,

And selling tea, alcohol, cattle, and sheep?
As for those [monks] who pull their robes up high like the leaves of a
    palm tree,[12]
And wield terrible tools and iron knives,
It would be right to chase them out now, but
These days there are more and more [of them]!

However, as Gendun Chophel's sarcasm about Naychong Trinlay ignoring such monks' transgressions points up, we need not see the dapdop as a "paradoxical group . . . [that] . . . seems to flaunt and make ridiculous the monastic system"

(Goldstein 1964: 125). They were rather the category of monks that most clearly illustrates the foundational importance of monastic subjectivity as the embodied acceptance of the mandalic order. As the monks who pushed the basic monastic limits on masculine behavior to their very edge, the dapdop were not a "paradoxical group" but a logical outcome of the system that supported the enabling performative hierarchy between monk and lay-male gender statuses. Even though they could hold the highest level of vows, as long as they fulfilled the most basic requirements of the system, serving the monastic order, their lifestyles did not threaten the categorical superiority of their monk status or the prestige of monasticism in general. Indeed, dapdop at Labrang played crucial roles in (literally) protecting the monastic order. As Huang Mingxin recalled in our interview, they served as a monastic "police force," accompanying high lamas on trips, backing up the eighty monastic officials in charge of administering the monastery's Lhade, and defending mandalic spaces from the crowds of worshippers at the annual festivals (cf. Ekvall 1959: 218; Norbu and Harrer 1960: 94; Goldstein 1964: 141).

Thus, from the perspective of Tibetan locals in the 1930s and 1940s, the behavior of the dapdop did not necessarily appear as categorically inimical to monkhood, because it was still a conventional form of masculinity, publicly marked as serving monasticism (cf. Norbu and Harrer 1960: 94; Goldstein 1964: 141). Mass monasticism worked in part because neither end of the monastic spectrum—warrior to scholar-monks—countered Tibetan heroic masculinity.

In fact, this was the basis for the great appeal of monasticism to lay families. It was seen as another career for "extra sons" (i.e., those with male siblings, ideally elder, who would inherit family property) or for those who showed proclivities for it, a career that had the bonus effect of increased merit for both the dedicating family and the son-turned-monk himself.[13] In effect, monkhood in the Labrang region maintained the prestige of the move to renunciation while allowing for much intermingling, alliance building, and commercial exchange among lay and monastic men. The reality was that monkhood sacralized the assumed basic male proclivity and masculine obligation to pursue mobility for the benefit of self and the community. Most monks did not remain sequestered in monasteries; instead, they moved frequently between natal homes and monasteries (especially those who joined monastic communities close to home), growing up playing with lay boys, and in adulthood traveling often between monasteries on pilgrimages, monastic business, or trading missions (cf. Snellgrove and Richardson 1986: 248).

DOMESTICATING MONASTIC SUBJECTS

"In general, nothing has changed," said the well-known trulku, a former monk who was a lay university professor in the 1990s. I had asked him about changes in monastic organization at Labrang in recent years. His face a smiling mask, he went on to insist (in Chinese) that "everything is exactly as it was." Yet, as Tshering Khar's anguish so poignantly illustrated above, young men who felt great responsibilities to participate in Tibetan Buddhist revitalization were squeezed between heightened imperatives to achieve heroic masculine ideals and the strong recognition of their fundamentally diminished capacity to do so. This was the context in which young monks in Labrang found themselves the objects of competing efforts to recreate ideal monastic subjects. I argue that state efforts to regulate monasticism, at the same time as local markets had been opened to domestic and international trade and tourism, had greatly altered the participation frameworks that maintained the basic gender hierarchy between monkhood and lay manhood. In the resultant "institutional vacuum," differently positioned people called upon the performative resources of monkhood in overlapping and clashing ways. A look at these contestations will help make sense of the newly controversial nature of monkhood and its relationship to Tibetan masculinities in Labrang.

As we saw in chapters 1 and 2, for Tibetans the gendered violence of Maoist "peaceful liberation" in the frontier zone generated stark categorical polarities of time and ethnic subjectivities. As in Tshering Khar's portrayal of Sherap Gyamtsho, in Tibetans' post-Mao practices of memory, the heroism of great men under such duress effectively erased the compromises, like those of Apa Alo in the 1920s or of the fifth Jamyang Shepa in the 1940s, that had tied the frontier zone ever closer to outside interests. Thus, in the early reform years, the status of monasticism was heightened as a form of masculinity that heroically marked a body as a public icon of anti-Maoist and pro-(pan-)Tibetan resolve—monasticism, especially in rural regions, had come to be associated with one of the most *individually agentive* moves an adult could make. As many told me, in those years, a "return" to monasticism, on the part of elderly men defrocked during the Maoist years, or on the part of households dedicating sons, was seen to be an essential part of a broader reorientation of agencies and exchange to the mandalic order under trulkus—a reconstruction of a mass monasticism that would resurrect a radically desecrated past (cf. Bass 1998: 105; Goldstein 1998b: 3).

The majority of young monks (aged between 20 and 35 years) I spoke to in Labrang took novice ordination at this time, when their rural communities began enthusiastically reconstructing local monasteries that had been branch monasteries (Tib. *dgon lag*) under the authority of Labrang. Li Dekuan, in his analysis of his fieldwork on reopened Tibetan Buddhist monasteries in Gannan prefecture, disapprovingly reports that by 1985 or 1986, not only were nomad residents of Gangya, Labrang's erstwhile grassland Lhade, visiting Labrang monastery several times annually to make offerings as individuals or household groups, but, contrary to state policy expressly forbidding it, they had also revived patron obligations to their local monastery of Drakar (seat of the female trulku Gungru Tshang). Lhade residents donated most of the 200,000 yuan needed to rebuild it, a total "religious burden," Li states, that reached dangerously excessive levels of between 15 and 33.7 percent of households' annual incomes that year (Li Dekuan 1989: 242; cf. Yang Ming 1992: 12).

Yet Li's statistics are presented in a framing historiography that jumps from 1949 to 1979, completely erasing the Maoist years. His concern about the economic "burden" of revitalization imposed by monastic elites thus misses the fact that for most rural Tibetans, weary and relatively impoverished from decades of upheaval, such expenditures on monasticism were seen to be a voluntary and particularly *disciplined* form of consumption—as we have seen, donations were investments in hoped-for personal and collective futures, exchange values only possible with the reestablishment of the basic hierarchy between (virtuous) monkhood and lay manhood. Young monks I spoke to who had entered monasteries at that time, regardless of their age at initial ordination, invariably expressed a sense of prideful agency at having participated so centrally by taking on monastic vows to become a field of merit for the laity. Akhu Konchok's parents urged him to become a monk at the local monastery at the age of seventeen in 1982, when he had finished Chinese-language middle school in their seminomadic region southeast of Labrang. He described that heady time during our interview, emphasizing his personal agency in the decision:

FROM FIELD NOTES: At that time, to talk about the general opinion, the attitude toward becoming a monk was very good. When it came to monks, whether their intentions were just to check it out [Tib. *bsam pa mgo rdog*], or whether they were talented and learned [Tib. *yon tan*], no matter what, they were considered to have moved to a superior status. Widely, no matter who it was, [monasteries] were seen as places to make merit. When I myself was young, I thought that they were places to make offerings and prostrations, and the best one to do that was the monk. Having seen that, I was inspired by great faith, and for that reason I voluntarily became a monk.

The "first blush" of monastic revitalization thus represented a resolute effort on the part of local Tibetans to return to a form of mass monasticism that would encompass a variety of men dedicated to the service of Buddhism and the community. For one thing, decisions for sons to enter monkhood were made along many of the same pragmatic lines as they were in the past. When in 1982 local governments in Gannan prefecture began the initial move to a household-responsibility system, the reallocation of land and livestock left most rural families, both farmers and nomads, with little household property relative to the past.[14] Thus many families could spare sons to join monasteries, where the influx of donations and demand for ritual services promised them a comfortable living. All the monks I spoke to who entered monkhood at that time did so either on their parents' initiative or with their enthusiastic support, and all of them were younger brothers in families with many (between 4 and 9) siblings. In contrast to nuns I interviewed, many fewer monks fled home to enter monastic life. Twelve out of eighteen nuns I spoke to who were ordained after the reforms fled home to enter the monastic life, while only two out of eighteen monks I interviewed who were ordained after the reforms had done so.

For another thing, the heightened prestige of monkhood and the acute sense of urgency after the desecrations of the Maoist years drew young men like Akhu Konchok in their mid- to late teens to monasticism, and contributed to a kind of "more is better" ethic in which robed bodies were deemed desperately needed in order to fill out the ranks of the decimated monastic community. Amnye Gompo, the eloquent and elderly former monk who, in our taped interview was so proud to hold forth on Buddhism and local Buddhist historiography, hit his stride when my assistant and I asked him about supporting monks through service and invitations to chant. He began a long, uninterruptible, fluent discussion of the essential importance of the Buddha Dharma by asserting unequivocally: "Without the monastic community, there is no [possibility for] meritorious action. Without the monastic community, without lamas, the Buddha wouldn't exist" (Tib. *dge 'dun med na dge med ni red/ dge 'dun med na . . . bla ma med na da sangs rgyas yod ni ma red*).

Akhu Tshultrim (aged 27) was from a small farming village northwest of Labrang in Qinghai. He proudly described for me how he had been inspired to leave the village school, where he said he had learned hardly more than the Tibetan alphabet, and enter monkhood at the age of fourteen in 1982. He said his parents had been very happy about his decision, and that back then, monks in the assembly at the local monastery could make up to a hundred yuan per day at peak festival times. But Akhu Tshultrim insisted the primary reason he became a monk was the freedom it gave him from lay manhood to make merit and study Buddhism: "An unmarried man is allowed to uphold vows [Tib. *mi rkyang sdom pa de mo bʐung na chog gi*]. If he stayed in [mundane] cyclic existence [Tib. *'khor ba*], then he— How is it said? He can't make merit, you know. He can't study and practice Buddhism."

In these ways, then, throughout the Labrang region, rural communities in the early reform years invested in reestablishing the basic performative difference between laymen and monks, sending as many preteen boys and teenagers as possible to local monasteries and supporting them with gifts of food and money. Li Dekuan, relying on statistics gathered through local Religious Affairs Bureaus and his own investigations, reports that in 1985 there were eighty-nine reopened monasteries in Gannan prefecture, the vast majority of which were Geluk, and that the number of monks by then unofficially reached almost five thousand (including 48 trulkus), almost double that recognized by the state, or around 4 percent of Tibetan males.[15] Li is especially concerned to report that even though reopened monasteries in Gannan were assigned quotas for numbers of monks they could accept, within five years numbers at most monasteries far exceeded their original quotas, including at Labrang, which, with an actual population of over fourteen hundred monks in 1987, had long surpassed its initial quota of 444. Further, Li calls attention to the "problem" of increasing numbers of monks under age eighteen in the early reform years, despite state policy expressly forbidding their acceptance into monastic communities. Comparing survey data collected in four counties, including Xiahe, Li reports that every monastery had young monks under eighteen, and in some monasteries such monks constituted up to 85 percent of their assemblies, while Labrang had the highest percentage of monks over age fifty (Li Dekuan 1989: 241; cf. Pu 1990: 506).

By the 1990s, the situation at Labrang monastery perhaps epitomized the ways in which this grassroots return to a mass monasticism ran counter to state efforts to control and utilize monasticism, rendering monkhood an unusually compromised status, even as it was associated more than ever with heroic anti-state opposition. In the early reform era, Tibetan men in Labrang had to live with the emasculating effects of Apa Gongjia's unprecedented military power and control of the means of production on the one hand, and the everyday ways in which their own interests ended up overlapping with state policy on the other. Despite Tibetans' efforts to revitalize masculine patrifilial authority in the valley, they also knew that, like the Eight Cavalrymen at the Great Prayer Festival, Tibetan lay elders' authority had been diminished and disarmed, even as state cadres still relied on them to keep order at the local level.

Young Tibetan men I knew were thus acutely aware that, for them, embodying heroic ethnic loyalties was not clear-cut. My lay male friend Wande (aged 30), a local-government cadre whose own father was a respected village elder, expressed this sentiment when he told me that the Tibetan term for "village head" (Tib. *sde dpon*, vs. Ch. *duizhang*) did not "fit" any more, because their power was nothing like it was when Tibetan lamas and lay leaders ruled. This was because, he said, they had no military might to support any opposition to the county government. Young Tibetan cadres like Wande, who felt no choice but to pursue social mobility through the avenues set forth by the state, had to grapple with the fact that they themselves embodied the domestication of Tibetan masculinities to its service (cf. Upton 1996). Wande, unlike our defiantly ethnic nomad student Gompo, who ended up painfully participating in a Shenzhen ethnic theme park, was drawing a salary close to his natal home in a Lhade village, and he told me he never wore Tibetan robes except occasionally on festival days. Such aspiring young cadres were thus positioned awkwardly vis-à-vis the time-honored pinnacles of Tibetan heroic masculinity: the nomad warrior and the learned monk, both of whom state policy and the tourism industry aimed to settle and contain— emasculate—as quaint and picturesque tokens of commodified Tibetan ethnic difference.[16]

In Labrang, such gendered tensions were particularly acute, because it was a place where monastic and state masculine authorities had historically confronted each other on the edge of nomad territory. As we have seen, Labrang was a model site in which Dengist "religion" policy sought to harness the taming power of Geluk monasticism to position Tibetan Buddhism as another "feminine hinge" on which to effect the shift from the past-oriented national heroism of Maoist revolutionaries to the future-oriented national heroism of risk-taking capitalist entrepreneurs. As Ann Anagnost has argued, "religion" (Ch. *zongjiao*) under Dengist reforms was the disciplinary category that attempted to proscribe all the irrational loyalties and selfish or wasteful consumption that were seen to constitute "feudal superstition" (Ch. *fengjian mixin*). Magic and superstition were the enemies, and essential Others, of the modernizing rational state and market; their proscription grounded Party leaders' claims that they headed a modern, yet *still Communist*, state (Anagnost 1987: 43). In this, Dengist leaders in fact followed in a long line of scholars, colonists, and missionaries in the frontier zone whose various claims to rationality confronted the dangerous "trope of the tribe" (Appadurai 1996: 162) in

Tibetans' unmanageable faith in the material efficacy of divine agents (e.g., Ekvall 1938, Tucci 1988, Li Anzhai 1989; cf. Schwartz 1994: 227).

Thus, in the early reform years, the 1978 charter for the administration of Labrang monastery under a "Democratic Management Committee" (Ch. Siyuan Minzhu Guanli Weiyuanhui *or* Siguanhui) was used as a standard for other reopening monasteries in Gansu. The sixth Jamyang Shepa (then 35 years old) and Gongtang Tshang (then 56 years old) were rehabilitated and given high positions in the provincial and national Buddhist Association (CBA) and Chinese People's Political Consultative Committees (CPPCC), and when the tenth Panchen Lama toured the monastery in 1980 and 1982, he appointed the two of them as heads of the reestablished Management Committee (cf. Wang Yunfeng 1997: 242). Further, Labrang was chosen as the site for the nationally funded Gansu province Buddhist Studies Institute, which was opened in 1985 to train monks and young trulkus from other Tibetan regions in Gansu to serve as teachers and Management Committee members at local monasteries.[17] By the early 1990s, "religion work" cadres from other provinces sought to emulate the apparent success of Labrang's monastic administration in supervising monks and implementing state policies (Tian 1991).

Thus, from the outset monastic revitalization at Labrang was structured to produce a particularly intense confluence of competing interests. Even as Labrang was supposed to model the ideal containment and domestication of monasticism to the service of the state, state officials' disproportionate focus on the monastery raised it to even greater regional prominence among Tibetans than it had had before. It was the only place where the few remaining lamas could be found to provide the crucial initiations and oral transmissions of the teachings. In addition, it was the only place with the initial funding to recreate some of the divine grandeur and mandalic pageants of the past.[18]

Ironically, the most powerful way in which state interests were able to co-opt those of the monastic elite was in appropriating the power of monasticism to tame Tibetan masculinities by legislating and redefining ideal monastic subjects. That is, state appeals to monastic law in order to define monks as devoted solely to a realm of pure and "normal" (Ch. *zhengchang*) "religion" coincided nicely with Geluk monastic elites' urgent interest in reestablishing the authoritative foundations of Buddhism in Labrang as a superior form of rationalized and moralized knowledge production. Of course, as illustrated by Qing rewards in the eighteenth century to Labrang's lay and monastic leaders for keeping their monks out of the Mongol uprisings, such a convergence of outside state and local monastic interests in the valley was not entirely new. Yet, if we recall Tibetans' adamant military resistance to Muslim attempts to intervene in monastic affairs in the 1920s, CCP religion policies under reforms represented unprecedented state interference in monastic administration.

In the 1978 Tibetan-language charter (KZC 1978) for Labrang's Management Committee, drawn up by the leadership of the Gansu province CBA under guidelines set forth by the national CBA, it is clear how Chinese state goals and Tibetan Buddhist monastic ideals coincided at the same time as new regulations were introduced that attempted to legislate an unprecedented distinction between monks and laity. The tone of the document reflects the risk to the state of reopening such a potentially powerful institution as Labrang. On the one hand the rules and regulations are an appeal to Buddhist monastic codes (cf. Ellingson 1990, Cabezón 1997). New monks must be able-bodied, attain the consent of their parents to join the order, respect their teachers and elders, wear proper robes, abide by the strictest decorum in monastic quarters, and earnestly uphold their vows so that the laity may see them as a proper field of merit:

> 3.7.3. [Monks] must strictly uphold the rules and regulations of the monastery. Because they are monks in the monastery, they must strictly undertake the three: getting teachings, thinking, and meditating [*or* cultivating]. In the morning and afternoon they will memorize texts; they will earnestly study the Duwa texts, philosophy, and logic. Having abandoned all greedy and harmful thoughts, they will generate the thought of enlightenment, and they must uphold the Duwa rules of Buddhism by doing good and accumulating merit.

On the other hand, the rules and regulations pay overwhelming attention to creating monks first and foremost as subjects of the state. As such, monks' primary allegiance should be to the state and its laws. They must simultaneously "love their country and love their religion" (Tib. *rgyal gces chos gces*, Ch. *aiguo aijiao*). In addition, they must be "self-sufficient" and not burden the "faithful masses" with their upkeep.

Thus, the regulations aim to alter the grounds for the recognition of monks by requiring quotas and stringent testing for new candidates, by setting the minimum age of ordination at eighteen, by legislating that monks study Party policy, by mandating that they engage in productive labor, and by ruling that all monks must study and grasp Buddhist teachings and refrain from any "superstitious" (Tib. *rmongs dad*, lit. "blind" or "delusional" faith) activities that exploit the gullible masses:

3.8. 2. [The monastery] must absolutely forbid such people as mediums [Tib. *lha ba*] and diviners [Tib. *mo ma*] from carrying out such superstitious activities inside Buddhist monasteries as calling deities or demons, curing illness by taming demons, or reading signs or letters, or divining in any way.

As epitomized in this effort to distinguish "mediums" and "diviners" from "monks," the intention is clearly not to return to monasticism the way it was, but to distill the community down to a group that most nearly approximates the ideal state monastic subject—stripping away the "monastic proletariat" (Tucci 1988), worldly monk officials, *and* trulku-tantrists, and leaving the monk-scholars to be dutiful students of a rationalized Buddhism settled and sequestered in a well-managed monastic institution that is segmented off from inappropriately consumptive exchange with laity.

In effect then, the Management Committee rules attempted to turn the performative resources of monkhood to the purposes of the post-Mao CCP state and capitalist moral economy by mandating the unprecedented enforcement of a (refigured) monastic ideal, thereby attempting to limit the potential of Geluk remandalization to recreate Labrang monastery's political and economic power among Tibetans. The rules after all demanded that "monks resemble monks" (Tib. *grwa ba de grwa bar 'dra ba zhig du 'gyur dgos*, Ch. *seng xiang seng*) and that "the monastery should work with dignity to make the region a place with beautiful surroundings and pleasing Buddhist activities." Further, citing a slogan widely used in education and birth-planning circles to express the reform-era imperative to channel resources toward nurturing a few to lead the rest into modernity, state policy insisted that in the process of monastic revitalization the emphasis should be on developing the "quality" (Ch. *suzhi*, Tib. *yon tan*) of monks, not the quantity (cf. Anagnost 1995, Bass 1998).

We could thus see this religion-policy emphasis on regulating monkhood as an unprecedented state challenge to the substantialized masculine transcendence so foundational to Geluk mandalization. That is, state attempts to make Labrang monastery an icon of ideally contained statist "religion" were efforts to emasculate trulkus and lamas, to curtail the practices that indexically linked their masculine agency to material efficacy in *this* world. The category "superstition" attempted to close off the ubiquitous exchanges, among monks and between monks and laity, that generated the great value attached to the worldly tantric prowess of trulkus and lamas. Instead, Buddhist monasticism as "religion" for the laity was supposed to be distilled down to the otherworldly role of merit making, effectively deferring Buddhist efficacy to people's *future* lives, an endeavor of judicious accumulation that nicely mirrored state visions for citizens' responsible investment in capitalist enterprise.

Amidst the reform-era push for "modernization," this policy emphasis resonated powerfully with the concerns of many Tibetan cadres and intellectuals who contended, in ways similar to some exiled intellectuals' critiques of Buddhism, that mass monasticism was incompatible with the demands of modernity, no longer empowering Tibetans but weakening them, keeping them "backward" and "passive" in a rapidly changing world:

> FROM FIELD NOTES: Wandikhar was a retired Tibetan Party official who greatly enjoyed acting as an ambassador for the Labrang region for the benefit of foreign visitors. In our long conversation one day, he was proudly telling me about the New Year's custom of burning incense and saying prayers on household rooftops at the stroke of midnight. I asked what the incense was for, and what benefit it had, and he answered vaguely: "So that the Buddha will protect them, I suppose" (Ch. *foye baoyou ba*). But I had heard that the incense was for dewa mountain deities, and I told him so, adding that I had also heard that people customarily went to favorite monk-lamas for annual "divination advice" (Tib. *lo rtsis*) at New Year's. Wandikhar's face went sour, and at first he pretended he didn't know what this meant. Then, he admitted: "Yes, those things are superstition [Ch. *mixin*], and Tibetans around here stubbornly believe in their efficacy." Finally, he shrugged in resignation and said: "It's their habit" (Ch. *xiguan le*).

Here, Wandikhar's initial representation of Tibetans' ritual practices attempted to reduce Buddhist efficacy to a mirror trope for the ideal state—a benign, otherworldly, paternal protection. Yet I would argue that such discursive efforts to delimit both monastic and state masculine authorities served such reform-minded Tibetans well in their attempts to envision a modernizing trajectory on Tibetan terms.

From the beginning of the reform era many Tibetan reformers, such as the controversial lay Amdo Tibetan scholar Danzhu Angben (1993), sought to direct development efforts away from monastic revitalization to secular concerns such as (state-sponsored) education in science and technology so that Tibetans could "catch up" (Ch. *ganshang*) with the "more advanced" Han Chinese. From the perspective of such earnest reformers, monks should make up only a minority of Tibetan men—well-educated preservers of Buddhist traditions as one aspect of

Tibetan culture. But these contemporary concerns were the very sentiments that had led to a rapprochement between some Tibetan men and Chinese regimes throughout the twentieth century (cf. Stoddard 1985), and they confronted the heightened conservatism and heroic prestige of the monastic elite in Labrang, who strongly believed that the "recovery" of Tibetan culture should begin with and emanate from the monastery.

In this context, young monks, drawn to Labrang in increasing numbers throughout the 1980s and early 1990s, found that their monastic bodies were the unprecedented measure of ethnic loyalties and social processes now seen to be arrayed in polarized oppositions, even as the choices they were presented with were not at all so neatly arranged. Akhu Konchok expressed this in the course of telling me how, in order to stay in Labrang, he frequently had to resist the pleas of village elders from his home region to come back and take up a leadership position in their local monastery, which lacked learned monks:

> We young people are really in a difficult position. The social pressure on us is intense, and it comes from many sides. On the one hand are the conservatives [Ch. *baoshou pai*]; on the other, the progressives [Ch. *jinbu pai*]. Since the "opening up," Tibetans have been allowed to recover their culture and religion, and this process must start with monasteries. Therefore, we young monks all have a great responsibility to participate.

Yet he went on to say that it was very hard to know how best to participate as a monk in order to both contribute to the revitalization of Tibetan culture and not get left behind by the demands and opportunities of the modern world.

CONTESTING ENTREPRENEURSHIPS: REFIGURING TIBETAN MASCULINITIES

By the early 1990s then, Labrang became a central arena in which contestations surrounding the nature of Tibetan masculinities came to a head. For one thing, state officials' efforts to contain monasticism there could not keep pace with the grassroots remandalization of surrounding regions that their own focus on Labrang had helped to attract. For another, when the "first blush" of monastic revitalization in outlying regions waned as rural households' standard of living increased and new opportunities opened up with the diversifying economy (cf. Kai 1995: 63), Labrang came to be the monastic center on which rural laity consolidated their merit-making activities and donations. This process helps to explain why the only two young monks I interviewed who had fled home to become ordained locally were the ones who had sought to enter monastic life in the late 1980s. The parents of both protested because they felt that the life of a monk was too hard. As Akhu Tshultrim told me, lay donations to rural monasteries declined a few years after the reforms, and by the time we were speaking (he said) a monk was lucky to make a thousand yuan a year from assembly attendance. Further, as Catriona Bass (1998) has recently demonstrated, Dengist modernization policies had disastrous effects on state-sponsored secular education in rural Tibetan regions, because the return to a "quality" approach to education (versus a "quantity" approach that emphasized providing basic education to the masses) channeled resources away from rural and primary levels toward urban and higher-education schools. At the same time, responsibility for funding education devolved onto local governments often unable, or unwilling, to earmark funds for schools.

Tibetans across the community complained to me either of the lack of secular schools in farming and nomad areas or of the abysmal state of school facilities and the irrelevance of the curriculum, much of which, especially after the military crackdown on Tibetan demonstrations in Lhasa, and the rise of campaigns to encourage "patriotism" among minorities, was aimed at molding Tibetan youth as good Chinese citizens, not at teaching useful vocations (cf. Upton 1996; Bass 1998: 97). Labrang was one of the few places in the region to have Tibetan primary and middle schools. However, Tibetan teachers who were good friends of mine complained about the low quality of the facilities and of the instruction. Further, county funding for education dried up in the mid-1990s, leaving a huge classroom building unfinished and empty, and teachers without salaries for months at a time. Thus, the concentration of resources on Labrang monastery supported what many locals came to see as the only good, prestigious, useful education in the region for those sons who could be spared, a phenomenon that helps to explain the marked increase in the number of preteen monks at Labrang by the early 1990s.

Perhaps most importantly though, the nature of Tibetan masculinities amidst state-sponsored monastic revitalization in the 1990s came to be the very pivot on which turned a reemerging high-stakes politics of *contesting entrepreneurships*—competing frameworks for masculine subjects accessing, controlling, and expanding capital. In Dengist state religion policy, the vision of a segmented monastic-secular spatial and political economic order in the valley constructed the monastery as an ideally disciplined capitalist firm (altruistically) operating on behalf of both the locality and the nation. The economist Kai Wa perhaps put it best in his study on Tibetan monastic economies in the PRC in the mid-1990s. Describing the new professional class of monks trained at monasteries and in trulku estates across Tibetan regions, he enthuses (1995: 63):

> They do not just dream about the past and deny reality; on the contrary, they have broadened their field of vision, and have boldly overcome obstacles in finding ways to do business with township enterprises, in both public and private economies, as well as with private-enterprise households. Experience has already proven their results to be remarkable. Thus they have greatly strengthened the power of "monastic self-sufficiency," lightening the burden of the broad masses and heightening enthusiasm for monasteries to participate in the market economy.

Here then, we find the capitalist heroic masculinity of the bold, yet civic-minded, entrepreneur applied to Tibetan monks and trulkus. In effect, such a policy emphasis on rationalized monastic capitalism as "self-sufficient" and thus nonexploitive amounts to attempts at appropriating the participation frameworks of a monastic moral economy for a state-sponsored capitalism in which new possibilities for consumption and voluntary generosity have elided both the exigencies of production and the everyday constraints of ongoing state discipline.[19] The dream here would seem to be, in the absence of state support for rural education, to harness the taming power of Tibetan monasteries in order to recruit and sedentarize young Tibetan monks as a loyal (patrifilial) and aspiring labor force for national capitalist advance. Indeed, in an article assigned to monk students at the Buddhist Studies Institute in Labrang while I was there, Zhi Hong, writing in a Chinese Buddhist magazine, urges young monks not to be like those "wild monks" (Ch. *ye heshang*) who use Buddhism to selfishly make money and travel around providing ritual services while enjoying modern amusements (1993: 3). And this dream, I would add, took on imperative proportions in the wake of the transnational Panchen Lama controversy in mid-1995.

Yet such statist attempts to define value by directing exchange and shaping future aspirations always already create their Other (or Others). Geluk remandalization by the 1990s, especially as directed by prominent monk-trulkus, positioned monk officials as oppositional entrepreneurs. That is, monk officials sought access to capital in order to reconstruct the frameworks of an ideally Tibetan patrifilial order, one in which rationality *depended* on the expanded space-time purviews of monks', lamas', and trulkus' masculine tantric prowess. At Labrang, the growth of the monastic economy as it diversified into commercial ventures, including tourism, along with the accumulation of capital by prominent trulkus like Gongtang Tshang, gave the monastic leadership great power to act as a set of private foundations on behalf of the Tibetan community, in effect stepping in at their discretion (in some ways as before) to give grants and loans to localities and individuals where corrupt and bankrupt governments could not. By the early 1990s, Labrang's Management Committee was reporting annual corporate incomes of over six hundred thousand yuan from its commercial enterprises alone, the majority of which went to paying monastic expenses, and the rest to various community causes.[20]

However, such monastic reports did not reflect the huge amounts of income, in money, goods, livestock, and donated labor, that the monastery as a whole and individual trulkus took in annually in the form of lay offerings, income that actually constituted the bulk of monastic wealth. In part, the amount of lay offerings that the monastery attracted reflected the increasing wealth of the surrounding nomad populations relative to farming regions by the 1990s (cf. Ma Jiang 1993). But as Li Dekuan reports, as early as 1984 the monastery was taking in an estimated 200,000 yuan annually from Lhade offerings alone (1989: 241). To give some indication of the scale of such offerings a decade later when I was there, throughout the year, but especially during the Great Prayer Festival, wealthy lay households or coalitions of nomad Lhade, as well as monks or lamas, gave Great Teas (Tib. *mang ja*) to the entire assembly of the main college at Labrang. In March 1995, they were being given every day, and Sodnam, my lay male friend who had married into one of the wealthiest households in town, told me there was a monthlong waiting list to give one. (He knew because his own household was in line.) Such "teas," at which a meal is served to up to six hundred monks and cash offerings are distributed to all according to rank, cost between twenty thousand and twenty-five thousand yuan, and were considered to generate prodigious merit for the donor. Great Teas were also given to the assemblies of other colleges or to particular trulkus' retinues.

By the mid-1990s, offerings to the monastic assemblies were so steady that a monk member could earn up to six hundred yuan a month, even in nonfestival periods, a sum that was twice the salary of a low-level cadre in Labrang. Further still, this income did not include that independently taken in by various trulkus, whose own disciples and former Lhade had taken on patron obligations to them. Gongtang Tshang's estate in the early twentieth century was among the wealthiest at Labrang.[21] By the 1990s Gongtang embodied the prodigious stature of heroic Tibetan monkhood; his resolve not to collaborate during the Maoist years was

FIGURE 18.
The newly rebuilt Great Liberation Stupa in Gongtang Tshang's
estate headquarters during the summer of 1993.

indexed most strongly for locals in his determination to remain a monk through his decades of imprisonment, a status that arguably elevated him to even higher prestige locally than the lay sixth Jamyang Shepa. As I heard from lay and monk officials working for him, his estate in the mid-1990s was worth millions (in U.S. dollars), most of which was not taxed. Gongtang was perhaps the most entrepreneurial of monk-trulkus in his remandalization efforts in the region. He directed a successful and diversifying milk-powder factory in his Lhade south of Labrang; he raised funds among wealthy Han disciples, and he donated tens of thousands of yuan to opening not only monasteries but also rural secular schools (cf. Liu Yu 1993, Wang Yunfeng 1997).

The most spectacular of Gongtang's efforts though was his success in rebuilding the Great Liberation Stupa that had stood on his estate grounds in the monastery. The stupa, with its four main altars, gold-plated Opakmay (Skt. Amitābha) temple on top, thousands of Buddha images, and displays of archived texts—some of which, officials insisted, were originals that had survived the Maoist years—was completed in 1993 to much fanfare. I was told it cost over five million yuan and required teams of artisans from all over the PRC. Some of the funds came from state bureaus, and Gongtang's wealthiest Chinese-American disciple, Miss Li, famously donated 200,000 yuan to the reconstruction.

But the bulk of the funds and supporting goods and labor came from local Lhade offerings. I was able to witness the vitality of a post-Mao Tibetan Buddhist "tournament of value" in Labrang when, in the summer of 1993, the town filled up with eager patrons ready to celebrate the completion of the stupa, and Lhade patriarchs lined up to make major offerings of funds and goods on behalf of their dewas, or to sponsor Great Teas for the monk assemblies conducting vivification rites for the stupa. Those exchanges, I found, were strongly structured by a vibrant patrifilial historicity, as people noted which patriarchs represented which dewas' traditional obligations, or traded stories about their relations to Gongtang's patrilines. Some of the most celebrated of young male visitors, like one princely layman from Sichuan, were the scions of former leader lines with close ties to Gongtang's estate. Labrang in the summer of 1993 was most definitely refigured as an Amdo fatherland under Gongtang:

> FROM FIELD NOTES: One afternoon during the preparations, Tshomo, Droko, and I sat in the office of Gongtang's chief accountant and watched as he wearily tried to keep track of the massive inflow of offerings. Remarking that his head hurt from it all, he asked Tshomo to help him draw up a chart to keep track of the various kinds of offerings from individuals and groups, ranging from flour to Buddha images, to robes, silk, and money—Droko even handed over the bracelets on her wrists. That day, the accountant was packing five thousand yuan in stacks of bills into a worn bag as payment for a shipment of meat to be served at the celebration feast. Some days, he exclaimed, he received so much cash—up to 210,000 yuan one day—that he could not fit it all into bags!

Hence the great danger Labrang monastery represented to the state: even as state policy sought to make Labrang a model for the domestication (and exploitation) of monasticism, it opened the way for the reestablishment of the patrifilial exchanges grounding the transcendent authority of heroic monk-trulkus. In 1995 and 1996, the unregulatable charisma of such men had contributed to the creation of independent monastic corporations—what amounted to great movements of capital—in the form of untaxed income and unregulated redistribution, outside state control. As Kai Wa (1995: 63) complains at the end of his article, the economies of the largest reconstructed monasteries in Tibetan regions did not in fact amount to ideal capitalist firms working on behalf of the state. He found that they were in actuality controlled by traditional hierarchies of Geluk monastic elites, in effect marginalizing the authority of Management Committees and channeling most monastic capital not to providing public services now abandoned by the state but to the recreation of the mandalic grandeur and scholarly curricula that were the basis of the great dignity and prestige of Tibetan Buddhist monkhood. Kai Wa thus ends his article by decrying the "closed and scattered capital" (Ch. *bisan zijin*) owned by large monasteries and trulkus for being *inaccessible and undirectable* to "economically beneficial" development projects (1995: 54).

At Labrang, the fifty monk representatives of the new Democratic Management Committee, ostensibly headed by Jamyang Shepa and Gongtang (neither of whom was actually in Labrang for most of the year), were under the ultimate direction of the county government and Party Religious Affairs offices. Yet I was told time and again that most monks of stature and learning did not want positions on the committee; in monastic circles it was not considered to be very prestigious, powerful, or particularly representative of the interests of the community.

By contrast, the Management Committee charter allowed for the reestablishment of monastic leadership within assemblies (i.e., the abbot, Tib. *khri pa;* the chief disciplinarian, Tib. *zhal ngo;* the assembly supervisor, Tib. *dge bskos;* and the chant master, Tib. *dbu mdzad*). Such senior monks and learned scholars, albeit greatly reduced in number, received the utmost respect and had much influence as role models among junior monks. They were the ones in the six colleges who presided over the close adherence to the schedule of "Dharma sessions" (Tib. *chos thog*) and intercessions (Tib. *chos mtshams*), to the curricula and methods of teaching and testing, and to daily strictures on monk behavior for displaying respect and monk virtue. All monks in assemblies had to wear the maroon-colored outfit of skirt, upper vest, outer robe, and traditional felt boots. No socks, sweaters, or sleeves of any kind could be worn, no matter what time of year. And when they went out, they could not wear glasses or hats. They could not be seen interacting with laywomen and nuns very often, or making frivolous trips into town, and they were not supposed to spend much time in worship practices such as circumambulation, which took time away from studying. The chief disciplinarian, shoulders massive with the wooden frame under his robe, still cut an awesome figure as he patrolled the assemblies and monk quarters during intercessions, and Labrang still had a reputation in Amdo regions as the monastery that demanded the strictest discipline of its monks.

Yet it was precisely in the control and discipline of young monks that the state's regulation had most emasculated monasticism in Labrang. And this, I argue, was the context in which Tibetan locals came to see the basic gender difference between monks and laymen as disturbingly blurred, threatening the hierarchical relationship between monastic and lay worlds, and giving new importance to recognizing the "real monks" (Tib. *akhu ngo ma, akhu kho thag*) among the "fake monks" (Tib. *akhu rdzun ma*), the "best or ideal monks" (Tib. *a tsa bo*) among the "worst" ones (Tib. *a ha ma*). In 1995, the Management Committee reported an official number of 757 monks and twenty-three resident trulkus in the monastery. However, there were actually more than twice that number of monks living in the monastery quarters and in town. As many Tibetans complained to me, from an illiterate nomad matriarch to a respected lama, the single most important way in which state efforts to curtail monasticism affected everyday life in Labrang was the enforcement of a quota on the number of monks permitted to enter the assemblies (cf. Tian 1991, Goldstein 1998a):

> FROM FIELD NOTES: "His being a monk is of no benefit at all!" The old nomad mother of my twenty-four-year-old monk friend Akhu Khedrup stated this unequivocally as we sat outside her tent. She complained to me that he was not allowed to join Labrang's assembly, and she worried about his frequent trips home (like this one with me) and his consequent lack of attention to his studies.

Even though the tenth Panchen Lama was eventually able to get the official quota of monks at Labrang raised to eight hundred in the late 1980s, that number still did not encompass all those seeking entrance by then. Acceptance to officially recognized status as a monk conferred great benefits in access to teachers, housing, and shares of assembly offerings. Further, such status was ostensibly for life for a monastic population the majority of which was under age thirty. Thus by the early 1990s, the monastery had very little leeway for (officially) accepting new monks.[22] In addition, the difficult and unprecedented testing and permit procedures that candidates for entrance had to undergo were major deterrents to young monks (cf. Tian 1991: 11). Finally, in the mid-1990s county officials attempted to diminish the regional draw of Labrang by limiting entrance to monks from Gansu province only. I was told that in 1994, of a hundred monks who underwent testing only two were accepted. In 1995, out of seventy monks tested only seven were accepted. Thus, most of the young monks I interviewed who had been living and studying at Labrang for years without entering assemblies held out little hope of ever being able to do so. Many complained that the chances for ordinary monks were further decreased by the special treatment given to monks with status or money—young trulkus and monks with connections (or the resources to make strategic bribes) among monastic elites and state officials could gain entrance by bypassing the testing system and age limits altogether. As Akhu Tshultrim told me by way of explaining why he would probably not test to get in, it was common knowledge that such monks as himself without "face" (i.e., status or connections, Tib. *ngo med gi*) or official residence status in Gansu must live in Labrang for at least ten years before they could even be considered for entrance into the assembly.

But such state limits could not restrain the strong inclinations toward monasticism among rural Tibetans, inclinations that by the mid-1990s had converged on Labrang. The clout of the monastic leadership meant that the state did not regulate the numbers of *ordinations* lamas conferred, nor the number of students they privately accepted, either as live-in disciples or as attendees at their lectures. Thus the monastic population when I was there was characterized by the unprecedented situation in which the majority of monks, both novice and fully ordained, did not participate in the assemblies of the monastery itself. Such monks lived outside the daily participation frameworks that structured monastic life, usually staying in borrowed rooms with relatives or friends from home regions. Since there were few senior monk teachers left, many young monks did not live with their teachers, and thus lacked the daily supervision a teacher traditionally provided.

Dargye, my educated lay male friend who had admonished me so vehemently not to forsake the gendered authority structures of monastic scholarship, put it clearest when he pointed out that monks in the reform era had a new dual nature: they were at once members of the monastic community and citizens of the state. Monks had "rights" (Ch. *quanli*) protected by the state, he explained, upon which the monastery could not impinge. If a monk wanted to go to town and see a movie, said Dargye, the monastery had no ultimate authority to stop him. Meanwhile, monks, even committee members themselves, would invariably scoff when I asked what the Management Committee was doing about monk discipline. In their view, committee representatives, most of whom were young themselves, had no authority with which to really influence young monks. As for the state's arm of local discipline, the Public Security Bureau, as long as monks did not participate in antistate activities, it did not concern itself with the everyday behavior of young monks deemed inappropriate by the Tibetan community.

Thus it was that Chinese state intervention in the Labrang region since the reforms created an "institutional vacuum" with ambiguous effects for young Tibetan men. Chinese state discipline had rendered the practice of Tibetan heroic masculinities profoundly problematic, yet the very limits or failings of those state apparatuses opened up spaces and created incentives for young men to pursue personal empowerment by deploying the performative resources of masculine ideals in new ways that ultimately threatened not only state interests but those of the Tibetan community itself. In the 1990s, both monastic and state officials had to grapple with the ultimate unmanageability of men's private aspirations and networks under capitalist imperatives, a process that underlay the indeterminacy of monastic recognition that all post-Mao authorities increasingly encountered in starker ways than ever before. As I argued in chapter 4, young men in this context often found the most viable and alluring route to masculine subjectivity to be that of the cosmopolitan entrepreneur—many young rural men did not aspire to become part of a monastic proletariat; they sought instead to participate in the cachet of mobile capital themselves.

Thus I found that perhaps the most basic aspect of masculinity that young Tibetan men held to in the face of their subordination under the predominance of the Chinese state and Han urbanites was the ability to *move*, through public spaces in pursuit of opportunities and networks, and away from the daily obligations of the household domain. As my lay male friend Damdrin put it one day, in the course of explaining the use of the Tibetan adverb *gzhung* ("essentially," "fundamentally"): "Men fundamentally will not touch the work internal to the household" (Tib. *byis lu cho khyim tshang gi nang gi las ka gzhung thug rgyu ma red*). As a realm of activity so profoundly and, as we saw in chapter 3, recently more intensively associated with women, household labor held out the most intimate and visceral threat of feminization for young men, so much so that Damdrin insisted that for fear of ridicule from their friends men would not help with such work even if the women were tired or sick.[23]

Importantly, with the intensifying masculinization of the private sector under reforms and increased access to global media, by the late 1980s such bottom-line masculinity for Tibetans increasingly came to be associated with the ability to demonstrate success in escaping the demands and limits of subsistence production. Young Tibetan men's aspirations for social mobility then turned to finding ways to secure earned income (Tib. *yong sgo*) through long-distance trade, wage labor, the salaries of a cadre, or other legal and illegal activities. As we have seen, both Tibetan men and women widely associated such income with the freedom or power (Tib. *dbang cha*) to move out of parochial and "backward" localities, to exercise individual choices in (preferably conspicuous) consumption, and thereby to participate in the globalizing economy of the "modern" world. This new emphasis in the performativity of Tibetan masculinity explains, in part, the decrease in the number of young men in the Labrang region choosing (or agreeing to) the monastic life at that time (cf. Kai 1995: 63). As old Akhu Sherap lamented in our 1995 interview, "nowadays boys refuse to become monks" (Tib. *byis lu cho da grwa pa byed kha mi nyan gi*) because they think the monastic life is too hard.

But I argue that the appeal of monkhood also lessened for young men because, in the face of the unprecedented domestication of monasticism under the CCP and the press of the new lay masculine entrepreneurial ideal, monkhood had been categorically *feminized* to an unprecedented extent.

This perspective, then, sheds further light on the appeal of the revived cult of mountain deities among young men in Labrang and elsewhere. In the context of state encouragement of capitalist motives and orientations to fantasies of future prosperity, mountain deities as mobile, if capricious, personal avatars who were (ironically) relatively free of state scrutiny were the ideal authorities to invoke and cajole as aids for men seeking to defeat competitors in achieving worldly success, even as they felt themselves to be subject to the winds of (market) fortune. Indeed, Tibetans refer to the capricious worldly fortune or "luck" that mountain deities can influence as "wind horse" (Tib. *rlung rta*), a conceptualization that would seem to jibe well with how locals perceived the workings of mobile capital in their lives. As hor gtsang 'jig med notes (2000: 70), men (and sometimes women) most often asked mountain deities for help in the worldly conquests and acquisitions of fights, business, gambling, and stealing. Men's exchanges with such deities in the 1990s then indexed the reemergence of the unmanageability, for both monastery and state, of young Tibetan men's entrepreneurial aspirations (Comaroff and Comaroff 2000: 316).

Yet the structural disadvantages young Tibetan men faced in the Labrang region meant that their consumption and networking practices did not often lead to any significant social mobility. Still, as against the Maoist state violence and the starkly exploitive avenues to personal wealth on the part of Maoist Tibetan cadres that they heard about from elders, young men in the 1990s could experience their communal private consumption and daily movements as appropriately (heroically) "Tibetan," in that they allowed for a powerful sense of resistance to or transcendence of state discipline. Successful Tibetan businessmen, taking up former niches of long-distance trade, could after all avoid the emasculating assimilation required of state cadres and travel throughout Tibetan regions relying on networks of close Tibetan friends and business partners. But in Labrang, for many young Tibetan men, single or married, the pursuit of masculine empowerment in this way amounted to movement limited to the daily trek out of the household, and consumption limited either to glimpsing the manly success of distant Others in contemporary Chinese and foreign videos, or to participating in the powerful male-bonding activity of drinking alcohol. These were the gendered processes, I argue, that underlay both the acute sense among elderly Tibetans, lay and monastic, of a generation gap separating them and young people, and the feeling expressed to me by Tibetans young and old of the increasing "chaos" of social change.

Such "chaos" was most importantly located in what people considered to be the *inappropriate* mobility and consumptive investments of young men—movements and exchanges that were seen to take them away from patrifilial masculine obligations to secure and provide for households and monasteries across space and time,[24] contributing to their lack of learned virtue or quality (Tib. *yon tan*, but people frequently used the Chinese word, *suzhi*, even in Tibetan conversation). My young laywoman friend Luji expressed this most clearly when I asked her what changes in men did she think there were. Relying on reports she had heard from elders, she insisted that before, men didn't used to "chaotically run around" (Ch. *luanpao*). Tibetans throughout Tibetan regions evinced bewilderment and disapproval at the unprecedented "laziness" of young men and the increasing presence of young men loitering in public spaces. Parents and wives especially complained about the selfishness of young men who did not use personal earnings to contribute to household expenses. For Apa Dondrup, the fifty-year-old farmer and former monk, the post-CCP lack of karmic justice was most strongly embodied in the undisciplined consuming bodies of young Tibetan men, in both nomad and village dewas. These days, he insisted, a son would ask his mother for money, go spend it, and then ask for more the next day, even stealing from her in order "to go all around having fun" (Tib. *la lung nga song ngas skyid po byed rgyu red*). And Akhu Konchok summed up one conversation on young men's spending habits by citing a saying: "Women earn money; men spend it" (Ch. *nude zhuan qian; nande hua qian*).

The unprecedented concentration of young laymen in town, hanging out in restaurants and bars, frequenting Tibetan brothels, gathering in the proliferating video halls to watch pirated foreign movies, loitering at pool tables in the streets, and fighting at night in drunken brawls, contributed to local villagers' fears of increasing crime and uncontrolled male violence in public spaces. I found that most local Tibetans, young and old, had very few explanatory apparatuses for these changes in the public performativity of masculinities. For them, it seemed only that the male penchant for violence and sex had escaped the confines of the spaces and times that had previously controlled or tamed it. Nowadays, as many told me, the masculine violence and transgressions that were associated with the itinerant population during festival times, and with spaces (e.g., grassland travel routes) outside Labrang, seemed to be affecting local boys at home.[25]

MONKS ARE MEN TOO: RESHAPING MONKHOOD

Yet as I demonstrated above, at the same time there were many incentives for young men to choose monkhood in Labrang between 1985 and 1995. I argue that it was the sanctioned mobility associated with the initially heightened heroic status of monkhood that caused the most determined of young Tibetan men in the region to converge on Labrang as monks. Thus, Labrang in the early 1990s was unique in the region for its concentration of young Tibetan men on the move— nomad and village laymen, and monks devoted to advancing through the monastic curricula, as well as monks looking to exploit the prestigious mobility associated with monkhood to gain access to the opportunities of the globalizing world.

Indeed, I found that another important draw for young monks in Labrang was the presence of large numbers of foreign tourists. Such tourists most often came equipped with notions of a new monk ideal, cultivated by Tibet activists abroad, of monks as emblems of a virtuous culture under siege, their heroism now seen to reside in their courageous *non*violence (as enacted in Lhasa and India in the high drama of genres of public protest adopted from Indian and Western models) in the face of the crushing might of the Chinese state (cf. Schwartz 1994). Foreign tourists I spoke to tended to focus on robed bodies as evidence of the greater ethnic-Tibetan character of Labrang relative to other Tibetan regions, and many chose to support "Tibet" by agreeing to teach English or to become "sponsors" on the model of Buddhist patronship for individual monks. After all, most of the monks we originally met were those who sought us out to teach English or to become their sponsors. Further, the fierce competition for lay support in Labrang and the decline in lay donations in rural areas meant that for monks with no access to assembly donations, securing a foreign sponsor was a great coup.[26] In that context, there were powerful pressures and incentives for young men both to assert the performative claim to the higher status of virtuous monkhood and to seek ways (both consciously and not) to alter its practice in order to participate in modern masculinity.

I argue that, within the "institutional vacuum" opened up by state intervention in the Labrang monastic community, the main way young monks (from the most devoted to the most cynical) accomplished this was to position themselves on a continuum of behavior that effectively distilled monkhood down to its most basic empowering aspect: young monks reinterpreted Buddhist discourse on the nature of monkhood and virtuous action to insist on more or less radical mobility as against their relative immobility in the post-Mao frontier-zone political economy. In fact, in the face of such emasculation pressures, a large part of the continued appeal of monkhood as heroically masculine was the possibility it held out for movement across spaces and social contexts in a status still *interstitial* to mainstream state apparatuses aimed at settling and assimilating Tibetans.

Thus, in my conversations with monks, all my interlocutors were greatly concerned to portray themselves as engaged in a personal quest for explicitly Tibetan scholarship, regardless of their level of vows or access to teachers, and that was why they came to Labrang. Even though some (usually in the most formal of interactive contexts, the taped interview) insisted monkhood is essentially the renunciation of nonvirtuous deeds (Tib. *mi dge ba*) in order to benefit all sentient beings, such things were very distant motivators for most. Instead, they drew on discursive emphases within the tradition of Tibetan Buddhist monasticism to focus on what was *gained* by passing into monkhood—the ability to act as an individual pursuing the life of the mind. All my young monk interlocutors, notwithstanding their age at initial ordination, portrayed their status as their own choice, and, just like nuns I spoke to, all expressed great pride in their agency at having overcome much adversity to strive in their studies.[27]

Importantly, the passage to monkhood for them most fundamentally indexed a mental orientation—the *intention* to strive in this way, one that not only allowed for the break from household obligations in rural areas where arranged marriage for women *and* men was again the norm, but that also constituted an internal essence that substantiated a monk as an individual and therefore could be taken anywhere. Akhu Gyamtsho (age 24) came from a family of relatively well-off cadres in an urban area north of Labrang. He defied his parents' strong opposition and left school, fleeing home to become a monk at the age of sixteen, in 1987. He was one of the most imprudent of monks Cain and I knew, talking too openly and often of his anti-state sentiments, and he was one of the most direct about recruiting us to be his "sponsors." In our interview, Akhu Gyamtsho proudly described the benefits of monkhood in terms of the mobility it provided him: "I have absolutely no household work" (Tib. *nga bab gi khyim las med*), he said, "no responsibility to a home" (Tib. *gnas gi nus pa med gi*). "Wherever I stay is my home" (Tib. *nga gang nas sdad na da nga'i yul red*).

Thus, especially for young monks like Akhu Gyamtsho seeking ordination in the late 1980s and early 1990s, the tradition's emphasis on monkhood, or virtuous action in general, as first and foremost an individual mental aspiration rather than as public action within particular participation frameworks (cf. Goldstein 1964, 1998a; Lopez 1996a), served well to legitimate their movement out of households at a time when monasticism had been severely compromised, and when criticism of young laymen's inappropriate mobility was on the rise. In addition, it worked to define monkhood as an inviolable internal (ethnic) essence that could not be touched by the reach of the state or the vicissitudes of the modern world. This after all was the logic that sustained the great monk and lama heroes who persevered in remaining monks throughout their forced defrocking in the Maoist years. And, I argue, in the face of local cadres' repeated attempts during those years to eradicate monkhood by forcing monks to marry, locals had come to associate the inner core of monkhood even more strongly with celibacy—that is, with the intention to refrain from heterosexual sex indexed most basically by a refusal to marry (cf. Welch 1972: 323).

As my laywoman friend Wanma Ji, who had been a teenager during the Cultural Revolution, adamantly described it while holding up her pinkie (indicating her lowest moral judgment) and pretending to spit, a "fallen monk" (Tib. *grwa log*) was widely looked down upon. But, she insisted, such dreadful "fallen" status was not necessarily indicated by his clothes; it was all right if he wore "Chinese clothes" (Tib. *rgya lwa gon na drag ni red*). The crucial thing was whether or not he had slept with a woman. Then, she said, he was considered to be a "fallen monk." In this, Wanma Ji was perhaps thinking of the few monks, some of them trulkus, who, unlike the sixth Jamyang Shepa, never married during the Maoist years yet continued to wear lay clothes after the reforms. Those among them who took up leadership roles in monastic administration were widely admired for their dedication to helping Tibetans. I was often told that those men were still "monks."

But I would argue that this legacy of the Maoist years amidst the shifting participation frameworks for masculinities under reforms also contributed to a new politics of recognition in the valley, one that held out the possibilities and the dangers of *delinking* transcendent masculine agency, indeed trulkuhood itself, from the local patrifilial frameworks of Geluk monasticism. I argued in the beginning of this book that trulkuhood in Labrang reproduced maleness as the performative ground for agents of the highest Buddhist exchanges, and that trulkus' transcendent authority as human Buddhas linking absolute and relative space-times relied on their claims to the powerfully flexible masculine agency of skillful means. Here, I emphasize that such an interpretive framework in the Labrang region, in which specific actions are to be interpreted as outcomes of the compassionate motivations of the omniscient, actually depended for its efficacy on the everyday disciplinary frameworks and public performativity of monkhood. As we saw, trulku recognition practices were always fraught with conflict among Tibetans, but in the heyday of Geluk monasticism at Labrang, especially under the powerful diarchy of the fifth Jamyang Shepa and his brother Apa Alo, none of those contests significantly threatened the *categorically* superior status of Buddhism or monasticism itself.

But in the 1990s, I found that in practice, the masculine "skillful means" of the ideally entrepreneurial subject threatened to diminish or delegitimize that of the trulku or lama in the absence of monasticism. Thus, the example set by heroic monks who withstood state repression and individually upheld their vows ironically worked to legitimize new uses of the discourse of monkhood among young men who felt such heroes to be impossibly distant role models. Thus, while Akhu Konchok used our formal interview to lecture me, in the closest appropriation of doctrinal language he could muster, on the nature of the monk ideal, he responded to my question about the fact that he had taken a salaried job as a cadre, and lived, still in robes, outside monastic quarters and discipline, by appealing to the inviolable and hence eminently movable essence of monkhood:

> Whether I live in the [work unit], whether I live in the monastery, whatever place I live in, even if I live as a villager, whatever I am, in the main, if I became a monk, I have taken vows, and that's how it should be explained. Thus, it doesn't matter whether or not I am called another name; I am in essence a monk [Tib. *nga gtso bo grwa pa red*].

Effectively then, the thrust of this cultural logic was to deny the vital importance of the ritualized participation frameworks that had both grounded monastic masculinity as a superior gender status across space and time, and constituted it in public performativity—that is, as an efficacious social relationship continually reproduced in everyday interactions. This move afforded some young monks great flexibility to both invoke the virtue of that gender status and push the limits of its performance in order to partake in what seemed to be the glittering new possibilities open to laymen. In this, they actually heightened locals' awareness of the embodied performativity of monkhood and masculinity as people sought to distinguish between "real" and "fake" monks.

In the reconstructed monastic community, not only was there no official place for most monks; there was no place for the vast majority of young men who did not have it in them to discipline masculine behavior enough to live as monk-scholars. In effect, the state attempted to emasculate Labrang monastery by eliminating those who did not "resemble" a monkly ideal, yet in so doing it compromised the ability of monasticism to domesticate Tibetan masculinities without providing any viable alternatives. As old Apa Thupten put it:, "You know all those young lay guys [Tib. *gsar bu cho*] hanging out in the streets and getting into trouble? They are the dapdop of before" (Tib. *de cho ldab-ldop gi kha ma red*).

Thus the monastic career in Labrang in some ways came close to a notion of monkhood as an individual endeavor, because for most, succeeding as a monk-scholar there had never before required such self-imposed initiative and discipline. In such a context, only a very few could hold to the practice of monkhood to the point of resisting the opportunities for masculine consumption in town. Indeed, among the laity, the unprecedented movements and consumptive practices of robed bodies across spaces and at times deemed inappropriate for monks constituted the phenomenon most subject to criticism and expressions of angry disgust, and contributed to their fears that young men in Labrang were increasingly out of control.

This after all was the context in which Akhu Konchok so eloquently insisted, during an English lesson one day: "Monks are men too!" That statement was his way of explaining why young monks at that time, even those within assemblies or those living with senior monks, felt compelled to go out and experience the novelties of the modern world. In his view, monkhood by then could not be expected to fully rein in the "natural" compulsions of males in the face of such new and pervasive temptations. Indeed, old Akhu Sherap lamented to me, with his young monk pupil, Gompo's brother, standing next to him, that in his youth monks never went out to participate in popular culture, but "these days the young [monks] go all the time, saying they can't help it" (Tib. *da deng sang gi chung chung cho khags med gi ʒer rgyu red*). He reprimanded his young charge for being out all afternoon in a restaurant the day before. Consequently, by 1996 in Labrang, red-robed bodies could be seen gathering in most of the places in which young laymen were congregating in increasing numbers.

In the daytime, many monks, even those who were in assemblies, but between "Dharma sessions," gathered in restaurants to eat and drink tea (rather than alcohol) with lay and monk friends. My laywomen friends who ran one of the restaurants they frequented commented that such monks with their assembly earnings were a large part of the restaurant's income. At night young monks would sneak out of the monastery and crowd into video parlors to watch movies or to attend lay dance and drama performances. In the late evening, I often saw groups of them returning to monastery quarters, singing and laughing, after a night on the town. Local Tibetans across the community were especially galled at the sight of young robed men openly playing pool on the streets, or sitting, heads covered, watching a particularly violent or erotic video. Yet Lhade patriarchs, erstwhile lay authorities, could do little to curb it. In 1994, a group of elder men from the Tawa Lhade approached the monastery with complaints about such monk behavior, to no avail. Harried senior monks with little time and curtailed authority felt resigned and powerless to stop it, even as they attempted to reach as many young monks as possible by accepting all monks who came, official or unofficial, to their individual lecture sessions.

These, then, were the circumstances under which some frustrated and angry Tibetan villagers, monks, and state cadres came to question the benefits of mass monasticism in Labrang, complaining in our conversations that there were "too many monks" (Tib. *a khu mang song*) nowadays and appealing to the terms of state discourse to argue that this was evidence that Tibetans must develop the quality of monks, not the quantity.[28] Importantly, the gist of local criticism was to reject monks' performative claims to the radical mobility and internality of monkhood and insist (in uneven ways) on locating "real" monkhood in the (idealized) participation frameworks that they imagined had constructed it as a separate and superior masculine gender status in the past. Indeed, part of the perception among locals that there were too many monks in Labrang was that there were too many robed bodies visible in traditionally unsuited places.

People's complaints and disgust focused on the bodily evidence of young monks' inappropriate mobility and public consumption, which to them seriously blurred the distinction between lay and monastic men, and indicated their selfish use of the monastic status for personal gain.[29] For example, Ama Karma, in her particularly vehement way, said she was especially appalled at the sight of young monks riding bikes and motorcycles. As her daughter nodded emphatically, she described how village children would yell at the passing monks: "You have no shame!" (Tib. *khyod ngo tsha rgyu med gi*). And Ama Wanma, with great disgust, was moved to contrast contemporary monks with a nostalgic view of monks before as ideally disciplined consumers: She described how in her day a real monk was one who owned only a bowl, and she demonstrated how all his possessions could be arranged around his body so that he didn't have to move from his recitation or meditation when he got *tsampa* [barley flour, the most basic of foods] to eat.

For those concerned about the urgent need to revitalize the monastery and monkhood as rationalized icons of the moral superiority of Tibetan culture, such behavior was refigured as transgressions with negative consequences that extended beyond individual karmic sin (Tib. *sdig pa, mi dge ba*) to the Tibetan minzu as a whole. This is so, I argue, because the movement of robed bodies out of the institutional frameworks of monasticism threatened to reduce the *general* meaning of that passage in public awareness from the bodily acceptance of a mandalic order to the strategies of opportunistic individuals. Yet the power and continued appeal of the transformation for many were precisely in the lasting capacity of the red robes, no matter how altered in the wearing, to index that order for an audience of Tibetan and foreign laity. Thus, despite intense lay criticism of young monks, the majority of monks Lhade villagers hired for indispensable ritual services came from the ranks of those not within assemblies. I found that the laity tended to prefer monks who lived in monastery quarters, official or not, but those monks tended to be the ones who were most devoted to their studies and hence less willing to perform ritual services for wages. Thus, especially around the new year, when households received their ritual obligations (Tib. *bca' ba*) from their lamas, monks qua robed bodies for hire were in great demand, and no one would have hired for such services a man who claimed to be a "monk" without wearing robes (see below).

Thus at Labrang, distinguishing between "real" and "fake" monks took on new importance for the Tibetan community. And in the context of the "institutional vacuum" there, that process was most importantly accomplished through the scrutiny and classification of robed bodies. Further, in direct opposition to appeals to monkhood as an individual, internal, movable essence, relative "realness" or authenticity of intentions was read from bodies that demonstrated degrees of commitment to Labrang monastery by adhering to the strictures on dress and behavior required of its assemblies. Young monks who regarded themselves as carefully upholding their vows, restricting their consumption, and striving for scholarly excellence resented being associated with monk transgressors. As Akhu Konchok pointed out, the laity mostly saw the monks who were behaving badly. They were the ones who were visible consuming in public spaces; those who lived a monastic life were invisible, because they tried to avoid such places. Not surprisingly, all the monks I interviewed who were not in assemblies were greatly concerned to portray themselves in our interactions as fundamentally different from the worst of monks. Despite their repeated contact with me, a woman, and the amount of time their pursuit of English took away from their studies of Buddhist texts, all of them depicted themselves as devoted to monastic scholarship at Labrang, their days filled with teachings, their bodily and consumptive discipline indexed by their proper monastic costumes. Akhu Gyamtsho, for example, was very embarrassed when I ran into him one cold evening at a monastic event during the Great Prayer Festival. He had just returned from his annual visit home and was wearing a sweater under his robe.

Monks and laity alike often strove to preserve the integrity of monasticism in Labrang by insisting that the worst "were monks from outside" (Tib. *phyi tsho nas yong no akhu*), not "from Labrang." The crucial distinction was not necessarily those who were part of the assemblies and those who were not. Rather, it was those whose bodies indexed their dedication to Labrang versus those whose bodies did not. Monks who still held out the hope of someday entering an assembly at Labrang, such as those from nearby nomad and village Lhade, strongly believed that their chances would be ruined if the Management Committee learned of their frequenting public spaces or modifying monastic dress for convenience or style.

As I walked through town one winter day with Akhu Khedrup, the young monk from a nomad Lhade who had been studying for years to enter the assembly, he shrugged off my suggestion that he must be cold without sleeves or jacket. He said: "We cannot wear such clothes, but those 'outsider' monks can." He pointed out robed men wearing street shoes, jackets, glasses, and hats. For him, his perseverance in adhering to proper monastic dress indexed the relative permanence of his commitment to monasticism and to Labrang. Meanwhile, modifications to the costume (from wearing maroon or red lay garments over the robes to leaving only the maroon skirt) were associated with the transient and strategic use of the monastic status by mobile and unconnected individuals. For locals, the worst of "fake" monks were those depicted in widespread rumors as donning monastic robes during the day and lay clothes at night in order to join the revelry of masculine consumption.

Yet, given the new pressures and meanings attached to the performativity of monkhood, and the cultural logic of monkhood as an internal essence, young men of varying degrees of commitment to monasticism were seeking ways to compromise on wearing robes at all while still remaining "monks." By the mid-1990s, most young monks who left Labrang on trips not marked as pilgrimage (Tib. *gnas skor la 'gro pa*) wore lay clothes to avoid the scrutiny of the state and the condescension of Han and Hui,[30] or to appear more modern and professional as business representatives of trulkus and monastery units. Gongtang Tshang had all the young monks who served in his estate dress in fine business clothes when they traveled in China to present a professional face to the outside world.

But for the majority of monks who traveled to urban areas individually there was little to keep them from "playing laymen" for that time, and enjoying the modern amusements available there. I was particularly embarrassed to find myself sitting next to such a monk at a movie, complete with graphic sex scenes, when he accompanied me and his lay Tibetan relative to the theater in Lanzhou. In Labrang, he had taken the vows of full ordination, always dressed in proper monastic costume, and was one of the few to live in the monastery under the care of a senior monk, his uncle. Finally, I encountered the logic of the internality and mobility of monkhood pushed to its radical extreme in the person of a "monk" living in Labrang monastery itself while dressed in lay clothes. I met this young man in town one day dressed in dapper lay attire and straddling a motorcycle. I had heard of him before, because he was one of those who frequently sought out foreign tourists.

He proudly told me in halting English that he had traveled abroad and had plans to do so again soon, but at present he lived in the monastery and was a "monk." When I asked him why he had not shaved his head or worn robes, he answered confidently: "Robes don't make the monk!" Yet such an individual appeal to a monastic identity with no visible bodily transformation seemed to reduce it to the fact that he did not happen to be married. My lay male friend Dopdan, who prided himself on his dedication to Tibetan secular and monastic education, was appalled when I told him about the encounter. He said that such a person did not really like being a monk (Tib. *a khu byed rgyu'o mi dga' gi*), and his representation of himself that way was a "disgrace to the minzu" (Tib. *mi rigs gi zhabs 'dren*).

Dargye was one of the most adamant and angry of lay critics. Even though he himself had chosen to pursue secular studies and had devoted himself to improving Tibetan secular education, he always emphasized his close ties to and great reverence for monk-lamas and Buddhist monastic scholarship. At his angriest, Dargye went so far as to say that Labrang monastery was no longer a "monastery" (Tib. *dgon pa*), because it was not the space of quiet contemplation and serious scholarship (Tib. *dpen sa*) required to qualify as one. In another conversation, he expressed deep anger and sadness that the behavior of some monks had divested the monastic costume of the *automatic* prestige and authority that had accompanied it. Dargye explained that monks were supposed to be above the laity, but their behavior reversed the roles, and polluted Buddhism (Ch. *wuran dao Fojiao*). He said that he often fantasized about asking monks in video parlors and restaurants why they were wearing robes if they wanted to come to town and behave that way. They should just dress like this (pulling at his own lay clothes). Why bother, he asked, to put the robes on at all, since their behavior was polluting a thousand years of Tibetan Buddhist history? Dargye, it seemed to me, had perceived the ultimate threat of such altered politics of monastic gender recognition—the potential semiotic shift that threatened the categorically transcendent nature of monastic masculinity in the frontier zone.

CONCLUSION: THE (EQUIVOCAL) VIOLENCE OF LIBERATION

Shortly after I returned to the United States, I received in friends' letters terrible news about three young Tibetan men I knew well in Labrang. I learned that only a few weeks after my departure, Dargye, my lay friend and self-designated mentor, and Drolma's husband, Tsonji, both died within days of each other. And Akhu Gendun (aged 20), one of the young monks I knew most committed to his studies at Labrang, fled to India in a panic after having been questioned by officers of the National Security Bureau (NSB) about the nature of his relationship with me.

The circumstances of the three incidents, so close together in space and time, seemed to me to encapsulate the tragic consequences for young Tibetan men of the massive social changes Chinese state intervention and capitalist marketization brought to the region. Tsonji drank himself to death at the age of twenty-seven. He had become increasingly despondent in the months before I left, vacillating between drinking binges and viciously beating his wife on the one hand and heartfelt regret on the other. Dargye died suddenly of illness, his parents unable to afford skyrocketing medical bills as hospitals privatized, leaving unfulfilled all the plans he had excitedly shared with me for collaborating with prominent lamas to improve Tibetan secular education. Akhu Gendun, who had begun living in his local monastery at age seven but never cut his close and affectionate ties with his mother, left behind all the material support his family provided to live in abject poverty in India. He told me he missed his family terribly and had not been able to reach them.

The three young men's different life paths and unfortunate turns of fate epitomized for me the predicament facing all young Tibetan men in China: they felt great pressures to seek forms of social mobility essential to Tibetan heroic masculinities, but for most there was nowhere ultimately to go in Labrang. As we saw, various efforts on the part of the Chinese state to tame Tibetan masculinities to its service had ambiguous effects for men, giving new vitality to nostalgic constructions of resolute heroism as the inviolable essence of an ethnically Tibetan masculinity, and heightening incentives for young men to defend it, yet profoundly compromising their ability to do so. The unforeseen consequence of this conundrum for young men was the marked increase in their mobility—in ways inappropriate and dangerous to both the state and the Tibetan community. By 1995, the uniquely powerful mandalic order reconstructed in Labrang drew a large percentage of lay offerings and young monks from surrounding Lhade and neighboring regions. But the "institutional vacuum" opened up by state regulations left few incentives for young monks to commit to staying in Labrang, to settling in a monasticism dedicated to its order.

Thus, at the same time as their rebuilt economic bases allowed monastic elites to control large circulations of capital outside the reach of the state, there were also great movements of monks outside both state and monastic institutional frameworks. With little to restrain them in the midst of the opened market and the unprecedented availability of global media, young monks mingled with laymen in new ways, pushing the performance of monastic masculinities to the point at which, in some cases, little remained to publicly distinguish them at all. In effect, Labrang had become a way station for extraordinary numbers of young men on the move. Seeking to participate in the wider parameters for social and karmic mobility embodied especially in the (Tibetanized) image of the heroic entrepreneur, their activities and networks threatened to take them away from patrifilial obligations to monasteries and households.

This, as I demonstrated above, was the context in which state and local Tibetan interests converged on the need to settle and contain monks by reducing their quantity and emphasizing their resemblance to a "high-quality" ideal. Yet beyond arresting and interrogating those suspected of expressing anti-state sentiments,[31] or those returning from India, state agents did little to police the large numbers of young monks now excluded from monastic jurisdiction—those for whom the tradition of mass monasticism did not require the complete suppression of masculine pursuits. In Labrang, there had never been the kind of overt public protests led by monks that there were in Lhasa. The scattered protests in the region since the mid-1980s were instead covert—usually anonymous handwritten messages on monastery walls calling for Tibetan independence. But, contrary to the assumptions of many foreign visitors, the "nonviolence" of these protests was not a consequence of something intrinsic to monkhood. Instead, it represented young monks' very practical recognition of the overwhelming domination of military force by the state. This, I argue, was the most emasculating aspect of state intervention in Tibetan monasticism.

This is so because, as we saw, the heroic masculinity of monks hinged on the ability to defend mandalic realms and conquer the enemies of Buddhism, and within the tradition of mass monasticism at Labrang, this had included the capacity to fight and kill when monasticism was vitally threatened (cf. Ma Haotian 1942–47; Welch 1972: 280; Huo Deyi 1991: 56). In the contemporary context, most young monks were not interested in repudiating lay masculinity to the extent of forsaking the potential for heroic violence. Indeed, one of the anonymous messages written on monastery walls while I was there was a warning to the Tibetan PSB officer widely rumored to have frequently participated in beating arrested monks. The message threatened him with physical retaliation if he did not mend his ways.

Much of the magnetic appeal of foreign videos for monks was after all the glorification of masculine violence they portrayed. I saw in several monks' quarters not only pictures of the Dalai Lama but also pictures of Rambo, his machine gun raised and ready, chest bared, ammo belts slung across his bulging muscles. Akhu Konchok studiously avoided public places, held out great respect for monastic scholarship, and was so politely diplomatic that he was often chosen to host visiting cadres and VIP Chinese tourists, yet he enthusiastically described for me one day his fascination with Rambo movies, which, he said, was so strong that he would drop everything and go see one if it was shown in Labrang. He explained that Rambo was great because he could take on whole armies by himself so bravely. Watching those movies, he said, made one feel strong, and he demonstrated by flexing his meager biceps. Hence the great appeal of Rambo: in Labrang, defending the monastery and openly attacking the state would be tantamount to taking on a whole army single-handedly, and yet Rambo succeeded on the sheer force of his hypermasculine strength and determination.

But the danger of the situation at Labrang was that, with the mitigation of the authority of monasticism to mediate and domesticate masculine violence, young monks in Labrang participated in acts of physical violence that differed little from those increasingly common among young laymen there. Their violence was not under the auspices of or in service to monasticism, but like that of laymen it was always spontaneous, and sometimes random. Tibetan PSB officers I spoke to expressed angry yet unsurprised concern at what they said was an increase in brutal fighting and murders among young Tibetan men. This they attributed to what they represented as the unschooled barbarity of young nomad men especially, who were coming to town to spend huge cash windfalls from sales of surplus livestock and other pastoralist products (cf. Zhang Jimin 1993).

While I was there, groups of young monks from different locales not infrequently fought in bloody brawls at night. In addition, monks participated in spontaneous outbreaks of violence that expressed major intra- and interethnic conflicts over the nature of moral exchange under the press of competing capitalist aspirations. The most contentious conflict in which monks participated was that between young Tibetan and Hui men. There were countless stories of fights, and I witnessed several myself, erupting between monks and young Hui merchants. These encounters usually occurred in or outside shops in which monks, resentful of the increasing presence and commercial power of the Hui in town, felt discriminated against or slighted in some way by the Hui proprietor. Within the tense cultural politics of Labrang, such individual clashes could provoke communal male violence as well. In the fall of 1992, after an alleged incident in which a Hui merchant was said to have struck a Tibetan monk, young monks and laymen rioted that night in town, destroying many of the Hui shops. And in March 1993, monks joined lay Tibetans in Labrang and in Hezuo to stage a legal march in which they protested Hui presence in "Tibetan" areas.

Thus, we could say that in the absence of viable frameworks for open attacks on the Chinese state among young lay and monastic Tibetan men, their efforts to participate in heroic masculine violence defending Tibetan fatherlands were deferred to occasions on which the threat of emasculation was immediately present and personified for them in the form of wives, Tibetan peers, or young Hui merchants (cf. Limón 1991: 130; Appadurai 1996: 45). Such young men were thus decidedly not apathetic or passive consumers of state-sponsored capitalist aspirations. Instead, as in their avid participation in mountain-deity worship, they simultaneously sought aid in efforts to advance their interests, and, like Tsonji, they recognized (and sought to manipulate) the dispersed and capricious nature of authoritative agencies impinging on them. But, as we have seen, the monastic mandalic authority that had once kept both Hui commerce and Tibetan masculine violence in check and in service to monasticism had been massively eroded. Many locals I spoke to thus viewed such spontaneous outbreaks not as welcome defensive gestures but as further evidence of the frightening social chaos accompanying an unprecedented number of young and mobile men of a variety of ethnicities and monastic proclivities gathering in town.

In this context then, it is easier to understand the heightened importance, to the state and to the Tibetan community, of the great monastic pageants such as the one with which I began this chapter. For state officials, they were gorgeous evidence, for a paying audience of foreign and Han tourists, of an ideally segmented sociospatial order in which "pure" and "normal" Tibetan Buddhism was freely performed under the auspices of the state at the same time as monasticism served national capitalist development. For most local Tibetans, they were the occasions on which the great pageantry operated as iconic indexes of both reconstituted patrifilial consumption and monastic capital, a time when the concentration of divine and human agents under corporate trulkus most effectively refigured the frameworks of Amdo fatherlands. In Labrang, the monastic community had been profoundly compromised, and Tibetan male authorities were required to make delicate decisions as they negotiated with, or themselves embodied, state authorities. But it was the ritual frames of such mandalic pageants, co-produced by the monks at their center and the worshipful laity on their peripheries, that provided the last remaining possibilities for moments in which this predicament facing Tibetan men in China could seem to be resolved.

In this light, we can see how the monk's attack on the Chinese photographer collecting state propaganda at the center of Opakmay's mandalic space was both legitimate and redemptive. Here, in contrast to the Cham Chen the next day, the monk directly and violently resisted the camera's claim to usurp both a primary point of view and a primary mode of exchange. The Bureau of Education cameramen's entrance into the space positioned the whole event within the hierarchical and fetishized frameworks of the state's *aiguo aijiao* order. And their guest permits operated for them as transparent indexes of a monetary contract for access to the (commodified) space. The monk's fist violently resisted that presumption, in effect policing access to monastic capital and commodification on local Buddhist terms. His bodily assault on an intrusive agent of the state, carried out on behalf of monasticism under lamas and trulkus centered in Labrang, thus embodied a Tibetan heroic masculinity that contrasted sharply with the weakened loyalties of the young men gathering in and passing through the valley, whose pursuit of "modern" masculinities in entrepreneurial mobility and consumption threatened to upend the hierarchy of masculinities and exchange that had maintained the lay-monastic relationship and the overarching prowess of trulkus. Ultimately, the process of monastic revitalization in Labrang was inextricable from such efforts to redeem Tibetan masculinities under Chinese rule. But those very efforts held the peril of a double-edged sword: they threatened in the end to both defend the monastic center and compromise out of existence its vital violence of liberation.

Epilogue

Quandaries of Agency

Toward the end of my summer 2002 visit to Labrang, I was in the home of my cosmopolitan lay male friend Kazang, enjoying the hospitality that had so often sustained me in my stays there over the past decade. Dinner was over, and family members were drifting off to bed when Kazang turned to me and asked in English: "Now, Charlene, I've been dying to know . . . What have you learned about Tibetans?" With exaggerated solemnity, he picked up a notebook and made as if to take notes. I was nonplussed to find myself suddenly under scrutiny, and having to express myself in English, when our conversations that summer had been almost exclusively in Tibetan. I hesitated as he prodded me, trying to gauge how serious he was. I finally decided that he was very serious, and that at some level he had wanted to turn the tables on me for a while. Later, in my own field notes, I recorded our "interview" like this:

> I started carefully and broadly. "Uh . . . I learned that there are many kinds
> of Tibetans, not only one." Kazang was not at all satisfied: "But every country
> is like that. What is different about Tibetans?" I tried again. "Uh . . . I learned
> that Tibetans are very loyal to their families." Stink bomb. Didn't fly. He
> shook his head sarcastically: "I don't agree. And lots of people are loyal to
> their families. What else?" I made a final stab—I knew where he was heading,
> what he wanted to hear, but it was also where I was heading: "I learned that
> Tibetans' faith is very, very deep." And he said: "Now we're getting to some-

thing. But why is Tibetans' faith so deep?" "Because it works," I answered (switching to Tibetan, *phan pa yod gi*). He nodded his approval, and I pressed on: "I learned that Tibetans' faith is real and substantial," knocking on the table to make the point, "that it's something you can feel, not something out there," looking up into the air. This Kazang liked. He finished the sentence with me.

In his mock appropriation of the metalinguistic authority of the English-language interview, Kazang had confronted me with the very serious stakes of both our decade-long collaboration and of Tibetans' Buddhist revival efforts in post-Mao China. For Kazang, as he went on to explain, the unique depth and substantiality of Tibetan faith was exemplified in his own dawning respect for the transcendent efficacy of trulkus' tantric prowess, an efficacy that for him escaped the objectification of both the statist social science and the capitalist commodification that my presence in Labrang in the 1990s and 2000s inevitably indexed. Immediately shifting to a personal narrative, Kazang described how it wasn't until he reoriented his family and entrepreneurial aspirations from urban India, where he grew up, to Labrang in 1985 that he began to understand the material efficacy of Tibetan faith through his growing relationship with Gongtang Tshang. Then, in his tumble of testimonials describing the various miraculous powers of Gongtang he had witnessed, Kazang framed his transformation as the process by which his "faith inevitably got deeper and deeper" (Tib. *dad pa je che je che a bud song ni red*) and he took on more and more responsibilities to Gongtang's estate. In effect, Kazang's narrative described his own gradual mandalization, his substantialization as a lay patriarch and patron of Gongtang's revitalizing order in Labrang, and thus as a privileged beneficiary of Gongtang's transcendent vision and compassionate tantric prowess.

Yet, in his mock reversal of our participant roles that evening, Kazang also pointedly implicated myself-as-ethnographer in the precarious quandaries of agency facing Tibetans in the post-Mao frontier zone. In this book, I have emphasized, following Webb Keane (1997) and others, that interpersonal hazard or risk is inherent, and indeed entailed, in all practices of communication, construed here as a cultural politics of mutual contextualization and recognition. But I would add that the risks of this kind of ethnography of communication are *not* limited to the potential dangers of ethnographers' empirical inaccuracies (*pace*, e.g., Silverstein 2001). More fundamentally, ethnographers of language and culture as social action risk deploying and embodying interpretive frameworks that, in conscious or unconscious collusion with local and global authorities, can radically relativize and thus delegitimize the very premises of locals' personhood—as global agents of authoritative metalanguage, ethnographers like me risk breaching local participation frameworks that keep key quandaries of agency provisionally at bay.

In this book, my attention to gender dynamics among Tibetans in Labrang led me to argue that Tibetan trulkus' absolute and abstractable power, so efficacious and personally orienting for Kazang, was in actuality intersubjectively constructed through the specific operation of local gendered frameworks for action and subjectivity. Trulkuhood under post-Mao reforms was a politics of Tibetan masculinities, asserted in tantric Buddhist remandalization practices as frameworks for transcendent authority and agency under the press of the Chinese state and globalizing market. My point in these chapters, as I tried to tell Kazang, was not to expose the unreality or insubstantiality of Tibetan Buddhist absolutes by insisting that they are always constructed relative to the human social. Instead, my focus on the gendered participation frameworks structuring national incorporation in Labrang pointed up the irreducibly material or embodied nature of *all* meaning production among local Tibetans and their interlocutors—the very possibility for efficacious transcendence for Tibetans is produced in locals' mutual recognitions of the (inherent) limits of human participation and agency.

By grounding my analyses of the gendered nature of post-Mao Buddhist revival on Erving Goffman's master trope of participation frameworks, I demonstrated the ways that for differently positioned locals, notions of sexed bodies worked on the one hand to embody or ontologize persons, concepts, times, and spaces locally, and on the other to link those categories to larger institutional and imagined contexts. Gender in this light is decidedly *not* a trivial or circumscribed social domain, relevant largely to "women." Instead, my approach positioned gender as fundamental to local-translocal relations, a particular politics of personhood for women *and* men that structured the rising stakes of frontier encounters in the PRC in the 1990s and early 2000s. In essence, I argued that local categories of sex, gender, and sexuality, along with their associated ideal manifestations and activities, provided Tibetans with discursive resources for a particularly subtle and broad-reaching *metapragmatics*. By this I mean—as in Apa Dondrup's insistence in the midst of our conversation about the Maoist years that "no older woman would ever be seen with her hair short"—the situated evocation of presumed norms linking linguistic categories to appropriate social contexts and actions (cf. Silverstein 2001: 383). Drawing on insights from linguistic anthropologists, I emphasized in the introduction that all signs or representations must be contextualized as practices. In the Sino-Tibetan frontier zone, I found that hierarchically arranged signs of sex and gender, unlike representations of other forms of social difference, operated as primary ontologizing icons and indexes of social positions, subjectivities, histories, and relationships amidst rapid social change. As such, they held the promise and peril for Tibetans of both naturalizing local ethnic and class orders, and devaluing them by enabling the universalizing thrust of competing national and global regimes of value.

Over the course of these six chapters, I developed an account of the particular configuration of sex and gender categories among Labrang Tibetans as they emerged in our interactions in the valley and beyond. In effect, the powerful legacy of Geluk mass monasticism in the Labrang region after reforms meant that for Tibetans, male monasticism, together with lay man- and womanhood, still operated as a third ideal gender status articulating with a hierarchical male-female sexual-karmic polarity. In this context, the masculine discipline and tantric prowess associated with Geluk monasticism worked to mediate and mitigate the limits of the Buddhist sexual-karmic polarity, allowing for the possibility of human-intentioned transcendence over bodily (and political) obstacles. However, as we saw in chapters 3 and 4 especially, the androcentric nature of Tibetan remandalization efforts under hypermasculinizing capitalist reforms in the 1990s also intensified a polarity of sex-gender categories among Tibetans that foregrounded trulkus as superior translocal agents of exchange in contradistinction to laywomen as inferior localized objects of exchange.

This approach, then, allowed me to rethink socioeconomic encounters since the founding of Labrang monastery in the Sino-Tibetan frontier zone as most importantly a clash between different types of "violence of liberation"—that is, competing yet mutually constituted participation frameworks for recruiting gendered subjects, and their associated production and exchange obligations, to the jurisdictions of transcendent masculine agencies. Throughout the six chapters, I thus conceptualized the traumatic process of national incorporation as emasculating for *all* Tibetans in the Labrang region—the "feminine hinge" was central to the violent imposition of and local collaboration in socioeconomic change, both during and after the Maoist years. As we saw in chapter 2 especially, the CCP only succeeded in imposing PRC nationhood on Labrang when "Democratic Reforms" beginning in 1958 enforced participation frameworks for emasculating trulkus and masculinizing women as state subjects. In this way, I worked to build an account of the spatial, temporal, and economic transformation of Amdo Tibetan fatherlands (Tib. *pha yul*) in the ongoing process of their incorporation into a reconfigured Chinese Fatherland (Ch. *zuguo*).

In chapter 5, we glimpsed the quandaries of agency this process created for Tibetan Geluk trulkus and monks. Under post-Mao economic reforms, as some trulkus worked to expand and globalize their revitalized mandalic orders, they risked participating in their own categorical containment within a newly seg-mented political and economic order that subordinated Buddhist exchanges to state and capitalist interests, and lured increasing numbers of young Tibetan men away from monastic careers. In chapters 3 and 4, I illustrated some of the quan-daries of agency facing Tibetan laywomen and nuns. As laymen and monks' translocal trajectories expanded and diversified in the 1990s, the burden of public scrutiny and social constraint locally fell on women and femininities. And yet, as Kazang was so concerned to tell me, Tibetans across the community in Labrang still looked to the transcendent "skillful means" of trulkus to meet and manipulate the terms of such rapid and often imposed social changes. Despite intensifying gender hierarchies under reforms, recourse to tantric masculine prowess grounded most men's and women's visions of Tibetan futures.

Indeed, as I discovered time and again, the omniscience of the fifth Jamyang Shepa, the last ruling lama who had reached adulthood before CCP intervention, extended over the decade of my fieldwork in Labrang and into the uncertain future. From the early 1990s and even into the 2000s, my presence elicited, from Tibetans of every ilk, various versions of an important "future story" (cf. M. Goodwin 1990: 231) for the Labrang region. In those narratives, recounted with varying degrees of certainty and hope, my interlocutors insisted that the "real" sixth Jamyang Shepa, the actual heir to the fifth's mandalic order and transcendent agency, was *not* the man who had been enthroned in 1952 and now lived in Lanzhou as a married layman and Chinese-educated cadre. Instead, citing accounts of the fifth Jamyang Shepa's deathbed prophecy about his own rebirth, narrators told me that the sixth Jamyang Shepa was none other than the president of the United States (at that time Bill Clinton).

It seemed to me that these stories amounted to a collective recognition of the profoundly emasculated status of Labrang's Tibetan Buddhist order under CCP rule. Yet, like Mipham's prayers to Gesar at the turn of the twentieth century, they were important components of local Tibetans' reform-era efforts to expand, indeed globalize, the scope of mandalization by relocating divine masculinity out-side the purview of local monasticism and in a contemporary embodiment of globalizing state and capitalist power, far away and foreign, yet dedicated nonethe-less to Labrang. However, that collective longing for a transcendent efficacy unat-tainable within the parameters of local Tibetan masculinity was precisely what was drawing many young Tibetan men away from the obligations and commitments that had been the patrifilial foundation of Geluk mandalization in the region. Indeed, as I discovered, my short time in Labrang was only a brief window on a rapidly changing situation.

As we have seen, by the early 1990s, when I first traveled to Labrang, Gongtang Tshang had emerged as the most powerful and central trulku in remandalization efforts there. His place-based history and reputation for unstained commitment to Geluk monasticism throughout his long imprisonment had elevated him to an unprecedented translocal status above even the sixth Jamyang Shepa. But by the end of my stay there, in 1996, the transnational controversy over the recognition of the next Panchen Lama tested the ailing Gongtang's integrity anew and prompted intensified central-government enforcement of its *aiguo aijiao* order locally. Gongtang's activities were greatly curtailed, and he was kept for the most part in Lanzhou. And, as I heard from Akhu Gendun in India, in the ensuing two years after I left, central Party officials brought their national "Patriotic Education Campaign" (Ch. *Aiguo Jiaoyu Zhengzhi Yundong*) to Labrang, almost two years after its launch in the great Geluk monasteries around Lhasa (cf. Bass 1998, Goldstein 1998a). Modeled on Maoist thought-work campaigns, this effort deployed county work teams for six months in Labrang to reeducate lamas, local Tibetan cadres, and officially recognized monks as to the properly subordinate relationship of Buddhism to the state. In his letter to me, Akhu Gendun, who had fled Labrang a few weeks before the work teams took up their duties, described the effects of the campaign as ineffectual efforts to resedentarize monks, in that unofficial (and thus inappropriately mobile) monks were supposed to return to home regions and lay life but instead temporarily moved elsewhere or traveled in unprecedented numbers to India.[1]

When I returned to Labrang in the summer of 2002, President Clinton's regime had not panned out as an extension of Jamyang Shepa's mandalic order, and the stakes of global political economic relations had heightened dramatically with the 9/11 terrorist attacks on American centers of state and capitalist power, and with the new Bush regime's retaliatory efforts in Afghanistan and Iraq. That summer, for the first time, as Akhu Konchok and I went up to the Sangkok grasslands, we encountered an elaborate Chinese-style gate over the road. I was "welcomed" to the grassland only after I paid the young Tibetan woman and received my "grassland tourist ticket." I also found my friend Kazang bereft with the death of his beloved Gongtang Tshang (in 2000) and angry at recent provincial initiatives, under a new central-government "Develop the West" (Ch. *Xibu Da Kaifa*) campaign, to destroy many village homes in the valley and push through a new highway that Gongtang had long blocked. In one moment of despair, Kazang shook his head at me and said: "It's all over now . . ." (Tib. *da tshar song*).

I was not surprised, then, when both Kazang and Apa Jikmay (the old former village leader who in 2002 had watched as homes around his were destroyed to make way for the new road) reconfigured the old story of the fifth Jamyang Shepa's prophecy so as to allow for the possibility that Labrang's Tibetan mandalic order might benefit from the new global hypermasculinity touted by President Bush. Indeed, echoing sentiments I had heard from Tibetans young and old that summer, Apa Jikmay enthused, in language that made Bush metonymic of the nation, that Bush's strong response to the terrorists showed that the United States was heroic, and thus a *morally* powerful nation (Tib. Meigo *dpa' bo red, rgyal khab ngar ba red*). Hence, in that and in a separate conversation with Kazang, both men jettisoned the earlier links Tibetans had drawn for me between the fifth Jamyang Shepa and President Clinton. Instead, they focused on the open-ended details of Jamyang Shepa's prophecy to turn their eyes hopefully to the future: "In my next life I will be reborn in America. I'll come in a plane to Labrang, and I will have light hair and light eyes. And you won't recognize me."

NOTES

INTRODUCTION

1. Over the course of my four research trips to the region between 1992 and 2002, I talked informally with hundreds of foreign visitors, tourists, students, and missionaries about their impressions of Labrang and their views of Tibetans. Yet the majority of tourists to Labrang in the 1980s and 1990s were actually Han Chinese urbanites. Here I mean only to elucidate some of the context in which I myself was perceived by local Tibetans.

2. This phrase among local Tibetans most often meant those visitors assumed to be white Europeans or Americans.

3. We were engaged but not officially married until we returned to the United States in 1996.

4. Note though that such census figures up to 1990 for Labrang do not reflect increasing numbers of migrants counted as residents elsewhere. "Hui" is an umbrella term used by the state to designate groups nationwide who can prove ancestry with Muslim groups that immigrated into China from the Tang dynasty on. There are other, smaller groups of Muslims in this region whose different *minzu* labels reflect different histories of migration into China: e.g., the Salars, or the Dongxiang (cf. Gladney 1991, Lipman 1997). According to the 1990 census, of the million Hui in Gansu, over half (some 575,000) lived in neighboring Linxia prefecture, where Han Chinese were still the majority (LHZ 1990; Zhang Tianlu 1993: 253; *Gansu Nianjian* 1994: 275).

5. At that time, some local stores I found sold books designated "for internal use only" (Ch. *neibu*). Those sources turned out to be particularly helpful in reconstruct-

ing the historiography of socialist transformation locally. By 2002 however, with increasing state efforts to control print media, I did not come across a single "neibu" book for sale privately.

6. Cain also had to transform himself somewhat in order to be perceived as a layman in interactions with Tibetans.

7. I mean "pivotal" here in the dual sense of "central" and "having the capacity to turn on an axis."

CHAPTER 1. FATHERLANDS

1. Here it is very appropriate to consider this term "subjects" in the dual sense Foucault underscored: as types of experiencing participants *and* as people under the rule of a regime.

2. Note that a popular website for Tibetans in the diaspora established in 2001 by a Tibetan man in India is called Phayul.com. The site is explicitly aimed at creating a deterritorialized global Tibetan community nonetheless centered on the territorialized notion of a Tibetan fatherland.

3. This designation as one of the six great Geluk monasteries locates Labrang in a broader spatialized historiography of the Geluk sect centered on Lhasa. The other five were the big three surrounding the central city of Lhasa—Drepung, Sera, and Ganden—Tashilunpo in Shigatse, the seat of the Panchen Lamas southwest of Lhasa, and Kumbum in Amdo, just north of Labrang, the monastery founded at the birthplace of Tshongkhapa, the lama claimed as the founder of the Geluk sect. Labrang monastery was also referred to as Amdo Tashi Gomang after the college at Drepung from which the first Jamyang Shepa graduated.

4. Female trulkus are rarely mentioned in foreign or Tibetan programmatic statements on the nature of trulkus. (Ngawang Zangpo 1997 is a partial exception.) In fact most as a matter of course refer to trulkus as male. Donald Lopez (1997) estimates that out of more than three thousand male trulku lines in existence in recent years, only a few were female. Further, while there are some cases of female-to-male incarnation across generations, trulku lineages were most often uniformly sexed across generations, and I have never heard of a male-to-female incarnation.

5. In Janet Gyatso's groundbreaking work (2003, 2005) on sex and gender categories in a variety of Tibetan medieval Buddhist and medical texts, she found that terms for maleness and femaleness associated with particular genital and other bodily "signs" (Tib. *mtshan*) functioned as master categories for all kinds of logical operations built on binaries (and their associated thirds).

6. The provenance of this unusual painting (here fig. 4) is somewhat mysterious. The portion of the temple where Andreas Gruschke took this photograph in the late 1980s was not built until 1907, and it survived the Cultural Revolution intact. My

inquiries through monk friends did not turn up anything; even the old monk caretaker of the temple did not know anything about the history of the paintings there. Patricia Berger, in a personal communication, says that the large figure is most likely the Mongol lord, since the costume he wears is typical of ornate garments given as gifts to Mongols for loyal service to the Qing court.

7. Recent scholars of the Qing imperial world have emphasized the Qing emperors' deliberate attempts at a flexible indexicality, especially the great Kangxi and his son the Qianlong emperor, as a crucial component of their successful expansionism. Qianlong, for example, styled himself in different contexts as imperial holder of the Chinese Mandate of Heaven, but also as a Mongol khan of khans, a Buddhist Cakravartin king, and a transcendent bodhisattva (cf. Hevia 1995: 30; Millward 1999; Berger 2003; Perdue 2005).

8. The most important of these junctures was what Louis Schram (1954–61: 34) called a "watershed" event in that region's history: after the Qing put down the Mongol uprising northwest of Labrang in 1723, the court rewarded the monastery's Mongol patrons and lama hierarchs for not participating (cf. Petech 1950). At the same time the Qing imposed punitive restrictions on monasteries north of Labrang. Danzhu Angben and Wang Zhouta (1993) argue that from this time on, Labrang monastery became the dominant monastic center in Amdo. Further, the monastery's expansion under the second, third, and fourth Jamyang Shepas occurred as the monastery exploited its neutral position amidst Muslim uprisings in Gansu (cf. Lipman 1990, 1997).

9. Note though that the Tibetan term for "country" here, *yul*, means an inhabited place associated with an essentialized notion of ethnicity and styles of governance. It does not necessarily correspond with the way "country" is used in English to mean a sovereign nation.

10. Even though in recent years Tibetan women have arguably been very active participants in new forms of media production among Tibetans in the PRC, these songs, like most public Tibetan media, were most often written or sung (or both) by men. Other gendered subjects of Nostalgia Songs are lamas, lovers, and mothers (see chapter 3).

11. After the capital was moved to Hezuo, it rapidly grew from a trading town about a fifth the size of Labrang to be the largest city in Gannan, with more than thirty-five thousand people in 1990 (cf. Li Anzhai 1982: 14).

12. In the Labrang region, the Geluk sect dominated among Tibetans by the late eighteenth century because of the power and influence of the two main Geluk monastic centers, Labrang and Chonay (Tib. Cone). Relying on statistics collected in 1988, Pu Wencheng (1990: 506) estimates that before 1949, there were a total of 369 monasteries in Gansu, with 16,900 monks, including 310 incarnate lamas. Of these, there were only ten or so Nyingma monasteries, two or three Sakya monasteries, and nine Bon temples.

13. I mean "abject" here not as "poor, miserable or pitiable," but in the way Butler, following Kristeva, used it: as an enabling category of inferior Other (1990: 133; cf. Gyatso 2003, 2005).

14. As Lopez (1997) notes, Tibetans considered the Vajrayāna to be a quicker path to enlightenment, providing ritual techniques for wielding especially potent power for both supramundane and mundane tasks. Yet it was thus also considered to be thereby more dangerous for the uninitiated.

15. Tibetan Buddhists distinguish between wrathful (Tib. *khro po*, lit. "angry," "rageful," to the point of violence) and peaceful (Tib. *zhi ba*) deities. Most of the main tutelary deities have many wrathful and peaceful emanations, and note that wrathful deities include female ones. At Labrang, most of the main protector deities of the monastery and its subunits were male-sexed, but Palden Lhamo, considered a wrathful emanation of the peaceful female deity Drolma (Skt. Tārā), was an important female protector (cf. Li Anzhai 1989: 159).

16. "Damjen" means "Vow Holder," referring to the deity's vow to Tshongkhapa that he would protect the Geluk. He, along with Gompo (Skt. Mahākāla) and Jikshay (Skt. Vajrabhairava), who were also considered to be wrathful emanations of Buddhas, were the only protector deities who resided in the *gonkhang* of all monastic colleges in the 1940s (cf. Nebesky-Wojkowitz 1956; Li Anzhai 1989: 159).

17. This brief summary does little justice to the great complexity of these events. For detailed descriptions and analyses of Tibetan Buddhist monastic dance, see Nebesky-Wojkowitz 1956, 1976; M. Duncan 1964; Montmollin 1988; Marko 1994; Schrempf 1994; Kohn 2001.

18. Hence the common epithets for the Jamyang Shepa lamas, "Supreme Protector" (or "Supreme Refuge," Tib. *skyabs mgon*) or "Omniscient One" (Tib. *kun mkhyen*). Note that their mysterious and overarching power for Labrang's subjects was in part constructed through the relative invisibility of their tantric prowess to ordinary patrons. At all the main public festivals, the participant role of the Jamyang Shepas was not as tantrist on display but as supreme presence spectating from above.

19. Indeed as many have pointed out, the intimacies of lama-disciple exchange are often expressed in a trope of father-son relation (cf. Samuel 1993).

20. Labrang's status as a tax haven as well as a refuge from violence in the increasingly chaotic frontier zone in part helps to account for the influx of Tibetan, Hui, and some Han migrants in the 1920s and 1930s (cf. Huang 1989; Lipman 1990, 1997; Chen Wei 1991).

21. From this perspective, we need not read, as Samuel (1993: 594) does, Tibetans' use of the term *dewa* to refer to both nomad and farming communities as an example of the "fluidity" of Tibetan sociospatial terminology. Instead, it indexes a history of sedentarization under Labrang monastic rule and the commensurate nature of those communities as corporate subjects of the monastery.

22. Wang Zhouta counts over eighty separate tribes under this grouping (1996a: 85). There were actually many more groups that maintained other types of relationship with the monastery (cf. Pu 1990). In its heyday during the nineteenth and early twentieth centuries, Labrang is said to have accumulated 108 branch monasteries. That number is actually symbolic; it is a sacred Buddhist number. Luo 1987, Danzhu Angben and Wang Zhouta 1993, and Apa Alo 1994 all list ninety-four Geluk branch monasteries, five Nyingma, and one Bon, grouped by the type of relationship they had with Labrang.

23. There were the so-called Eighteen Mansions (Tib. *nang chen bco brgyad*) at Labrang, the buildings of which towered over the ordinary monks' quarters (see fig. 7). In actuality, trulkus from Labrang's "branch" monasteries came to study and over the years built permanent residences within monastic space. By 1949, there were thirty trulku "mansions" at Labrang, and sixty-eight trulkus in residence (Pu 1990: 508; Danzhu Angben and Wang Zhouta 1993; Ma Denghun and Wanma 1994; Wang Zhouta and Chen 1994).

24. Joseph Rock (1956: 37) states that this burden came to a tribe about every ten years, and it entailed support of the seventh-month prayer festival as well. Li Anzhai (1982: 7–8) attempted to tally in KMT yuan the amount of money required to appropriately provide for a "Great Tea" for the monk assembly during the Great Prayer Festival in the early 1940s. He estimates that it cost the patron tribe over forty-six thousand yuan, and opines that this was a far heavier burden than any "modern income tax."

25. By the 1940s Tawa town included over a thousand households and some thirty-five hundred people, over half of whom were Han and Muslim Chinese. Population statistics for the farming dewa in the valley before CCP intervention are of course only rough estimates. Li Anzhai (1992a: 92) based these numbers on statistics collected in the Tawa dewas by the KMT government in 1941 for tax purposes, so I consider them to be the closest to accurate numbers available. Wang Zhouta (1996a: 386), citing statistics collected by Chinese work teams in 1958 and giving no numbers on non-Tibetan residents, estimates that the Tibetan population in Labrang's so-called Four Patron Tribes consisted of a total of a thousand sedentary households, or 3,046 laypeople. Of those, the Tawa dewa had 410 Tibetan households, or 1,090 people.

26. Zhang Guangda (1993a) says that in the early twentieth century the wealthiest of trulkus could have capital of up to a million *baiyang* (Yuan Shikai silver dollars) in addition to owning herds and farmland. Pu Wencheng (1990) lists property owned by the monastery as a whole just before Communist intervention. Labrang monastery rented 21,700 square mu (about 3,580 acres) of farmland. In addition, the monastery had 36,500 head of sheep in the Xiahe county region, 7,400 head of cattle, and 9,540 horses, and rented 5,100 houses. See also Gao Changzhu 1942, Zhang Qiyun 1969, GGK 1987, Luo 1987, Ji Wenpo 1993, Danzhu Angben and Wang Zhouta 1993.

27. Muslim soldiers garrisoned Labrang for eight years after besting Apa Alo's

Tibetan nomad troops in a series of brutal battles (1917–27). See also Rock 1930; Lipman 1984, 1990, 1997; Luo 1987; Huang 1989: 21; Nietupski 1999.

28. The new county's claimed territory did not correspond with the ranges of Labrang's patron tribes (cf. Rock 1956: 65; Zhang Guangda 1993b).

29. Ma Haotian (1942: 76) complained in 1936 that county officials never had direct access to Jamyang Shepa.

CHAPTER 2. FATHER STATE

Portions of this chapter were previously published in "Speaking Bitterness: Autobiography, History and Mnemonic Politics on the Sino-Tibetan Frontier," in *Comparative Studies in Society and History* 47(1): 40–78. Copyright © 2005 by the Society for Comparative Study of Society and History. Reprinted with the permission of Cambridge University Press.

1. Early CCP overt and subtle efforts to appropriate Tibetan Buddhist images and discourse and recruit Tibetans to the (unacknowledged) divination of Mao Zedong were controversial among Communist policymakers and not widely successful (Welch 1972: 267–97).

2. Here I agree with Stevan Harrell (1995) that the Chinese term *minzu*, with its long history of appropriation from Japanese contexts, and its multiple connotations of "race," "ethnicity," "lineage," and "nationality," is virtually untranslatable in English. I thus choose to leave it untranslated in the rest of the book.

3. The smallest recognized minzu groups consisted of a few thousand people, while the largest, the Han, consisted of hundreds of millions.

4. According to the 1990 census, there were 2,096,000 Tibetans registered in the TAR, while a total of 2,478,000 Tibetans were registered in Gansu, Qinghai, Sichuan, and Yunnan. There were 367,000 Tibetans in Gansu, 912,000 in Qinghai, 1,088,000 in Sichuan, and 111,000 in Yunnan. All regions, but especially Qinghai and Sichuan, showed large increases in Tibetan population from the 1981 census (cf. Zhang Tianlu 1993: 107).

5. Some people registered under the label "Zangzu" do not speak Tibetan at all.

6. This is not to say that Han do not experience any limitations and potential political ramifications in memorializing the Maoist years (see for example Feng 1991, Judd 1994, Schwarcz 1994, Watson 1994b, Jun 1999, Rofel 1999). Yet since the early 1980s Han citizens could participate in conferences and publish fiction and autobiographical memoirs (i.e., the "wounded literature" and "seeking roots literature" movements).

7. Elinor Ochs and Lisa Capps argue that narrative is a fundamental speech genre because it is culturally universal and emerges early in childhood speech development. Provided only that they present sequences of events, Ochs and Capps assert that the term "narrative" covers verbalized, visualized, or performed versions (1996: 19).

8. This is a vast literature. Tibetans in exile typically worked closely with Americans

or Europeans to produce autobiographical accounts of CCP intervention in Tibetan regions. As Hugh Richardson (1998) pointed out, the Dalai Lama himself spearheaded the move to oppositional personal accounts in exile (Tenzin Gyatso 1962), and his oldest brother quickly followed suit (Norbu 1960). Accounts produced under Chinese government auspices have been equally numerous in both Chinese and English. They can be found as core components of most literature produced for foreign audiences, but see for example Anna-Louise Strong 1959, Israel 1983, Liu Qizhong and Chen 1991.

9. To list only the main campaigns that directly affected ordinary Tibetans in Labrang: "Democratic Reforms." including class labeling and land reform (1957–61), the Great Leap Forward (1958), "Antifeudalism" campaigns (1958–62), socialist education campaigns (1962–66), and the Cultural Revolution (1966–68).

10. Uses of revolutionary testimonials were already being developed and modified during Communist work-team-led land-reform and socialist education campaigns among Han villagers in the "liberated areas" prior to 1949 (see for example Hinton 1966, Crook and Crook 1979, Chan et al. 1984, Friedman et al. 1991). In the Labrang region, Han Chinese regions of neighboring counties underwent the land-reform process in 1952–53, five years before Labrang (GGK 1987).

11. In all my interactions with Tibetans in the Labrang region over a ten-year period, such commentary concerning misrecognitions of other Tibetans' sex-gender status was extremely rare, and I never heard commentary about the equivocal status of a Tibetan male.

12. Note that the sources do not give numbers of Tibetan women who participated in the first Fulian meetings in Labrang in the early 1950s; evidence suggests they may well have been in the minority (GZZ 1999: 1155; XXZ 1997: 645).

13. These minority minzu cadres included the handful of young Tibetans who had joined the CCP before 1949, local Tibetan leaders, and young people who attended short-term training classes for Zangzu and other minority minzu at what was to become the Northwest Minzu Institute (Huang 1989, XDZ 1991). According to the school's statistics, before 1966 the cadre-training class graduated forty-one classes and several thousand "minority cadres" from all over Gansu and some from Qinghai. Of these, 242 were reported to be women graduating from the "women's training classes" (XMXY 1984). In most cases, the classes were only a few months long and focused on politics and policies of the new regime.

14. Warren Smith asserts that the CCP by the end of 1957 had already committed eight PLA divisions and over a hundred and fifty thousand troops to the suppression of rebellions in eastern Tibetan regions (1996: 431). Tenzin Palbar states that in the eight months it took the PLA to put down the uprising, Tibetans in Gannan had clashed 996 times with PLA troops (1994: 107).

15. The life-size clay sculpture exhibit in Lhasa, "Wrath of the Serfs," was commissioned in the early 1970s as a traveling exhibit. It represented vignettes of brutal

exploitation of Tibetan serfs by "the big three"—Tibetan aristocracy, government, and monasteries—and was based on speaking-bitterness narratives elicited by a team of Chinese and Tibetan artists sent from Beijing from a hundred "liberated serfs." Importantly, Tibetan women are depicted in the exhibit as foregrounded revolutionary agents who go from "victim to victor" by the end of the cycle. Indeed, the main revolutionary woman in the exhibit is pictured on the cover of the exhibit catalogue (Harris 1999: 130; cf. *Rent Collection Courtyard* 1976; Topping 1980: 126).

16. Leonard Van der Kuijp notes that fragments exist of the earliest Tibetan historiographic works from the seventh, eighth, and ninth centuries (1996: 40). These early texts reveal an intense interest in record keeping, including royal and family genealogies and archives.

17. I am grateful to Amdo Lekshay Gyamtso for his excellent index of this text and for his invaluable help in translating portions of it.

18. Apa Alo (Huang Zhengqing) in his memoir gives a poignant and detailed account of the dread, confusion, and grief experienced by Tibetans across the community after the fifth Jamyang Shepa's sudden death in 1947. He writes that locals associated his death with local historiography, telling of inauspicious things always happening the first few years after the deaths of Jamyang Shepas (1989: 57, 103; cf. Yin 1948).

19. Zhabs drung frequently uses the first-person pronoun (Tib. *kho bo*) to record his own presence at key events in Jamyang Shepa's life (cf. Gyatso 1998: 108).

20. In a head count of Tibetan circumambulators around the monastery over a two-week period in the summer of 2002, I found that old women accounted for the vast majority of Tibetans wearing robes, and far more old women wore robes than did old men.

21. I have talked with hundreds of laypeople throughout the main villages surrounding the monastery, as well to monks and nuns in Labrang, over the course of my fieldwork there. But I refer here only to those Tibetans born before 1949 (people in their mid-forties and older) who told detailed stories of their lives. Of those, twenty-six were men (3 monks and 7 former monks, including an incarnate lama), and twenty-eight were women (3 nuns). The majority, over thirty of them, were sixty years of age and older.

22. Harris (1999) documents this process visually, noting that before 1959 realist paintings and self-portraits of lamas—not to mention depictions of ordinary Tibetans' lives—were almost unheard of. In Amdo especially the 1980s saw an explosion of vernacular literature and video production depicting ordinary lives, including first-person accounts (Tsering Shakya 2000, Upton 2000).

23. Of the twenty-five oppositional testimonials I heard, seventeen were offered almost immediately after we met. My experience was perhaps a pale echo of the tenth Panchen Lama's and Apa Alo's, both of whom described similar reactions when they separately traveled to Amdo regions to talk with Tibetans in 1961.

24. Of those twenty-five, only three were cadres at the time. (One woman, Ama Drolkar mentioned above, studied in Lanzhou but did not become a cadre.) During the Maoist years, ten were labeled class enemies (and were struggled for being monks, landlords, rich traders, or rebels), and the rest were farmers. There were fourteen men and eleven women, about evenly distributed by gender between fifty and seventy years old.

25. I originally met many of these people while walking the circumambulation path around the monastery. Most of them undertook three or four circuits of the monastery per day, taking several hours to do it.

26. Tsering Shakya notes that monks at Labrang were recruited as early as 1950 to translate Chinese policy documents and speeches for the first Tibetan-language newspaper in Amdo (1994: 158).

27. Indeed a particularly tragic historical index of these personal crises of agency and morality during the Maoist years is the number of stories of Tibetan friends and relatives committing suicide (a phenomenon previously almost unheard of among Tibetans) beginning just after the summer speaking-bitterness meetings in 1958 (Tenzin Palbar 1994: 208).

28. Tibetan dialects belong to the minority of world languages known as ergative languages. In these languages, a grammatical marker usually distinguishes agents of transitive verbs from both subjects of intransitive verbs and objects of transitive verbs (Duranti 1994; Ahearn 2001: 22).

29. June Dreyer notes that when the Party began to crack down on local media in minority areas in the aftermath of the anti-rightist campaign (1957) and the run up to the Great Leap Forward (1958), investigators were horrified to find non-Han translations of Party and government materials in a variety of minority minzu languages that rendered the CCP in old imperial terms (1976: 158).

30. "Gongma" ("high one") can refer to the Buddha and to particular trulkus and scholars, as well as to emperors.

31. An important indication of the political vicissitudes of this respatialization is the frequency with which districts within the valley were renamed and reapportioned between 1958 and 1980 (cf. Ma Denghun and Wanma 1994: 176; XXZ 1997: 780).

32. When village temples were rebuilt in Labrang Lhade in the 1980s and 1990s, trulkus from the monastery conducted vivification rites for mountain-deity images just as they did for Buddha images.

33. Both the tenth Panchen Lama in his 1962 report (1997) and Tenzin Palbar (1994: 136) assert that this was the case throughout Tibetan regions in Gansu and Qinghai.

34. Apa Alo's daughter, Tshering dpal skyid (b. late 1920s), was a young woman in her twenties in 1949. She may have been among the first girl students in the Labrang girls' school her father established with Li Anzhai and Yu Shiyu in 1940. As the 1955 graduation picture Ama Drolkar showed me confirms, Apa Alo's daughter was sent to study in the first minority minzu cadre-training classes established in Lanzhou soon

after the PLA deposed her father and trulku uncle in 1949 (cf. Huang 1989: 59; Tenzin Palbar 1994: 50).

35. Tenzin Palbar (1994: 136) asserts that between 1959 and 1961 half a million Chinese settlers from the eastern provinces of Henan, Anhui, and Shandong were made to immigrate to Tibetan regions in Qinghai and Gansu. He does not cite a source. Warren Smith cites a 1959 article in the journal *Chinese Agriculture and Reclamation* stating that forty thousand Chinese youths were "sent down" to Tibetan regions of Qinghai in 1956 in order to help "reclaim wastelands" (1996: 442; also see Rohlf 2003).

36. In the booming leather and wool trade under monastic auspices in the 1930s, KMT county officials could extract capital only by taxing exports controlled by Hui merchant families (cf. Gu and Lu 1938; Gao Changzhu 1942; Chai 1956; Zhang Qiyun 1969; Zhang Guangda 1993a: 87).

37. This rite of passage for girls was widespread in Amdo regions. Li Anzhai (1992b) says it was not held in Khams regions to the south. In Labrang, there was no equivalent rite of passage for lay boys (see chapter 5).

38. One of the main ritual duties of women in Labrang then and in the post-Mao years was to keep the household Stove Deity (Tib. *thab lha*) happy, thus helping to maintain household harmony and prosperity, by maintaining a clean and pure stove and regularly burning incense offerings (cf. Tucci 1988: 188).

39. Plowing in Labrang, as elsewhere among Tibetans, was one of the few agricultural tasks restricted to men.

40. "Wesang" is a local idiom, spelled *be sang*, that may well be an old transliteration of the pre-Communist Chinese term for the common folk, *bai xing*, "hundred names."

41. Duizhang, or production-team leaders, were the lowest-level government cadres in the commune system (cf. Dhondup Choedon 1978).

42. One of the most important ritual duties of household patriarchs and sons during the Losar festivities was to make the first offerings of elaborate Losar foods to the household's deities at the altar and to burn incense offerings to the Lhade mountain deity at the village temple, along with prayers for the well-being of the household in the coming year.

43. Ideally, as many told me, men were exclusively in charge of making the main offerings and negotiating the vivification rites (Tib. *rab gnas*) and arrangement of altar images. Women were not supposed to touch image-receptacles and were charged with daily "maintenance" offerings on behalf of the household (cf. Lhamo mtsho 1995).

CHAPTER 3. MOTHER HOME

Portions of this chapter were previously published in "Gendered Boundaries in Motion: Space and Identity on the Sino-Tibetan Frontier," in *American Ethnologist* 30(4): 597–619. Copyright © 2003 by the American Anthropological Association.

1. Between 1985 and 1995 Xiahe county reported a total of 180,000 tourist visits to Labrang, 13 percent (or about 24,000) of which were made by foreigners. A total of over six million yuan came in, with a gross profit of almost two million yuan (XXZ 1997: 475; cf. Yang Ming 1992: 13; *Gansu Nianjian* 1994). The increase in domestic and foreign tourist visits in Labrang was part of a larger phenomenon affecting all Tibetan regions in the PRC (cf. Zhang Zhongli 1996).

2. See Turnbull 1992 for just such a romantic conflation of anthropology, tourism, and pilgrimage.

3. According to Pu Wencheng (1990), all other major Amdo Geluk monasteries (i.e., Kumbum, Rongwo, Gonlung, and Chonay) had "recovered" on a much smaller scale than Labrang in the 1980s, some with little or no state support. Labrang had the greatest concentration of qualified teachers, so that even if a local monastery had a relatively large number of monks, they had to travel to Labrang to seek further teachings and initiations (see chapter 5).

4. I am grateful to Amdo Lekshay Gyamtso for his invaluable help in translating this and other Tibetan texts.

5. In Buddhist and popular discourses, *lu* or *naga*s are powerful, long-lived, serpentlike beings who inhabit bodies of water and often guard great treasure.

6. As early Marxist translators in Tibetan regions well knew, the metaphor of the sun for Mao Zedong inevitably recalled the way Tibetans referred to the Dalai Lama as the sun (Tib. *nyi ma*).

7. This was true of many of the Han Chinese tourists I spoke with. Han urbanites from Lanzhou liked to get away to Labrang for the weekend or even for the day, especially in the summer. Foreign tourists by contrast tended to stay somewhat longer, but most remained in Labrang for less than a week before moving on to their next stop.

8. Note that many of my Tibetan friends who spoke Chinese referred to regions east of Labrang as the "interior" (Ch. *neidi*).

9. In 1994, Lanzhou had within its overall economy the highest percentage in the country of industry and raw-material processing (*Gansu Nianjian* 1994).

10. According to early CCP statistics, 70 percent of the Tibetan population of Xiahe county was engaged in nomadic pastoralism, while 30 percent were engaged in agriculture (Ya Hanzhang 1991: 40). In the 1990s, the majority of Tibetans in the county were still engaged in pastoralism, but that percentage has decreased with the migration of Tibetans to towns and cities. In 1990, about 30 percent of the county's population was registered as nonagricultural (urban), while about 64 percent of the county's GDP in 1994 was from primary industry (i.e., farming and pastoralism: Marshall and Cooke 1997: 1360; *Gansu Pucha* 1993).

11. Gesang Daji did fieldwork on booming township enterprises in the ethnically mixed yet historically Tibetan township of Wanggatang just east of Labrang in 1993.

He found that these enterprises were monopolized by sons and daughters of cadres and argues that they were corrupt and inefficient.

12. Again, I am grateful to Amdo Lekshay Gyamtso for his invaluable help in translating this and other Tibetan texts.

13. For a quintessential example of this, see Ellen Bruno's 1993 film about Tibetan nuns, *Satya: A Prayer for the Enemy.* Such images are also rife in the great upsurge of music-video production among Tibetans in Amdo since the late 1990s.

14. The depoliticizing function of such tropes of femininity may in part explain why the Chinese term for the national homeland, *zuguo* (lit. "patrilineal ancestor land," translated here as "Fatherland" to capture the crucial masculinity of that notion in the Chinese context), has most often been rendered in English as "Motherland."

15. Even though precise percentages of men in Tibetan monasteries is a point of some debate, Goldstein argues that whereas in Tibet just prior to Chinese intervention this "mass monasticism" had resulted in 10–15 percent of the male population in monasteries, Buddhist monasteries in Thailand held only 1–2 percent of men.

16. Yu Xiangwen (1943), in his analysis of kinship and marriage in a nomad dewa just west of Labrang, found that monks represented 16 percent (21 out of 133 men) of the male population there.

17. Collected by Wang Qingshan (cf. Makley et al. 2000). Proverbs (Tib. *gtam dpe*), usually structured in parallelisms that express basic conceptual similarities and oppositions, are a vital part of local Tibetan culture. They are rarely written down (although several collections of "Tibetan proverbs" have recently been published in Qinghai and Gansu) but are passed along through frequent citation in everyday interactions and in more formal rhetorical exchanges such as comedic duets (Tib. *kha shags*) and speeches.

18. Note that this gendered inside-versus-outside dichotomy among Tibetans historically did not necessarily map onto the cultural politics of "public-versus-private" dichotomies assumed in capitalist Western countries.

19. *Skye dman* (lit. "low birth") is a phrase, albeit not in wide colloquial use in Labrang, denoting "female" or "woman" (cf. Aziz 1988, Havnevik 1990). Perhaps indexing the influence of Maoist Fulian discourse, my Tibetan interlocutors, men and women, were often embarrassed by the stark hierarchy expressed by this term, and women especially objected to its very pejorative connotations.

20. After the prayer wheels were rebuilt in the early 1990s, Labrang monastery had hundreds of them lining its shikor. The largest and most elaborate of these, built with donations from monks and laity, were some two and a half feet high, requiring considerable arm strength to turn, and cost up to ten thousand yuan each.

21. In 1993, the National Tourism Bureau named the traditional summer monastic debates (Tib. Dunpi Rikdra) and picnic festival (Tib. Shinglong) in Labrang a "select

tourism festival" (Ch. *jingxuan luyou jiehui*) for marketing to foreign and domestic tourists (*Gansu Nianjian* 1994: 129).

22. Foreign visitors to Labrang I met there and in the United States often complained to me about the limitations on their movements through monastic spaces imposed on them by restrictions on tourists.

23. Elderly women and men working on a circumambulation standard on the shikor walked from two to six circuits or hours a day over a period of three to six years. For those working on standards around temples within monastic space, practitioners would walk from twenty to seventy circuits a day.

24. In contrast to other revitalized Geluk monasteries in Amdo, at Labrang women, as tourists, were allowed onto monastic grounds even during the summer retreat (Tib. *dbyar mtsham*). As Akhu Konchok sheepishly explained in a letter, the monastery considered tourism to be too important as income for it to ban women during the peak tourist season.

25. This demographic roughly fits written descriptions of gendered participation in circumambulation in the decades prior to Chinese Communist intervention in Labrang (cf. Ma Haotian 1942–47, Ekvall 1964b, Li Anzhai 1989) as well as oral accounts I heard from older Tibetans.

26. Still, this great increase is difficult to interpret, because it is unclear whether or not monks in the monastery were included in this number. Monks with official status at Labrang may or may not have had permanent-residence status in the valley, and there were great numbers of unofficial monks in town at any one time.

27. The increase in Tibetan population may also be partly due to Tibetans' (especially nomad Tibetans') relative immunity from state birth-control policies in the 1980s. Data from the 1990 census suggest that natural population increases in the relatively large grassland townships of Sangkok and Gangya southwest and north of Labrang town were much greater than those in the urbanizing valley. In addition, the 2000 census marks a significant decrease in reported numbers of Hui in town, a change that might suggest younger generations of Hui were leaving Labrang households to find opportunities elsewhere, perhaps in booming Linxia.

28. The 2000 census reports that 33 percent of immigrants in Labrang were women. Further, in a sample of 862 extraprovincial immigrants in the townships of Gannan, the vast majority (760) were in Labrang town. Of those, fully 71 percent were from neighboring Qinghai province, suggesting that these were mostly Tibetan immigrants to town, a number that would include monks, nuns, and laypeople.

29. Many young urban women lamented to me that they did not have more time to complete circumambulations, something I never heard from young village men, and I often talked with village women young and old who would snatch the time off from in the fields during inclement weather to circumambulate.

30. Since village women did the majority of farm work, fields could also be such a space for women (except during the winter). Women from different households, usually relatives but also friends in mutual-aid networks within or across villages, would help one another with stages of the agricultural process. Throughout the spring and summer, women spent much time in fields working in small groups with children nearby. Fields however are arguably not "public" spaces but part of the household domain.

31. It was also almost exclusively Tibetan Lhade matriarchs and their daughters who performed regular cleaning labor around the shikor as a form of "merit work."

CHAPTER 4. CONSUMING WOMEN

Portions of this chapter were previously published in "On The Edge of Respectability: Sexual Politics on the Sino-Tibetan Frontier," in *positions: east asia culture critique* 10(3): 575–630. Copyright © 2002 by Duke University Press. All rights reserved. Used by permission of the publisher.

1. Tibetan Buddhism, in its emphasis on tantric forms of yogic practice that crucially utilize sexual metaphors for liberation based on a refigured, although not entirely inverted, notion of male-female sex-gender polarity, perhaps epitomizes this more than other Buddhist cultures (cf. Gyatso 2003, 2005).

2. Zhang Qiyun asserts in fact that the majority of such wage laborers were women who were making at most two jiao per day in very unreliable forms of work. But since his numbers often do not jibe with the majority of other reports, it is hard to tell whether this assertion reflects less the numerical reality and more the marked and thus more visible status of such women for Zhang. However, I did find that all the population statistics reported for the valley from the 1930s to the most recent PRC census in 2000 report more males than females in Labrang town, with the situation reversing in surrounding rural districts, including Jiujia township (cf. XXZ 1997: 215).

3. The Chinese verb *duoluo*, which I translate as "to degenerate," has connotations of moral corruption. *Duoluo fengchen* means "to be driven to prostitution."

4. The wives and daughters of the American and European Christian missionaries who accompanied their husbands and fathers to settle in Labrang and elsewhere along China's frontier zone prior to 1949 rarely left their mission compounds, while the men went out daily to proselytize, network, and travel (Wayne and Minnie Persons, personal communication, 1997; also cf. Rijnhart 1901, Nietupski 1999).

5. Li Anzhai was an anthropologist and professor at Yanjing University who had trained for two years in the United States in the mid-1930s. XDZ 1991 claims he was at the time working as an underground CCP operative in Labrang.

6. See Ma Haotian 1942–47, Li Anzhai 1982, Huang 1989, Yu Shiyu 1990c. The XDZ editors state that upon Apa Alo's initiative, the girls' school opened in 1940 with twenty students and Apa Alo's wife, Tshering Lhamo, as principal, and eventually had

eighty students, including Han and Hui girls, and two women teachers (1991: 107; cf. Tuttle 2005).

7. The most commonly used word for the body in Labrang, *phung bo*, "heap," reflects the influence of Buddhist karmic morality on popular thinking.

8. Note that Gyatso (2003, 2005), in her structuralist analysis of sex and gender categories in the Vinaya, finds a wide variety of sex-gender "Others" arrayed against a presumed male standard. Yet she ends by suggesting that females operate as a master Other category.

9. Even the iconoclast Gedun Chopel in his *Treatise on Passion* was careful not to transgress dictums on secrecy concerning tantric sexual practices (dge 'dun chos 'phel 1992: 42).

10. To date, except for a couple of publications by Melvyn Goldstein, there is very little information on homosexual practice in Tibetan Buddhist monasteries, but some scholars assert that traditional monastic codes singled out heterosexual activity as the paradigmatic form of sexual transgression (Goldstein 1964; Zwilling 1992: 209; Goldstein et al. 1997; Ross and Rapp 1997: 156; Gyatso 2003, 2005).

11. Tibetan beliefs about incest follow the lines of the kinship system, which counts members of both lineages equally and divides them into generations in relation to ego. Thus all relations of one's own generation (siblings and cousins) are symbolically equal and therefore would be incestuous lovers. All relations of ego's parents' generation, including affines (i.e., mother- and father-in-law), are symbolically parents and thus would be incestuous lovers.

12. Perhaps because historically the weight of social controls on sexuality in Buddhism has focused on regulating monks, and morality is considered to be largely an individual matter, in contrast to other religious cultures, direct Buddhist regulation of lay sexuality and household affairs is uncommon (cf. Gyatso 2005).

13. Li Anzhai (1992b) noted that girls did not necessarily marry immediately after undergoing the "letting down the hair" rite. The rite also made girls "socially sexual"—that is, they could then (discreetly) take lovers.

14. The German missionary Matthias Hermanns (1953) describes the practice he saw among Tibetan nomads west of Labrang in the 1940s, which he translates (into German) as "marrying a girl to heaven." His description closely mirrors that given by the missionary Louis Schram (1954–61: 78), who lived among the Tibetanized Mongours just north of Labrang in the 1920s. Both describe a practice in which unmarried daughters went through a marriage rite in order to sanction their liaisons with male guests and any resulting children. Schram asserts that any child of such a union was referred to as a "child of heaven." Neither Hermanns nor Schram gives the Tibetan terms for those expressions.

15. Note that in Tibetan regions to sell the body in this way was exclusively associated with women. There was no equivalent word for men.

16. Such liaisons were contracted between Tibetan women and itinerant Han Chinese and Hui traders, as well as between Tibetan women and Tibetan men. While some of these "marriages" were the result of love matches that ultimately lasted lifetimes, others represented a man buying exclusive access to a favorite lover for a certain contract period. Travel writers and other observers attest to these types of practices in most towns along the Sino-Tibetan frontier.

17. See TIN 1999 for a paradigmatic example of this type of social analysis. However, a more recent TIN publication, reporting the results of interviews with Tibetans in Lhasa on their views of the contemporary scene there, states that there were more than seven thousand Tibetan prostitutes in Lhasa, ranging in age from fifteen to forty-five, and that they far outnumbered Chinese prostitutes in the city (TIN 2000).

18. Hence the spate of accounts in the international news media following the release of the 1999 TIN report on prostitution, which depicted it as a Chinese state "plot" against Tibetans. One such account, probably echoing the politically charged rumor mill among Tibetans there, states that "the Chinese authorities" had been secretly teaching Chinese prostitutes Tibetan and training them to "target" monks in Lhasa (J. Morris 1999; cf. Becker 1999).

19. According to my estimates, there were about two hundred nuns affiliated with the Labrang nun communities in 1995, at least 80 percent of whom were under the age of forty. This was more than twice the number of nuns reportedly living in Labrang just prior to the Communist victory in 1949 (Geng 1993: 217; KHBG 1993: 47; see Makley 2004).

20. Observers have noted the great expansion and diversification of markets in sexual services provided by women throughout China by the early 1990s, ranging from poor rural women kidnapped into sexual slavery, to university students making extra money on the side, to high-priced escorts exclusively targeting wealthy businessmen and cadres (see Evans 1997, Hershatter 1997, Dutton 1998, Davis 1999).

21. Notably, by the summer of 2005, this had already changed, so that Tibetan women singers and dancers were baring more and more skin during performances and in music videos.

22. This perhaps explains the fact that the only place I saw advertisements for STD treatment, ubiquitous in Chinese cities, was on the outside posts of the prayer-wheel buildings along the circumambulation path around the monastery—where all visiting pilgrims pass.

23. The state was implicated in this as well, in that state family-planning policies widely assumed that women alone were responsible for contraception, and they focused on making contraception proper and available to married women, not to young women before marriage.

24. Rape did occur in the Labrang region, but it was relatively rare. Or else it was rarely reported to the police!

25. Apa Sangye was most disgusted by this practice in the Tawa villages, saying vehemently that he felt no woman should touch the ritual offerings to mountain deities, and that no one would do such a thing in his home region. He opined that the reason such an unprecedented practice began was that women had kept up offerings during the violence of the Maoist years. And yet as we have seen, the peculiar nature of the Tawa dewas prior to CCP intervention, with men frequently gone, and women often staying in natal households, there could have been a fair number of households without grown men or resident patriarchs. Thus the practice could have begun out of expedience. Other lay residents of the Tawa dewas I spoke to said that women could carry the arrows, but only men could actually place the arrow in the deity's cairn. And dewa patriarchs still presided over and organized major communal offerings.

26. It is difficult to gauge just how widespread violence against wives was among Tibetans. In my experience, I found actual violence against wives to be fairly rare, especially in nomad and more remote farming regions. It seemed however that the incidence of wife beating increased in urban settings, where, I argue, women had made inroads into salaried jobs or careers as state cadres. In our building alone, four of the five young Tibetan wives, three of whom were low-level cadres, endured beatings of various degrees of ferocity and frequency, and one finally sued her husband for divorce, even though that move left her homeless and with little property of her own.

CHAPTER 5. MONKS ARE MEN TOO

1. As I argue elsewhere, I found that locals treated nunhood *not* as a categorically ideal gender status in its own right but in fact as a maverick, and thus uniquely vulnerable, gender status for females in imitation of ideal monkhood (see Makley 2004).

2. In contrast to Apa Alo's projects to set up lay schools, Jamyang Shepa's idea to set up a school for young monks with KMT funding met with great opposition from monks and monastic leaders. According to Huang Mingxin, the Han former monk at Labrang and head teacher at the monk school, whom I interviewed in 1995, there were only two classes of students, totaling about a hundred monks. By his account, the school was so hotly opposed by monastic leaders that it was closed immediately upon Jamyang Shepa's death in 1947; the monks all returned to monastic routines, and Huang Mingxin himself was forced to leave Labrang (cf. Yin 1948; Li Anzhai 1982: 24; Huang 1989: 42; Upton 1999: 74–79). Note as well that in state-sponsored historiography, the monk school is depicted as founded by the KMT Education Bureau, not Jamyang Shepa (XXZ 1997: 782, 788).

3. Indeed, the very end of Mipham's lifetime, in the first decade of the twentieth century, during the reign of the great modernizer the thirteenth Dalai Lama, was a time of cataclysmic changes in the status of "Tibet" as a nation (cf. Sperling 1976; Stoddard 1985; Klieger 1992; Tsering Shakya 1993, 1999; Schwartz 1994; W. Smith 1996).

4. Men like Tsonji frequently made offerings to their birth gods on behalf of them-

selves *and* of their sons. When a son is born, as several laywomen friends explained it, one of the father's jobs is to make offerings to the dewa birth gods on behalf of the boy. This was not done for girls.

5. In Labrang, both laymen and monks would participate in *labtse* rites to mountain deities.

6. Robert Ekvall (1964a: 1127) describes the lifestyle of nomad men as "training for war" (cf. Ekvall 1952, Zhang Jimin 1993).

7. Ambitious students in the Thisamling college wishing to move up in the various levels of "grades" were busy dawn to late at night preparing, memorizing, and meditating, and the completion of the curriculum could take several decades. Each of the other five colleges had between a hundred and two hundred monks at any one time. Four of those colleges specialized in tantric practice and study, while the medical college offered a program of study in the lineages of Tibetan medical knowledge and practice (cf. Li Anzhai 1982, 1989; Stoddard 1985; Yonten Gyatso 1988).

8. Goldstein (1964: 125) says 95 percent of monks in the Lhasa region entered monasteries in their mid-teens. In the Labrang region it was probably also true that the majority of boys entered monasteries around this time—this allows young boys to stay in natal homes longer and provides the household with the benefit of their labor longer. This continued to be true after monasteries were reopened in the 1980s (see below).

9. The detailed ranking of life indemnities levied in cases of murder graphically illustrates the weighting of more or less authoritative and pure bodies. Victims were ranked according to high, middle, and low status, ranging from the highest trulkus to lowly butchers. The life indemnity for female victims was counted as half that of the equivalent status for a male (cf. Wang Zhouta 1996a: 412).

10. Ekvall (1959, 1964b) says that in the Labrang region such monks were also called *ban log* (lit. "fallen monk"), a term that indexed their lack of virtuous restraint. He says they wore robes though, and unlike *grwa log*, men who had returned to lay life, they were still addressed and referred to as "monks" (Tib. *a khu*; cf. Goldstein 1964).

11. I am grateful to Amdo Lekshay Gyamtsho for his invaluable help in translating this and other Tibetan texts. See dge 'dun chos 'phel 1990 for a reprint of the entire poem.

12. That is, *dapdop* who pulled the skirts of their monk robes up so that they hung down over their belts. Ordinary monks were not supposed to show their ankles or waist belts.

13. This is not to say that some families did not resist the dedication of sons to the monastic life in that region of small family sizes and chronic labor shortages.

14. The amount allocated per person varied with the amount of land and livestock owned by a collective. Lhade villagers did not receive much. As Ama Drolkar complained to me one day, her family had controlled five mu of land before collectiviza-

tion, but they received only two mu in the reallocations of 1982, because their household had only four members (cf. GGK 1987: 117).

15. In contrast to Li's findings, *Gannan Gaikuang* (GGK 1987: 102) reports that in 1984 there were only thirty-nine monasteries open in Gannan prefecture.

16. By the 1990s, state development policy advocated by Han economists emphasized the eventual settlement of nomads in permanent dwellings and improving their attendance in state schools (cf. Ma Guangrong 1990, Ma Jiang 1993).

17. The Buddhist Studies Institute (Ch. Foxueyuan, Tib. Nangten Lobdra) received provincial and national subsidies to support about a hundred monk students in a four-year program. The students lived apart from other monks in their own compound but received teachings from lamas in the monastery and sometimes participated in monastic debates with monks in the Thisamling college. Most of their study time, including political study, history, and instruction in Chinese, was done in the school compound. In a book published to commemorate its tenth anniversary, the school reports having accepted a total of 241 students from eighty-five monasteries in Gansu, 141 of whom had graduated and been assigned to fifty or more monasteries (KZNT 1996: 36).

18. This is most likely the reason why Li Dekuan (1989: 241) found that in 1982 Labrang monastery had the smallest number of "underage" (i.e., younger than 18, the state age limit) monks in residence relative to other newly reopened monasteries in Gannan prefecture.

19. In a recent *People's Daily* article (April 2001) praising the selfless entrepreneurship and management skills of the monk general manager of Tashilunpo monastery's transnational corporation, the author notes with great approval that seventeen hundred monasteries across the TAR operated their own businesses.

20. In addition to revenue from ticket sales to tourists, in 1995 Labrang monastery as a corporation was also earning money in several stores and restaurants, a guesthouse for foreign tourists, a bus line to several nomad regions, a printing factory, a carpentry shop, an herbal-pill factory, and a Tibetan hospital. In its 1995 report to the county CPPCC, the Management Committee claimed to have donated 70,000 yuan in monastic funds to "beautifying the environment" and 130,000 yuan to the new county hydroelectric dam, as well as funds to various local schools and monasteries. In addition, it reported sending monks to plant hundreds of thousands of trees and to help fix the road east of town (cf. Li Dekuan 1989, Tian 1991, Suo Dai 1992, Yang Ming 1992).

21. Danzhu Angben and Wang Zhouta (1993: 235) state that in the first half of the twentieth century the Gongtang estate included five hundred households of Lhade, about two hundred mu of land, three regions of forests, six hundred horses, three thousand cattle, five hundred sheep, and over a million yuan of capital accumulated from trade and loan business (cf. Liu Yu 1993, Zha Zha 1993, Dor Zhi 1995, Wang Yunfeng 1997).

22. Initially, the provincial and county Religious Affairs Bureaus provided small living subsidies to senior monks who returned to Labrang and were granted "official residence registration" (Ch. *hukou*) there. By the mid-1990s, officials limited state responsibility for monks and lamas by refusing to change their residence registration from that of their home regions. Thus, while eight hundred monks and lamas were officially recognized as members of Labrang's assemblies, most did not have official residence status there (cf. Goldstein 1998a). I do not have information on whether or not senior monks continued to collect living subsidies from the state.

23. It should be noted that household work could be a very public affair in Labrang, because courtyards and villages often shared a water source, caring for children or shopping for meals was carried out on the main streets of the town or in village commons, and agricultural subsistence production was undertaken in fields for all to see. In nomad dewa, the gendered division of labor was even more striking, and young men were rarely in the encampment at all during the day. Cain still talks about his discomfort at doing the laundry in our courtyard as Tibetan and Chinese male workers there watched and whispered among themselves.

24. Tibetan laymen after all, in their categorical roles as ideal household heads and heirs to family property in patrilocal marriages, were the ones who (theoretically) "stayed" while women married out.

25. Several elder laity and former monks contrasted the relatively predictable behavior of Tibetan grassland bandits (Tib. *jag pa*) in the old days with the unpredictable behavior and wide range of victims associated with modern-day thieves (Tib. *rkun ma*).

26. I found that monks in general received more support in the form of money and food from their families than did nuns, and because of the increasing wealth of nomad households relative to village ones, monks from nomad families were generally better supported than those from villages.

27. All the young monks I interviewed, except one who took up residence in the local monastery at age seven, took novice ordination in their mid- to late teens.

28. This despite the fact that, by my estimates, in the mid-1990s there were actually far fewer monks relative to the lay population (less than 12%) than just prior to Communist victory (around 37%). By the mid-1990s, both Gongtang Tshang and the sixth Jamyang Shepa had begun to publicly advocate a "quality" over "quantity" approach to monasticism as well.

29. Significantly, such criticism of monk bodies did not focus, as it did for nuns, on assumptions of illicit sexual behavior. This is particularly striking in light of the heightened importance of celibacy as the bottom-line requirement for monkhood.

30. Note that I never saw or met a nun who did this. For the most part, nuns did not travel except on pilgrimage, and they always wore monastic dress. By contrast,

monks who could afford it would travel to Lanzhou or Lhasa on business or to see friends, and many tried to make it to India while I was there.

31. In the mid-1990s, a few monks were arrested every year in Labrang under suspicion of such political "crimes." Depending on the nature of the allegations against them, they were held without trial and interrogated for possible ties to any organized underground resistance movement. Such monks were sometimes beaten and imprisoned, usually for a short "reeducation" term of a few weeks to several months in the PSB detention center in Labrang, and then released. More serious cases were sent to prison for longer sentences in Hezuo.

EPILOGUE

1. At his monastery in southern India alone, he said, there were more than a hundred monks who were once at Labrang.

REFERENCES CITED

Adams, Vincanne. 1992. The Production of Self and Body in Sherpa-Tibetan Society. In *Anthropological Approaches to the Study of Ethnomedicine*, edited by Mark Nichter. Philadelphia: Gordon and Breach Science.

—————. 1999. *Equity of the Ineffable: Cultural and Political Constraints on Ethnomedicine as a Health Problem in Contemporary Tibet*. Cambridge, Mass.: Harvard Center for Population and Development Studies.

Agha, Asif. 1993. *Structural Form and Utterance Context in Lhasa Tibetan: Grammar and Indexicality in a Non-Configurational Language*. New York: Peter Lang.

Ahearn, Laura M. 2001. Language and Agency. *Annual Review of Anthropology* 30: 109–37.

AKS. [*a mdo'i kha shags* (Comedic Duets from Amdo)]. 1993. Xining: Qinghai Minzu Chubanshe.

Allione, Tsultrim. 1984. *Women of Wisdom*. London: Routledge and Kegan Paul.

Alonso, Ana Maria. 1994. The Politics of Space, Time and Substance: State Formation, Nationalism and Ethnicity. *Annual Review of Anthropology* 23: 379–405.

Alonso, Mary Ellen, ed. 1979. *China's Inner Asian Frontier*. Cambridge, Mass.: Peabody Museum.

Ama Adhe [Adhe Tapontsang]. 1997. *Ama Adhe, the Voice That Remembers: The Heroic Story of a Woman's Fight to Free Tibet*. As told to Joy Blakeslee. Boston: Wisdom Publications.

Anagnost, Ann. 1987. Politics and Magic in Contemporary China. *Modern China* 13(1): 40–61.

————. 1989. The Transformation of Gender in Modern China, Gender and Anthropology: Critical Reviews for Research and Teaching. Amherst: Project on Gender and the Curriculum.

————. 1994. The Politics of Ritual Displacement. In *Asian Visions of Authority: Religion and the Modern States of East and Southeast Asia*, edited by Laurel Kendall, Charles Keyes, and Helen Hardacre. Honolulu: University of Hawaii Press.

————. 1995. A Surfeit of Bodies: Population and the Rationality of the State in Post-Mao China. In *Conceiving the New World Order: The Global Politics of Reproduction*, edited by Faye Ginsburg and Rayna Rapp. Berkeley and Los Angeles: University of California Press.

————. 1997. *National Pastimes: Narrative, Representation and Power in Modern China*. Durham: Duke University Press.

Anderson, Benedict. 1990. *Language and Power: Exploring Political Cultures in Indonesia*. Ithaca: Cornell University Press.

Anonymous. 1958. The Black Wickedness of the Deceiving Reactionaries Belonging to the Religious Establishments Is Quite Intolerable. *Minzu Tuanjie* [Nationalities Unite], November 22.

Anzaldua, Gloria. 1987. *Borderlands/La Frontera: The New Mestiza*. San Francisco: Aunt Lute Book Company.

Apa Alo [Apa A blo (Huang Zhengqing)]. 1994. *a blo spun mched kyi rnam thar*. [Biography of A blo and His Brother]. Beijing: Minzu Chubanshe. [See also Huang Zhengqing 1989.]

Appadurai, Arjun. 1986. Introduction. In *The Social Life of Things: Commodities in Cultural Perspective*, edited by Arjun Appadurai. Cambridge: Cambridge University Press.

————. 1996. *Modernity at Large: Cultural Dimensions of Globalization*. Minnesota: University of Minnesota Press.

Ardussi, John, and Lawrence Epstein. 1973. The Saintly Madman in Tibet. In *Himalayan Anthropology: The Indo-Tibetan Interface*, edited by James Fisher. The Hague: Mouton.

Aris, Michael. 1992. *Lamas, Princes and Brigands: Joseph Rock's Photographs of the Tibetan Borderlands of China*. New York: China Institute in America.

Asad, Talal. 1993. Towards a Genealogy of the Concept of Ritual. In *Genealogies of Religion*. Baltimore: The Johns Hopkins University Press.

Avedon, John. 1984. *In Exile from the Land of the Snows*. New York: Vintage.

Axel, Brian. 2002. *From the Margins: Historical Anthropology and Its Futures*. Durham: DukeUniversity Press.

Aziz, Barbara. 1975. Tibetan Manuscript Maps of Dingri Valley. *The Canadian Cartographer* 12: 28–38.

———. 1976. Reincarnation Reconsidered: The Reincarnate Lama as Shaman. In *Spirit Possession in the Nepal Himalayas*. New Delhi: Vikas Publishing House.

———. 1978a. *Tibetan Frontier Families*. New Delhi: Vikas Publishing House.

———. 1978b. Maps and the Human Mind. *Human Nature* 1(8): 50–59.

———. 1988. Women in Tibetan Society and Tibetology. In *Tibetan Studies: Proceedings of the 4th Seminar of the International Association for Tibetan Studies, Schloss Hohenkammer, Munich, 1985*, edited by Helga Uebach and Jampa L. Panglung. Munich: Kommission fur Zentralasiatische Studien, Bayerische Akademie der Wissenschaften.

Bakhtin, Mikhail. 1981 [1937–38]. *The Dialogic Imagination*. Translated by Caryl Emerson and Michael Holquist. Austin: University of Texas Press.

Barlow, Tani. 1994. Theorizing Women: Funu, Guojia, Jiating, In Angela Zito, *Body, Subject and Power in China*. Chicago: University of Chicago Press.

Bass, Catriona. 1998. *Education in Tibet: Policy and Practice since 1950*. New York: St. Martin's.

Bateson, Gregory. 1972. A Theory of Play and Fantasy. In *Steps to an Ecology of Mind*. New York: Ballantine Books.

Bauman, Richard, and Charles Briggs. 1990. Poetics and Performance as Critical Perspectives on Language and Social Life. *Annual Review of Anthropology* 19: 59–88.

Bauman, Richard, and Joel Sherzer. 1975. The Ethnography of Speaking. *Annual Review of Anthropology* 4: 95–119.

Becker, Jasper. 1999. Prostitution Undermining Tibet Culture. *South China Morning Post*, August 12.

Behar, Ruth. 1993. *Translated Woman: Crossing the Border with Esperanza's Story*. Boston: Beacon Press.

Bell, Catherine. 1992. *Ritual Theory, Ritual Practice*. Oxford: Oxford University Press.

Bell, Sandra, and Elisa Sobo. 2001. Celibacy in Cross-Cultural Perspective. In *Celibacy, Culture and Society: The Anthropology of Sexual Abstinence*, edited by Sandra Bell and Elisa Sobo Madison: University of Wisconsin Press.

Bentor, Yael. 1993. Tibetan Tourist Thangkas in the Kathmandu Valley. *Annals of Tourism Research* 20: 107–37.

———. 1997. The Horseback Consecration Ritual. In *Religions of Tibet in Practice*, edited by Donald S. Lopez, Jr. Princeton: Princeton University Press.

Berger, Patricia. 2003. *Empire of Emptiness: Buddhist Art and Political Authority in Qing China*. Honolulu: University of Hawaii Press.

Bishop, Peter. 1989. *The Myth of Shangri-la*. Berkeley and Los Angeles: University of California Press.

———. 1993. *Dreams of Power: Tibetan Buddhism and the Western Imagination*. London: Athlone Press.

———. 1994. The Potala and Western Place Making. *Tibet Journal* 19(2): 5–22.

blama bstan po. 1962 [1820]. *The Geography of Tibet: The Mirror Which Illuminates All the Inanimate and Animate Things and Explains Fully the Great World ('dẓam gling rgyas bshad), by blama bstan po (d. 1839)*. Trans. Turrel Wylie. Rome: Istituto Italiano per il Medio ed Estremo Oriente.

Blum, Susan. 2000. *Portraits of Primitives: Ordering Human Kinds in the Chinese Nation*. New York: Rowman and Littlefield.

Bordo, Susan. 1993. Postmodern Subjects, Postmodern Bodies, Postmodern Resistance. In *Unbearable Weight: Feminism, Western Culture, and the Body*. Berkeley and Los Angeles: University of California Press.

Bourdieu, Pierre. 1984. Introduction. In *Distinction: A Social Critique of the Judgment of Taste*. Translated by Richard Nice. Cambridge, Mass.: Harvard University Press.

Bray, John. 2001. Nineteenth- and Early Twentieth-Century Missionary Images of Tibet. In *Imagining Tibet*, edited by Thierry Dodon and Heinz Rather. Boston: Wisdom Publications.

Briggs, Charles. 1986. *Learning How to Ask: A Sociolinguistic Appraisal of the Role of the Interview in Social Science Research*. Cambridge: Cambridge University Press.

Bryant, Barry. 1993. *The Wheel of Time Sand Mandala: Visual Scripture of Tibetan Buddhism*. New York. Samaya Foundation.

Buffetrille, Katia. 1989. La restauration du monastère de bsam yas: Un exemple de continuité dans la relation chapelain-donateur au Tibet? *Journal Asiatique*. 277(3–4): 363–411.

Bulag, Uradyn. 2002. *The Mongols at China's Edge: History and the Politics of National Unity*. Lanham: Rowman and Littlefield.

Butler, Judith. 1988. Performative Acts and Gender Constitution: An Essay in Phenomenology and Feminist Theory. *Theatre Journal* 40(4): 519–31.

———. 1990. Gender Trouble, Feminist Theory and Psychoanalysis. In *Feminism/Postmodernism*, edited by Linda Nicholson. New York: Routledge.

———. 1993. *Bodies That Matter: On the Discursive Limitations of Sex*. New York: Routledge.

Cabezón, José Ignacio. 1992. Introduction. In *Buddhism, Gender and Sexuality*, edited by José Ignacio Cabezón. Albany: SUNY Press.

———. 1997. The Regulations of a Monastery. In *Religions of Tibet in Practice*, edited by Donald S. Lopez, Jr. Princeton: Princeton University Press.

Campbell, June. 1996. *Traveller in Space: In Search of Female Identity in Tibetan Buddhism*. New York: Braziller.

Carrasco, Pedro. 1959. *Land and Polity in Tibet*. Seattle: University of Washington Press.

Carrier, James G., and Josiah M. Heyman. 1997. Consumption and Political Economy. *Journal of the Royal Anthropological Institute* 3(2): 355–73.

Castelli, Elizabeth. 1991. 'I Will Make Mary Male': Pieties of the Body and Gender Transformation of Christian Women in Late Antiquity. In *Body Guards: The Cultural Politics of Gender Ambiguity*, edited by Julia Epstein and Kristina Straub. London: Routledge.

Chai Bozi. 1956. Zai Gannan Zangzu Zizhi Qu [In Gannan Tibetan Autonomous Region]. In *Xibei Heshan Xunshi* [An Inspection tour in the Mountains and Rivers of the Northwest]. Hong Kong.

Chan, Anita, Richard Madsen, and Jonathan Unger. 1984. *Chen Village: The Recent History of a Peasant Community in Mao's China*. Berkeley and Los Angeles: University of California Press.

Chang, Julian. 1997. The Mechanics of State Propaganda: The People's Republic of China and the Soviet Union in the 1950's. In *New Perspectives on State Socialism in China*, edited by Timothy Cheek and Tony Saich. Armonk: Sharpe.

Chang, Won Ho. 1989. *Mass Media in China: The History and the Future*. Ames: Iowa State University Press.

Chang Chih-jang [Zhang Zhirang]. 1959. A Much-Needed Marriage Law. In *The Marriage Law of the PRC Together with Other Relevant Articles*. Beijing: Foreign Languages Press.

Chang Qiuying. 1991. Xiahe Gongwei Fulian Zhuren Chang Qiuying Tongzhi Shengping Jianjie [Brief Introduction to the Biography of Comrade Chang Qiuying, Head of the Xiahe Party Committee Women's Association]. In *Xiahe Dangshi Ziliao* 1 [Materials on the History of the Communist Party in Xiahe, vol. 1], edited by Zhang Qingyou. Lanzhou: Zhonggong Xiahe Xian Wei Dangshi Ziliao Zhengji Bangongshi.

Chao, Emily. 2003. Dangerous Work: Women in Traffic. *Modern China* 29(1): 71–107.

Cheek, Timothy. 1997. Introduction: The Making and Breaking of the Party-State in China. In *New Perspectives on State Socialism in China*, edited by Timothy Cheek and Tony Saich. Armonk: Sharpe.

Chen, Nancy, Constance D. Clark, Suzanne Z. Gottschang, and Lyn Jeffery, eds.

2001. *China Urban: Ethnographies of Contemporary Culture*. Durham: Duke University Press.

Chen Guangguo. 1991. Zangzu Xiguan Fa zai Panchu Xingshi Anjian Zhong de Zuoyong Taolun [A Discussion of the Function of Tibetan Customary Law in Sentencing Cases]. *Minzuxue Yanjiu* [Ethnological Research] 10: 215–29.

Chen Qingying. 1990. *Zhongguo Zangzu Buluo* [Tibetan Tribes of China]. Beijing: Zhongguo Zangxue Chubanshe.

———. 1991. Lcang-skya Rolpa'i rDo-rje and Emperor Qianlong. In *Theses on Tibetology in China*, edited by Hu Tan. Beijing: Zhongguo Zangxue Chubanshe.

———. 1995. *Zangzu Buluo Zhidu Yanjiu* [Research on Tibetan Tribal Systems]. Beijing: Zhongguo Zangxue Chubanshe.

Chen Wei. 1991. The Origin and Vicissitudes of the Mongolian and Tibetan Tribes in Hainan of Qinghai. *Tibet Studies: Journal of the Tibetan Academy of Social Sciences* 3(2): 70–83.

Chen Xiaomei. 1999. Growing Up with Posters in the Maoist Era. In *Picturing Power in the People's Republic of China: Posters of the Cultural Revolution*, edited by Harriet Evans and Stephanie Donald. Oxford: Rowman and Littlefield.

Cohn, Bernard, and Nicholas Dirks. 1988. Beyond the Fringe: The Nation-State, Colonialism, and the Technologies of Power. *Journal of Historical Sociology* 1(2): 225–29.

Collier, Jane, and Sylvia Yanagisako. 1987. Theory in Anthropology since Feminist Practice. *Critique of Anthropology* 9(2): 27–37.

Colomina, Beatriz, ed. 1992. *Sexuality and Space*. Princeton: Princeton University School of Architecture.

Comaroff, Jean. 1997. The Empire's Old Clothes: Fashioning the Colonial Subject. In *Situated Lives: Gender and Culture in Everyday Life*, edited by Louis Lamphere, Helena Ragone, and Patricia Zavella. New York: Routledge.

Comaroff, Jean, and John L. Comaroff. 2000. Millennial Capitalism: First Thoughts on a Second Coming. *Public Culture* 12(2): 291–342.

Corrigan, Philip Richard, and Derek Sayer. 1985. *The Great Arch: English State Formation as Cultural Revolution*. Oxford: Blackwell.

Crapanzano, Vincent. 1996. Self-Centering Narratives. In *Natural Histories of Discourse*, edited by Michael Silverstein and Greg Urban. Chicago: University of Chicago Press.

Croll, Elisabeth. 2001. Chinese Women Organizing: Cadres, Feminists, Muslims, Queers. In *New Spaces, New Voices: Women Organizing in Twentieth-Century China*, edited by Ping-chun Hsiung, Maria Jaschok, Cecilia Milwertz, and Red Chan. Oxford: Berg.

Crook, David, and Isabel Crook. 1979. *Ten Mile Inn: Mass Movement in a Chinese Village.* New York: Pantheon.

Dai Jinhua. 1996. Redemption and Consumption: Depicting Culture in the 1990's. *positions: east asia culture critique* 4(1): 127–41.

———. 1999. Invisible Writing: The Politics of Chinese Mass Culture in the 1990's. *Modern Chinese Literature and Culture* 11(1): 34–57.

Dan Qu [dam chos]. 1993. *Labuleng Si Jianshi* [A Brief History of Labrang Monastery]. Lanzhou: Gansu Minzu Chubanshe.

Daniel, Valentine. 1996. *Charred Lullabies.* Princeton: Princeton University Press.

Danzhu Angben [don 'grub dbang phan] and Wang Zhouta ['brug thar]. 1993. Lishishang de Labuleng Si [Labrang Monastery in History]. In *Zangzu Wenhua Sanlun* [Collected Writings on Tibetan Culture]. Beijing: Zhongguo Youyi Chuban Gongsi.

Davis, Deborah, ed. 1999. *The Consumer Revolution in Urban China.* Studies on China, 22. Berkeley and Los Angeles: University of California Press.

de Certeau, Michel. 1984. *The Practice of Everyday Life.* Berkeley and Los Angeles: University of California Press.

de Lauretis, Teresa. 1987. *Technologies of Gender: Essays on Theory, Film and Fiction.* Bloomington: Indiana University Press.

———. 1999. Oedipus Interruptus. In *Feminist Film Theory: A Reader,* edited by Sue Thornham. New York: New York University Press.

Desjarlais, Robert. 1992. *Body and Emotion: The Aesthetics of Illness and Healing in the Nepal Himalayas.* Philadelphia: University of Pennsylvania Press.

dge 'dun chos 'phel. 1990. *dge 'dun chos 'phel gyi gsung rtsom* 1–3 [The Collected Works of Gendun Chophel, vols. 1–3]. Compiled by Hor khang bsod nams dpal 'bar. Lhasa: Xizang Wengu Ji Chubanshe.

———. 1992 [1938]. *'dod pa'i bstan bcos* [Treatise on Passion]. Trans. Jeffrey Hopkins. In *Tibetan Arts of Love: Sex, Orgasm, and Spiritual Healing.* Ithaca: Snow Lion.

Dhondup Choedon. 1978. *Life in the Red Flag People's Commune.* Dharamsala: Information Office of His Holiness the Dalai Lama.

Diamond, Norma. 1988. The Miao and Poison: Interactions on China's Southwest Frontier. *Ethnology* 21(1): 1–25.

Dikotter, Frank. 1995. *Sex, Culture and Modernity in China: Medical Science and the Construction of Sexual Identities in the Early Republican Period.* London: Hurst.

Dirks, Nicholas. 1992. Introduction: Colonialism and Culture. In *Colonialism and Culture,* edited by Nicholas Dirks. Ann Arbor: University of Michigan Press.

Dirlik, Arif. 1978. *Revolution and History: The Origins of Marxist Historiography in China, 1919–1937.* Berkeley and Los Angeles: University of California Press.

dkon mchog bstan pa rab rgyas. 1987 [1865]. *mdo smad chos 'byung* [History of Buddhism in Domay]. Lanzhou: Gansu Minzu Chubanshe.

dkon mchog rgyal mtshan [dbal mang pandita]. 1985 [1800]. *bla brang bkra shis 'khyil gyi gdan rabs lha'i rnga chen.* [The Great Sacred Drum: The History of Labrang Monastery (*Labuleng Si Zhi* [Gazetteer of Labrang Monastery])]. Lanzhou: Gansu Minzu Chubanshe.

Dodin, Thierry, and Heinz Rather, eds. 2001. *Imagining Tibet: Perceptions, Projections, and Fantasies.* Boston: Wisdom Publications.

Dor Zhi [Duo Shi]. 1995. Di Shi Ci Shilun Jingang Guanding Fahui Jianjie [A Brief Introduction to the Tenth Kalacakra Initiation Ceremony]. *Xianmi* 1: 3–8.

Douglas, Mary. 1966. *Purity and Danger: An Analysis of Concepts of Pollution and Taboo.* New York: Praeger.

Draper, John. 1994. Lama Knows: Religion and Power in Sherpa Society. In *Tantra and Popular Religion in Tibet.* New Delhi: International Academy of Indian Culture.

Dreyer, June. 1976. *China's Forty Millions.* Cambridge, Mass.: Harvard University Press.

Du Pengcheng. 1991. Wo zai Xiahe de Rizi li [My Days in Xiahe]. In *Xiahe Dangshi Ziliao* 1 [Materials on the History of the Communist Party in Xiahe County, vol. 1]. Lanzhou: Zhonggong Xiahe Xian Weidangshi Ziliao Zhengji Bangongshi.

Duan Deyi, Qi Yuling, and Li Yangrui, eds. 1982. *Gansu Luyou Zhinan* [A Tourism Guide to Gansu]. Beijing: Zhongguo Luyou Chubanshe.

Duara, Prasenjit. 1995. *Rescuing History from the Nation: Questioning Narratives of Modern China.* Chicago: University of Chicago Press.

———. 1998. The Regime of Authenticity: Timelessness, Gender, and National History in Modern China. *History and Theory* 37(3): 287–308.

Duncan, Marion. 1964. *Customs and Superstitions of Tibetans.* London: Mitre.

Duncan, Nancy. 1996. Renegotiating Gender and Sexuality in Public and Private Spaces. In *Bodyspace: Destabilizing Geographies of Gender and Sexuality,* edited by Nancy Duncan. London: Routledge.

Duozang Caidan. 1992. *Labuleng Si: Luyou Zhinan* [Labrang Monastery: A Tourism Guide]. Chengdu: Sichuan Minzu Chubanshe.

Duranti, Alessandro. 1994. *From Grammar to Politics: Linguistic Anthropology in a Western Samoan Village.* Berkeley and Los Angeles: University of California Press.

———. 1997. *Linguistic Anthropology.* Cambridge: Cambridge University Press.

Dutton, Michael. 1992. Policing and Punishment in China: From Patriarchy to 'the People.' Cambridge: Cambridge University Press.

————. 1995. Dreaming of Better Times: 'Repetition with a Difference' and Community Policing in China. *positions: east asia culture critique* 3(2): 414–47.

————. 1998. *Streetlife China*. Cambridge: Cambridge University Press.

Edgar, J. H. 1924. Geographical Control and Human Reactions in Tibet. *Journal of the West China Border Research Society,* 14–16.

Ekvall, Robert. 1938. *Gateway to Tibet*. Harrisburg: Christian Publications.

————. 1939. *Cultural Relations on the Kansu-Tibetan Border*. Chicago: University of Chicago Press.

————. 1952. *Tibetan Skylines*. New York: Farrar, Straus, and Young.

————. 1959. Three Categories of Inmates within Tibetan Monasteries: Status and Function. *Central Asiatic Journal* 5(3): 215–18.

————. 1960. The Tibetan Self-Image. *Pacific Affairs* 33: 375–82.

————. 1964a. Peace and War among the Tibetan Nomads. *American Anthropology* 66: 1119–48.

————. 1964b. *Religious Observances in Tibet: Patterns and Function*. Chicago: University of Chicago Press.

————. 1968. *Fields on the Hoof*. New York: Holt, Rinehart and Winston.

————. 1979. *The Lama Knows: A Legend Is Born*. New Delhi: Oxford and IBH Publishing.

Ellingson, Ter. 1990. Tibetan Monastic Constitutions: The Bca'-yig. In *Reflections on Tibetan Culture,* edited by Lawrence Epstein and Richard F. Sherburne. Lewiston: Mellen.

Elliot, Mark. 2000. The Limits of Tartary: Manchuria in Imperial and National Geographies. *Journal of Asian Studies* 59(3): 603–46.

Enloe, Cynthia. 1989. Nationalism and Masculinity. *Bananas, Beaches and Bases: Making Feminist Sense of International Politics*. Berkeley and Los Angeles: University of California Press.

Epstein, Israel. 1983. *Tibet Transformed*. Beijing: New World Press.

Epstein, Julia, and Kristina Straub. 1991. Introduction. In *Body Guards: The Cultural Politics of Gender Ambiguity,* edited by Julia Epstein and Kristina Straub. London: Routledge.

Epstein, Lawrence. 1982. On the History and Psychology of the 'Das-Log'. *Tibet Journal* 7(4): 20–85.

Epstein, Lawrence, and Peng Wenbin. 1994. Autumn Ganja and Murdo: The Social Construction of Space at Two Pilgrimage Sites in Eastern Tibet. *Tibet Journal* 19(3): 21–40.

Escobar, Arturo. 1995. *Encountering Development : The Making and Unmaking of the Third World*. Princeton: Princeton University Press.

Evans, Harriet. 1997. *Women and Sexuality in China: Dominant Discourses of Female Sexuality and Gender since 1949*. Cambridge: Polity.

―――. 1998. The Language of Liberation: Gender and *Jiefang* in Early Chinese Communist Party Discourse. *Intersections*, Inaugural Issue. http://wwwsshe.murdoch.edu.au/intersections/back_issues/harriet.html. [Accessed Jan. 20, 2002.]

―――. 1999. Comrade Sisters: Gendered Bodies and Spaces. In *Picturing Power in the People's Republic of China: Posters of the Cultural Revolution*, edited by Harriet and Donald Evans. Oxford: Rowman and Littlefield.

Fairbank, John, and Albert Feuerwerker, eds. 1986. *Cambridge History of China*, vol. 13, part 2, *Republican China, 1912–49*. Cambridge: Cambridge University Press.

Faure, Bernard. 1998. *The Red Thread: Buddhist Approaches to Sexuality*. Princeton: Princeton University Press.

―――. 2002. *The Power of Denial: Buddhism, Purity and Gender*. Princeton: Princeton University Press.

Fausto-Sterling, Anne. 1997. How to Build a Man. In *Gender/Sexuality Reader*, edited by Roger Lancaster and Micaela di Leonardo. New York: Routledge.

Fei Xiao-tong. 1981. On the Social Transformation of China's National Minorities, and Ethnic Identification in China. In *Toward a People's Anthropology*. Beijing: New World Press.

Felman, Shoshana, and Dori Laub. 1992. *Testimony: Crises of Witnessing in Literature, Psychoanalysis, and History*. New York: Routledge.

Feng Jicai. 1991. *Voices from the Whirlwind: An Oral History of the Chinese Cultural Revolution*. New York: Pantheon.

Fletcher, Joseph. 1978. Ching Inner Asia ca. 1800. In *Cambridge History of China*, vol. 10, part 1, *Late Ch'ing, 1800–1911.*, edited by John Fairbank and Denis Twitchett. Cambridge: Cambridge University Press.

Foucault, Michel. 1977. *Discipline and Punish: The Birth of the Prison*. New York: Vintage.

―――. 1978. *The History of Sexuality*, vol. 1, *An Introduction*. New York: Vintage.

―――. 1984. Docile Bodies. In *The Foucault Reader*, edited by Paul Rabinow. New York: Pantheon.

Friedman, Edward, Mark Pickowicz, and Mark Selden. 1991. *Chinese Village, Socialist State*. New Haven: Yale University Press.

Gal, Susan. 1991. Between Speech and Silence: The Problematics of Research on

Language and Gender. In *Gender at the Crossroads of Knowledge: Feminist Anthropology in the Postmodern Era*, edited by Micaela di Leonardo. Berkeley and Los Angeles: University of California Press.

Gansu Tongji Nianjian [Gansu Statistical Yearbook]. 1994. Beijing: Chinese Statistics Press.

Gansu Pucha [Gansu Census]. 1993.

Gao Changzhu. 1942. Di 22 Ti: Labuleng: Jinkuang ji qi Kaifa Yijian [The 22nd District: Labrang: Some Perspectives on Its Current Situation and Development]. In *Bianjiang Wenti Lunwen Ji* [Collected Writings on Frontier Issues]. Taipei: Zhengzhong Shuju.

Gao Zhanfu. 1992. 1949 Yilai de Gansu Minzu Yanjiu [Research on Gansu Minzu since 1949]. *Xizang Yanjiu Huixun* [Tibetan Studies Newsletter] 14: 20–24.

Gaubatz, Piper Rae. 1996. *Beyond the Great Wall: Urban Forms and Transformation on the Chinese Frontiers.* Stanford: Stanford University Press.

Geertz, Clifford. 1980. *Negara: The Theater State in Nineteenth-Century Bali.* Princeton: Princeton University Press.

Geng Fu. 1993. Xiahe Luyou Ziyuan Jianjie [A Brief Introduction to Xiahe's Tourism Resources]. In *Xiahe Wenshi Ziliao* 1 [Data on the History of Xiahe County, vol. 1]. Xiahe: Zhongguo Renmin Zhengxie Shanghuiyi Xiahe Xian Weiyuanhui Wenshi Ziliao Weiyuanhui.

Germano, David. 1998. Re-membering the Dismembered Body of Tibet. In *Buddhism in Contemporary Tibet: Religious Revival and Cultural Identity*, edited by Melvyn Goldstein and Matthew Kapstein. Berkeley and Los Angeles: University of California Press.

Gesang Daji [skal bzang dar rgyas]. 1993. Gannan Zangzu Zizhizhou nongmu qu Diaocha Yanjiu Baogao [Report on Field Research in Nomadic and Farming Regions of Gannan Tibetan Autonomous Prefecture]. *Zhongguo Zangxue (China Tibetology)* 3: 52–63.

GGK [*Gannan Zangzu Zizhizhou Gaikuang* (Introduction to Gannan Tibetan Autonomous Prefecture)]. 1987. Lanzhou: Gansu Minzu Chubanshe.

Gibbons, Todd. 1995. Review: The Wild and the Tame in Tibet. *History of Religions* 34(3): 281–91.

Giddens, Anthony. 1971. *Capitalism and Modern Social Theory: An Analysis of the Writings of Marx, Durkheim and Weber.* Cambridge: Cambridge University Press.

Gillette, Maris. 2001. *Between Mecca and Beijing: Modernization and Consumption among Urban Chinese Muslims.* Stanford: Stanford University Press.

Gilmartin, Christina. 1990. Violence against Women in Contemporary China. In

Violence in China: Essays in Culture and Counterculture, edited by Jonathan Lipman and Stevan Harrell. Albany: SUNY Press.

Gladney, Dru. 1991. *Muslim Chinese: Ethnic Nationalism in the PRC*. Cambridge, Mass.: Harvard University Press.

———. 1994. Representing Nationality in China: Refiguring Minority/Majority Identities. *Journal of Asian Studies* 53(1): 92–123.

———. 1995. Tian Zhuangzhuang, the Fifth Generation, and Minorities Film in China. *Public Culture* 8(1): 161–75.

———. 2004. *Dislocating China: Muslims, Minorities, and Other Subaltern Subjects*. Chicago: University of Chicago Press.

Goffman, Erving. 1979. *Gender Advertisements*. Cambridge, Mass.: Harvard University Press.

———. 1981. *Forms of Talk*. Philadelphia: University of Pennsylvania Press.

Goldstein, Melvyn. 1964. A Study of the Ldab Ldop. *Central Asiatic Journal* 9: 125–41.

———. 1989. *A History of Modern Tibet, 1913–1951: The Demise of the Lamaist State*. Berkeley and Los Angeles: University of California Press.

———. 1997. *The Snow Lion and the Dragon: China, Tibet, and the Dalai Lama*. Berkeley and Los Angeles: University of California Press.

———. 1998a. The Revival of Monastic Life in Drepung Monastery. In *Buddhism in Contemporary Tibet: Religious Revival and Cultural Identity*, edited by Melvyn Goldstein and Matthew Kapstein. Berkeley and Los Angeles: University of California Press.

———. 1998b. Introduction. In *Buddhism in Contemporary Tibet: Religious Revival and Cultural Identity*, edited by Melvyn Goldstein and Matthew Kapstein. Berkeley and Los Angeles: University of California Press.

Goldstein, Melvyn, and Matthew Kapstein, eds. 1998. *Buddhism in Contemporary Tibet: Religious Revival and Cultural Identity*. Berkeley and Los Angeles: University of California Press.

Goldstein, Melvyn, William Siebenschuh, and Tashi Tsering. 1997. *The Struggle for Modern Tibet: The Autobiography of Tashi Tsering*. Armonk: Sharpe.

Goldstein, Melvyn, and Tsarong Paljor. 1985. Tibetan Buddhist Monasticism: Social, Psychological and Cultural Implications. *Tibet Journal* 10(1): 14–31.

Goodwin, Charles, and Alessandro Duranti. 1992. Rethinking Context: An Introduction. In *Rethinking Context: Language as an Interactive Phenomenon*, edited by Charles Goodwin and Alessandro Duranti. Cambridge: Cambridge University Press.

Goodwin, Marjorie. 1990. *He-Said-She-Said: Talk as Social Organization among Black Children*. Bloomington: Indiana University Press.

Graeber, David. 2001. *Toward an Anthropological Theory of Value: The False Coin of Our Own Dreams*. London: Palgrave.

Griebenow, Marion. 1938. Traveling with a God of Tibet. *Alliance Weekly* 73(20), May 14.

Grimshaw, Patricia. 1997 [1989]. New England Missionary Wives, Hawaiian Women and 'the Cult of True Womanhood.' In *Gender in Cross-Cultural Perspective*, edited by Caroline Brettell and Carolyn Sargent. London: Prentice-Hall.

Gross, Rita. 1993. *Buddhism after Patriarchy*. New York: SUNY Press.

Gu Zhizhong and Lu Yi. 1938 [1935]. *Dao Qinghai Qu* [En route to Qinghai]. Shanghai: Shangwu Yinshu Guan.

Gumperz, John J. 1992. Contextualization and Understanding. In *Rethinking Context: Language as an Interactive Phenomenon*, edited by Charles Goodwin and Alessandro Duranti. Cambridge: Cambridge University Press.

Guo Lu. 1995. Gannan Zhou Funu Fazhan Xianzhuang [Perspectives on the Current State of Women's Development in Gannan, parts 1–4]. *Gannan Bao* [Gannan News], September 19–21.

Gupta, Akhil, and James Ferguson. 1992. Beyond 'Culture': Space, Identity and the Politics of Difference. *Cultural Anthropology* 7(1): 6–23.

Gutschow, Kim. 2001. The Women Who Refuse to Be Exchanged: Nuns in Zangskar, Northwest India. In *Celibacy, Culture and Society: The Anthropology of Sexual Abstinence*, edited by Sandra Bell and Elisa Sobo. Madison: University of Wisconsin Press.

Gyatso, Janet. 1987. Down with the Demoness: Reflections on a Feminine Ground in Tibet. In *Feminine Ground: Essays on Women and Tibet*, edited by Janice Willis. Ithaca: Snow Lion.

———. 1996. Drawn from the Tibetan Treasury: The gTer ma Literature. In *Tibetan Literature: Studies in Genre*, edited by José Ignacio Cabezón and Roger R. Jackson. Ithaca: Snow Lion.

———. 1998. *Apparitions of the Self: The Secret Autobiographies of a Tibetan Visionary*. Princeton: Princeton University Press.

———. 2000. Juicing the Other: Comparative Study of the Role of the Female Partner in Tantra. Paper presented at "The Tantric Turn in Buddhism," Buddhist Studies Conference, University of Michigan.

———. 2003. One Plus One Makes Three: Buddhist Gender, Monasticism, and the Law of the Non-Excluded Middle. *History of Religions* 43(2): 89–115.

————. 2005. Sex. In *Critical Terms for the Study of Buddhism*, edited by Donald S. Lopez, Jr. Chicago: University of Chicago Press.

GZZ [*Gannan Zhou Zhi* (Gazetteer of Gannan Prefecture)]. 1999. Beijing: Minzu Chubanshe.

Hall, Jacquelyn Dowd. 1998. You Must Remember This: Autobiography as Social Critique. *Journal of American History* 85(2): 439–65.

Hanks, William. 1989. Text and Textuality. *Annual Review of Anthropology*. 18: 95–128.

————. 1990. *Referential Practice: Language and Lived Space among the Maya*. Chicago: University of Chicago Press.

————. 1996. Exorcism and the Description of Participant Roles. In *Natural Histories of Discourse*, edited by Michael Silverstein and Greg Urban. Chicago: University of Chicago Press.

Hannerz, Ulf. 1996. When Culture Is Everywhere: Reflections on a Favorite Concept. In *Transnational Connections*. New York: Routledge.

Harding, Harry. 1987. The Legacy of Mao Zedong. In *China's Second Revolution: Reform after Mao*. Washington, D.C.: The Brookings Institute.

Harrell, Stevan. 1995. Introduction: Civilizing Projects and the Reaction to Them. In *Cultural Encounters on China's Ethnic Frontiers*, edited by Stevan Harrell. Seattle: University of Washington Press.

Harris, Clare. 1999. *In the Image of Tibet: Tibetan Painting after 1959*. London: Reaktion.

Havnevik, Hanna. 1990. *Tibetan Buddhist Nuns: History, Cultural Norms and Social Reality*. Oslo: Norwegian University Press.

Heng, Geraldine, and Janadas Devan. 1992. State Fatherhood: The Politics of Nationalism, Sexuality and Race in Singapore. In *Nationalisms and Sexualities*, edited by Andrew Parker, Mary Russo, Doris Sommer, and Patricia Yaeger. New York: Routledge.

Herberer, Thomas. 1989. *China and Its National Minorities: Autonomy or Assimilation?* Armonk: Sharpe.

————. 2001. Old Tibet a Hell on Earth? The Myth of Tibet and Tibetans in Chinese Art and Propaganda. In *Imagining Tibet*, edited by Thierry Dodon and Heinz Rather. Boston: Wisdom Publications.

Hermanns, Matthias. 1953. The Status of Women in Tibet. *Anthropological Quarterly* 26(3): 67–78.

Hershatter, Gail. 1997. *Dangerous Pleasures: Prostitution and Modernity in Twentieth-Century Shanghai*. Berkeley and Los Angeles: University of California Press.

————. 2001. The Remembered Self: Gender and Early Socialism in the Life Stories of Rural Shaanxi Women. Paper presented at the conference "Gender in Motion: Division of Labor and Cultural Change in Late Imperial and Modern China," University of California, Berkeley, October 5–7.

Hershatter, Gail, Emily Honig, Jonathan N. Lipman, and Randall Stross, eds. 1996. *Remapping China: Fissures in Historical Terrain.* Stanford: Stanford University Press.

Hessler, Peter. 1999. Tibet through Chinese Eyes. *Atlantic Monthly,* February: 56–66.

Hevia, James. 1995. *Cherishing Men from Afar: Qing Guest Ritual and the Macartney Embassy of 1793.* Durham: Duke University Press.

Hinton, William. 1966. *Fanshen: A Documentary of Revolution in a Chinese Village.* New York: Vintage.

Honig, Emily, and Gail Hershatter. 1988. *Personal Voices: Chinese Women in the 1980's.* Stanford: Stanford University Press.

hor gtsang 'jigs med. 2000. bod kyi gzhi bdag gi skor la nyams zhib phran bu byas ba'i zin bris [Some Brief Notes from Research on Tibetan Mountain Deities]. *Nor mdzod* [Treasury] 2: 49–99.

Hostetler, Laura. 2001. *Qing Colonial Enterprise: Ethnography and Cartography in Early Modern China.* Chicago: University of Chicago Press.

Hsiung, Ping-chun, Maria Jaschok, and Cecilia Milwertz, eds. [with Red Chan]. 2001. *Chinese Women Organizing.* Oxford: Oxford University Press.

Huang Zhengqing [A pa A blo]. 1989. *Huang Zhengqing Yu Wushi Jiamuyang* [Huang Zhengqing and the Fifth Jamyang Shepa]. Lanzhou: Gansu Minzu Chubanshe. [See also Apa Alo 1994.]

Huber, Toni. 1992. A Tibetan Map of lHo-kha in the South-Eastern Himalayan Borderlands of Tibet. *Imago Mundi: The Journal of the International Society for t he History of Cartography* 44: 9–23.

————. 1994a. Why Can't Women Climb Pure Crystal Mountain? Remarks on Gender and Space at Tsa-ri. In *Tibetan Studies: Proceedings of the Sixth Seminar of the International Association for Tibetan Studies, Fagernes, 1992,* vol. 1, edited by Per Kvaerne. Oslo: Institute for Comparative Research in Human Culture.

————. 1994b. Putting the gnas Back into gnas-skor: Rethinking Tibetan Buddhist Pilgrimage Practice. *Tibet Journal* 19(2): 23–60.

————. 1999. *The Cult of Pure Crystal Mountain: Popular Pilgrimage and Visionary Landscape in Southeast Tibet.* Oxford: Oxford University Press.

Humphrey, Caroline. 1994. Remembering an 'Enemy': The Bogd Khaan in Twenti-eth-Century Mongolia. In *Memory, History, and Opposition under State Socialism,* edited by Rubie S. Watson. Santa Fe: School of American Research Press.

Hunter, Alan, and John Sexton. 1999. *Contemporary China*. New York: St. Martin's.

Huo Deyi. 1991. Xiahe Gongwei Diyi Ren Shuji Huo Deyi Tongzhi Zishu [The Personal Account of Comrade Huo Deyi, the First Party Secretary of Xiahe County]. In *Xiahe Dangshi Ziliao* 1 [Materials on the History of the Communist Party in Xiahe, vol. 1], edited by Zhang Qingyou. Lanzhou: Zhonggong Xiahe Xian Wei Dangshi Ziliao Zhengji Bangongshi.

Hyde, Sandra. 2001. Sex Tourism Practices on the Periphery: Eroticizing Ethnicity and Pathologizing Sex on the Lancang. In *China Urban: Ethnographies of Contemporary Culture*, edited by Nancy Chen, Constance D. Clark, Suzanne Z. Gottschang, and Lyn Feffery. Durham: Duke University Press.

Hymes, Dell. 1975. Breakthrough into Performance. In *Folklore: Performance and Communication*, edited by Dan Ben-Amos and Kenneth S. Goldstein. The Hague: Mouton.

ICT [International Campaign for Tibet]. 1996. *bod kyi shar phyogs sa khul khag* [Map of Eastern Tibetan Regions]. Washington, D.C.

Iredale, Robyn, and Fei Guo. 2003. Overview of Minority Migration. In *Chinese Minorities on the Move*, edited by Robyn Iredale and Fei Guo. Armonk: Sharpe.

Irvine, Judith. 1979. Formality and Informality in Communicative Events. *American Anthropologist* 81: 773–90

———. 1996. Shadow Conversations: The Indeterminacy of Participant Roles. In *Natural Histories of Discourse*, edited by Michael Silverstein and Greg Urban. Chicago: University of Chicago Press.

Jacka, Tamara, and Josko Petkovic. 1998. Ethnography and Video: Researching Women in China's Floating Population. *Intersections*, Inaugural Issue, September, http://wwwsshe.murdoch.edu.au/intersections/back_issues/tampt1.html. [Accessed Jan. 20, 2002.]

Jakobson, Roman. 1990 [1957]. Shifters, Verbal Categories and the Russian Verb. Excerpted in *On Language*, edited by Linda R. Waugh and Monique Monville-Burston. Cambridge, Mass.: Harvard University Press.

Jamyang Norbu. 1992. Atrocity and Amnesia: Another Assault on Goldstein's Attempt at Revising Tibetan History. *Tibetan Review* 27(5): 22–24.

———. 1999. Rangzen Charter: The case for Tibetan Independence. http://www.rangzen.net/eng/charter/contents.html.

Ji Wenpo. 1993. Xiahe Xian Lidai Tunken yu Liangshi Jiaoyi Gaikuang [Introduction to the History of Agricultural Colonies and Grain Trade in Xiahe County]. In *Xiahe Wenshi Ziliao* 1 [Data on the History of Xiahe County, vol. 1]. Xiahe: Zhongguo Renmin Zhengxie Shanghuiyi Xiahe Xian Weiyuanhui Wenshi Ziliao Weiyuanhui.

Jia Zhuoping. 1995. Gaibian Guannian, Tuokuan Silu: Wanmao Xiang Funu Jiji Canyu Jingzheng [Change Beliefs and Widen Minds: Women of Wanmao Township Enthusiastically Participate in Economic Competition]. *Gannan Bao,* September 7.

Judd, Ellen. 1994. *Gender and Power in Rural North China.* Stanford: Stanford University Press.

Jun Jing. 1999. Villages Dammed, Villages Repossessed: A Memorial Movement in Northwest China. *American Ethnologist* 26(2): 324–43.

Jurists [International Commission of Jurists]. 1960. *Tibet and the Chinese People's Republic: A Report to the International Commission of Jurists.* Geneva: International Commission of Jurists.

Kai Wa. 1995. Lun Dangqian Zangzu Siyuan Jingji ji qi Daoxiang Wenti [On the Economy of Contemporary Tibetan Buddhist Monasteries and the Problem of Guiding It]. *Qinghai Minzu Xueyuan Xuebao* [Journal of the Qinghai Nationalities Institute] 4: 59–63.

Kansteiner, Wulf. 2002. Finding Meaning in Memory: A Methodological Critique of Collective Memory Studies. *History and Theory* 41(2): 179–97.

Kapferer, Bruce. 2003. Sorcery and the Shapes of Globalization Disjunctions and Continuities: The Case of Sri Lanka. In *Globalization, the State and Violence,* edited by Jonathan Friedman. Walnut Creek: Altamira.

Kaplan, Martha, and John Kelly. 1990. History, Structure, and Ritual. *Annual Review of Anthropology* 19: 119–51.

Kapstein, Matthew. 1997. Turning Back Gossip. In *Religions of Tibet in Practice,* edited by Donald S. Lopez. Princeton: Princeton University Press.

———. 1998. Concluding Remarks. In *Buddhism in Contemporary Tibet: Religious Revival and Cultural Identity,* edited by Melvyn Goldstein and Matthew Kapstein. Berkeley and Los Angeles: University of California Press.

Karan, Pardyumna. 1976. *The Changing Face of Tibet: The Impact of Chinese Communist Ideology on the Landscape.* Lexington: University Press of Kentucky.

Karmay, Samten. 1994. Mountain Cults and National Identity in Tibet. In *Resistance and Reform in Tibet,* edited by Shirin Akiner and Robert Barnett. Bloomington: Indiana University Press.

Keane, Webb. 1997. *Signs of Recognition: Powers and Hazards of Representation in an Indonesian Society.* Berkeley and Los Angeles: University of California Press.

Kessler, Suzanne, and Wendy McKenna. 1978. *Gender: An Ethnomethodological Approach.* Chicago: University of Chicago Press.

Keyes, Charles. 1983. Introduction: The Study of Popular Ideas of Karma. In

Karma: An Anthropological Inquiry, edited by Charles Keyes and Valentine Daniel. Berkeley and Los Angeles: University of California Press.

―――. 1984. Mother or Mistress but Never a Monk: Buddhist Notions of Female Gender in Rural Thailand. *American Ethnologist* 11(2): 223–41.

―――. 1986. Ambiguous Gender: Male Initiation in a Northern Thai Buddhist Society. In *Gender and Religion: On the Complexity of Symbols,* edited by Caroline W. Bynum, Stevan Harrell, and Paula Richman. Boston: Beacon.

Khandelwal, Meena. 2001. Sexual Fluids, Emotions, Morality: Notes on the Gendering of Brahmacharya. In *Celibacy, Culture and Society,* edited by Elisa Sabo and Sandra Bell. Madison: University of Wisconsin Press.

KHBG. [kan lho'i bod rgyud nang bstan dgon sde so so'i lo rgyus mdor bsdus (Gannan Zangchuan Fojiao Siyuan Gaikuang [zhongji] [Brief Introduction to Tibetan Buddhist Monasteries in Gannan])]. 1993. In *Gannan Wenshi Ziliao (di 10 ji)* [Data on the History of Gannan Prefecture, vol. 10]. Hezuo.

Klieger, P. Christiaan. 1992. *Tibetan Nationalism: The Role of Patronage in the Accomplishment of a National Identity.* Meerut: Archana Publications.

Kohn, Richard. 1997. A Rite of Empowerment. In *Religions of Tibet in Practice,* edited by Donald S. Lopez, Jr. Princeton: Princeton University Press.

―――. 2001. *Lord of the Dance: The Mani Rimdu Festival in Tibet and Nepal.* Albany: SUNY Press.

Kornman, Robin. 1997. Gesar of Ling. In *Religions of Tibet in Practice,* edited by Donald S. Lopez, Jr. Princeton: Princeton University Press.

Kuhn, Annette. 1985. *The Power of the Image.* London: Routledge.

Kvaerne, Per. 1994. The Ideological Impact of Tibetan Art. In *Resistance and Reform in Tibet,* edited by Shirin Akiner and Robert Barnett. Bloomington: Indiana University Press.

KZC [kan su'u zhing chen gyi nang bstan dgon pa do dam byed rgyu'i tshod lta'i lag len byed thabs (Preliminary Methods for the Management of Buddhist Monasteries in Gansu Province)]. 1978.

KZNT. [kan su'u zhing chen nang bstan slob grwa'i gnas tshul mdor bsdus, 1986–96 (Brief Introduction to the Situation of the Gansu Buddhist Studies Institute, 1986–96)]. 1996. Labrang: nang bstan slob grwa.

Lakoff, Robin. 1995. Cries and Whispers: The Shattering of Silence. In *Gender Articulated: Language and the Socially Constructed Self,* edited by Kira Hall and Mary Bucholtz. London: Routledge.

Lancaster, Roger. 2003. *The Trouble with Nature: Sex in Science and Popular Culture.* Berkeley and Los Angeles: University of California Press.

Laub, Dori. 1992. Bearing Witness; or, the Vicissitudes of Listening. In *Testimony: Crises of Witnessing in Literature, Psychoanalysis, and History,* edited by Shoshana Felman and Dori Laub. New York: Routledge.

Levine, Nancy. 1988. *The Dynamics of Polyandry: Kinship, Domesticity and Population on the Tibetan Border.* Chicago: University of Chicago Press.

Lhamo mtsho [Lamao cuo]. 1995. Qinghai Zangzu Funu zai Shehui Jingji Shenghuo Zhong de Diwei yu Zuoyong [The Status and Function of Qinghai Tibetan Women in Socioeconomic Life]. *Qinghai Minʐu Xueyuan Xuebao* [Journal of the Qinghai Nationalities Institute] 4: 64–68.

Lhamo skyabs. 1986. kan lho'i lo rgyus steng byung ba'i bod kyi mkhas mchog 'ga'i 'khrungs 'das ngo sprod phran bu [A Brief Introduction to the Lives of the Superior Tibetan Scholars in the History of Gannan]. *ʐla ʐer* [Moonlight] 3: 59–64.

LHZ [*Linxia Huiʐu Ziʐhiʐhou Zhi* (Gazetteer of Linxia Hui Autonomous Prefecture)]. 1990. Lanzhou: Gansu Minzu Chubanshe.

Li, Xiaoping. 1998. Fashioning the Body in Post-Mao China. In *Consuming Fashion: Adorning the Transnational Body,* edited by Anne Brydon and Sandra Niessen. Oxford: Berg Press.

Li Anzhai. 1982 [1957]. *Labrang: A Study in the Field.* Tokyo: Institute of Oriental Culture.

———. 1989 [1957]. *Zangʐu Zongjiao Shi ʐhi Shidi Yanjiu* [Ethnographic Research on the History of Tibetan Religion]. Beijing: Zhongguo Zangxue Chubanshe.

———. 1992a [1941]. Chuan, Gan Shu Xian Bianmin Fenbu Gaikuang (1941–42) [The Distribution of Frontier Peoples in Several Counties of Gansu and Sichuan Provinces (1941–42)]. In *Li Anʐhai Zangxue Wenlun Xuan* [Selected Tibetan-Studies Writings of Li Anzhai]. Beijing: Zhongguo Zangxue Chubanshe.

———. 1992b [1946]. Xikang Dege zhi Lishi yu Renkou [The History and Population of Derge in Xikang]. In *Li Anʐhai Zangxue Wenlun Xuan* [Selected Tibetan-Studies Writings of Li Anzhai].. Beijing: Zhongguo Zangxue Chubanshe.

Li Dekuan. 1989. Gannan Zhou Zangchuan Fojiao Xianzhuang de Diaocha [Fieldwork on the Current Situation of Tibetan Buddhism in Gannan Prefecture]. *Xibei Minʐu Yanjiu* [Northwest Nationalities Research] 2: 238–42.

Li Shijin. 1948. Labuleng zhi Renkou [The Population of Labrang]. *Bianjiang Tongxun* [Frontier News] 5(2): 13–17.

Lichter, David, and Lawrence Epstein. 1983. Irony in Tibetan Notions of the Good Life. In *Karma: An Anthropological Inquiry,* edited by Charles Keyes and Valentine Daniel. Berkeley and Los Angeles: University of California Press.

Limón, José. 1991. Representation, Ethnicity and the Precursory Ethnography: Notes of a Native Anthropologist. In *Recapturing Anthropology: Working in the Present,* edited by Richard G. Fox. Santa Fe: School of American Research Press.

Lin, L. H. M. 1999. Sex Machine: Global Hypermasculinity and Images of Asian Woman in Modernity. *positions: east asia culture critique* 7(2): 277–306.

Lipman, Jonathan. 1980. The Border World of Gansu, 1895–1935. Ph.D. dissertation, Stanford University.

———. 1984. Ethnicity and Politics in Republican China: The Ma Family Warlords of Gansu. *Modern China* 10(3): 285–316.

———. 1990. Ethnic Violence in Modern China: Hans and Huis in Gansu, 1781–1929. In *Violence in China: Essays in Culture and Counterculture,* edited by Jonathan Lipman and Stevan Harrell. Albany: SUNY Press.

———. 1997. *Familiar Strangers: A History of Muslims in Northwest China.* Seattle: University of Washington Press.

Litzinger, Ralph. 2000. *Other Chinas: The Yao and the Politics of National Belonging.* Durham: Duke University Press.

Liu Qizhong and Chen Gengtao. 1991. *Profiles of Fifty Tibetans* [*Jinri Xizang ren*]. Beijing: Xinhua.

Liu Yu. 1993. Jinxi Dashi Gongtang Cang [The Great Golden Throne Teacher Gongtang Tshang]. *Tuoling* 4: 8–50.

Lonely Planet Travel Survival Kit—China. 1996. Hawthorne, Victoria: Lonely Planet Publications.

Long Rangxiong. 1959. Xizang Funu de Xinsheng [New Life for Tibetan Women]. *Zhongguo Funu* [China's Women] 19: 16–17.

Lopez, Donald S., Jr. 1995. Introduction. In *Buddhism in Practice,* edited by Donald S. Lopez, Jr. Princeton: Princeton University Press.

———. 1996a. 'Lamaism' and the Disappearance of Tibet. *Comparative Studies in Society and History.* 38(1): 3–25.

———. 1996b. *Elaborations on Emptiness: Uses of the Heart Sutra.* Princeton: Princeton University Press.

———. 1997. Introduction. In *Religions of Tibet in Practice,* edited by Donald S. Lopez, Jr. Princeton: Princeton University Press.

———. 1998. *Prisoners of Shangri-La: Tibetan Buddhism and the West.* Chicago: University of Chicago Press.

Luo Faxi, ed. 1987. *Labuleng Si Gaikuang* [An Introduction to Labrang Monastery]. Lanzhou: Gansu Minzu Chubanshe.

Ma Denghun and Wanma Duoji [pad-ma rdo-rje]. 1994. *Gannan Zangzu Buluo*

Gaikuang [An Introduction to the Tibetan Tribes of Gannan]. Hezuo: Zhongguo Renmin Zhengxie Shanghui Gannan Zangzu Zizhizhou.

Ma Guangrong. 1990. Gannan Zangzu Zizhizhou Jingji Fazhan Zhanlue Yanjiu [Research into Strategies for the Economic Development of Gannan TAP]. In *Gansu Minzu Diqu Jingji Fazhan Zhanlue Yanjiu* [Research on the Prospects for the Development of Gansu Minority Regions], edited by Teng Pingwen. Lanzhou: Gansu Minzu Chubanshe.

Ma Haotian. 1942–47 [1936]. *Gan Qing Zang Bianqu Kaocha Ji* [Travel Record of Investigations in the Border Regions of Gansu, Qinghai, and Tibet]. 3 volumes. Shanghai: Commercial.

Ma Jiang, ed. 1993. *Gannan Zangzu Zizhizhou Shoumu Zhi* [Gazetteer of Pastoralism in Gannan Tibetan Autonomous Prefecture]. Lanzhou: Gansu Minzu Chubanshe.

MacFarquhar, Roderick. 1983. *The Origins of the Cultural Revolution*, vol. 2, *The Great Leap Forward, 1958–1960*. New York: Columbia University Press.

Macgranahan, Carole 1996. Miss Tibet, or Tibet Misrepresented? The Trope of Woman-as-Nation in the Struggle for Tibet. In *Beauty Queens on the Global Stage: Gender, Contests, and Power*, edited by Colleen Ballerino Cohen, Richard Wilk, and Beverly Stoeltje. New York: Routledge.

Makley, Charlene. 1994. Gendered Practices and the Inner Sanctum: The Reconstruction of Tibetan Sacred Space in 'China's Tibet.' *Tibet Journal* 19(2): 61–94.

———. 1997. The Meaning of Liberation: Representations of Tibetan Women. *Tibet Journal* 22(2): 4–29.

———. 1998. The Power of the Drunk: Humor and Resistance in China's Tibet. In *Linguistic Form and Social Action*, edited by Jennifer Dickinson and Mandana Limbert. Michigan Discussions in Anthropology 13: 39–79.

———. 1999. Embodying the Sacred: Gender and Monastic Revitalization in China's Tibet. Ph.D. Dissertation, Department of Anthropology, University of Michigan.

———. 2004. The Body of a Nun: Nunhood and Gender in Contemporary Amdo. In *Women of Tibet*, edited by Hanna Havnevik and Janet Gyatso. New York: Columbia University Press.

Makley, Charlene, Keith Dede, Hua Kan, and Wang Qingshan. 2000. Labrang Amdo Dialect: A Phonology. *Linguistics of the Tibeto-Burman Area* 22(1): 97–127.

Makransky, John. 1996. Offering (mChod pa) in Tibetan Ritual Literature. In *Tibetan Literature: Studies in Genre*, edited by José Ignacio Cabezón and Roger R. Jackson. Ithaca: Snow Lion.

Malkki, Lisa. 1997. National Geographic: The Rooting of Peoples and the Territorialization of National Identity among Scholars and Refugees. In *Culture, Power,*

Place: *Explorations in Critical Anthropology*, edited by Akhil Gupta and James Ferguson. Durham: Duke University Press.

Manderson, Lenore, and Margaret Jolly. 1997. Introduction. In *Sites of Desire, Economies of Pleasure: Sexualities in Asia and the Pacific*, edited by Lenore Manderson and Margaret Jolly. Chicago: University of Chicago Press.

Mannheim, Bruce, and Dennis Tedlock. 1995. Introduction. In *The Dialogic Emergence of Culture*, edited by Bruce Mannheim and Dennis Tedlock. Chicago: University of Illinois Press.

Marcus, Julie. 1992. Racism, Terror and the Production of Australian Auto/biographies. In *Anthropology and Autobiography*, edited by Judith Okeley and Helen Callaway. New York: Routledge.

Marko, Ana. 1994. 'Cham: Ritual as Myth in a Ladakhi Gompa. In *Tantra and Popular Religion in Tibet*, edited by Geoffrey Samuel, Hamish Gregor, and Elisabeth Stutchbury. New Delhi: International Academy of Indian Culture and Aditya Prakashan.

Marshall, Steven D., and Susette T. Cooke. 1997. *Tibet outside the TAR*. Washington, D.C.: International Campaign for Tibet. [CD-ROM]

Mauss, Marcel. 1990 [1925]. *The Gift: The Form and Reason for Exchange in Archaic Societies*. New York: Norton.

Maynes, Mary Jo, Ann Waltner, Birgitte Soland, and Ulrike Strasser, eds. 1996. *Gender, Kinship, Power: A Comparative and Interdisciplinary History*. New York: Routledge.

McClintock, Ann. 1995. *Imperial Leather: Race, Gender and Sexuality in the Colonial Contest*. New York: Routledge.

McDermott, R. P., and Henry Tylbor. 1995. On the Necessity of Collusion in Conversation. In *The Dialogic Emergence of Culture*, edited by Dennis Tedlock and Bruce Mannheim. Chicago: University of Illinois Press.

McLagan, Meg. 2003. Human Rights, Testimony, and Transnational Publicity. *The Scholar and Feminist Online* 2(1). http://www.barnard.edu/sfonline/ps/mclagan.htm.

Miller, Beatrice. 1980. Views of Women's Roles in Buddhist Tibet. In *Studies in the History of Buddhism*, edited by A. K. Narain. Delhi: BR Publishing.

Mills, Martin. 2003. *Identity, Ritual and State in Tibetan Buddhism*. London: RoutledgeCurzon.

Millward, James. 1999. Coming onto the Map: 'Western Regions' Geography and Cartographic Nomenclature in the Making of Chinese Empire in Xinjiang. *Late Imperial China* 20(2): 61–98.

Mitchell, Timothy. 1992. Orientalism and the Exhibitionary Order. In *Colonialism and Culture*, edited by Nicholas Dirks. Ann Arbor: University of Michigan Press.

Montmollin, Marceline de. 1988. Some More on the Shaba Sha Khyi 'cham—A Bhutanese 'cham on the Conversion of the Hunter mGon po rDo rje by Mi la ras pa. In *Tibetan Studies: Proceedings of the 4th Seminar of the International Association for Tibetan Studies, Schloss Hohenkammer, Munich, 1985,* edited by Helga Uebach and Jampa L. Panglung. Kommission fur Zentralasiatische Studien, Bayerische Akademie der Wissenschaften.

Morris, Jenny. 1999. China Uses Prostitutes to Bring Shame on Tibetan Monks. *The Telegraph* (London), May 10.

Morris, Rosalind. 1995. All Made Up: Performance Theory and the New Anthropology of Sex and Gender. *Annual Review of Anthropology* 24: 567–92.

Mueggler, Erik. 2001. *The Age of Wild Ghosts: Memory, Violence, and Place in Southwest China.* Berkeley and Los Angeles: University of California Press.

Mulvey, Laura. 1975. Visual Pleasure and Narrative Cinema. *Screen* 16(3): 6–18.

Munson, Todd. 1999. Selling China: www.cnta.com and Cultural Nationalism. *The Journal for Multimedia History* 2. http://www.albany.edu/jmmh/.

Nakane, Chie. 1966. A Plural Society in Sikkim—A Study of the Interrelations of Lepchas, Bhotias and Nepalis. In *Caste and Kin in Nepal, India and Ceylon,* edited by Christoph von Fürer-Haimendorf. New Delhi: Sterling.

Nalanda Translation Committee. 1997. A Smoke Purification Song. In *Religions of Tibet in Practice,* edited by Donald S. Lopez, Jr. Princeton: Princeton University Press.

Nebesky-Wojkowitz, Rene de. 1956. *Oracles and Demons of Tibet: The Cult and Iconography of the Tibetan Protective Deities.* London: Oxford University Press.

———. 1976. *Tibetan Religious Dances: Tibetan Text and Annotated Translation of the 'Chams yig.* Delhi : Pilgrims.

Nee, Victor. 1983. Between Center and Locality: State, Militia and Village. In *State and Society in Contemporary China,* edited by Victor Nee and David Mozingo. Ithaca: Cornell University Press.

Newland, Guy. 1996. Debate Manuals (*Yig cha*) in dGe lugs Monastic Colleges. In *Tibetan Literature: Studies in Genre,* edited by José Ignacio Cabezón and Roger R. Jackson. Ithaca: Snow Lion.

Ngawang Zangpo. 1997. *Enthronement: The Recognition of the Reincarnate Masters of Tibet and the Himalayas.* Ithaca: Snow Lion.

Nietupski, Paul. 1999. *Labrang: A Tibetan Buddhist Monastery at the Crossroads of Four Civilizations.* Ithaca: Snow Lion.

Nora, Pierre. 1989. Between History and Memory: Les Lieux de Mémoire. *Representations* 26: 7–24.

Norbu, Thubten Jigme, and Heinrich Harrer. 1960. *Tibet Is My Country*. London: Hart-Davis.

Nowak, Margaret. 1984. *Tibetan Refugees: Youth and the New Generation of Meaning*. New Brunswick: Rutgers University Press.

Oakes, Timothy. 1997. Ethnic Tourism in Rural Guizhou: Sense of Place and the Commerce of Authenticity. In *Tourism, Ethnicity and the State in Asian and Pacific Societies*, edited by Michel Picard and Robert Woods. Honolulu: University of Hawaii Press.

———. 1998. *Tourism and Modernity in China*. New York: Routledge.

———. 2000. China's Provincial Identities: Reviving Regionalism and Reinventing 'Chineseness.' *Journal of Asian Studies* 59(3): 667–92.

Ochs, Elinor, and Lisa Capps. 1996. Narrating the Self. *Annual Review of Anthropology* 25: 19–43.

Ohnuma, Reiko. 2005. Gift. In *Critical Terms for the Study of Buddhism*, edited by Donald S. Lopez, Jr. Chicago: University of Chicago Press.

Ortner, Sherry. 1978. *Sherpas through Their Rituals*. Cambridge: Cambridge University Press.

———. 1983. The Founding of the First Sherpa Nunnery and the Problem of 'Women' as an Analytic Category. In *Feminist Re-Visions: What Has Been and Might Be*, edited by V. Patraka and L. Tilly. Ann Arbor: University of Michigan Women's Studies Program.

———. 1989. *High Religion: A Cultural and Political History of Sherpa Buddhism*. Princeton: Princeton University Press.

———. 1996. Borderland Politics and Erotics: Gender and Sexuality in Himalayan Mountaineering. *Making Gender: The Politics and Erotics of Culture*. Boston: Beacon.

Osterhammel, Jürgen. 1997. *Colonialism: A Theoretical Overview*. Princeton: Wiener.

Page, Jeremey. 2002. China Buffs Image in Tibet with Beauty Contest. Reuters (WTN), August 24.

Palden Gyatso. 1997. *The Autobiography of a Tibetan Monk*. Translated by Tsering Shakya. New York: Grove.

Panchen Lama VII. 1997 [1962]. *A Poisoned Arrow: The Secret Report of the 10th Panchen Lama*. London: Tibet Information Network.

Parker, Andrew, Marry Russo, Dorris Sommer, and Patricia Yaeger, eds. 1992. *Nationalisms and Sexualities*. New York: Routledge.

Paul, Diane. 1985 [1979]. *Women in Buddhism: Images of the Feminine in the Mahayana Tradition*. Berkeley and Los Angeles: University of California Press.

Paul, Robert. 1982. *The Tibetan Symbolic World: Psychoanalytic Explorations*. Chicago: University of Chicago Press.

Peletz, Michael. 1995. Kinship Studies in Late Twentieth-Century Anthropology. *Annual Review of Anthropology* 24: 343–72.

Perdue, Peter. 2005. *China Marches West: The Qing Conquest of Central Eurasia*. Cambridge, Mass.: Harvard University Press.

Petech, Luciano. 1950. *China and Tibet in the Early Eighteenth Century: History of the Establishment of Chinese Protectorate in Tibet*. Leiden: Brill.

———. 1988. Yuan Organization of the Tibetan Border Areas. In *Tibetan Studies: Proceedings of the 4th Seminar of the International Association for Tibetan Studies, Schloss Hohenkammer, Munich, 1985*, edited by Helga Uebach and Jampa L. Panglung. Kommission fur Zentralasiatische Studien, Bayerische Akademie der Wissenschaften.

Powers, John. 2004. *History as Propaganda: Tibetan Exiles versus the People's Republic of China*. London: Brill.

PRC State Council. 2001. *White Paper: Tibet's March towards Modernization*. Online at http://www.china-embassy.org/eng/zt/zgxz/News%20About%20Tibet/t37001.htm.

Pu Wencheng. 1990. *Gan Qing Zangchuan Fojiao Siyuan* [Tibetan Buddhist Monasteries of Gansu and Qinghai]. Xining: Qinghai Renmin Chubanshe.

Rahul, R. 1969. The Role of Lamas in Central Asian Politics. *Central Asiatic Journal* 12(1): 209–27.

Rappaport, Roy. 1979. *The Obvious Aspects of Ritual, Ecology, Meaning and Religion*. Richmond: North Atlantic.

Ren Naiqiang and Zewang Duoji. 1989. Duo Gan Si Kao Lue [A Brief Study of mdo-khams]. *Zhongguo Zangxue (China Tibetology)* 1: 136–40.

Rent Collection Courtyard: A Revolution in Sculpture, 1967. 1976. *China Reconstructs*, special supplement.

RFA [Radio Free Asia]. 2002. Planned Miss Tibet Contest Sparks Controversy. Radio Free Asia (WTN), May 3.

Richardson, Hugh. 1998 [1986]. Foreword. In *Tashi Khedrup: Adventures of a Tibetan Fighting Monk*. Translated by Hugh Richardson. Montreal: Orchid.

Ricoeur, Paul. 1981. Narrative Time. In *On Narrative*, edited by W. J. T. Mitchell. Chicago: University of Chicago Press.

Rijnhart, Susan. 1901. *With the Tibetans in Tent and Temple*. Cincinnati: Foreign Christian Missionary Society.

Robertson, Jennifer. 1998. *Takaraᶎuka: Sexual Politics and Popular Culture in Modern Japan*. Berkeley and Los Angeles: University of California Press.

Robinson, James Burnell. 1996. The Lives of Indian Buddhist Saints: Biography, Hagiography and Myth. In *Tibetan Literature: Studies in Genre*, edited by José Ignacio Cabezón and Roger R. Jackson. Ithaca: Snow Lion.

Rock, Joseph. 1930. Seeking the Mountains of Mystery: An Expedition on the China-Tibet Frontier to the Unexplored Anmyi Machen Range, One of Whose Peaks Rivals Everest. *National Geographic* 57: 131–85.

———. 1956. *The Amnye Ma-Chhen Range and Adjacent Regions: A Monographic Study*. Rome: Istituto Italiano per il Medio ed Estremo Oriente.

Rofel, Lisa. 1994. Yearnings: Televisual Love and Melodramatic Politics in Contemporary China. *American Ethnologist* 21(4): 700–722.

———. 1999. *Other Modernities: Gendered Yearnings in China after Socialism*. Berkeley and Los Angeles: University of California Press.

Rohlf, Greg. 2003. Dreams of Oil and Fertile Fields: The Rush to Qinghai in the 1950s. *Modern China* 29(4): 455–89.

Ross, Ellen, and Rayna Rapp. 1997. Sex and Society: A Research Note from Social History and Anthropology. In *The Gender/Sexuality Reader*, edited by Roger N. Lancaster and Micaela di Leonardo. New York: Routledge.

Rubin, Gayle. 1975. Traffic in Women: Notes on the 'Political Economy' of Sex. In *Toward an Anthropology of Women*, edited by Rayner Reiter. New York: Monthly Review Press.

Samuel, Geoffrey. 1993. *Civiliᶎed Shamans: Buddhism in Tibetan Societies*. Washington, D.C.: Smithsonian Press.

———. 1994. Gesar of Ling: Shamanic Power and Popular Religion. In *Tantra and Popular Religion in Tibet*, edited by Geoffrey Samuel, Hamish Gregor, and Elisabeth Stutchbury. New Delhi: International Academy of Indian Culture and Aditya Prakashan.

Scharping, Thomas. 2003. *Birth Control in China, 1949–2000: Population Policy and Demographic Development*. New York: Routledge.

Schein, Louisa. 1997. The Consumption of Color and the Politics of White Skin in Post-Mao China. In *The Gender/Sexuality Reader*, edited by Roger N. Lancaster and Micaela di Leonardo. New York: Routledge.

———. 2000. *Minority Rules: The Miao and the Feminine in China's Cultural Politics*. Durham: Duke University Press.

———. 2001. Urbanity, Cosmopolitanism, Consumption. In *China Urban: Ethnographies of Contemporary Culture*, edited by Nancy Chen, Constance D. Clark, Suzanne Z. Gottschang, and Lyn Feffery. Durham: Duke University Press.

Schram, Louis. 1954–61 [1920s]. The Mongours of the Kansu-Tibetan Frontier. Parts 1–3. *Transactions of the American Philosophical Society*, vols. 44, 47, and 51.

Schrempf, Mona. 1994. Tibetan Ritual Dances and the Transformation of Space. *Tibet Journal* 19(2): 95–120.

Schwarcz, Vera. 1992. Memory and Commemoration: The Chinese Search for a Livable Past. In *Popular Protest and Political Culture in Modern China: Learning from 1989*, edited by Jeffrey N. Wasserstrom and Elizabeth J. Perry. Boulder: Westview Press.

———. 1994. Cultural Dilemmas and Political Roles of the Intelligentsia—Memory and Commemoration: The Chinese Search for a Livable Past. In *Popular Protest and Political Culture in Modern China*, 2nd ed., edited by Jeffery N. Wasserstrom and Elizabeth J. Perry. Boulder: Westview Press.

———. 1996. How to Make Time Real: From Intellectual History to Embodied Memory. In *Remapping China: Fissures in Historical Terrain*, edited by Gail Hershatter, Emily Honig, Jonathan N. Lipman, and Randall Stross. Stanford: Stanford University Press.

Schwartz, Ronald. 1994. *Circle of Protest: Political Ritual in the Tibetan Uprising, 1987–1992*. New York: Columbia University Press.

Scott, Joan. 1988. *Gender and the Politics of History*. New York: Columbia University Press.

———. 1991. Experience. In *Feminists Theorize the Political*, edited by Judith Butler and Joan Scott. New York: Routledge,

Shaw, Miranda. 1994. *Passionate Enlightenment: Women in Tantric Buddhism in India*. Princeton: Princeton University Press.

Silverstein, Michael. 1976. Shifters, Linguistic Categories, and Cultural Description. In *Meaning in Anthropology*, edited by Keith Basso and Henry Selby. Albuquerque: University of New Mexico Press.

———. 1997. The Improvisational Performance of Culture in Realtime Discursive Practice. In *Creativity in Performance*, edited by R. Keith Sawyer. Greenwich: Ablex.

———. 2001 [1977]. The Limits of Awareness. In *Linguistic Anthropology: A Reader*, edited by Alessandro Duranti. Oxford: Blackwell.

Smith, Richard. 1998. Mapping China's World: Cultural Cartography in Late Imperial Times. In *Landscape, Culture and Power in Chinese Society*, edited by Wen-hsin Yeh. University of California, Berkeley: Institute of East Asian Studies.

Smith, Warren. 1996. *Tibetan Nation: A History of Tibetan Nationalism and Sino-Tibetan Relations*. Boulder: Westview Press.

Snellgrove, David, and Hugh Richardson. 1986. *A Cultural History of Tibet*. Boston: Shambala.

Soja, Edward. 1989. *Postmodern Geographies: The Reassertion of Space in Critical Social Theory.* London: Verso.

Spain, Daphne. 1992. *Gendered Spaces.* Chapel Hill: University of North Carolina Press.

Sperling, Elliot. 1976. The Chinese Venture in K'am, 1904–1911, and the Role of Chao Erh-feng. *Tibet Journal* 1(2): 10–36.

———.1990. Ming Ch'eng-tsu and the Monk Officials of Gling-tshang and Gongyo. In *Reflections on Tibetan Culture,* edited by Lawrence Epstein and Richard F. Sherburne. Lewiston: Mellen.

———. 1993. The Yuan-Ming Transition in Sino-Tibetan Relations: Notes on Frontier Affairs. Paper presented at the Tibetan Studies Colloquium, University of Washington.

Spiro, Melford. 1970. *Buddhism and Society: A Great Tradition and Its Burmese Vicissitudes.* New York: Harper and Row.

Sponberg, Alan. 1992. Attitudes toward Women and the Feminine in Early Buddhism. In *Buddhism, Sexuality and Gender,* edited by José Ignacio Cabezón. Albany: SUNY Press.

Stacey, Judith. 1983. *Patriarchy and Socialist Revolution in China.* Berkeley and Los Angeles: University of California Press.

Stein, R. A. 1972. *Tibetan Civilization.* London: Faber and Faber.

Stevenson, Mark. 1999. Wheel of Time, Wheel of History: Cultural Change and Cultural Production in an Amdo Tibetan Community. Ph.D. dissertation, University of Melbourne.

Stoddard, Heather. 1985. *Le mendiant de l'Amdo* [The Beggar of Amdo]. Paris: Société d'Ethnographie.

———. 1986. Tibet from Buddhism to Communism. *Government and Opposition* 21: 70–95.

———. 1993. Tibetan Publications and National Identity. In *Resistance and Reform in Tibet,* edited by Robert Barnett and Shirin Akiner. Bloomington: Indiana University Press.

Stoler, Ann. 1991. Carnal Knowledge and Imperial Power: Gender, Race, and Morality in Colonial Asia. In *Gender at the Crossroads of Knowledge,* edited by Micaela di Leonardo. Berkeley and Los Angeles: University of California Press.

Strong, Anna Louise. 1959. *Tibetan Interviews.* Peking: New World Press.

Stubel, Hans. 1958 [1936]. *The Mewu Fantzu.* New Haven: HRAF Press.

Stuchbury, Elisabeth. 1994. The Making of Gonpa: Norbu Rinpoche from Kardang and Kunga Rinpoche from Lama Gonpa. In *Tantra and Popular Religion in Tibet,* edited by Geoffrey Samuel, Hamish Gregor, and Elisabeth Stutchbury. New Delhi: International Academy of Indian Culture and Aditya Prakashan.

Sun Zhenyu. 1993. Labuleng Shihua [Introduction to Labrang]. In *Xiahe Wenshi Ziliao* 1 [Data on the History of Xiahe, vol. 1]. Xiahe: Zhongguo Renmin Zhengxie Shanghuiyi Xiahe Xian Weiyuanhui Wenshi Ziliao Weiyuanhui.

Suo Dai. 1992. *Labuleng Si Fojiao Wenhua* [The Buddhist Culture of Labrang Monastery]. Lanzhou: Gansu Minzu Chubanshe.

Tambiah, Stanley. 1968. The Magical Power of Words. *Man* 3(2): 175–208.

———. 1976. *World Conqueror and World Renouncer: A Study of Buddhism and Polity in Thailand against a Historical Background*. Cambridge: Cambridge University Press.

Taussig, Michael. 1980. *The Devil and Commodity Fetishism*. Chapel Hill: University of North Carolina Press.

———. 1987. *Shamanism, Colonialism and the Wild Man: A Study in Terror and Healing*. Chicago: University of Chicago Press.

Tedlock, Dennis. 1995. Interpretation, Participation, and the Role of Narrative in Dialogical Anthropology. In *The Dialogic Emergence of Culture*, edited by Bruce Mannheim and Dennis Tedlock. Chicago: University of Illinois Press.

Teichman, Eric. 1921. *Travels of a Consular Officer in North-West China*. Cambridge: Cambridge University Press.

Teng Pingwen. 1990. Jianchi Gaige, Jianli Wanshan Minzu Diqu Shehui Zhuyi Shangpin Jingji Xin Tizhi, (Persevere in Carrying Out Reform, Establishing and Perfecting the New System of Commodity Economics in Minzu Regions). In *Gansu Minzu Diqu Jingji Fazhan Zhanlue Yanjiu* [Research on Economic Development Plans for Gansu Minority Regions], edited by Teng Pingwen. Lanzhou: Gansu Minzu Chubanshe.

Tenzin Gyatso [H. H. the Dalai Lama]. 1962. *My Land and My People*. New York: McGraw-Hill.

Tenzin Palbar [alags tsa yus tshang]. 1994. *nga'i pha yul gyi ya nga ba'i lo rgyus* [The Tragic History of My Fatherland]. Dharamsala: Narthang.

Thongchai, Winichakul. 1994. *Siam Mapped: The History of the Geo-Body of a Nation*. Honolulu: University of Hawaii Press.

Tian Wei. 1991. Dui Labuleng Si de Kaocha [Investigations on Labrang Monastery]. *Sichuan Tongyi Zhanxian* [Sichuan's United Front] 6: 11–12.

TIN [Tibet Information Network]. 1999. *Social Evils: Prostitution and Pornography in Lhasa*. Tibet Information Network Briefing Paper 31. Online at http://www.tibetinfonet.net/.

————. 2000. Personal View: Tibetan Perspectives on Lhasa Today. Online at http://www.tibetinfonet.net/ (December).

Topping, Audrey. *1980. The Splendors of Tibet. New York: Sino.*

Tsering Shakya. 1993. Whither the Tsampa Eaters? *Himal,* Sept.–Oct.: 8–11.

————. 1994. Politicisation and the Tibetan Language. In *Resistance and Reform in Tibet,* edited by Robert Barnett and Shirin Akiner. Bloomington: Indiana University Press.

————. 1999. The Dragon in the Land of the Snows. New York: Columbia University Press.

————. 2000. The Waterfall and Fragrant Flowers: The Development of Tibetan Literature since 1950. *Manoa* 12(2): 28–40. [Special Issue: *Song of the Snow Lion: New Writing from Tibet.*]

Tsing, Anna. 1993. *In the Realm of the Diamond Queen: Marginality in an Out-of-the-Way Place.* Princeton: Princeton University Press.

Tucci, Giuseppe. 1988 [1970]. *The Religions of Tibet.* Berkeley and Los Angeles: University of California Press.

Turnbull, Colin. 1992. Postscript: Anthropology as Pilgrimage, Anthropologist as Pilgrim. In *Sacred Journeys: The Anthropology of Pilgrimage,* edited by Alan Morinis. Westport: Greenwood Press.

Tuttle, Gray. 2005. *Tibetan Buddhists in the Making of Modern China.* New York: Columbia University Press.

Unger, Jonathan. 1993. Introduction. In *Using the Past to Serve the Present: Historiography and Politics in Contemporary China.* Armonk: Sharpe.

Upton, Janet. 1996. Home on the Grasslands? Tradition, Modernity, and the Negotiation of Identity by Tibetan Intellectuals in the PRC. In *Negotiating Ethnicities in China and Taiwan,* edited by Melissa J. Brown. University of California, Berkeley: Institute of East Asian Studies.

————. 1999. Schooling Sharkhog. Ph.D. dissertation, University of Washington.

————, trans. 2000. Rivers of Change and Oceans of Tears: Three Contemporary Poems from the Amdo Region. *Manoa* 12(2): 9–17. [Special Issue: *Song of the Snow Lion: New Writing from Tibet.*]

Van der Kuijp, Leonard. 1996. Tibetan Historiography. In *Tibetan Literature: Studies in Genre,* edited by José Ignacio Cabezón and Roger R. Jackson. Ithaca: Snow Lion.

Volosinov, V. N. 1986 [1929]. *Marxism and the Philosophy of Language.* Cambridge, Mass.: Harvard University Press.

Wang, Xiangyun. 2000. The Qing Court's Tibet Connection: Lcang skya rol pa'i rdo rje and the Qianlong Emperor. *Harvard Journal of Asiatic Studies* 60(1): 125–64.

Wang Shaogang and Hu Angang. 1999. *The Political Economy of Uneven Development: The Case of China*. Armonk: Sharpe.

Wang Yunfeng. 1997. *Huofu de Shijie* [The World of a Living Buddha]. Beijing: Minzu Chubanshe.

Wang Zhouta ['brug thar]. 1996a. *Gansu Zangzu Buluo de Shehui yu Lishi Yanjiu* [Research on the Social History of Gansu Tibetan Tribes]. Lanzhou: Gansu Minzu Chubanshe.

———, ed. 1996b. *Labuleng Si yu Huangshi Jiazu* [Labrang Monastery and the Huang Family]. Lanzhou: Gansu Minzu Chubanshe.

Wang Zhouta ['brug thar] and Chen Xiaoqiang. 1994. *De 'er long Si yu Libei Saicang Huofu* [Derlong Monastery and the Setshang Incarnate Lamas]. Beijing: Zhongguo Zangxue Chubanshe.

Watkins, Joanne. 1996. *Spirited Women: Gender, Religion and Cultural Identity in the Nepal Himalaya*. New York: Columbia University Press.

Watson, Rubie. 1994a. Introduction. In *Memory, History and Opposition under State Socialism*. Santa Fe: School of American Research Press.

———, ed. 1994b. *Memory, History and Opposition under State Socialism*. Santa Fe: School of American Research Press.

Welch, Homer. 1972. *Buddhism under Mao*. Cambridge, Mass.: Harvard University Press.

Weston, Kath. 1991. *Families We Choose: Lesbians, Gays, Kinship*. New York: Columbia University Press.

———. 1993. Do Clothes Make the Woman? Gender, Performance Theory, and Lesbian Eroticism. *Genders* 17: 1–21.

White, Hayden. 1981. The Value of Narrativity in the Representation of Reality. In *On Narrative*, edited by W. J. T. Mitchell. Chicago: University of Chicago Press.

Whyte, Martin. 1979. Small Groups and Communication in China: Ideal Forms and Imperfect Realities. In *Moving a Mountain: Cultural Change in China*, edited by Godwin Chu and Frank Hsu. Honolulu: Published for the East-West Center by the University Press of Hawaii.

Williams, Raymond. 1977. *Marxism and Literature*. Oxford: Oxford University Press.

Wolf, Margery. 1985. *Revolution Postponed: Women in Contemporary China*. Stanford: Stanford University Press.

Wrath of the Serfs [exhibition catalogue]. 1976. Beijing: Foreign Languages Press.

XDZ [*Xiahe Dangshi Ziliao* 1 (Data on the History of the Communist Party in Xiahe County, vol. 1)]. 1991. Lanzhou: Zhonggong Xiahe Xian Wei Dangshi Ziliao Zhengji Bangongshi.

XMXY [*Xibei Minzu Xueyuan Yuanshi, 1950–1984* (The History of the Northwest Nationalities Institute, 1950–1984)]. 1984. Xining: Qinghai Renmin Chubanshe.

XXZ [*Xiahe Xian Zhi* (Gazetteer of Xiahe County)]. 1997. Lanzhou: Gansu Minzu Chubanshe.

Ya Hanzhang. 1991 [1950]. Jiefang Chu Xiahe Jianzheng de Jingyan he Jiaoxun [Lessons and Experiences from the Winning Over of Xiahe at the Beginning of Liberation]. In *Xiahe Dangshi Ziliao* 1 [Data on the History of the Communist Party in Xiahe County, vol. 1], edited by Zhang Qingyou. Lanzhou: Zhonggong Xiahe Xian Wei Dangshi Ziliao Zhengji Bangongshi.

Yang, C. K. 1959. The Ascendancy of the Status of Women in the Family. In *Chinese Communist Society: The Family and the Village*. Cambridge, Mass.: M.I.T. Press.

Yang, Mayfair. 1999. From Gender Erasure to Gender Difference: State Feminism, Consumer Sexuality, and Women's Public Sphere in China. In *Spaces of Their Own: Women's Public Sphere in Transnational China*, edited by Mayfair Yang. Minneapolis: University of Minnesota Press.

Yang Ming. 1992. Shixi Labuleng Si Chaosheng Dui Jingji de Yingxiang [Some Preliminary Analyses of the Effect of Labrang Monastery's Pilgrims on the Economy]. *Xizang Yanjiu* [Tibet Research] 4: 12–14.

Yi Haozhong. 1993. Xiahe Xian Gonglu Fazhan Gaikuang [Introduction to the Development of Highways in Xiahe County]. In *Xiahe Wenshi Ziliao (di yi ji)* [Data on the History of Xiahe County, vol. 1]. Xiahe: Zhongguo Renmin Zhengxie Shanghuiyi Xiahe Xian Weiyuanhui Wenshi Ziliao Weiyuanhui.

Yin Jingyuan. 1948. Guoli Labuleng Si Qingnian Lama Zhiye Xuexiao zhi Zhanwang. [The Prospects for the State-run Labrang Monastery Young Monk Vocational School]. *Bianjiang Tongxun* [Frontier News] 4: 10–11.

Yonten Gyatso. 1988. Le monastère de Bla-brang bkra-shis 'khyil [The Monastery of Labrang Tashikhyil]. In *Tibetan Studies: Proceedings of the 4th Seminar of the International Association for Tibetan Studies, Schloss Hohenkammer, Munich, 1985*, edited by Helga Uebach and Jampa L. Panglung. Munich: Kommission für Zentralasiatische Studien, Bayerische Akademie der Wissenschaften.

Yu, Frederick T. C. 1964. *Mass Persuasion in Communist China*. New York: Praeger.

Yu Shiyu. 1990a [1943]. Zangmin Funu [Tibetan Women]. In *Yu Shiyu Zangqu Kaocha Wenji* [Collected Writings of Yushiyu on Her Research in Tibetan Regions]. Beijing: Zhongguo Zangxue Chubanshe.

———. 1990b [1943]. Labuleng Zangmin Funu zhi Shufa [The Hairstyles of Labrang Tibetan Women]. In *Yu Shiyu Zangqu Kaocha Wenji* [Collected Writings of Yushiyu on Her Research in Tibetan Regions]. Beijing: Zhongguo Zangxue Chubanshe.

————. 1990c [1944]. Jieshao Zangmin Funu [Introducing Tibetan Women]. In *Yu Shiyu Zangqu Kaocha Wenji* [Collected Writings of Yushiyu on Her Research in Tibetan Regions]. Beijing: Zhongguo Zangxue Chubanshe.

Yu Xiangwen. 1943. Hequ Zangqu Youmu Zangmin zhi Jiating Zuzhi [The Marriage System among Tibetan Nomads in the Bend of the Yellow River]. *Dongfang Zazhi* [Eastern Magazine] 39(1): 41–45.

Yuval-Davis, Nira. 1997. Theorizing Gender and Nation. In *Gender and Nation*. Sage: London.

ZDPG [*zhal 'don phyogs bsgrigs (zhal 'don nyer mkho phyogs sgrig ces bya ba bzhugs so* [Collected Recitations])]. 1990s.

Zha, Jianying. 1996. *China Pop: How Soap Operas, Tabloids and Bestsellers Are Transforming a Culture*. New York: New Press.

Zha Zha [bkra bkra]. 1993. Labuleng Si Si Da Saichi Shixi Shulue [Brief History of the Four Golden Throne Lamas of Labrang Monastery]. *Anduo Yanjiu*, Chuankan hao [*Amdo Research*, Inaugural Issue]: 68–76.

————. 1994. Qing Wei Labuleng Jiqi Zhoulin Diqu Dashi Ji [A Collection of Major Events in Labrang and Neighboring Regions at the End of the Qing Dynasty]. In *Xibei Minzu Xueyuan Xuebao* [Journal of the Northwest Minzu Institute] 1: 84–89.

zhabs drung tshang [skal bzang dkon mchog rgya mtsho]. 1952. *kun mkhyen po rje brtsun blo bzang 'jam dbyangs ye shes bstan pa'i rgyal mtshan dpal bzang po'i rnam par thar ba dpag bsam ljon pa zhes bya ba* [The Wish-Fulfilling Tree: The Biography of the Fifth Jamyang Shepa]. [Woodblock impression from blocks at Labrang monastery.]

Zhambu, Doje. 1992. Reform Wave Sweeps Tibet. *China's Tibet* 3(4): 16–18.

Zhang Guangda. 1993a. Jiefang Qian, Hou Labuleng Minzu Jinrong Shulue [A Brief Discussion of the Financial Situation in Labrang before and after Liberation]. In *Xiahe Wenshi Ziliao* 1 [Data on the History of Xiahe County, vol. 1]. Xiahe: Zhongguo Renmin Zhengxie Shanghuiyi Xiahe Xian Weiyuanhui Wenshi Ziliao Weiyuanhui.

————. 1993b. Labuleng Zangxue Yanjiu qu—Yin Jingyuan Xiansheng Xiaozhuan [The Labrang Tibetan Studies Research Group—A Brief Biography of Mr. Yin Jingyuan]. In *Xiahe Xian Wenshi Ziliao* 1 [Data on the History of Xiahe County, vol. 1]. Xiahe: Zhongguo Renmin Zhengxie Shanghuiyi Xiahe Xian Weiyuanhui Wenshi Ziliao Weiyuanhui.

Zhang Jimin. 1993. *Qinghai Zangqu Buluo Xiguan Fa Ziliao Ji* [Collected Materials on Traditional Law among the Tibetan Tribes of Qinghai]. Xining: Qinghai Minzu Chubanshe.

Zhang Keji. 1993. Labuleng Zangzu Funu de Chengnian Liyi [The Coming-of-Age Rite for Tibetan Women in Labrang]. In *Xiahe Xian Wenshi Ziliao* 1 [Data on the History of Xiahe County, vol. 1]. Xiahe: Zhongguo Renmin Zhengxie Shanghuiyi Xiahe Xian Weiyuanhui Wenshi Ziliao Weiyuanhui.

Zhang Qingyou. 1991. Jiefang Chuqi Xiahe Gongwei Fushi yu Fan Fushi Douzheng Shiwei [A Synopsis of Corruption within the Xiahe Party Committee and the Struggle against It during the Early Liberation Period in Xiahe]. In *Xiahe Dangshi Ziliao* 1 [Data on the History of the Communist Party in Xiahe County, vol. 1]. Lanzhou: Zhonggong Xiahe Xian Wei Dangshi Ziliao Zhengji Bangongshi.

Zhang Qiyun. 1969 [1930s]. *Xiahe Xian Zhi* [Xiahe County Gazetteer]. Taibei: Zhongguo Fangzhi Yeshu.

Zhang Tianlu, ed. 1993. *Zhongguo Minzu Renkou de Yanjin* [The Evolution of the Population of China's Nationalities]. Beijing: Haiyang Chubanshe.

Zhang Zhongli. 1996. Zang Wenhua: Qingzang Gaoyuan Luyou ye de Linghun [Tibetan Culture: The Soul of the Tourism Industry on the Qingzang Plateau]. *Qinghai Minzu Xueyuan Xuebao* [Journal of the Qinghai Nationalities Institute] 3: 11–15.

Zhao Jialie. 1965. Xizang Funu de Xinsheng [New Life for Tibetan Women]. *Zhongguo Funu* [China's Women] 4: 126–28.

Zhi Hong. 1993. Lue Tan 'Seng Xiang Seng' [A Brief Discussion of the Policy of 'Monks Resembling Monks']. *Taizhou Fojiao* [Taizhou Buddhism] 4: 2–4.

Zito, Angela. 1994. Silk and Skin: Significant Boundaries. In *Body, Subject and Power in China*, edited by Angela Zito. Chicago: University of Chicago Press.

Zong Zidu. 1956. Xizang Funu he Ertong de Xin Shenghuo [The New Life of Tibetan Women and Children]. *Zhongguo Funu* [China's Women] 4: 6–8.

Zwilling, Leonard. 1992. Buddhism and Homosexuality as Seen in Indian Buddhist Texts. In *Buddhism, Gender and Sexuality*, edited by José Ignacio Cabezón, Albany: SUNY Press.

INDEX

Italicized page numbers indicate figures and maps.

agency: of Apa Gongjia, 121; broadened
    frameworks for female, 208–9; in cir-
    cumambulation, 173–75; consumption
    as, 183–84, 215–16; in karmic status,
    173–74, 177–78; in monasticism, 250;
    patrifiliality delinked from, 273–75;
    prostitutes as reprising, 212, 219. *See
    also* quandaries of agency
agriculture: female-headed households
    in, 200; men's work in, 302n39;
    nomadic pastoralism vs., 80, 303n10;
    women's work in, 120, 121, 306n30
Akhu Gendun (pseud.), 246, 280, 290
Akhu Gyaltshan (pseud.), 112
Akhu Gyamtsho (pseud.), 171, 272–73,
    278
Akhu Jamyang (pseud.), 106
Akhu Khedrup (pseud.), 266, 278
Akhu Konchok (pseud.): on female
    trulkus, 38; on inheritance and mar-
    riage, 198–99; on Labrang and state,
    14; on men's spending, 270; on monk-
    cameraman incident, 235–36; on

monkhood, 251, 252, 259, 274, 275;
    on monk's consumption, 277; on
    Rambo, 282; on state violence, 1;
    on tigers, 232; on women and ritual
    space, 166, 177, 305n24
Akhu Sherap (pseud.), 30, 153, 275
Akhu Tshultrim (pseud.), 252–53, 260,
    267
Alak Gungru Tshang, 38, 115
alcohol: male consumption of, 215–16,
    222, 270, 280; proverb about, 243
All-China Women's Federation (Zhong-
    guo Funu Lianhe Hui, or Fulian):
    cadres trained by, 90–92, 115; journal
    of, 120; modern women and, 89–91;
    Tibetan women in, 299n12; women's
    labor and, 170–71
altars, household, 129–34
Ama Damdrin (female, pseud.), 212
Ama Deji (pseud.): on Apa Gongjia,
    106; on communal kitchens, 118–19;
    on confiscations, 117–18; on village
    temples, 113–14; on wealth, 126

349

Ama Dorje (pseud.), 111, 120–21

Ama Drolkar (pseud.), 91, 301n24, 310–11n12

Ama Drolma (pseud.):

Ama Dukar (pseud.), 110, 121

Ama Gazang (pseud.), 110, 121, 122, 128–29

Ama Karma (pseud.), 128, 133, 213, 276

Ama Lhamo (pseud.): appearance of, 89; arrest of, 121; cadre training of, 114–15; circumambulation of, 164; gender confusion of, 5–6; literacy of, 91

Ama Luji (pseud.), 96, 124, 132, 133, 270

Ama Metok (pseud.), 209–12

Ama Tsholo (pseud.), 104, 109, 110–11, 127, 132

Ama Tshomo (pseud.), 169, 264

Ama Wanma (pseud.), 276–77

Amdo (region): access to villages in, 145–46; depictions of ordinary lives in, 300n22; *Lonely Planet* on, 2; people's self-identification of, 80; remapping of, 46, 47; stereotypes of, 72–73. *See also* Labrang (Xiahe county seat); Mother Home; *phayul* (fatherland)

Amdo Tibetan (dialect): commitment to learning, 18–20; literary journal in, 217; media productions in, 241; newspaper in, 301n26; as self-reference, 80; transliteration of, xv–xvi

Amnye Gompo (pseud.), 125–26, 167, 252

Amnye Shalak (deity), 222

Anagnost, Ann, 30, 88, 102, 210, 254–55

antifeudalism campaigns (1958–62), 92–93, 117, 299n9

anti-rightist campaign (1957), 301n29

Apa Alo. *See* Huang Zhengqing (Apa Alo)

Apa Cheka (pseud.), 124

Apa Denzin (pseud.): on Apa Gongjia, 105–6, 107–9; arrest of, 120–21; on cadres, 123, 129; on lack of choice, 122; mentioned, 111

Apa Dondrup (pseud.): on Apa Gongjia, 106; on confiscations, 117–18; on gender and village temples, 112–14; on *jundray*, 132; on karmic justice, 270; on reciprocity relations, 125; on women's dress, 191, 287

Apa Gongjia (Father State): as agent of suffering, 122–29; attempt to recontextualize, 136–37; cadres as extension of, 126–29; Chinese state as, 105–10; circumambulation as resistance to, 155; continued hegemony of, 167; economic reforms as will of, 146–47; emasculation of men by, 115–17, 120–21, 123–24, 166; Great Prayer Festival juxtaposed to, 233–36; ideal absence from Tibetan homes, 140; invalid narratives of, 110–11; karmic justice vs. authority of, 134; merit threatened by, 174; resources and remuneration for, 114, 117–18; sexual regime under, 203–6; spatiotemporal terms in narratives about, 130–34. *See also* Chinese Communist Party (CCP)

Apa Gyalo (pseud.), 98, 133–34

Apa Jikmay (pseud.): altar of, 132; on Apa Gongjia's continued actions, 109; on patriliny, 110–11; on prophecy, 291; on women's work, 120; on year of rupture, 104

Apa Sangye (pseud.): on confiscations, 115–16; on gender complementarity, 126; on lack of choice, 122; on secret circumambulation, 157; on temporary marriage, 213; on women and ritual practices, 309n25

Apa Thamki (pseud.), 121, 122, 127, 128, 133

Apa Thupten (pseud.), 216, 275

Appadurai, Arjun, 78

Arik Lenpa: folktales about, 173–74

Aris, Michael, 21

asceticism: desacralization of, 204–5;

sex-gender hierarchy and, 189–96; sexuality juxtaposed to, 150–55, 182–83. *See also* celibacy

assimilation: emasculation in, 269–70; objectification in, 8, 24; resistance to, 237; sexual regime in, 203–6; socialist androgyny reframed as ethnic, 100; violence of, 7–8

autobiographical pact, 87, 130

bad attitudes (Tib. *rnam gyur mi sra gi*), 30

Bakhtin, Mikhail, 59, 97

bandits: use of term, 128

Bass, Catriona, 260

Bauman, Richard, 78

Baywatch (television program), 4

Bentor, Yael, 154

Berger, Patricia, 295n6

birth control, 210, 220, 305n27, 308n23

Bod: Bopa people, 80; *bod rigs* (Worik), 80; use of term, 81

bodhisattvas, 34–35, 38, 55

bodily markers: confusion about, 5–6; of nomad men, 29–30; *rawa* (head-dresses) as, 118, *119*, 121, 126, 169–70; of respect and status inferiority, 160–61, 175–77; of Tibetan laywomen, 19. *See also* dress

body: Buddhist ambivalence about, 34–35; cultural politics of, 190–96; hidden history in, 104–5; of lamas, 59; in mind-body opposition, 192–93; sexed, as participation framework, 182–85; term for, 307n7. *See also* female bodies; Tibetan sexedness

body-space, gendered: concept of, 150–51; dapa in practice defined by, 163–65

borderlands discourse, 20–21. *See also* boundaries; center and periphery; frontier zone

boundaries: of lay-monastic interactions, 155–59; pollution as indexing, 192–93; sexuality on frontier and, 185–88

Bourdieu, Pierre, 184

Briggs, Charles, 78, 86

Bruno, Ellen, 304n13

Buddha images, 228–29

Buddhism: body-mind opposition in, 192–93; Dharma in, 26–27, 132–33; egalitarian nature of, 163–64, 169, 171; gendered historicity of, 129–34; Mahāyāna school of, 34, 95–96; rational knowledge of, 17, 255–56; role of mothers in, 149–50; sexuality as central problematic of, 34–35, 182–83. *See also* Tibetan Buddhism

Buddhist Studies Institute, 17, 255, 311n15

Bureau of Education, 234–36, 284

Bush, George W., 290, 291

Butler, Judith, 10–11, 296n13

capitalist modernization telos: commodification of sexuality in, 183–84, 207, 308n20; dilemmas of, in centralized state, 143–47; gender as critical to understanding, 11–13; masculinization of, 166–67, 212, 219–20, 268–69, 288; sedentarist vision juxtaposed to, 225–27; women's burdens in, 175–79. *See also* consumption; market economy; modernity and modernization; reform and opening up (Ch., *gaige kaifang*)

Capps, Lisa, 298n7

CBA (China Buddhist Association), 237, 255

CCP. *See* Chinese Communist Party (CCP)

celibacy: bodily discipline of, 197; de-sacralization of, 204–5; as deviant, 186; as monastic requirement, 17, 56, 150–51, 273; reconstituting efficacy of, 206–7; sex-gender hierarchy and, 189–96; sexuality juxtaposed to, 150–55, 182–83. *See also* asceticism center and periphery: Labrang situated in, 20, 22–27

Cham Chen (Great Monastic Dance): centering force of, 61–62; eradication of, 75; festival context of, 228–29; gendered spatial politics context of, 68–72; as public mandalization, 60–61, *63*; recontextualization of, 81

Chao, Emily, 166–67

chaos: use of term, 270

Chegyal. *See* Damjen Chegyal (deity)

Chiang Kai-shek (Jiang Jieshi), 75, 187. *See also* KMT (Guomindang)

China Buddhist Association (CBA), 237, 255

China News Digest, 210

China's Women (Fulian journal), 120

Chinese Communist Party (CCP): agendas of, 49–53; campaigns of, 299n9; dispute arbitration and, 244–45; enlightenment of, 141–42; erasure of, 96–97, 99–100; forgetting by, 81–82, 135–38; lama-scholar's positions in, 237–38; Marxist historiography in, 100–101, 103; mistakes of, 109, 111, 136; nationalist spatial frameworks of, 49–50, 78–81; as project in practices of embodiment, 23–24; recent campaigns of, 290–91; remembering by, 87–95; reversal of moral consequences of, 104–5; sexual regime under, 85–86, 203–6, 209–10; "thought work" of, 52, 88; United Front policies of, 50–52, 93. *See also* Apa Gongjia (Father State); Maoist campaigns; reform and opening up (Ch., *gaige kaifang*)

Chinese language: "Fatherland" in, 304n14; transliteration of, xv–xvi

Chinese people. *See* Han Chinese; Hui Chinese (Muslim Chinese)

Chinese People's Political Consultative Committees (CPPCC), 255

Christian Missionary Alliance, *151*

chronotopes: trulkus as, 97

circumambulation: advertisements visible on, 308n22; agency and benefits of, 173–75; bodily commitments to, 164–65, 177; body-space and dapa in, 163; burden of encircling and, 175–79; contested circuits in, 155–59; gendered ethnic differences delineated in, 137–38; as gendered spatial practice, 138–40, 305n25; as mandalic social geography, 155; path of, illustration, *139*; prayer wheels of, 304n20; standards of, 305n23

circumambulators, Tibetan: author's meeting of, 301n25; bodily markers of, 156–57; boundaries reclaimed by, 158–59; gender and appearance of, 163, 165–66, 174, 300n20, 305n29; illustration, *139*; secrecy of, 122, 157

CITS (state's international travel service), 7

civility: promotion of, 48–49

class politics: among Tibetans, 102–3; confiscations in narrative of, 114; reconstitution of, 121–29; struggle in, as alien concept, 102–3; subjectivity in, iconicity of, 90

Clinton, Bill, 289, 290

collectives and collectivization: break-up of, 146; communal kitchens in, 118–19; confiscations in, 114, 115–16, 117–18, 127; famine of, 109–10, 121, 122; implementation of, 95; remuneration system in, 117–18; respatialization in, 110–21; secret circumambulation in, 122, 157; sumptuary restrictions in, 183; as violent expropriation by Other (CCP), 108–9. *See also* rupture of 1958

commerce and commercialization: acquiescence to, 250; of monasteries, 191,

260–65, 311n17. *See also* consumption; tourism, state-supervised; wealth

commodification: aesthetics of, 6–13, 20; of customs and culture, 7, 8, *9*, 10, 159–61; of female bodies, 184–85, 193–94, 208, 210–11, 214–17; forced transition to, 117; monastery tour ticket prices and, 159; of narratives, 117; of sexuality, 183–84, 207, 308n20

commodity voyeurism: allure of, 182; female bodies in, 214–17; intensification of, 223–24; participation in, 7; playing card images as example of, 181; training in, 48–49; types of consumers and, 184

communication: as gendered process, 4–5; inherent risks in, 286–87. *See also* discourse genres; narratives; video and media productions

competence: as masculine attribute, 241–42

complementary filiation: concept of, 66

consumption: agency of, 183–84, 215–16; criticism of monks for, 210–11, 276–80; Deng's call for, 146, 168–69, 183–84, 220–21; fines for conspicuous, 192; foreigners as models of, 4, 10; male venues of, 215–16, 221–22; merit making as, 257–58; offerings as disciplined form of, 251; "scopofilia" of, 214; sedentarist vision juxtaposed to, 225–27; of sexuality, 181–85; state's need for flexibility and control of, 137–38, 143–47; structural limits in, 269–71; therapeutic, for China's citizens, 6–7; as transgression, 276–80. *See also* commodity voyeurism

contextualization: in cartography, 41–42; consumption of sex and, 181–85; cultural politics of, 12, 31–32; gender and spatial, in participation frameworks, 61–62; maṇḍalas as tools in, 56–57; masculinities as defensive, 236, 284;

micropolitics of sex and, 138–40, 225–28; ritual as situated event in, 54; sex as key cue in, 55–56. *See also* decontextualization; recontextualization

Cooke, Susette T., 145, 159

corporality. *See* body; female bodies

country: use of term, 295n9

CPPCC (Chinese People's Political Consultative Committees), 255

crime: grassland bandits vs. modern thieves, 312n23; increase of, 282–84; murder, 310n9; "political," 313n29; prostitution as, 211–12

"cross-ethniking": concept of, 18

cultural politics: of body, 190–96; in frontier zone, 20–27; of gendered recognition, 6–13; of kinship, 64; at Labrang monastery, post-Mao, 162–65; of mapping, 33; of masculinity and space, 12, 31–32; of mobility, 226–27; of national incorporation, 76–82; of sexuality, 181–85. *See also* sexual politics

Cultural Revolution (1966–68): circumambulating in, 122; destructiveness of, 76; gender-neutral dress in, 204–5; lama-scholar's humiliation in, 237; liberated funu in, 90; painting's survival of, 39–40, *41*, 294–95n6; village temples destroyed in, 113–14

cyclicity: femininity and, 147–55; gendered idealization of, 169–70

ḍiākinīs, 196

Dalai Lama, His Holiness the Fourteenth: Beijing trip of, 129; fact-finding delegation from, 135–36, 227; flight and exile of, 2, 8–9, 80; Geluk sect of, 22, 25; images of, 282; issues highlighted by, 4; Panchen Lama recognition by, 234, 235, 261; personal account of, 298–99n8

Damdrin (male, pseud.), 268

Damjen Chegyal (deity): peaceful Buddha vs., 228–29; recontextualization of, 81; ritual for, 60–61, 63; vow of, 296n16

Danzhu Angben, 258–59, 295n8, 311n19

dapa (Tib. *dad pa;* faith): bodily performance as indicative of, 164–65, 176; depth and substantiality of, 286; production/performance of, 162–63; ritual work of, 173–75

dapdop (warrior monks), 247–49, 275

Dargye (pseud.): on author's methodology, 18; death of, 280; monks criticized by, 279–80; on monks' duality, 267; on shameful action, 207

Daser (journal): drawing of mother in, *149*; poetry on fatherland in, 141–43, 147, 177, 226; poetry on mother home in, 147–49

decontextualization: politics of, 76–82. *See also* contextualization

deities: access to and recognition of, 230; of dewas, 113–15; foreigners compared with, 4, 10; kitchen-related, 119, 302n38; of Lhade tribes, 114–15; mandalas as evoking, 56–57; material receptacles of, 115; as objects of exchange, 162; proper orientation to, 19–20; protector types of, 55–63, 69–71; recognition and embodiment of, 153–55; substantialization of, as guests, 57–58; wrathful vs. peaceful types, 228–29, 296n15. *See also* mountain deities

Democratic Management Committee: behaviors of, 206; charter and rules of, 255–57, 265; festival passes of, 234–36; incomes of, 262–64, 311n18; marginalization of, 265; role of, 158

Democratic Reforms (1958 on), 81–82, 92–93, 98, 108, 288, 299n9. *See also* collectives and collectivization; rupture of 1958

Deng Xiaoping: birth-planning policies of, 210; on consumption, 146, 168–69, 183–84, 220–21; Four Modernizations of, 143; monastery's revitalization and, 14–15, 76; southern tour of, 159. *See also* reform and opening up (Ch., *gaige kaifang*)

Develop the West campaign, 290–91

dewas (administrative units): census of, 74–75; deities of, 113–15; heads of, 124–25, 254; as participation framework, 67–68, 297n25; revitalization's effects on, 125; sedentarization and, 296n21; statistics on, 297n25. *See also* Lhade tribes

Dharamsala: beauty pageant in, 217

discourse genres: de- and recontextualization of, 77; framing type of, 52–53; gendered hierarchy of, 131; interstices in, 14–15; linguistic anthropological approach to, 59; as participation framework, 12; state and, 21–22, 90. *See also* interviews; life stories; narratives; oppositional testimony; speaking bitterness; testimony

dissident activities: anxieties in, 215; crackdown on, 217, 260; nonviolence in, 271, 281–82

divinity: attempt to assign to Mao, 130, 298n1; lamas and trulkus as categories of, 24–25; recognition and discipline in, 227–28; of trulkus, 36

divorce, 211, 309n26

domestication: cadres' and ordinary folks' interests in, 227; by KMT, 188; of masculinities, 40–48; of monastic subjects, 250–59; of Tibetan nationality as Zangzu, 46, *47*. *See also* taming (Tib. *'dul pa*) project

Dondrup Gyal, 217

Donpa: thangka of, *229*

Dopdan (pseud.), 279

Drangchar (literary journal), 217

dress: care of men's, 152–53; of circumambulators, 300n20; earrings as markers in, 19; fines for women wearing pants, 192; gender-neutral, 89–90, 204–5; KMT reading of, 187–88; of lay guards, 230, 232–34; of laywomen, 19, 217; of monks, 194, 273–80, 310n12; of nuns, 216, 312–13n28; *rawa* (headdresses) and, 118, *119*, 121, 126, 169–70; of tourists, 216; transformation of, 113; of women cadres, 93, 113, 116; of young male nomad, 29–30. *See also* bodily markers

Dreyer, June, 118, 301n29

Droko (pseud.), 264

Drolma (deity), 296n15

Drolma (pseud.), on care of men's clothing, 152–53; on covers on Buddha images, 197; death of husband, 280; factory job of, 117–18; family picnic of, 180–81, 224; on foreign sexuality, 223–24; husband's violence against, 222; on inflation, 146; on lamas and lovers, 189; marriage of, 201–3; on prostitutes, 214; refusal to be interviewed, 82–87, 99, 100; on sex differences, 171–72; on sexual discretion, 220–21; work and income of, 169; on year of rupture, 104–5

Duara, Prasenjit, 81, 187, 188

Dutton, Michael, 184, 209–10

duwa, 53, 238, 244. *See also* domestication; taming (Tib. *'dul pa*) project

earrings. *See* dress

economic development: dilemmas of, 140–47; monasteries' support for, 262, 311n18; zones for, 30, 168. *See also* capitalist modernization telos; tourism, state-supervised

education: locals working in, 279, 280; monasteries' support for, 262; for monks, 231, 309n2; secular schools and, 192, 306–7n6; shortcomings of,

260; socialist, 52, 88, 91–92, 111, 204, 299n9, 299n13; state campaigns of, 290

Eight Cavalrymen of Namtisay, 69–70, 230, 234–35, 253–54

Eight Lhade Tribes, 231

Ekvall, Robert, 64, 137, 155, 186, 310n6, 310n10

Elliot, Mark, 42

emasculating secularization: by Apa Gongjia, 115–17, 120–21, 123–24, 166; assimilation and, 269–70; components of, 32; concept of, 14–15; national incorporation and, 93, 95, 236–41, 288; trulkus resexed in, 27

embodiment: of deities, gendered politics in, 153–55; of Dharma, 132–33; of ethnic authenticity and modernity, 10–13; in frontier zone, 20–27; of lamas and trulkus, 24–25, 58–59; of space, 138–40; in Tibetan fatherland, 32–40. *See also* body; body-space, gendered

entrepreneurs and entrepreneurship: contestations of, 259–71; delinking agency from patrifiliality in, 273–75; masculinization of, 166–67; prostitutes as, 212, 219; Tibetanized image of, 281. *See also* market economy

Epstein, Julia, 11

ethnic difference: brochure's representation of, 8, *9*, 10; commodity aesthetics and, 6–13; regendering across categories of, 16–20. *See also* minzu (nationality or national ethnic group)

Evans, Harriet, 120, 210

everyday contexts: assumptions about monkhood in, 243; deity images preferred in, 154–55; depictions of, 300n22; dilemmas of, 206; heroic role models in, 237–38; heterosexual contact in, 180–81; lamas as agents in, 59; ritual linked to, 54–55; said and unsaid in, 97; spatial categories in, 152–55;

everyday contexts *(continued)*
tigers in, 233. *See also* ordinary folks;
sex-gender hierarchy
exchange systems: as dynamic and negotiated, 58–59; men as specialists in,
66–67

famine, 109–10, 121, 122
fanzi (lit. "aborigine" or "barbarian"):
use of term, 63
fatherlands. *See phayul* (fatherland)
fathers: authority of, 65–66, 111; respectful address of, 106. *See also*
patrifiliality
Father State (Apa Gongjia). *See* Apa
Gongjia (Father State)
female bodies: commodification of, 184–
85, 193–94, 208, 210–11, 214–17; corporality of, 172–75; enclosure of, 197–
98; male desire for young, virgin, 196;
as markers of sexual disarray, 186–87;
masculinities maintained via, 190–96;
pollution of, 171–72; translocal mobility of, 212–13; unmarried, as prostitutes, 211–12; in videos, 214–15
femaleness: circumscribed nature of,
149–50; corporality and, 172–75; as
marked and impure, 26, 140, 152–53,
193; terms for, 294n5
feminine hinge: Buddhism as, 254–55;
concept of, 82, 288; consequences of,
90, 120–21; global role of sexuality
in, 207; monasticism as, 227; reconfigured under reforms, 137–38, 167
femininities: contested role of, 85–86;
cyclicity and, 147–55; depoliticizing
function of tropes of, 304n14; as icons
of commodities, 184–85; markers of,
19; prostitutes vs. Tibetan ideal, 213;
shifting of, 88–89
Feng Yuxiang, 73–74
fetishization, 101, 210, 300n22
fieldwork: macro/micro and local/

translocal links in, 27–28; official
permission for, 4; regendering and,
14–20. *See also* linguistic anthropology; narratives; participation
frameworks
Folk Cultural Village (Shenzhen), 30
folktales: Arik Lenpa in, 173, 174; cautionary, 173–74, 210, *211*, 223–24;
wild animals in, 233
foreigners: gender assumptions of, 5–6,
185–86; as models of consumption, 4,
10; as sponsors of monks, 271, 272;
Tibetans' view of sexuality of, 184,
212–13, 215, 223; as unintelligible to
locals, 1–6. *See also* missionaries
foreign tourists: desires of, 2–3, 8; dress
of, 216; length of stay, 303n7; monastery tours for, 159–61, 175–77; monk
ideal of, 271; Tibetans' view of sexuality of, 184, 212–13, 215
Foucault, Michel, 31, 42, 181, 294n1
Four Lhade Tribes, 67–68, 115
framing cues: concept of, 13; gender as,
54–55; theory of, 28. *See also* participation frameworks
frontier zone: competing outsiders in,
182; concept of, 21–22; consumption
and sedentarist vision juxtaposed in,
225–27; cultural politics of mapping,
33; dynamic context of, 31–32; Geluk
mandalization in, 62–72; mapping
national space in, 43–48; participation
frameworks and, 23–27, 287–88; population changes in, 167–68; rational
vs. trope of tribe in, 254–55; sexuality
in, 185–88
Fulian. *See* All-China Women's Federation (Zhongguo Funu Lianhe Hui, or
Fulian)
funu (Zangzu modern women), 89–91

Gangjan Oser, 148–49, 153
Gannan Bao (newspaper), 168, 170

Gannan Tibetan (or Zangzu) Autonomous Prefecture: administrative structure of, 80; folk customs commodified
in, 7, 8, *9,* 10; household-responsibility system in, 252; map of, 40–41, *44–*
45; minzu relegated to, 79; official histories of, 97; rebuilding monasteries
in, 251, 253, 311n13; tourists in, 1–2;
women's organization in, 91–92. *See*
also Labrang (Xiahe county seat);
People's Congress (Gannan prefecture); Xiahe county
ganpo: use of term, 124
Gansu province: map of, *44–45;* monasteries in, 255, 295n12; population of,
298n4; tourist commodification of,
159. *See also* Gannan Tibetan (or
Zangzu) Autonomous Prefecture
Geertz, Clifford, 53–54
Geluk sect/lineage: dominance of,
295n12; expansion of influence, 62–
63; maṇḍala of, *35;* mapping by, 42–
44; peaceful Buddhas and teachings
of, 228–29; power of, 22, 25; Qing
emperors' relationship with, 39–40,
41. See also Dalai Lama, His Holiness
the Fourteenth; Jamyang Shepa (lineage); Labrang Tashi Khyil monastery;
mandalization
gender and gender categories: in accounts
of Apa Gongjia (Father State), 108–
10; biological and karmic categories
of, 37–38; celibacy in context of, 189–
96; contextualization viewed via, 31–
32; in fatherland, 37–40; of foreigners, 5–6; as framing cues, 13, 54–55;
as ongoing recognition process, 11–
13; reconstitution of, 121–29; recontextualization of, 102; reform trajectories and, 135–38; in ritual roles, 125–
26; spatialized polarities of, 196–201;
statist concept of, 87–95; Tibetan
women vs. monk ritualists as, 8; as

unavailable to reflection, 14. *See also*
sex-gender hierarchy
gender complementarity: karmic justice
and, 132–34; public performativity of,
126; respatialization of, 111–14
Gendun Chopel: on celibacy, 191; mentioned, 230; secrecy maintained by,
307n9; on sexual arts, 195–96; on
warrior monks, 247–49
generational differences: gendered
processes underlying, 270–71; males
and females mixing in public and,
207–22; in views on state violence,
1, 134
Geng Fu, 159–60
geography/history/power dialectic:
approach to, 32; fatherland concept
and, 32–40; mapping national space
in, 40–48; national incorporation in
context of, 76–82; oppositional practice of time in, 95–100. *See also*
socialist transformation
Gesang Daji, 145–46, 303–4n11
Gesar (warrior hero), 239–40, 289
gestures: of lowest moral judgment, 273;
shameful action indicated by, 181, 190,
191, 224
globalization. *See* capitalist modernization telos; market economy; reform
and opening up (Ch., *gaige kaifang*)
Goffman, Erving, 12–13, 28, 138–39,
287–88
Goldstein, Melvyn, 136, 150, 196, 304n15,
307n10, 310n8
Gompo (deity), 296n16
Gompo (young male, pseud.), 29–30,
32, 46, 48
Gongtang Tshang (trulku): death of,
290; dispute arbitration by, 245; dress
of monks under, 279; karmic justice
and, 134; popularity and power of,
25–26, 286; portrait of, 129, 132,
133; position of, 265; "quality" over

Gongtang Tshang *(continued)*
"quantity" advocated by, 312n26;
rehabilitation of, 255; return of, 158;
stories about, 96; stupa of, 15, *263*;
wealth of, 262–64, 311n19
Gong Xikui, 144
Great Leap Forward (1958), 116–17,
120–21, 299n9, 301n29. *See also* collectives and collectivization; rupture
of 1958; women's liberation
Great Liberation Stupa, 15, 262–*63*
Great Prayer Festival: circumambulation
in, 157; crowd control at, 231–36;
Great Teas in, 262, 264, 297n24; lay
people's and merchants' duties reiterated in, 71–72; mandalic order asserted in, 229–36; offerings in, 262–
63; participant obligations in, 69;
sedentarization and, 70; thangkas
displayed in, 228–29; transformed
premises for, 76–77. *See also* Cham
Chen (Great Monastic Dance)
Griebenow, Marion, 37, 72, *151*
Gruschke, Andreas, 294–95n6
Guo Lu, 168, 170
Guomindang. *See* KMT (Guomindang)
Guru Rinpoche, 55
Gu Zhizhong, 188
Gyaplo (pseud.), 124, 126–27, 128,
133
Gyatso, Janet: on life stories, 95–96; on
sex, 182–83; on sex-gender Others,
307n8; on tantric yogic practice, 193;
on Tibetan terms for maleness and
femaleness, 294n5

Han Chinese: as cadres, 90–92, 204–6,
244–45; condescension toward robed
monks, 278; education of, 258–59;
inheritance and marriage practices
of, 198–99; as leaders, 79; on Maoist
years, 298n6; mediators between
Tibetans and, 70–71, 145; migration
of, 167–68; pants-wearing style of,
191–92; as participants in Maoist campaigns, 116–17; population of, 7–8;
socialist nostalgia of, 105; speaking-
bitterness campaigns among, 299n10;
Tibetan sexuality compared with,
186–87; Tibetans' view of sexuality
of, 184; as tourists in Tibet, 2, 4, 160–
61, 175–77, 293n1, 303n7; urban, as
norm, 22
Hanks, William, 13, 161–62
Harrell, Stevan, 298n2
Harris, Clare, 300n22
Hermanns, Matthias, 307n14
heroic masculine role model, 236–41,
242–43, 250, 261, 268–70, 280–84
Hershatter, Gail, 218
heterosexuality: bodily discipline of,
197–201, 222–24, 273; compulsive
masculine, and Buddhist ritual, 183,
193–96; as paradigmatic transgression, 307n10; vision of hypereroticized, 207–14. *See also* asceticism;
celibacy
Hevia, James, 40
Hezuo: development of, 295n11; as prefecture capital, 49
historiography: alternative, oppositional,
101–10; of Labrang monastery, 35–
36, 294n3; Marxist, 100–101, 103;
Tibetan interests in, 95, 300n16
history: as gendered practice of time,
83–84; references to, in time, 99;
testimony on, 82–87
home (Tib. *nay*): altars in, 129–34;
Father State's ideal absence from,
140; household work of, 268, 272–73,
312n21; kitchen-related deities of,
119, 302n38; Labrang monastery as
supreme, 156; layers of connotations
of, 154; sexed bodies and mobilities

vis-à-vis, 151–55; spatial arrangement of, 180–81, 197

homosexuality, 197, 307n10

honest and straightforward (terms): meanings of, 111–12, 126–27, 133

Hopkins, Jeffrey, 196

household-registration system, 144

household-responsibility system, 145, 146, 252

Huang family: lay-monastic relationships of, 50–52

Huang Amang Tshang, 50

Huang Amgon, *51*

Huang Mingxin, 247, 249, 309n2

Huang Zhengqing (Apa Alo): on death of fifth Jamyang Shepa, 300n18; defeat of, 297–98n27; family of, 91, 115–16; lay-monastic relationships and, 50, *51*, 72; meetings required of, 234; memoir of, 52, 300n18; monastic discipline and, 230; as Namtisay, 75; political negotiations of, 61, 73–74, 250; portrait of, 126; secular schools established by, 192, 306–7n6

Huber, Toni, 25, 154

Hui Chinese (Muslim Chinese): condescension toward robed monks, 278; as economic mediators, 70–71, 145; ethnic identity of, 237; gender confusion of, 5–6; housing of, 4; migration of, 167–68, 305n27; population of, 7–8; Tibetan men's conflict with, 283; Tibetan sexuality compared with, 186–87; use of term, 293n4

Huo Deyi, 50–52

Hu Yaobang, 136

hwawo (hero; Tib. *dpa' bo*). *See also* heroic masculine role model

iconicity: of class subjectivity, 90; concept of, 38; of maleness, 38–39

imagined community: *dewa* and, 67–68

"imagined cosmopolitanism": concept of, 9–10

incest, 307n11

incorporation: use of term, 77–78. *See also* national incorporation

industrialization, 116–17

institutional vacuum: increase of crime in, 282–84; monks' behavior and appearance changes in, 272; in post-Mao reforms, 267–68, 281; real and fake monks in, 277–78

interviews: dissenting stories in, 103–10; refusals of, 82–87, 99, 100; reversal of, 285–87; threats and violence associated with, 16. *See also* life stories; oppositional testimony; testimony

Jampiyang (bodhisattva), 60

Jamyang Nagri (Ch. Wu Zhengang), 50–51, 52–53

Jamyang Norbu, 33

Jamyang Shepa (trulku lineage): common epithets for, 296n18; as embodiment of ideally disciplined masculinity, 229–36; mandalic field of action of, 156; protector deity as extension of, 61–62; Qing emperors' relationship with, 39–40, *41*; recognition of, 36–37; repairing stupas of, 132; seat of, 35–36, 165; stories about, 96; studies of, 245–46

Jamyang Shepa (first), 33, 39–40, *41*

Jamyang Shepa (second), 70

Jamyang Shepa (fourth): commercialism under, 191; on competition, 70–72; death of, 73; Lhade tribes and, 67–68, 115; monastic discipline and, 230–31, 309n2; monastic government reorganization of, 62, 71–72

Jamyang Shepa (fifth Lozang Jamyang Yeshe Tanpa): biography of, 96–97; census by, 74–75; commercialism

Jamyang Shepa *(continued)*
under, 191, 250; deathbed prophecy
of, 289–91; death of, 300n18; dream
of, 72–75; lay and family relationships
of, 50, *51*; monastic consolidation
under, 229–30; tantric rituals and, 58
Jamyang Shepa (sixth): detained by
CCP, 95; enthronement of, 96; meetings required of, 234; portrait of, 132,
133; position of, 265; "quality" over
"quantity" advocated by, 312n26;
"real," 289–91; rehabilitation of, 255;
residence of, 165
Japan: invasion by, 188
Jiang Jieshi (Chiang Kai-shek), 75, 187.
See also KMT (Guomindang)
Jikshay (deity), 296n16
Jiujia township, 7–8. *See also* Labrang
(Xiahe county seat)
Ju Mipham, 238–40, 289, 309n3
jundray: concept of, 132

Kai Wa, 260–61, 264–65
karmic justice: ideas of, 131–34; lack of,
post-Mao, 270
karmic status: agency in, 173–74, 177–
78; gendered division of labor based
in, 152–53. *See also* merit and merit
making
Kazang (pseud.): on folktales, 174; on
foreign sexuality, 223–24; hospitality
of, 285–87; on karmic justice, 134;
love songs and, 198, 218; on monks
and sexuality, 194–95; on recent state
campaigns, 290
Keane, Webb: on power, 52, 54;
quandary of agency concept of, 26,
62, 103–5, 286; on ritual and power,
54, 68
Keyes, Charles, 149–50, 177–78
kinship, 64, 66, 307n11. *See also* complementary filiation; patrifiliality;
patriliny; patrilocality

KMT (Guomindang): aspirations of,
146–47; census by, 168; defeat of, 61;
Education Bureau of, 231, 309n2;
Labrang occupation and militarization
of, 73–75, 297–98n27; sex-gender
hierarchy under, 185–88, 191–92, 205;
taxation by, 302n36
knowledge: continuity of, 64–65; emasculating secularization of, 14–15; folk
vs. Buddhist, 18; rational source of,
17, 254–56; testimony as producing,
86–87
Konchok Tanpa Rabgye, 43, 46
Kornman, Robin, 239
Kristeva, Julia, 296n13

labor: exploitation of women's, 119–21,
166–67; gendered division of, 152–53,
268, 272–73, 312n21; militarization of,
116–17; recommodification of, 170–
71; as resource for Father State, 117–
18; ritual practice and leisure in context of, 165–66; state's need for flexibility and control of, 143–47
Labrang (Xiahe county seat): appeal
of, 2; asymmetric local-translocal
encounters in, 9; as center and periphery, 20, 22–27; economic and administrative role of, 72–73; as fatherland,
33–34; as feminine object, 188;
"future story" of, 289–91; hotel in,
7; as locality, 31–32; mandalization
of, 33, 53–61; name of, 36; national
incorporation in, 24–25; occupation
of, 73–75, 297–98n27; official histories of, 97; population of, 7–8, 167–
68; protests in, 281–82; public shower
incident in, 5–6; schools of, 260;
shops of, *83*; speaking bitterness in,
88–89; state anxieties evidenced in,
16; tax status of, 67, 296n20; tourism
resources of, 159–61; urbanization of,
9, 13; young mobile men in, 271–80

Labrang studies: use of term, 15

Labrang Tashi Khyil monastery: area surrounding, 1–2, *72*, *151*; branch monasteries of, 67, 297n22; as center and periphery, 20–21; as center of fatherland, 140–43; continuity from Lhasa, 22, 43, 46; cultural politics at, post-Mao, 162–65; desecration and closure of, 21, 26–27, 95, 157; expansions of, 62–63, 295n8; historiography of, 35–36, 294n3; objectification of, 15; official reopening of, 76, 157–58; power of, 22–23, 295n12; rebuilding of, 158–59, 207, 227; remandalization of, 155–59; revitalization of, 14–15, 254–59; rural laity's offerings to, 259–60; secular and state intrusions into, 158, 165; "select tourism festival" of, 304–5n21; taming rituals at, 54–63; tours of, 114, 159–61, 175–77; wealth of, 102–3, 297n23, 297n26, 311n18. *See also* Democratic Management Committee

labtse rites, 240–41, 310n5

laity: assumed sexuality of, 189; bodily discipline of sexual discretion among, 197–201; festivals of, 19, 216, 277, 302n42; fines for, 191–92; as guards for monastic functions, 230, 231–32, *233*; mandalization of, 69–70; obligations of, 62–63, 68, 69, 70, 164–65. *See also* offerings

Lama Chopa (Offerings to the Lama ritual), 58–59, 193–94

lamas: authoritative words of, recorded, 17–18; as cultural heros, 25; disciples' relationships with, 296n19; dispute arbitration by, 244–45; embodiment of, as media of transvaluation, 58–59; life stories of, 96–97, 101; as objects of exchange, 162; proverbs about, 189; speaking bitterness at, 93, 95, 205; tantric ritual practices of, 53–61;

teaching of, 267; transcendence of, 130–34; use of term, 24. *See also* asceticism; celibacy; *trulkus* and trulkuhood

Lama Tsanpo, 43

land reform campaigns, 91–92, 108, 299n10

language: choice of, 101–2. *See also* Amdo Tibetan (dialect); Chinese language; Mandarin Chinese

Lanzhou: economy of, 303n9

lay-monastic relationships: altering participation frameworks in, 250–59; attenuated nature of, 238–39; blurring distinctions in, 266, 276–80; boundaries and public space in, 155–59; celibacy and sexuality juxtaposed in, 150–55, 182–83; competition for control of, 68–72; complexities of, 242; delinking connections in, 273–75; exchange specialists in, 66–67; hierarchy of, 230, 231–36, 244–45; as intense yet detached, 189; legitimate violence controlled and dispensed via, 62, 232–36; monks' celibacy in context of, 189–96; performative binary in, 245; revitalization of, 125–29, 153–54, 158–59; in 1950s, 50–52; terminology in, 17

Levine, Nancy, 65, 66

Lhade tribes: complaints of, regarding monks' behavior, 276; *dewa* as participation framework and, 67–68, 297n25; funds for thangkas from, 231; as "God Dewa," 115; Losar festivities of, 216, 302n42; monastic order and, 67–68, 125; monks hired by, 277; number of, 297n22; offerings of, 251, 262–64; patrilineal historicity of, 64–65; reallocations for, 252, 310–11n12; trulku's taming power over, 61–62, 69–72

Lhamo mtsho, 171

Lhasa: beauty pagent, 217; demonstrations in, 260, 281; Labrang's continuity from, 22, 43, 46; monasteries in area of, 150, 294n3; Patriotic Education Campaign in, 290; stereotypes of Amdowans by, 72–73; women working in, 168

Li Anzhai: background of, 306n5; on cost of Great Tea, 297n24; on female-headed households, 200; on fines for laity, 191–92; on rites of passage, 302n37, 307n13; on Tawa dewas, 297n25; on Thisamling college, 58; on Tibetan sexuality, 186

liberation: life stories on, 88–89; of non-Han men from local masculinities, 79–81; rational basis of, vs. irrational religion, 52–53; Tibetan Buddhist metaphors for, 306n1. *See also* violence of liberation; women's liberation

Li Dekuan, 251, 253, 262, 311n16

life indemnities, 310n9

life stories: erasures in, 96–97, 99–100; function of, 95–97, 101; on oppression and liberation, 88–89

linguistic anthropology: on discourse genres, 59; on narrative, 84–85; on participation, 24, 28, 78; signs/representations as dialogic in, 11–13, 287–88

lions, 233

lishaypa. See Tibetan cadres

Li Shijin, 200

literacy, 91

Lobsang Samten, 135–36, 227

locality: feminine cyclicity and, 147–55; Labrang as, 31–32; women's maintainence of, 140. *See also* mobility; patrilocality; translocality

Lonely Planet Travel Survival Kit, 2

Lopez, Donald S., Jr., 294n4, 296n13

Losar festivities, 216, 302n42

Lumo (pseud.), 218–19, 220

Lu Yi, 188

MacFarquhar, Roderick, 119

Ma Haotian, 74, 157, 187, 298n29

Mahāyāna Buddhism, 34, 95–96

maleness: authority and violence linked to, 61; iconicity of, 38–39; as pure and unmarked, 26–27, 37–38; terms for, 294n5

Malkii, Lisa, 225

maṇḍalas: borders of, as "ritual battlefronts," 232–36; as contextualization tools, 56–57; female bodies as conduits and commodities in, 193–94; Geluk lineage, 35; photograph compared with, 156

mandalization: centering and sedentarism in, 61–72; challenges to, 89, 257–58; commercialization juxtaposed to, 191; concept of, 53; in constructing patrifiliality, 230–31; function of, 33; KMT domestication resisted in, 188; in monastic festivals, 59–61, 63, 229–36; monk's gender status in, 226; oppositional practice of time in, 97; sexual-karmic polarity and, 153; social geography in, 154–55; success of, 150; tantric idiom in structure of, 193–96; violence of liberation in, 53–61, 173. *See also* remandalization

Mandarin Chinese: use of, 4

manikhang. See village temples

Maoist campaigns: invalid narratives of, 110–11; land reform, 91–92, 108, 299n10; population decline in, 116; reversals of, 143; specific: antifeudalism campaigns, 92–93, 117, 299n9; anti-rightist campaign, 301n29; Democratic Reforms, 81–82, 92–93, 98, 108, 288, 299n9. *See also* collectives and collectivization; Cultural

Revolution (1966–68); Great Leap Forward (1958); women's liberation

Mao Zedong: on class struggle, 103; death of, 2; divination attempts for, 130, 298n1; images of, 26–27; lamas' meeting with, 129; on marriage, 92, 204, 210; state violence under, 24; on women, 120. *See also* Apa Gongjia (Father State); Chinese Communist Party (CCP); Maoist campaigns

maps and cartography: KMT role in intensification of, 74; as representations and assertions, 33; retrospective claims in, 52; statist goals in, 40–48

Ma Qi (warlord), 73–74

market economy: anxieties about, 122; ethnicity and modernity juxtaposed in, 6–13; expanding sexual services in, 308n20; legitimate vs. illegitimate wealth in, 127–29; masculinization of, 166–67, 212, 219–20, 268–69, 288; monastery's role in, 157–58; reconstituting PRC subjects in, 143–47; Tibetan female ideal in, 120–21; training to participate in, 48–49; women's burdens in, 175–79; women working in, 168–69. *See also* capitalist modernization telos; consumption; modernity and modernization; reform and opening up (Ch., *gaige kaifang*); tourism, state-supervised

Marko, Ana, 60

marriage and marriage arrangements: bodily discipline of, 196, 199–201; CCP law on, 92, 204, 209–10; forced, for monks, 205; inheritance and, 198–99; KMT trope of ideal, 188; love as basis for, 201–3; missionaries on, 307n14; revival of networking and exchange practices in, 152; "temporary" type of, 200, 213, 308n16; variety of, 66, 189–90

Marshall, Steven D., 145, 159

masculinities: CCP as morally suspect type of, 105–10; compulsions of, 183, 193–96, 275; consumption in shoring up, 215–16, 221–22; delinking patrifiliality from, 273–75; "diarchy" of, 59; domestication of, 40–48, 250–59; emasculation of, 78, 79–81, 93, 95, 205; embodiment of ideally disciplined, 229–30; heroic role models in, 236–41, 242–43, 250, 261, 268–70, 280–84; hierarchies of, 55, 61–62; local social order and, 9–10; mandalization of Labrang and, 53–61, 287; misrecognitions of, 49–53, 73–75; mobility and, 30–32, 46, 48, 61–72; as pivot in contesting entrepreneurships, 260–71; reclaiming space for, 124–29; recognition and discipline in, 227–28; reconstruction of, women's role in, 160–61, 172–77; refiguring of, 259–71; state-local conflict of, 123–24; Tibetan fatherlands and, 32–40; wild animals linked to, 231–32, 238. *See also* monastic masculinities

mass monasticism: consequences of, 281–84; context of, 245, 249; ethic of, 150, 196; gender status in, 288; merit making in, 258; questioning benefits of, 276; revitalization as return to, 250, 252, 253–54; statistics on, 304n15. *See also* remandalization

memory and mimesis: of bodies and state violence, 24; gendered spaces in, 110–21; gendered violence and, 87–95; historicizing power of, 86–87; misrecognitions in, 237–38, 250; oppositional telling of, 97–98; public performances of, dangers of, 84–87, 298n6; recontextualization of, 82–84

merit and merit making: accumulation of, as consumption, 257–58; Apa Gongjia as threat to, 174; circum ambulation as, 163–64, 174–75;

merit and merit making *(continued)*
cleaning work around shikor as, 306n31; gender differences in, 152–53, 172, 178–79; Labrang as center of, 259–60; monkhood as freedom to make, 253; offerings in, 262–64. *See also* karmic status

micropolitics of sex: consumption and, 181–85; contextualization and, 138–40, 225–28

migrants and migration: destination of, 167–68, 302n35, 305n27; forced, 302n35; women as percentage of, 305n28

militarization: of local labor, 116–17; of local population, 124, 127

minority nationalities, 6–7, 22, 24. *See also* minʐu (nationality or national ethnic group)

Minwei (Commission on Minʐu ["Nationality"] Affairs), 77–78. *See also* tourism, state-supervised

minʐu (nationality or national ethnic group): appropriations of speech of, 99–100; category of, 78–79; Han cadres and, 88–89; as medium of statist forgetting, 81–82; minority women cadres of, 91–92, 299n13; recognition of, 79–81; size of groups in, 298n3; social research on, 101, 102–3; use of term, 298n2

Minʐu Unite (CCP journal), 118

misrecognitions: of masculinities, 49–53, 73–75; in memories, 237–38, 250; rehierarchizing in, 142–43; in rituals, possibilities of, 68–72; of wife as prostitute, 202–3, 220–21. *See also* recognition

missionaries, 199, 306n4, 307n14

"Miss Tibet" contest, 217

mnemonic communities: concept of, 95–96. *See also* life stories; memory and mimesis

mobility: as basic aspect in masculinity, 268–69; competence linked to, 241–42; consumption's promise of, 184; expanding possibilities of, 207; foreign missionaries and, 306n4; gender asymmetries in, 151–55, 167–69, 171, 189–90; gendered cultural politics of, 226–27; mandalization and, 61–72; of monks, 271–80; quandaries of agency in, 289–90; sacralization of, 249; sedentarist vision juxtaposed to, 225–27; spatial vs. social, 190; state's need for flexibility and control of, 137–38, 140–47, 170–71, 208, 280–84; structural limits in, 269–71; subjecthood in context of, 46, 48

modernity and modernization: dilemmas of development and, 140–47; framing discourse for accepting, 52–53; maintenance of Tibetanness vs. participation in, 207–8; pants-wearing style linked to, 191–92; shifts in sexuality and consumption in, 182; women's liberation as symbol of, 90

monasteries: as capitalist businesses, 191, 260–65, 311n17; leadership structure of, 158, 265–66; rebuilding of, 251, 253, 259–60; as repoliticized spaces, 16; tax-exempt status of, 43; wealth of, 102–3, 261–65, 297n23, 297n26, 311n18; women excluded or allowed in, 159–61, 166, 171–75, 305n24. *See also* Labrang Tashi Khyil monastery; monasticism; monks and monkhood

monasticism: appeal of, 249, 251–53, 310n11; author as outsider to, 18; authoritative context of, 14–15; authority of, emasculated, 253–54; bodily discipline of, 196–97; celibacy in, 17, 56, 150–51; internal, mental intention as discursive emphasis in, 272–80; proper orientation to, 19–20; scholarly ideal and trulkus in, 25–26;

state's emasculation of, 265–66; status of, 250–52

monastic law, 230, 255–56

monastic masculinities: domestication of, 250–59; maṇḍala's borders and, 228–36; mandalization of Labrang and, 53–61; negotiations of, 225–28; speaking bitterness as displacement of, 93, 95, 205; as tamed to service of Buddha, 241–49; unmarked nature of, 225

Mongol lords, 39–40, *41*, 295n8

monks and monkhood: arrests and imprisonment of, 95, 255, 313n29; behavioral changes among, 272–80; decision to become, 251–53; domestication of, 227; dress of, 194, 273–80, 310n12; dual nature of, 267–68; family support for, 312n24; femininization of, 269–70; fights of, 283–84; as gendered subject category, 8, 17, 38, 242, 288; income of, 262–64; internal intention and mobility as essence of, 272–80; levels of vows of, 245–47; number and age of, 206, 227, 253, 266–67, 269, 311n16; participation frameworks in, 242–49; as percentage of men, 150, 304nn15–16; public consumption of, 210–11; reshaping of, 271–80; rules and regulations for, 255–57, 265–67; school for, 231, 309n2; standards for bodily performance of, 207; statistics on, 305n26; tantric practitioners among, 58; testing and permit procedures for, 266–67; as tour guides, 160–61, 162, 175–77; as translators, 301n26; warrior, hypermasculine type (dapdop), 247–49, 310n10; wealth of, 102–3, 297n23, 297n26. *See also* lay-monastic relationships; monastic masculinities

Mother Home: burden of encircling and, 175–79; concept of, 147; corporality of female and, 165–75; feminine cyclicity and, 149–55; poetry about, 147–49; remandalization of Labrang monastery and, 155–59

"Mother Love" (drawing), *149*

mothers and mothering: in Buddhism, 149–50; merit work compared with, 178–79; Nostalgia Songs for, 147–49, 153; nurturance and altruism ideal for, 147–49, 214; renewed focus on, 169–71, 172

mountain deities: incense burning for, 258; male-only rites for, 240–41, 310n5; men's worship of, 222, 269, 283

movies. *See* video and media productions

Mueggler, Eric, 105

murder: sentences for, 310n9

music and songs, 198, 218, 221, 241. *See also* Nostalgia Songs (Tib. *dran glu*); video and media productions

Muslim Chinese. *See* Hui Chinese (Muslim Chinese)

Namtisay (deity), 69–70, 75

narratives: autobiographical, 298–99n8; autobiographical pact and, 87, 130; co-constructions of, 85, 104, 110–11; as commodities, 117; folktales as, 173–74, 210, *211*, 233; as participation framework, 85; as speech genre, 84–85, 298n7; state-sponsored practices in, 87–90, 93. *See also* discourse genres; interviews; life stories; oppositional testimony; speaking bitterness; testimony

national incorporation: concept of, 78; emasculating nature of, 93, 95, 236–41, 288; gendered cultural politics of, 76–82; statist remembering and, 87–95. *See also* incorporation

National Security Bureau (NSB), 16, 280

National Tourism Bureau, 304–5n21

nation-state: domestication of masculinities in space of, 40–48; embodiments of and by, 24; religion subsumed under, 15; sovereignty and, 33, 54; *trulkus* violent resexed in process, 26–27. *See also* Apa Gongjia (Father State)

nay, Buddhist, 171–75. *See also* home (Tib. *nay*)

Naychung (deity), 171

Naychung Trinlay (deity), 248–49

Negara (Indonesian state), 53–54

neibu books, 293–94n5

networks of men, 30–32, 215–16, 218. *See also* lay-monastic relationships; masculinities

New Life Movement, 187

New Year's activities, 258, 277

9/11 terrorist attacks, 290–91

nomads and nomad regions: drawing of, *149*; farmers vs., 80, 303n10; female-headed households among, 200; grassland conflicts of, 244–45; love songs of, 198; male training in, 310n6; map of, *44–45*; as object lessons, 174; others' views of, 201; sedentarism process and, 63–72; self-sufficiency of, 146; state policies on, 311n14

Northwest Minzu Institute, 299n13

nostalgia: under national incorporation, 236–41

Nostalgia Songs (Tib. *dran glu)*: for mothers, 147–49, 153; oppositional Tibetanness of, 48; women's production of, 295n10

NSB (National Security Bureau), 16, 280

nuns and nunneries: decision to become, 252; dress of, 216, 312–13n28; family support for, 312n24; as gendered subject category, 37–38, 211–12, 309n1; on going out at night, 221; increased number of, 209, 218, 308n19; levels of vows of, 246; on mothering vs. merit work, 178; sexuality of, 212–13

objectification: of Buddhism, 52–53; of deities and lamas, 162; of female bodies, 193–94, 210–22; of Labrang, 188; of monastery, 15; of Tibetanness, 6–7, 8, 14, 20, 24, 48, 238–39, 240

Ochs, Elinor, 298n7

offerings: ambivalence about, 57–58; as danger to state, 264–65; as disciplined form of consumption, 251; household altars and, 131; Labrang as center of, 259–60, 262–64; Labrang's tax status and, 67, 296n20; to men's birth gods, 309–10n4; men's handling of, 302n43, 309n25; political and economic stakes in, 69–72; ritual of, 58–59; state filming of, 235–36; to warrior hero Gesar, 239–40

Offerings to the Lama ritual (Lama Chopa), 58–59, 193–94

"old people": dissenting testimony of, 104–10

"on-the-spot fieldwork" (Ch. *shidi diaocha*), 4

Opakmay (deity), 234–36

oppositional testimony: dissenting stories in, 103–10; gendered spaces in, 110–21; knowledge production in, 86–87; truth claims in, 130–34

ordinary folks (Tib. *besang*): monasticism as viewed by, 227; on rebuilding monastery, 159; reconstituting gender of, 121–29; as unintelligible to foreigners, 1–6; young monks criticized by, 275–80. *See also* everyday contexts

Others and Otherness: abjectness of, 55; androgyny as, 89; Apa Gongjia as, 105; CCP as, 107; female bodies as, 214–17; interviewer as, 17–18; multiple gendered categories of, 10–13;

ritual linked to, 54; sexuality in tropes of, 185–86; sexual respectability in distinctions of, 201; Tibetan nomads as, 63

Palden Lhamo (deity), 296n15
Panchen Lama: appointments by, 255; arrival of, 135, 158, 227; Beijing trip of, 129; quota and, 266; recognition of, 234, 235, 261, 290; on sexual regime under CCP, 205, 206
participation frameworks: capacity to arbitrate, 78; complex interactions of, 161–65; concept of, 12–13, 28, 287–88; of ethnic authenticity and modernity, 10–13; flexibility in, 61–62; formalized speech events, 12; gender and spatial contextualization in, 61–62; global agents' impact on, 286–87; negotiating alignments in, 139–40; patrilineal type of, 66–67; physicality, substance, and contiguity in, 25; socialist androgyny as, for ethnic assimilation, 100; tensions between, 23; trulkus' role in, 25, 27. See also framing cues; quandaries of agency; specific frameworks (e.g., circumambulation; mandalization)
pastoralism, 303n10. See also nomads and nomad regions
patrifiliality: bodily contiguity and, 176–77; challenges to, 89, 93, 95; ideas of karmic justice and, 131–34; mandalizing pageants in constructing, 230–31; masculine agency delinked from, 273–75; obligations and benefits of, 67–72; re-presentation of, 100; respatialization as conquest of, 114–21; revitalization of, 121–29, 153–54, 264–65; revival of rites related to, 169–70. See also lay-monastic relationships
patrilineality, 64

patriliny, 110, 170
patrilocality, 152, 169, 312n22
Patriotic Education Campaign, 290
People's Congress (Gannan prefecture), 117
People's Daily, 119, 311n17
People's Liberation Army (PLA), 21, 93, 128, 299n14
People's Militia, 124, 127
People's Republic of China (PRC): map of, xviii; modernity discourse of, 21–22; national unity of, as temporal construction, 79; Tibetan regions in, mapped, 47. See also Chinese Communist Party (CCP); nation-state
personhood: capitalist vision of, 183–84; essential gender equality in, 163–64; speech as component of, 98–99. See also agency; femininities; masculinities; monastic masculinities
Persons, Wayne, 63, 72, 119, 151, 229
Phakwa Gyab, 140–43, 147, 177, 226
phayul (fatherland): alienation from, 48; concept of, 32–33; gendered embodiment in, 33–40; Labrang refigured as, 264; mandalization as reorganizing, 64–65; narrative repositioning of, 90; pageantry's role in, 283–84; praise poem for, 140–43, 147, 177, 226; refigured as national space, 40–48, 288; Tibetan authority grounded in, 242; Tibetanness juxtaposed to, 80
pilgrims and pilgrimage practices: footprints/handprints and physicality in, 59; mandalic social geography in, 154–55; as object lessons, 174; tourists distinguished from, 162–63
PLA (People's Liberation Army), 21, 93, 128, 299n14
poetry: about warrior hero, 239–40, 289; on fatherland, 140–43, 147, 177, 226; on mother home, 147–49, 153

politics: of access to ritual space, 76–77, 234–36, 283–84; of minzu, 78–79; of recognition, 273–75; of time, 81–82. *See also* class politics; cultural politics; micropolitics of sex; sexual politics

pollution, 171–72, 192–93, 214, 219

pornography, 210

PRC. *See* People's Republic of China (PRC)

prophecies, 23, 96–97, 289–91

prostitutes and prostitution: altruistically motivated sex vs., 200; assumptions of, 186; CCP regime and, 203, 205; crackdown on, 210; criminalization of, 211–12; dress and, 191–92; exotic "minority" vs. Chinese, 218; gendered definition of, 307n15; interviews of, 218–19, 220; KMT views of, 187–88; misrecognition of wife as, 202–3, 220–21; reports on, 203, 308nn17–18; Tibetans' views of, 212–13; trope for, 214

PSB (Public Security Bureau), 15–16, 267, 282–83

public monastic festivals: circumambulation in, 156–57; heightened importance of, 283–84; Jamyang Shepa's role in, 296n18; lay-monastic patrifilial relations in, 230–31; as mandalization effort, 59–61, 63; open resistance to state in, 236; struggle meetings as counter to, 93; transformed premises for, 76–77. *See also specific festivals*

Public Security Bureau (PSB), 15–16, 267, 282–83

public space: compulsory meetings in, 27, 93; delegitimation of, 112; desacralization of, 212–13; female bodies scrutinized in, 216–17; males and females mixing in, 207–22; politics of access to, 76–77, 234–36;

rehistoricized, 135–36; young monks in, 275–80. *See also* circumambulation; dress; speaking bitterness

Pu Wencheng, 295n12, 297n26, 303n3

Qing dynasty and emperors: fall of, 23; flexible indexicality of, 295n7; mapping in service of, 42, 43; nation-state claims to areas of, 78–79; patriarchal legacy of, 187; trulkus' relationship with, 32, 39–40, *41*

quandaries of agency: in recognition, 26, 62; socialist transformation and, 103–5; summary of, 286–91

Rambo (movie character), 282

rape, 308n24

Rapp, Rayna, 197

reciprocity relations: obligations of, 20; reimagining of, 111–12; revitalization of, 125

recognition: altering grounds of monastic, 256–57; contested nature of, 24, 234, 235; of deities, gendered practices, 153–55, 240–41; gendered, 6–13; history as aspect in, 85–87; as local and translocal, 36–39; of minzu, 79–81; of prostitutes, 219; quandary of agency in, 26, 62; ritual as situated event in, 54; of sexed bodies, 151–52. *See also* misrecognitions

recontextualization: of Apa Gongjia, 136–37; of Cham Chen, 81; of discourse genres, 77; of gender, 102; of memory and testimony, 82–84; of public space, 93, 95, 101; of space and time, 136–38; in tourism development, 159–61; of Wencheng (princess), 149

reform and opening up (Ch., *gaige kaifang*): bodily performance and recognitions in, 207–22; institutional vacuum created in, 267–68; local remembering and statist forgetting in, 135–38; male-to-female transformation stories and, 174; quandaries of agency in, 289–90; reallocations in, 252, 310–11n12; religion under, 254–56, 260–61; sexuality in context of, 182–85, 191, 201–3; standards of living and opportunities in, 259–60; time-space compression in, 144–45; tourism resources in, 159–61; township enterprises and, 303–4n11; use of term, 2. *See also* market economy; revitalization

regime of value: concept of, 108–9

religion: as category of the state, 15; under Dengist reforms, 254–56, 260–61; feudalism linked to, 89; freedom of, post-Mao guarantee of, 14–15; irrationality of, vs. rational liberation, 52–53; slogan on, 15, 143, 256

Religious Affairs Bureau, 312n20

remandalization: androcentrism of, 288; dangers of, 177–79; of Labrang monastery, 155–59; precarious nature of, 206–7; state control vs. pace of, 259, 261–62; unmarked nature of monkhood as ground for, 225. *See also* mandalization; mass monasticism

resources: Father State's appropriation of, 117–18; for internal use, 293–94n5; Labrang and monastery as, 159–61; Tibetan Buddhist sites as, 7, 8, *9*, 10. *See also* tourism, state-supervised

respatialization: gendered spaces of memory vs., 110–21

revitalization: competing interests in, 254–59; of cult of *zhidak*, 240–41; ideas of karmic justice in, 129–34; lay donations in, 251; ordinary folks vs. cadres in, 121–29; reconstructing gendered spaces in, 110–21; as return to mass monasticism, 252; of smaller monasteries, 303n3; women's role in,

153–54. *See also* Labrang Tashi Khyil monastery

Richardson, Hugh, 299n8

Rimay (Tib. *Ris med*) movement, 238

rites of passage: for female coming-of-age, 118, *119*, 121, 126, 169–70, 198–99, 200–201, 213, 243, 307n13; for marriage, 199–200; for passage to monkhood, 243–44, 245, 310n8

ritual practices: disrupting cycles of, 165; for emplacing deities, 115; of everyday worshipful encounters, 154–55; gender categories in, 125–26; household altars and, 129–34; monks hired for, 277; on New Year's, 258; participant obligations of, 62–63, 69, 164–65; proper orientation to, 18–20; shinglong season and, 180–81; as situated events, 54; tourism trumped by, 162–63; vulnerabilities of, 68–69. *See also* circumambulation; laity; offerings; tantric ritual practices; *specific festivals*

road and bridge construction: limits of, 145–46; through monastery, 158, 165; violence of, 109, 290–91; women's work in, 120

Robertson, Jennifer, 18

Rock, Joseph, 297n24

Rofel, Lisa, 100

Ross, Ellen, 197

Rubin, Gayle, 13

rupture of 1958: gender reversals from, 112–21; narratives of, 100–110; respatialization in, 110–11; sexual regime imposed in, 204–5; Tibetans' roles in, 115–16, 122–29. *See also* collectives and collectivization; Democratic Reforms (1958 on)

Satya: A Prayer for the Enemy (film), 304n13

Schein, Louisa, 9, 81, 82, 167

Schram, Louis, 295n8, 307n14

Schrempf, Mona, 53
secrecy, 16, 56, 122, 157, 196, 307n9
sedentarization: *dewa* in context of,
296n21; mandalization and patrifiliality in, 63–72; mobility and consumption juxtaposed to, 225–27; monks'
mobility juxtaposed to state's aim in,
272; rewards for, 70
sex: gender vs., 13; as key contextualization cue, 55–56; micropolitics of, 138–
40, 181–85, 225–28
sex-gender hierarchy: access to monastic
space and, 171–75, 177; benefits of,
222–23; centrality of, 287–88; dialectic of, 13; flexibility of, 189–96; under
KMT, 185–88, 191–92, 205; in leisure
time, 165–66; in local-translocal encounters, 5–6, 9–13; mixing and mingling dangers in, 207–22; as ontological ground, 9–10, 17; participation
frameworks in context of, 175–79;
spatialization of, 196–201
sexual intercourse, 195–96
sexuality: celibacy in context of, 189–96;
commodification of, 181–85, 207,
308n20; containment and taming of,
196–201, 207–8; on frontier, 185–88;
misrecognitions of, 201–3. *See also*
heterosexuality; homosexuality
sexual-karmic polarity: concept of, 306n1;
gendered division of labor based in,
152–53; ideal gender statuses in, 226;
maintaining male authority in, 190–96
sexually transmitted diseases (STDs),
308n22
sexual politics: boundary and transgression in, 185–88; under Chinese state,
203–6; consumption and contextualization in, 181–85; flexibility in,
190–96
Shabdrong Tshang, 96–97
"Shambala Miss Tibet" contest, 217
shameful actions: as community disgrace, 207; gesture indicating, 181,
190, 191; performative burden of,
213–14, 224
Shenzhen (economic zone): folk village
in, 30; women working in, 168
Sherap Gyamtsho, 237–38, 250
shikor (outer circuit; Tib. *phyi skor*), 137,
155–57, 304n20, 306n31. *See also*
circumambulation
shinglong season, 180–81
slogans: on collectivization, 119; of
KMT, 74; on mobility and rootedness,
145, 170–71; on nation and religion,
15, 143, 256; on resources, 257; on
women, 120
Smith, Warren, 299n14, 302n35
socialist androgyny: as ethnic assimilation, 100; as participation framework,
85–86, 108–10; passive experience of,
121; public performance of, 204–5;
recognition of, 89–91; repudiation of,
136; of speaking bitterness, 93, 95, 101
socialist transformation: alternative historiography of, 100–110; misrecognition
of masculinities in, 49–53; oppositional practices of time and, 95–100;
quandary of agency in, 103–5; respatialization in, 110–21; speaking-bitterness narratives in, 87–95. *See also* violence of liberation; women's liberation
Sodnam (pseud.), 218, 220, 262
Soja, Edward, 31
sovereignty, 33, 54
space and spatialization: cultural politics
of, 31–32; domestication of masculinities in, 40–48; embodiment of, 138–
40; of gender polarities, 196–201;
household altars and, 129–34; memories of gendered, 110–21; recontextualization of, 77, 93, 95, 101; restrictions in protector-deity temples, 55–
56; sedentarism process and, 63–64.
See also public space; respatialization

speaking bitterness: actual content of, 104; appropriations of, 99–100, 130; mandatory participation in, 88, 101, 112; as participation framework, 87–95; as response to Tibetans' opposition, 97; sculpture based on, *94*, 299–300n15; suicides and, 301n27; as "tournaments of value," 117; in village temples, 113–14

Stove Deity (Tib. *thab lha*), 119, 302n38

Straub, Kristina, 11

struggle (Ch. *douzheng*): use of term, 77

struggle meetings, 93, 104. *See also* speaking bitterness

subjects and subjecthood: biological and karmic categories of, 37–38; de- and recontextualization of, 77; domestication of monastic, 250–59; dual sense of, 294n1; "fragile abstractions" of, translocally, 78; heroic role models in, 238; as ongoing recognition process, 11–13. *See also* femininities; masculinities; monastic masculinities

suicides, 301n27

sumptuary restrictions, 183, 191–92

sun metaphor, 142, 303n6

superstition, 256–58

Tambiah, Stanley, 53–54

taming (Tib. *'dul pa*) project: concept of, 43, 46; emasculating moves in, 227; prestige of, 241–49; protector-deities and, 55–63. *See also* domestication

tantric ritual practices: compulsive masculine heterosexuality and, 183, 193–96; misrecognitions in, 68–72; offerings to warrior hero in, 239–40; secrecy of, 196, 307n9; sex-gender system and, 37–38; of trulku recognition and embodiment, 33–34; violence of liberation in, 53–61

tape-recordings: of lamas, 17–18

TAR, 80, 298n4. *See also* Tibet

Tashi Ji (pseud.), 201, 208

Tawa town: administrative structure of, 80; description of, 185–86; People's Commune in, 157; population of, 167–68, 297n25; sexually available women in, 200, 218

Teng Pingwen, 144

Tenzin Gyatso. *See* Dalai Lama, His Holiness the Fourteenth

Tenzin Palbar, 67, 299n14, 302n35

testimony: dissenting stories in, 103–10; narrating vs. narrated selves in, 112; as participation framework, 86–87. *See also* oppositional testimony; speaking bitterness

Thai Buddhism, 53–54

thangkas: displays of, 60–61, *63*, 197, 228–29; of Donpa, *229*; vivification rite of, 234–36

Thisamling college, 58, 160, 245–46, 310n7, 311n15

Tibet: author's travel to, 4; call for independence of, 281–82; foreign support for, 271; as reified periphery, 22; status of, 309n3

Tibetan Buddhism: authoritative center of, 14–15; civilizing project of, 43, 46; conflict over control of, 22–23; depth and substantiality of, 286; gendered positioning in, 163; heroic lama theme in, 55; historicity and karmic justice in, 129–34; historiographic interests of, 95, 300n16; internal, mental intention as discursive emphasis in, 272–73; lama as human agent in, 34; objectification of, 52–53; power of speech in, 98–99; taming in, 56; tantric yogic practice in, 183, 193–96, 306n1; values of, 140

Tibetan cadres (Tib. *las byed pa*): dispute arbitration and, 244–45; dress of, 93, 113, 116; as extension of Apa Gongjia, 126–29; heroic masculinities and, 254;

Tibetan Buddhism *(continued)*
as illegitimate patriarchs, 127; income of, 127–29, 262; karmic justice and, 132–34; locals' fear of, 114; on monasticism, 227; ordinary folks vs., 121–29; on rebuilding monastery, 159; on sexual regime, 204–5; training of, 90–92, 114–15. *See also* women's liberation

Tibetan culture: assumptions about, 144; commodification of, 7, 8, 9, 10, 159–61; festishization of, 101, 300n22; proverbs in, 151, 189, 194–95, 243, 256, 304n17; as tensions between participation frameworks, 23

Tibetan language: entry into monastic space and, 163, 175–77; as ergative language, 301n28; literary journal in, 141–43, 147–49, 177, 226. *See also* Amdo Tibetan (dialect)

Tibetan men: birth god offerings of, 309–10n4; bodily markers of, 29–30; careers reconfigured by, 208; consumption of, 215–16, 268–71; domestication of, 48–49; emasculation of, 115–17, 120–21, 123–24; as exchange specialists, 66–67; as gendered subject category, 37–38; institutional vacuum for, post-Mao, 267–68; labor obligations of, 68, 70; legitimized violence of, against women, 221–22, 309n26; mandalization of, 69–70; military crackdown on, 95, 108, 114–16; mobility of, 61–72, 167, 168, 189–90; monks as percentage of, 150, 304nn15–16; resistance of, 49–53, 81, 93; shortage of marriageable, 199; structural disadvantages, post-Mao, 269–71, 280–84; violence increasing among, 282–84. *See also* lay-monastic relationships; maleness; masculinities; networks of men; monks and monkhood

Tibetanness: gendered markers of, 19–20; global modernities vs. mainte-

nance of, 207–8; Nostalgia Songs and, 48, 295n10; objectification of, 6–7, 8, 14, 20, 24, 48, 238–39, 240; phayul juxtaposed to, 80; revival of, 7–8; tourists' search for, 2–3, 8

Tibetan people: categorization of, 6–7, 63–64; decontextualization of, 79–81; diaspora of, 33, 294n2; divisions among, 122–29; education of, 258–59; gender confusion of, 5–6; maps of, 42–43; occupations of, 200, 303n10; pan-regionalism among, 240; population of, 7–8, 298n4; regendering within context of, 16–17; regions in PRC, mapped, 47; separatists among, 2–3; structural disadvantages of, 144–47, 269–71, 280–84. *See also* everyday contexts; laity; monks and monkhood; narratives; nomads and nomad regions; ordinary folks; sex-gender hierarchy

Tibetan sexedness: assertions about, 140; in market economy context, 166–67; as participation framework, 182–85; reproduction and Buddhism linked to, 148–49; ritual work of dapa feminized in, 173–75; women's burdens in, 177–79. *See also* sex-gender hierarchy

Tibetan Studies Institute, 4, 15, 17

Tibetan women: burdens of, 177–79, 184–85, 206–22; commodification of, 208; discreet sexual activities of, 199–200, 210–11, 223; drawing of, 149; as gendered subject category, 8, 37–38; gender equality model idealized by, 169; headdresses of, 118, 119, 121, 126, 169–70; legitimized male violence against, 221–22, 309n26; markers of, 18–19; media productions of, 295n10; mobility of, 189–90; recommodification of labor of, 170–71; as responsible for maintaining locality, 140; social stability and labor provided by, 120–

21; as "third party," 210; as trulkus, 37, 38, 115, 251, 294n4. *See also* dress; femaleness; femininities; nuns and nunneries; women's liberation

Tibet Daily, 211

Tibet Information Network, 203, 308nn17–18

tigers, 231–32, 235–36

time: Apa Gongjia and, 105–6; of Dharma and prophecies, 96–97; history as gendered practice of, 83–84; history as safe place in, 125–26; keyed to ritual cycles, 169–70; oppositional practices of, 95–100, 129–34; politics of, 81–82; radical restructuring of, 111–12

tourism, state-supervised: authoritative context of, 14–15; brochures for, 7, 8, *9,* 10, 217, 227; commodity aesthetics in, 6–7, 20; cultural politics and negotiation of, 162–65; dilemmas of, 140–47; distancing fostered in, 3–4; elisions of, 241, 304–5n21; of grasslands, 290; monastery tours and, 159–61, 175–77; pageantry in, 217; rituals filmed and, 77–78; statistics on, 303n1. *See also* foreign tourists; Labrang Tashi Khyil monastery

transgression: consumption as, 276–80; heterosexuality as paradigmatic, 307n10; against monastic discipline, 248–49; prostitutes' appearance as, 219; sexual politics in, 185–88

translocality: "fragile abstractions" in, 78; local links to, 5–6, 9–13, 27–28; masculinities and, 31–32; state authority and, 101; of trulkus, 39–40, *41. See also* mobility

tribes. *See dewas* (administrative units); Lhade tribes; nomads and nomad regions

trulkus and trulkuhood: as chronotopes, 97; competition among, 68–72; as

contested and unmanageable, 36–37; dispute arbitration by, 244–45; embodiment of, 32–40, 58, 132–33; as exchange specialists, 66–67; female, 37, 38, 115, 251, 294n4; Gesar (warrior hero) as, 239–40; as key shifters and interpretive pivots, 26; life stories of, 96–97, 101; marginalization of, 78; patrifiliality delinked from, 273–75; popularity and power of, 25–27, 287; portraits of, 129, *133;* recognition of, 36–39; speaking bitterness at, 93, 95, 205; transcendence of, 130–34; use of term, 24; violent resexing of, 26–27; wealth of, 102–3, 297n23, 297n26

Tsering Shakya, 301n26

Tshering (pseud.), 7, 8, *9,* 10

Tshering dpal skyid (Apa Alo's daughter), 115–16, 301–2n34

Tshering Khar (pseud.), 236, 237–38, 250

Tshering Lhamo (Apa Alo's wife), 91, 192, 306–7n6

Tshongkhapa (lama), 43, 46, 56, 229

Tsonji (pseud.), 201–3, 222, 280

urbanization: expansion of, 72–73; "imagined cosmopolitanism" of, 9–10; Labrang as vital node in, 167–68; legitimate vs. illegitimate wealth in, 127–29; patrifilial exchange and, 70; population changes in, 167–68, 305n28; state funds directed to, 260

Vajrayāna practice, 296n13

Van der Kuijp, Leonard, 300n16

video and media productions: availability of, 104; on exploitation of Tibetans, *94,* 299–300n15; of female singers, 308n21; feminine cyclicity in, 148–49; of festival, by state, 234–36, 284; "Folk Cultural Village" as, 30; labtse rites in, 241; models and sexuality in,

video and media productions *(cont.)*
214–15; monks' viewing of, 276, 279,
282; official memory in, 97; Other
viewed in, 270; by Tibetan women,
295n10; women as minzu subjects in,
90–91
village temples, 113–15, 118–19, 301n32
violence, legitimate: heroic masculinities
and, 242–43; of men against women,
221–22, 309n26; of monks against
others, 228–36, 247–49, 284
violence of liberation: Apa Gongjia as
father of, 105–10; emotional toll of,
103–10; gendered effects of, and statist remembering, 87–95; history as
aspect of, 83; in mandalization, 53–61,
173; as moral battle, 88, 288; population changes linked to, 167–68; socialist transformation and, 48–53; Tibetan men enacting, 282–84; Tibetans'
roles in, 115–16, 122–29
Vocational School for Young Monks,
231, 309n2

Wande (pseud.), 171, 254
Wandikhar (pseud.), 258
Wanggatang: enterprises in, 303–4n11
Wang Zhouta, 295n8, 297n22, 297n25,
311n19
Wanma Ji (pseud.), 273
wealth: household altars as index of, 131;
legitimate vs. illegitimate, post-Mao,
126, 127–29, 212; mobility's role in,
268–69; monastic, 102–3, 261–65,
297n23, 297n26, 311n18; of monks
entering monastery, 267. *See also*
sumptuary restrictions
weed broth (Tib. *ldum bu*), 109–10
Weixing People's Commune (Tawa), 157
Wencheng (princess), 149
wesang. See ordinary folks
wild black yak, *233*
women: exploiting labor of, 119–21,
166–67; as percentage of immigrants,
305n28; as revolutionary minzu subjects, 90–91; trivialization of, 16. *See
also* femaleness; femininities; nuns and
nunneries; Tibetan women
women's liberation: as emasculation of
men, 115–17, 120–21, 123–24, 166;
erasure of, 100; in Han vs. Tibetan
communities, 92–93, 299n10; implications of, post-Mao, 208–9; labor exploitation in, 119–21; organizations
of, 90–92. *See also* speaking bitterness
Worik (*bod rigs*): use of term, 80
"Wrath of the Serfs," *94*, 299–300n15
Wulsin, Frederic, 185–86
Wylie, Turrell, 43

Xiahe county: appeal of, 2; CCP headquarters in, 158; founding of, 191;
map of, 40–41; marginalization of,
21; "peaceful liberation" of, 52; population decline in, 116; population of,
7–8; renaming in, 301n31; tourism
in, statistics, 303n1; tourism resources
of, 159–61; women's organization in,
91. *See also* Labrang (Xiahe county
seat)
Xizang Zangzu Autonomous Region
(Tibet or the TAR), 80, 298n4. *See
also* Tibet

Ya Hanzhang, 49–50
Yang, Mayfair, 90
Yu Shiyu, 192
Yu Xiangwen, 304n16

Zangzu: definition of, 79–81
Zhang Guangda, 297n26
Zhang Qingyou, 52, 205–6
Zhang Qiyun, 64, 186, 306n2
zhidak, cult of, 240–41
Zhi Hong, 261
Zong Zidu, 120

Text	10.25/14 Fournier
Display	Fournier
Compositor	BookMatters, Berkeley
Cartographer	Bill Nelson
Indexer	Margie Towery
Printer and binder	Thomson-Shore, Inc.